7·20·

W9-CNW-263

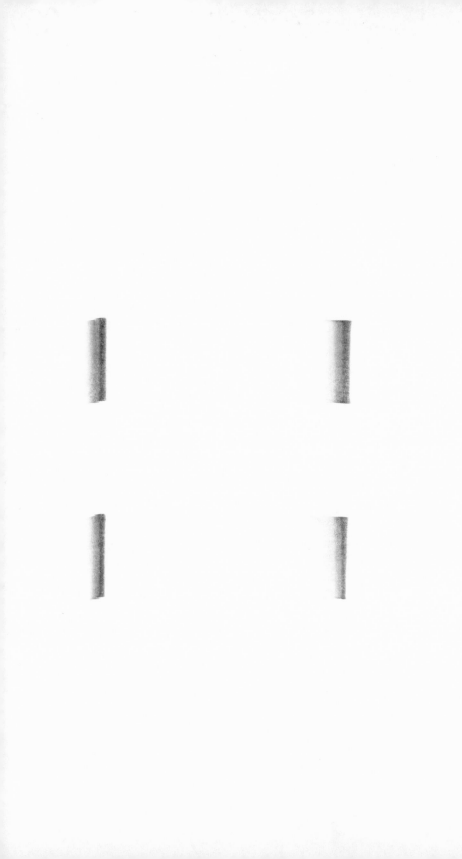

THREE   SCREENPLAYS

PUBLISHING FOR THE WORLD
125 Years
THE JOHNS HOPKINS UNIVERSITY PRESS

E. L. Doctorow

THREE SCREENPLAYS

With a Preface by the Author

Introduction, Commentaries, and Interviews

by Paul Levine

THE JOHNS HOPKINS UNIVERSITY PRESS

BALTIMORE AND LONDON

© 2003 The Johns Hopkins University Press

Preface and screenplays (Daniel, Ragtime,

Loon Lake) © 2003 E. L. Doctorow

All rights reserved. Published 2003

Printed in the United States of America on acid-free paper

2   4   6   8   9   7   5   3   1

The Johns Hopkins University Press

2715 North Charles Street

Baltimore, Maryland 21218-4363

www.press.jhu.edu

Library of Congress Cataloging-in-Publication Data

Doctorow, E. L., 1931–

[Screenplays. Selections]

Three screenplays / E.L. Doctorow ; introduction, commentaries,

and interviews by Paul Levine.

p. cm.

Includes bibliographical references.

Contents: Daniel—Ragtime—Loon Lake

ISBN *0-8018-7201-4 (hardcover : alk. paper)*

1. Motion picture plays. 2. Trials (Espionage)—Drama.

3. New York (State)—History—1865–   —Drama. 4. Adirondack

Mountains (N.Y.)—Fiction. I. Levine, Paul. II. Title.

PS3554.03 A6 2003

791.43′75—dc21   2002029674

A catalog record for this book is available from the British Library.

Contents

Preface

E. L. DOCTOROW

THESE FILM SCRIPTS adapted from my novels *The Book of Daniel, Ragtime,* and *Loon Lake* are published not for the general public but for students of film, who might find the comparison of novel and film useful to their studies. There can be no other rationale for publishing them. They were not intended for the eyes of readers but were prepared as a kind of map by which directors and their actors might find their way to a pictorial rendering of compositions made of English sentences.

All that is left of a screenplay's words in a finished film is the fraction the dialogue comprises. And in contemporary film drama, at least as it comes out of Hollywood, the words the characters speak will be heavily anticipated by the physical presentation of the actors and their surroundings. Add some music, and the emotional thrust of a scene can be inferred before a character says anything.

It must be said too that these screenplays were prepared not in any state of creative passion, for that had already been expended with the novels. They were motivated only by my desire to protect my work from oversimplification, bowdlerization, and general mauling by other hands. What ruled me, in short, was a paranoia made no less ignoble because I was being well paid for my efforts.

I can't help remembering how unhappy I was doing these adaptations. Had I undertaken an original screenplay from scratch this would not have been the case. But I was tracing my own work. I was a writer repeating himself. I was working without that generative excitement that propels you through a novel—without the experience of unfolding discovery as the novel makes itself known to you.

That I went ahead, nevertheless, not once, but on three separate occasions, is indication only of the arrogance of the high-wire walker who feels he can tiptoe across any abyss, however wide.

These scripts were usually put together within a year after each book's publication. With the construction of the last of them, *Loon Lake*, and with a history of exciting collaborations with people in the film industry, only one of which had led to an actual motion picture, I put the film scripts away and forgot about them. In looking them over now I find that for their intended purposes they are not without an integrity of their own. At the same time I challenge the film student to decide if they are reductions or potential filmic realizations of the novels on which they are based.* The large theoretical question is whether or not all adaptations inevitably simplify their source material, or whether, as produced film, they can visually attain the complex realities of rendered language.

I should confess, finally, that while my forays into the film business from the governing solitude of the novelist's life have not brought much in the way of creative satisfaction, they have given me an appreciative understanding of the screenwriter's art. I am gratified that my scriptwriting has entitled me to be a member of the Writers' Guild of America, the enlightened union run by screenwriters themselves which has slowly over the years brought them closer to the full recognition they deserve from the film industry.

There is a never-ending debate on the crucial yet self-erasing role of writers in the making of movies. Writing to create imagery that displaces their words, scriptwriters are seen as subalterns of the filmmakers whom they inspire. But their vision lingers in the finished film, the characterizations they invent are embodied by actors, the ideas that propel their writing, the comic spirit, or social anger—all of that is what is transmuted by directors into the light and motion of a film. The struggle for the entitlement of screenwriters is symbolized by the famous story (apocryphal, according to Capra's biographer, Joseph MacBride) of Robert Risken, Capra's collaborator on several films. Having heard one too many times about the "Capra touch," which had ele-

---

*Editions of *The Book of Daniel, Ragtime,* and *Loon Lake* are published in hardcover by Random House and in trade paperback by Plume Books.

vated the director to iconic status in Hollywood, Riskin slapped a hundred and twenty blank pages on Capra's desk one day and said to him "Put the Capra touch on this!" Still, directors and producers and studio executives use the inherent self-sacrifice of the writers' work to maintain a hierarchy of creative privilege. Screenwriters are beat about the head with the paradox of their invisible writing, though they are no less seminal to the making of films than composers are to the performance of their symphonies. In both cases notes on the page lead to a rendition by others in a different realm of sensation.

Professor Paul Levine, a film and American studies scholar at the University of Copenhagen, has contributed the scholarly apparatus for this volume. While I am not in entire agreement with some of his commentaries—and, of course, neither he nor I expected that I would be—I'm appreciative of the spirit in which they are proposed. Professor Levine's scrupulous attention to these scripts and the learning he brings to them have my admiration.

THREE   SCREENPLAYS

Introduction

E. L. DOCTOROW'S published work includes fiction, poetry, drama, and prose, but Doctorow has also chosen to write film scenarios of his own novels. Though many important American novelists have worked in Hollywood, no one else, to my knowledge, has adapted as many of his own major works. These scripts provide a unique opportunity to examine the process of artistic alchemy by which a novel is translated into another medium by its own creator. The function of this book is, then, twofold: to make available a new facet of the oeuvre of a major American writer and to follow the metamorphosis of his work from fiction into film.

As it happens, each screenplay has suffered a different fate. Doctorow's script of *Daniel*, begun in 1973, was made into a movie by Sidney Lumet in 1983. His mammoth screenplay of *Ragtime* was written in 1980 for director Robert Altman, who was prepared to turn it into a six-hour film and a ten-hour television miniseries. But Altman's movie was never made; instead, another director, Milos Forman, fashioned a more conventional film from a completely different script. Doctorow's adaptation of *Loon Lake* was written in 1981 and is perhaps his most complex screenplay. It still awaits film treatment. This book presents all three screenplays, including the original version of *Ragtime,* which Doctorow has revised for publication.

MOVIES have often played an important role in Doctorow's fiction. For instance, in *Ragtime* there is a key scene in which Tateh, the immigrant silhouette artist turned exploited factory worker, decides to exchange the ideal of socialist solidarity for the dream of commercial success. "Thus did the artist point his life along the lines of flow of American energy. Workers would strike and die but in the streets of cities an entrepreneur could cook sweet potatoes in a bucket of hot coals and sell them for a penny or two. Phil the Fiddler, undaunted by the snow, cut away the fingers of his gloves and played under the lighted windows of mansions. Frank the Cash Boy kept his eyes open for a runaway horse carrying the daughter of a Wall Street broker."[1] In the spirit of Horatio Alger, the silhouette artist decides to make moving pictures.

Tateh's story is an American parable: the artist is both rejuvenated and corrupted by his contact with the movies. He affirms his renewal by celebrating Alger's dream of success in his films. Like Gatsby, he is reborn. As the Baron Ashkenazy, he makes his fortune in the first silent pictures and invests the profits in the Buffalo Nickel Photoplay, Incorporated, a company whose very name is derived from the coin of the realm. During World War One he produces commercially successful propaganda films, then moves to California, where he creates a series of popular short films about an interracial group of street urchins reminiscent of the "Our Gang" comedies. They are both a touching reminder of his lost idealism and an ironic example of his corrupted sensibility.

As Tateh knows, film is a curious amalgam of dream, reality, and commerce. "In the movie films, he said, we only look at what is there already. Life shines on the shadow screen, as from the darkness of one's own mind. It is a big business." But movies aren't simply a source of escapist entertainment; they are also a means of assimilation. "People want to know what is happening to them," Tateh explains. "For a few pennies they sit and see their selves in movement, running, racing in motorcars, fighting and, forgive me, embracing one another. This is most important today, in this country, where everybody is so new. There is such a need to understand."[2]

In Doctorow's other novels, the careers of his young protagonists are often shaped by their lives in the movies. In *Loon Lake,* Joe is educated not in schools but in movie theaters. "My luxuries were cigarettes and movies," Joe says. "I liked to go to the movies and sit there; you could see two features and a newsreel for a dime. I liked comedies and musicals and pictures with high style. I always went alone. In my mind was the quiet fellow trying to see himself, hear what he sounded like."[3]

Just as socialist Tateh reinvents himself as Baron Ashkenazy, so proletarian Joe of Paterson recomposes himself as a son of the ruling class, Joseph Bennett. "He fitted himself out in movie stars he discarded them." Thus, Joe is socialized by watching movies. His idea of style and self comes from film; he is an actor who becomes the role he plays. "I was interested in the way I instantly knew who the situation called for and became him."[4]

In our interview, Doctorow suggests that Joe's film experience in the 1930s paralleled his own as a much younger child growing up in the Bronx. Similarly, in the partly autobiographical *World's Fair*, young Edgar's education is shaped as much by popular culture as by books. Once again, the experience of movies provides lessons in life. For instance, Edgar is disturbed when he discovers the resemblance between Adolph Hitler and his hero, Charlie Chaplin. "I loved Charlie Chaplin. We had the same taste in women, like the blind flower girl, whom we both found very beautiful and kind. He had helped her, as I would have. He was a wonderful little guy, he never got as mad at other people as they did at him, even when they were fighting, although he was often hurt by them." But the unfortunate resemblance takes on added resonance when he adds, "My father had a moustache too; they all three had moustaches."[5] One night Edgar dreams that his father is a ventriloquist with dummies of Chaplin on one knee and Hitler on the other. Later on, he tries to learn ventriloquism himself. First you learn to throw your voice; then you learn to create a new voice.

In Doctorow's most recent novel, *City of God*, the narrator is a writer named Everett who is also possessed by the movies. "I love movies," he says. "They make themselves out of the actual materials of the world, you see. They lift the world's appearances from the world as you would lift with your knife tip the iridescent blue-green coloration of the rainbow from the rainbow trout . . . leaving the substance of the world unchanged but rendered in exact homologous equivalence of itself."[6] Film is seductive, but Everett believes it also threatens to colonize our imaginations and usurp reality. "Movies are using up the cities, the countrysides, the seas, and the mountains. Someday every inch of the world will be on film." Everett fears the imperializing power of film, but he cannot resist turning his own fiction into imagined screenplays. "Life will not be simultaneous, it will be sequential, one story after another, story after story, as if all the DNA of every living thing were extended, on one strand, one byte at a time, to infinity."[7]

IF MOVIES play a significant role in Doctorow's novels it is because they are quintessential examples of American culture. In *Democracy in America*,

Alexis de Tocqueville noted that democracies differed from aristocracies in their attitude toward culture. In aristocratic societies, in which wealth is limited to a small group, craftsmen create rare works of art for a select clientele. But in democracies, in which wealth is more evenly spread, utility is prized above uniqueness by a larger public. Thus, the artisan in a democracy operates on a different premise: "In an aristocracy he would seek to sell his workmanship at a high price to a few; he now conceives that the more expeditious way of getting rich is to sell them at a low price to all." The result is that more goods of a lower quality are produced for a wider audience. Tocqueville observed that "when none but the wealthy had watches, they were almost all very good ones: few are now made which are worth much, but everybody has one in his pocket. Thus the democratic principle not only tends to direct the human mind to the useful arts, but it induces the artisan to produce with greater rapidity a quantity of imperfect commodities, and the consumer to content himself with these commodities."[8] In the 1830s, Tocqueville had already detected the popular strain in our culture.

Intrinsic to our idea of democracy is the connection between culture and commerce, but the notion that culture is indivisible in other ways is also typically American. Ralph Waldo Emerson characterized American culture as pragmatic and demotic. "I embrace the common, I explore and sit at the feet of the familiar, the low," he wrote.[9] Emerson's disciple, Walt Whitman, argued that American culture should be inclusive and democratic, not exclusive and elitist. "I should demand a program of culture, drawn out, not for a single class alone, or for the parlors or lecture rooms, but with an eye to practical life, the west, the workingmen . . . and with reference to the perfect equality of women."[10]

In *Highbrow/Lowbrow* Lawrence W. Levine notes that before the Civil War Americans shared a common public culture less fragmented and hierarchical than the one we have now. But by the end of the nineteenth century, the processes of industrialization, urbanization, and economic incorporation had created the cultural divisions we still see today. "Increasingly," observes Levine, "as public life became everywhere more fragmented, the concept of culture took on hierarchical connotations along the lines of Matthew Arnold's famous definition of culture—'the best that has been thought and known in the world . . . the study and pursuit of perfection.' "[11] At the beginning of the twentieth century two new words, borrowed from the pseudoscience of phrenology, entered the language of cultural description: *highbrow* and *lowbrow*.

Still, the boundary between highbrow and lowbrow culture is more porous in America than elsewhere. Whereas in Europe *Kultur* is still determined from the top down, in America culture is often shaped from the bottom up. The philosopher and film critic Stanley Cavell notes that people often wonder, "How is it that a professor of philosophy gets to thinking about Hollywood films?" For him the more natural question is, "How is it that someone whose education was as formed by going to the movies as by reading books, gets to thinking about philosophy professionally?"[12]

While others assume that highbrow philosophy and lowbrow movies have nothing in common, Cavell believes that educated Americans normally share a culture that contains both elements. Perhaps this accounts for the special character of American books like *Walden* and *The Adventures of Huckleberry Finn*, which blend serious and popular, metaphysical and demotic elements. Echoing Emerson and Whitman, Cavell concludes: "Every art, every worth-while human enterprise, has its poetry, ways of doing things that perfect the possibilities of the enterprise itself, make it the one it is; each of the arts has its own poetry, of course, so has each sport, and so, I am sure, have banking and baking and surgery and government."[13]

For Doctorow, too, the genius of American culture lies in its popular roots, which flourish in the rich soil of ordinary life. In *Ragtime* he shows how modern American culture was created from the bottom up. Ragtime and motion pictures, vaudeville and baseball were all nourished by contributions from the marginalized group of immigrants and blacks. But Doctorow is aware of the difference between an organic and creative popular culture and a mechanical and manufactured mass culture. In our interview, he expresses concern about how mass culture colonizes our imagination, hence his ambivalence about the relationship between the writer and the movies.

In *City of God* Doctorow writes, "When movies began they were shown in storefronts, dumps, you paid a nickel and sat down on a bench. They were silents, of course, one-reelers, and everyone made them, they were cheap to make, people made them about their own lives."[14] But as movies evolved from their humble beginnings in popular culture to a mass-based commercial business, they manifested less individual expression and more corporate will. Thus, says Doctorow, Hollywood was founded "to generate on an orderly industrial basis these corporate movies, which, whatever their period, contemporary or historical or futuristic, demonstrated to the audience watching them, now sitting in dark, palatial theaters built just for the purpose, that movies were a form of life to which life must aspire, as it has now shown every sign of doing."[15]

WHEN it comes to culture Americans profess democracy, but writers have always patronized filmmakers. Indeed, it is easy to condescend to the movies. Everyone has his favorite story about Hollywood gaucheries, and most of them concern writers. There's the one about Sam Goldwyn and Maurice Maeterlinck. Goldwyn hired the Belgian Nobel Prize winner, who did not speak English, to adapt his novel *La Vie des abeilles*, and when the screenplay was translated, Goldwyn was shocked to discover that the hero of the film was a bee. In another instance, Goldwyn revealed his true feelings toward writers when he tried to hire Louis Bromfield. "Sure, you're a great novelist but how many people have heard of you?" asked Goldwyn. "If you write two or three successful pictures, the name of Bloomfield will be known all over the world!"[16]

Writers often repaid the compliment. Though he chose to work in Hollywood, Aldous Huxley despised the studio system that forced him to deal with inferior collaborators. "What a disgust and a humiliation! It seems one worse, if possible, than the theatre," he complained. "I shall stick to an art in which I can do all the work by myself, sitting alone, without having to entrust my soul to a crowd of swindlers, vulgarians and mountebanks."[17] Huxley's lament has been echoed by countless novelists who felt stifled in the industrial organization and artistic claustrophobia of the Hollywood system.

American fiction is replete with examples of the novelist's hostility to the movies, especially by writers who have worked in Hollywood. In *The Deer Park*, Norman Mailer likens filmmakers to prostitutes. In Michael Tolkin's *The Player*, a screenwriter threatens to murder a studio executive in the name of all the exploited writers in Hollywood; instead, the executive murders the screenwriter. In *The Day of the Locust*, Nathanael West describes a film studio as a dream junkyard: "A Sargasso of the imagination! And the dump grew continually, for there wasn't a dream afloat somewhere which wouldn't sooner or later turn up on it, having first been made photographic by plaster, canvas, lath and paint."[18]

The idea of Hollywood as a dream factory is also irresistible. When filmmakers replaced poets as the acknowledged legislators of the American dream, the writer found himself in a position of reduced circumstances. F. Scott Fitzgerald, who spent his final years in Hollywood in the mistaken belief that he could master screenwriting, became obsessed with the power of visual images. In *The Last Tycoon,* he depicts producer Monroe Stahr (who is based on the legendary producer Irving Thalberg) teaching a brilliant lesson in the esthetics of film writing to a snobbish English writer named Boxley (who is reminiscent of Huxley). But Fitzgerald was also aware of the dangers that film posed to fiction. In *The Crack-Up,* he wrote:

I saw that the novel, which at my maturity was the strongest and supplest medium for conveying thought and emotion from one human being to another, was becoming subordinated to a communal art that, whether in the hands of Hollywood merchants or Russian idealists, was capable of reflecting only the tritest thought, the most obvious emotion. It was an art in which words were subordinate to images, where personality was worn down to the inevitable low gear of collaboration. As long past as 1930, I had a hunch that the talkies would make even the best-selling novelist as archaic as silent pictures.[19]

So writers have lived in uneasy propinquity to the movies. In the 1930s, great novelists like West, Fitzgerald, and Faulkner went to Hollywood out of economic necessity. For them, screenwriting was an imposition. But today young novelists take up screenwriting eagerly while established authors like Paul Auster, Joan Didion, and Norman Mailer choose to commute between fiction and film. Meanwhile, Doctorow observes, film people have become perhaps the smartest readers of fiction in the country. In recent years the movie and book worlds have developed a symbiotic commercial relationship as well: successful novels are translated into films, successful films are transformed into novels. Today Fitzgerald's prophesy has been fulfilled. "Movies changed our world forever," argues novelist Gore Vidal in *Screening History.* "Henceforth, history would be screened; first, in meeting houses known as movie houses; then at home through television. As the whole world is more and more linked by satellites, the world's view of the world can be whatever a producer chooses to make it."[20]

THOUGH writers grumble about the cultural hegemony of the movies and the commercial tyranny of the Hollywood system, the debate over film authorship is relatively new. When Gore Vidal was a contract writer at MGM in the 1950s, the power pyramid looked like this: "Apparently the ambitious man became a producer (that's where the power was). The talented man became a writer (that's where the creation was). The pretty man became a star." And the director? "The director is the brother-in-law," he was told.[21]

In the days of silent pictures, "the director was king," argues Vidal. "But once the movies talked, the director as creator became secondary to the writer."[22] In the postwar period, however, French *cinéastes* reversed the argument, claiming that film was the product of the director's vision in much the same way as fiction was the product of the writer's imagination. In the United States, where critics have a *faible,* a weakness for French theory, the idea of the director as *l'auteur,* the author of the film, was soon taken up by reviewers like Andrew Sarris. For Sarris, the *auteur* theory was a way of organizing our sense of film history rather than explaining how films were actually made. Not surprisingly, the decrees of the *auteur* critics have met with stiff resistance from film scholars, who point out the collective industrial character of American film production.[23]

Clearly, the simple notion of a single author does not adequately explain the operation of a communal medium like film. Leo Braudy suggests that instead of the French *auteur* we use the Spanish *autor,* "with its implication of the head of a company or the manager of a group, like the actor-managers ('autores') of the sixteenth century."[24] Moreover, the film director may possess organizational ability and inspirational talent but he is still dependent on the quality of the script. In *Making Movies,* Sidney Lumet claims that good films are the product of creative negotiation between writer and director. He notes approvingly that important novelists like William Styron, Don DeLillo, and Doctorow have all written for the movies.

But Doctorow worries about the toll that screenwriting takes on the novelist. He compares adapting his own fiction to mechanical drawing. It is an instrumental act of imaginative repetition that artists should avoid. He says, "when you do that, you see, you're doing something risky, it's a kind of self-negation as a writer that you would do well not to do too often." Compared to composing novels, he argues, adapting them for the screen is technical and reductive work because language in film is always secondary to image. In *City of God* he notes that "the term *film language* is an oxymoron. The literary experience extends impression into discourse. It flowers to thought with nouns, verbs, objects. It thinks. Film implodes discourse, it deliterates thought, it shrinks it to the compacted meaning of the preverbal impression or intuition or understanding. You receive what you see, you don't have to think it out."[25]

CINEMA and literature were not always so antagonistic. In the beginning, films and novels were both rooted in realist esthetics. Echoing Joseph Conrad's famous credo, D. W. Griffith claimed that above all he wanted to make his audience "see" the world as it is. But Griffith's vision was closer to the Victorian spirit of Dickens than to the modern spirit of Conrad. At the very moment that Griffith was creating the film language of American cinema, the modern novel was repudiating its Victorian roots by fracturing narrative, rejecting sentimentality, and introducing ambiguity. "The seeming concurrence of Griffith and Conrad splits apart under analysis," noted George Bluestone, "and the two arts turn in opposite directions. That, in brief, has been the history of the fitful relationship between novel and film: overtly compatible, secretly hostile."[26]

Novelists have always been clear on the reasons for this divorce. They insist that fiction and film achieve their effects in significantly different ways. The most obvious difference is one of medium. The novel is written in language; the film is composed of images. Doctorow compares the function of language in screenplays to "the rocket boosters in space launches: they get the film up and then they fall away. The only words left are the words that the characters speak." But dialogue is only one aspect of film composition, whose language is essentially nonverbal.

A second major difference writers point to is the treatment of time. The novelist may use three tenses while the filmmaker has only one. "The essential characteristic of the image is its presentness," says novelist Alain Robbe-Grillet; "by its nature, what we see on the screen is in the act of happening, we are given the gesture itself, not an account of it."[27] This presentness of the image accounts for film's visceral immediacy and for its apparent lack of reflection. For this reason Doctorow considers film a temporal medium as the novel is not, "more relentlessly time-driven than theater."

A third significant difference is in their treatment of space. The novel reproduces both inner and outer space; the film represents exterior space. This affects the different ways that film and fiction treat characterization. A novel deals with experience: how the world looks to the protagonist; a film deals with behavior: how the protagonist looks to the world. Whereas novels excel at exploring the psychological depths of their subjects, films excel at examining the physical dimensions of their objects. Sidney Lumet believes that great novels cannot be successfully adapted in the movies because "you would never be able to portray the inner life of a character with the depth that a novelist can." Doctorow agrees. "Fiction goes everywhere, inside, outside, it stops, it goes, its actions can be mental," he writes in *City of God.* "Films out of Hollywood are linear. The narrative simplification of complex morally consequential reality is always the drift of a film inspired by a book. Novels can do anything in the dark horrors of consciousness. Films do close-ups, car drive-ups, places, chases, and explosions."[28]

Finally, both writers and filmmakers are aware that movies and novels are created under different circumstances and speak to different audiences. Films require large investments and industrial organization. Novels are still individual creations until they become commercial products. Doctorow once joked that it cost him 145 dollars to write *Billy Bathgate* whereas Hollywood spent 45 million dollars making it into a mediocre movie. Writers believe that while they are free to explore ambiguity for a limited readership, Hollywood moviemakers are forced to exploit a set of formulas accessible to their mass audience. What finally separates film and fiction is less means than aims: they interpret reality in different ways.

In the world of classical cinema, "reality" is characterized by its clarity, coherence, and consistency. Hollywood movies typically operate in a circumscribed world of cause and effect. "The classical Hollywood film presents psychologically defined individuals who struggle to solve a clear-cut problem or to attain specific goals," explains David Bordwell. "In the course of this struggle, the characters enter into conflict with others or with external circumstances. The story ends with a decisive victory or defeat, a resolution of the problem and a clear achievement or nonachievement of the goals."[29] Whereas contemporary novels typically develop in a discontinuous and dialogic fashion that resists closure, Hollywood movies tend to remain linear, transparent, and terminal. "In the beginning of the motion picture," writes one screenwriter, "we don't know anything. During the course of the story, information is accumulated, until at the end we know everything."[30]

It is this one-dimensional character of mainstream American filmmaking that alienates writers. "What is it about movies?" asks Robert Stone, another novelist who has written screenplays. "Stalin and Hitler loved them, all the major liars and tyrants seem to have been fans. They are beloved of all simplifiers, the purveyors of ideologies and alibis. Do they really exercise some gravitational impulse on life that flattens out character and extracts obviousness from the myriad chambers of reality?"[31] Novelists worry about the tendency of film to reduce the significance of those qualities they prize most—language, characterization, moral complexity—in favor of narrative.

But if writers remain wary, they also acknowledge the cinema's impact on the evolution of modern fiction. Doctorow says that "everyone who writes now, everyone who has written since James Joyce, has been affected by films." He points, for instance, to the lessons that novelists have drawn about unnecessary exposition. "We can, as writers, make the same compact with the reader that the filmmaker makes with the audience: the story will unfold without explanation, with minimal exposition; it may jump around quite a bit and you may not know what's happening, but it will become clear eventually."

But fiction has influenced moviemaking, as well. In *Narration in the Fiction Film*, David Bordwell shows how both classical and avant-garde art cinema are deeply indebted to literary sources. According to Bordwell, classical narration in American film, with its emphasis on realism, is rooted in late-nineteenth-century popular fiction and drama, whereas art-cinema narration in postwar European film takes its cue from modernist fiction, which questions traditional definitions of the real. "Here new aesthetic conventions claim to seize other 'realities': the aleatoric world of 'objective' reality and the fleeting states that characterize 'subjective' reality."[32]

Cinema challenged the novel as the pre-eminent cultural form in the Age of Mechanical Reproduction because filmmaking united art, commerce, and technology in appealing to a mass public. We know that one result of the Modernist revolution was to collapse the distinctions between high and low; another was to transform the relationship between the artist and his or her audience. No longer could viewers be passive in the face of baffling works, which challenged them to fill in the spaces that artists had left blank. Recent critical theory also emphasizes the crucial role of the reader or viewer in the collaborative creation of a work of fiction or a motion picture. But collaboration must begin somewhere; namely, with the *ur*-text that the writer creates.

"In every film there are at least four films," observes Leo Braudy; "the one written, the one cast, the one shot, and the one cut."[33] This book is primarily about that first film. The script is the starting point in any discussion of filmmaking because, as Milos Forman remarked, "screenplays do come first, and they really are the foundations of movies."[34] In reading these film adaptations by E. L. Doctorow the reader is invited to participate in the process of creation and engage in a dialogue with author, director, and critic about movie versions made, revised, and still to come.

NOTES

1. E. L. Doctorow, *Ragtime* (New York: Random House, 1975), 111.

2. Ibid., 215.

3. E. L. Doctorow, *Loon Lake* (New York: Random House, 1980), 8.

4. Ibid.

5. E. L. Doctorow, *World's Fair* (New York: Random House, 1985), 132.

6. E. L. Doctorow, *City of God* (New York: Random House, 2001), 155.

7. Ibid., 107.

8. Alexis de Toqueville, *Democracy in America* (New York: Colonial Press, 1899), 2: 52.

9. "The American Scholar," *Selected Writings of Ralph Waldo Emerson*, ed. William H. Gilman (New York: Bantam Books, 1965), 238.

10. "Democratic Vistas," *The Collected Writings of Walt Whitman: Prose Works, 1892*, vol. 2, ed. Floyd Stovall (New York: New York Univ. Press, 1964), 396.

11. Lawrence W. Levine, *Highbrow/Lowbrow: The Emergence of Cultural Hierarchy* (Cambridge: Harvard Univ. Press, 1988), 223.

12. Stanley Cavell, "The Thought of Movies," *Themes Out of School: Effects and Causes* (San Francisco: North Point Press, 1984), 4.

13. Ibid., 14.

14. Doctorow, *City of God*, 236.

15. Ibid., 238.

16. Quoted in Garson Kanin, *Hollywood* (New York: Limelight Editions, 1974), 343‑ 44.

17. Quoted in Ian Hamilton, *Writers in Hollywood, 1915–1951* (New York: Harper & Row, 1990), 136.

18. *The Complete Works of Nathanael West* (New York: Farrar, Straus & Cudahy, 1957), 353.

19. F. Scott Fitzgerald, *The Crack-Up*, ed. Edmund Wilson (New York: New Directions, 1956), 78.

20. Gore Vidal, *Screening History* (Cambridge: Harvard Univ. Press, 1992), 32.

21. Gore Vidal, "Who Makes the Movies?" in *The Second American Revolution and Other Essays* (New York: Random House, 1982), 134.

22. Ibid., 133.

23. See, for instance, Thomas Schatz, *The Genius of the System: Hollywood Filmmaking in the Studio Era* (New York: Pantheon, 1988).

24. Leo Braudy, *The World in a Frame* (Garden City, N.Y.: Doubleday, 1976), 45.

25. Doctorow, *City of God*, 214.

26. George Bluestone, *Novels into Film: The Metamorphosis of Fiction into Cinema* (Berkeley: Univ. of California Press, 1957), 2.

27. Quoted in Geoffrey Wagner, *The Novel and the Cinema* (Rutherford, N.J.: Fairleigh Dickinson Univ. Press, 1975), 180.

28. Doctorow, *City of God*, 214.

29. David Bordwell, *Narration in the Fiction Film* (Madison: Univ. of Wisconsin Press, 1985), 157.

30. Quoted ibid., 160.

31. Robert Stone, "Oliver Stone's USA," *New York Review of Books*, Feb. 15, 1994, 24.

32. Bordwell, *Narration in the Fiction Film*, 206.

33. Braudy, *The World in a Frame*, 201.

34. Milos Forman, *Turnaround: A Memoir* (New York: Villard Books, 1994), 187.

From *The Book of Daniel*
to the Film of *Daniel*

E. L. DOCTOROW'S third novel, *The Book of Daniel*, was published in 1971, at the end of one of the most turbulent political periods in American history. The novel appeared at the culmination of a decade of radical resurgence that had begun in 1960 with the student sit-ins against segregation in Greensboro, North Carolina, and the student demonstrations against the House Un-American Activities Committee in San Francisco. As the student protests grew into a national movement expressed in nascent student-based organizations like SDS and SNCC, a new generation of young radicals appeared on the scene who challenged not merely the corporate power structure but the left-wing political establishment as well.

The New Left wrote a new chapter in the history of American radicalism. However, although the student movement was generous in its instincts, it was often self-destructive in its actions. When American society showed few signs of political change at the end of the sixties, student enthusiasm waned. The New Left fell as spectacularly as it had risen, undermined by the same sort of factional disputes and internecine warfare that had plagued the Old Left. Having attempted to abolish History, the young radicals became its victim instead. "When the New Left started it made much of the difference between it and earlier radicals," observed William O'Neill. "It was open, undoctrinaire, independent where they had supposedly been conspiratorial, dishonest, and sectarian. But in scarcely more than eight years the New Left recapitulated practically the whole history of American radicalism."[1]

It is against this turbulent background that Doctorow fashioned *The Book of Daniel*. He says:

> In the late Sixties I found myself thinking about the Rosenberg case, and it seemed to me that the more I found myself thinking about it, I saw that it was something that I could write. And not knowing why or how or what conclusions I was going to come to, I started to write that book and discovered I could hang an awful lot on it—not only the explicit and particular story of two people who were trapped in this way, but also the story of the American left in general and the generally sacrificial role it has played in our history.[2]

The Book of Daniel is, then, a meditation on American politics in the form of a novel, an imaginative revisioning of the Cold War years which bridges the generation gap between the Old and New Left by reconnecting the new radicalism to its history. It is not simply a fictional account of the Rosenberg case but a threnody on what Christopher Lasch called "the agony of the American Left."[3] In the final analysis, as Doctorow suggests, the book is not about the Rosenbergs but about the *idea* of the Rosenbergs. As Doctorow explains, "the specific dramatic interest I had was solely in terms of what happens when all the antagonistic force of a society is brought to bear and focused on one or possibly two individuals. What kind of anthropological ritual is that?"[4]

Here it matters little that Doctorow has changed some of the facts of the case: that the Rosenbergs are now called the Isaacsons; that their two sons have been transformed into a brother and sister, Daniel and Susan; that the crucial witness against them has been changed from a family member, David Greenglass, to a family friend, Selig Mindish. It also matters less whether the accused are innocent or guilty—in the novel Daniel never finds out—than that they have been cast as scapegoats in a ritual drama beyond their comprehension. Instead, the Isaacsons come to symbolize the legacy that one generation leaves another: the legacy of the Cold War, on the one hand, and of the Old Left, on the other. The subject of the novel is this legacy, Daniel's legacy, and that is why it is Daniel's book. "DANIEL'S BOOK: A Life Submitted in Partial Fulfillment of the Requirements for the Doctoral Degree in Social Biology, Gross Entomology, Women's Anatomy, Children's Cacophony, Arch Demonology, Eschatology, and Thermal Pollution."[5]

From *The Book of Daniel* to the Film of *Daniel*

The Book of Daniel was published in 1971 to critical acclaim, but it was neither a bestseller nor an obvious candidate for film adaptation. As Doctorow explains in our interview, the film version was a long time in gestation, from Haskell Wexler's early interest expressed in 1973 to Sidney Lumet's completed film a decade later.

"A SCREENPLAY is a story told in pictures." In *The Screenwriter's Workbook*, Syd Field analyzes the creative process of producing film scenarios. "Writing a screenplay is a step-by-step process," he explains. "First, find the subject, then structure the idea, then do character biographies, then do any research you need, then structure the first act on 3 × 5 cards; then write the screenplay, day by day, first Act I, then Act II and Act III."[6]

How different this is from the art of fiction, wherein the novelist discovers his story and characters in the process of writing. Doctorow has said that he writes to find out what he is writing about. "Anybody who finds himself in the situation of writing to a prescribed notion or to illustrate or fill in what he already knows should stop writing." Here, for instance, is Doctorow's description of the genesis of *The Book of Daniel:*

> I started to write the book in the third person, more or less as a standard, past tense, third person novel, very chronologically scrupulous. And after one hundred fifty pages I was terribly bored. That was a moment of great despair in my life, because I thought if I could really destroy a momentous subject like this, then I had no right to be a writer. That moment, when I threw out those pages and hit bottom, was when I became reckless enough to find the voice of the book, which was Daniel. I sat down and put a piece of paper in the typewriter and started to write with a certain freedom and irresponsibility, and it turned out Daniel was talking, and he was sitting in the library at Columbia, and I had my book.[7]

The finished novel is neither a standard third-person narrative nor chronologically scrupulous. Rather, its fractured chronology and fragmented narrative voice reflect the narrator's own sense of dislocation and outrage; this is very much Daniel's book and it contains his feelings of pain and outrage. The first problem facing the filmmaker is to find a cinematic equivalent of Daniel's voice.

While the novel begins with Daniel's voice, in the screenplay Daniel first appears in the seventh scene. We start with brief vignettes of the meeting and courtship of Daniel's parents in the radical political milieu of the 1930s; Doctorow deftly creates their world of immigrant aspirations, collegiate polemics, and Popular Front slogans. The romance of Paul and Rochelle Isaacson is tied up with the romance of Communism. Doctorow comments ironically on this revolutionary romanticism in a streetcar scene in which Paul lectures Rochelle on "the historical mission of the modern proletariat" while the camera pans to the other passengers: "an old woman, a couple of derelicts, a black man holding a bundle of rags." (In the film this camera pan is missing.) Daniel's voice first appears in the scene of Bukharin's show trial, which Daniel mockingly calls "Great Moments in Soviet Sports." (This scene is also missing from the film.) The difference between Daniel's cynicism and his parents' naiveté is immediately established; for the first time, but not for the last, the ideologies of the thirties and the sixties clash. Now the screenplay moves into the present and Daniel's visit to the hospital, which is the opening scene of the novel.

The finished film begins somewhat differently. Lumet starts with an extreme close-up of Daniel's eyes as he delivers a monologue on the physics of electricity and its application to the electric chair. (This speech will be repeated near the end of the film during his parents' execution.) While Daniel speaks, the camera moves back to reveal his entire face; as he explains the principles of the electric chair we have a brief glimpse of someone being taken to the execution chamber. (Later we learn it is Daniel's father.) Then we hear Paul Robeson singing the spiritual "Who Will Be a Witness?" as the screen goes black and the title DANIEL appears in large letters. We next see documentary footage of an antiwar demonstration, presumably the 1967 March on the Pentagon; then the scene shifts to the Lewin dinner table, where Daniel and Susan argue over their legacy. Finally, we see the 1930s scenes with which the screenplay begins. Here Lumet lovingly recreates the ambience of the radical thirties, for instance, in the artless square dance celebrating the Popular Front slogan "Communism Is Twentieth-Century Americanism." It is noteworthy that Doctorow and Lumet make no concessions to the "average" moviegoer, who is expected to recognize Earl Browder, Paul Robeson, and the Popular Front.

Why has Lumet made these changes? Clearly, the opening close-up is an arresting image that underpins Daniel's verbal assault on the audience. The brief glimpse of the execution chamber is a mystery that will not be explained

From *The Book of Daniel* to the Film of *Daniel*

until the end of the movie, when Daniel "does" the execution of his parents. (Lumet used a similar technique in his adaptation of Edward Lewis Wallant's novel *The Pawnbroker*.) The following scenes of the 1930s and 1960s are reshuffled to simplify the narrative's chronology. The time shifts are registered by filter alterations—the thirties in warm hues, the sixties in cool—to suggest the range of emotional worlds in the film.

Daniel's monologue, the changing color registers, and the swift editing are all attempts to find visual correlatives to Daniel's voice in the novel as he moves from alienation to acceptance. From the beginning, Lumet was aware that he would have to find "the visual equivalent of Edgar's poetry, of Edgar's non-reality. How do you make the picture seem real? But you can't use reality. It's not a realistic novel." In some cases, Lumet believes he has succeeded, particularly in the scenes with the children. But he has misgivings about the opening, as he suggests in our interview.

The film departs from the book in one major respect. It omits an important incident that appears in both the novel and the screenplay. This is the scene in which Daniel visits the New Left radical Artie Sternlicht, who trashes the Old Left in similar words in both book and script. According to Lumet, "it's a crucial scene, at the heart of one of the things that Edgar is talking about in that book, which is: This is why we have no American left today, because it cut itself off from its roots." Lumet thought the scene was so important that he actually shot it twice despite his modest budget. But he never managed to make the scene work.

Despite the best intentions, films often turn out differently from their scenarios because of accidents, errors, or budget limitations. Such gaps often require the reconstruction of the narrative and its meaning. For instance, Sternlicht's absence demands a significant revision in the film text. It creates a hole in the middle of the picture which the viewer senses whether or not he has read the book. When Daniel finds the poster of his parents in Susan's car, he must decide what to do with it. In the novel the poster becomes his letter of introduction to Sternlicht. In the screenplay Daniel walks to Sternlicht's apartment with the poster in his hand as he ponders his situation. But Sternlicht discards the poster, confirming the New Left's rejection of its own history. In the film we see Daniel carrying the poster in the street, but he never delivers it. Instead of Daniel's interior monologue Lumet substitutes Susan's voice. When Daniel finally hangs the poster on Susan's wall the action is logically consistent but its meaning is reduced to self-justification. Without

Sternlicht, *Daniel* becomes more a film about a family inheritance and less a film about a generational legacy.

Another significant change occurs at the end of the film. In the novel Doctorow provides three endings. In the first, Daniel returns to his parents' house only to discover that he is a stranger viewed with suspicion by the present poor black occupants. In the second, Daniel buries his sister and, at the same time, relives his parents' funeral. In a moving scene, he has Kaddish, the Jewish prayer for the dead, said over their graves. "I hold my wife's hand," he says. "And I think I am going to be able to cry." Having buried the dead and come back to life, Daniel must return to the present. But as he begins to write the last page, someone announces that the library is closed. It is 1968 and student radicals are closing down Columbia University in protest against the Vietnam War. "Close the book, man," he is told, "what's the matter with you, don't you know when you're liberated?"[8] This is finally what Daniel must do: close the book and re-enter the world.

In the screenplay, Doctorow moves directly from the execution to the funeral and then to a political demonstration in the summer of 1970. Daniel and Phyllis stand on the sidelines with their child and then the family joins the march. "The camera pans back, loses them in the immense crowd flowing through the city." Lumet films the scene pretty much as written, taking advantage, at Doctorow's urging, of the huge antinuclear rally that took place in New York's Central Park in 1983. Today Lumet feels that the ending fails to find an appropriate visual form for Daniel's rebirth. "I think I was depending on, or at least jumped at the crutch of, a political rally," Lumet says. "Not that that was a bad idea; it's just that somehow or other I should have been able to find a simpler, more beautiful way."

But perhaps the problem lies elsewhere. Doctorow, who takes responsibility for the idea, says "it turned out to make for a very soft ending." I think he's right. The beauty of the novel's ending is its openness. Like Daniel, the reader is led back to the real world of social relations, where the multiplicity of endings suggests the ongoing process of both self-realization and history. Instead, the film delivers the viewer and Daniel into the certitude of a political demonstration in which doubt and self-doubt are eliminated.

Despite its "soft ending," *Daniel* is a powerful motion picture, one that makes few concessions to popular taste. Compared to *Reds*, its more celebrated contemporary, it treats the complexities of radical politics with respect. Though conservative critics harshly attacked *Daniel* as historically revisionist, the film actually defies conventional ideological categories. Doctorow is careful to distinguish between the historical Rosenbergs as putative spies and the *idea* of the Rosenbergs embodied in the Isaacsons as complicitous victims in their own radical martyrdom. To his credit, Lumet instinctively recognized that he was dealing with an imaginative treatment of a resonant political-cultural event, unlike Haskell Wexler, who wished to turn *The Book of Daniel* into a documentary account of the Rosenbergs' trial and execution.

But any discussion of politics in film is likely to underestimate the mysterious power of the medium to move people in unintended ways. The classic Western *High Noon* has been variously interpreted as an attack on McCarthyism and a defense of Cold War militarism. In the final days of the first Polish elections in 1989, it was construed differently. For its final campaign poster, Solidarity appropriated the image of Gary Cooper as a resolute sheriff standing in front of the union logo with the caption "High Noon" underneath. The meaning was unmistakable, notes Ronald Brownstein: like Cooper, "Solidarity was tough, incorruptible, and coming to dispense justice."[9]

In the case of *Daniel*, Sidney Lumet feels that in 1983 the film was misunderstood and that much of the criticism was politically motivated. But seen today, more than a decade after the fall of the Berlin Wall, as we begin to assess the true costs of the Cold War, it may look like a very different film. Finally, Lumet still feels that *Daniel* is a "wonderful movie." He says, "Despite its critical and financial failure, I think it's one of the best pictures I've ever done."[10]

NOTES

1. William O'Neill, *Coming Apart* (New York: Quadrangle Books, 1971), 298.

2. *E. L. Doctorow: Essays and Conversations*, ed. Richard Trenner (Princeton: Ontario Review Press, 1983), 61.

3. Christopher Lasch, *The Agony of the American Left* (New York: Alfred A. Knopf, 1969).

4. Trenner, ed., *E. L. Doctorow*, 61.

5. E. L. Doctorow, *The Book of Daniel* (New York: Random House, 1971), 302.

6. Syd Field, *The Screenwriter's Workbook* (New York: Dell, 1984), 119, 10.

7. Trenner, ed., *E. L. Doctorow*, 38, 62.

8. Doctorow, *The Book of Daniel*, 302.

9. Ronald Brownstein, *The Power and the Glitter: The Hollywood-Washington Connection* (New York: Pantheon, 1990), 14.

10. Sidney Lumet, *Making Movies* (New York: Alfred A. Knopf, 1995), 45.

DANIEL

A Screenplay

EXT.   GREENE STREET RALLY. DAY. WINTER '38

We open on mounted New York City police breaking up a rally at City Hall Park. We're in the 1930s. Cops spur their horses into the crowd, lean over, swing their clubs. We hear screams, cursing. People scatter, placards are thrown to the ground.

The camera picks out one skinny YOUNG MAN *shouting through his cupped hands and then raising his fist defiantly. He is on the fringes of the crowd, out in the open, and he doesn't see a cop on horseback, stick upraised, bearing down from behind. A* GIRL's *voice screams "Look out!" and the young man turns and ducks just as the club whistles over his head and the horse canters by. But the horse has brushed him and he's fallen to the ground. The young woman helps him up.*

Together they are running, among others, through City Hall Park across the street to Park Row. They duck into a subway kiosk and stand inside the shell.

They are breathing heavily. The young man has a cut on his face, which he rubs with his sleeve. He is poorly dressed, a jacket with a wool scarf and slacks, although it is autumn and cold. He presses his horn-rimmed glasses up to the bridge of his nose with his middle finger, an apparently characteristic gesture. He finds the young woman looking at him. He laughs.

YOUNG MAN   The cossacks.

She laughs in return. She's obviously as poor as he, but somehow neater, with a threadbare coat which she now brushes assiduously. She's a not quite pretty girl

25

with a certain primness about her, but strength too. We hear the sound of sirens, horse hooves, distant screams. The two young people, their names are PAUL *and* ROCHELLE, *look at each other again, somewhat more aware now of each other's presence above and beyond the situation. He notices a button on her lapel. It says* OUST ROBINSON.

PAUL   You go to City?

ROCHELLE   At night.

PAUL   Me too!

INT./EXT.   CITY COLLEGE. DAY. WINTER '38

City College basement dining hall—oak tables, fake Heidelberg decor. Packed with students, many of whom eat their lunch from wax-paper wrapping. Room resounds with discussion. Intense thirties-type students, poor, first-generation American, burdened with books.
   At one crowded table PAUL *and* ROCHELLE *in earnest discussion with others. Next to* PAUL, *arguing on his side, is a gentle, prematurely balding boy,* BEN COHEN.

PAUL   The Fascists are taking Europe. The world is dying! And you're playing Trotskyist politics.

STUDENT   There would be no Hitler today if not for Stalin. True or not true?

BEN COHEN   That is simplistic.

STUDENT   Where was Stalin when a United Front in Germany could have kept Hitler from seizing power? Now you're all big antifascists!

ROCHELLE   We're prepared to grant you your righteousness.

Laughter from the table.

   What then?

STUDENT   Remember how you broke up our meeting at the Garden? Your people threw chairs. I remember. Yesterday we were social fascists. Today we're your comrades.

PAUL   You're a simplistic sectarian.

STUDENT   No I'm not, I'm Jewish!

Laughter.

PAUL   *(leaning forward.)* Then maybe you'll explain to the Jews in Nazi concentration camps the fine points of your dialectic.

The argument continues, taken over by others, as PAUL *and* ROCHELLE *talk to each other.* ROCHELLE *has finished her sandwich and sipped the last of her container of milk through a straw. She neatly folds her brown paper bag and puts it in her purse for use again.*

ROCHELLE   I have to get home.

PAUL   I'll see you home.

ROCHELLE   Don't be foolish. All the way to the Bronx? Then you first have to ride downtown.

PAUL   So what?

ROCHELLE   I'm tired. I can't invite you in. My mother . . .

PAUL   I'll picket your mother!

ROCHELLE *laughs.*

EXT.   MAY DAY PARADE. DAY. SPRING '38

May Day Parade. The marchers marching toward us raising their fists in rhythm. Red flags and American flags. This scene is silent. Along the line of marchers we find PAUL *and* ROCHELLE. *Next to* PAUL *is one of the students from the cafeteria,* BEN COHEN. *All three of them are exhilarated, joyful. Many banners and placards in the parade:* END THE ARMS EMBARGO. *Also,* COMMUNISM IS TWENTIETH-CENTURY AMERICANISM. *Also a YCL banner, union local banners, etc.*

EXT./INT.   STREETCAR. NIGHT. FALL '38

Night, and a streetcar is pulling uphill, its lights flickering, its wheels whining on their tracks.

Inside the streetcar, half empty, PAUL *and* ROCHELLE *sitting next to each other on the long bench that runs from front to back. Each has books and a paper bag with lunch.* PAUL *hunches over, reading aloud from a small book.* ROCHELLE *listens, studying him as he reads.*

PAUL   "The possibility of securing for every member of society through social production an existence which is not only fully sufficient from a material standpoint and becoming richer from day to day, but also guarantees to them the completely unrestricted development and exercise of their physical and mental faculties—this possibility now exists.

PAUL *glances up at* ROCHELLE *as one sharing a beautiful poem he's reading.*

"The seizure of the means of production by society puts an end to commodity production and therewith to the domination of the produce over the producer . . . To carry through this world-emancipating act is the historical mission of the modern proletariat. And it is the task of scientific socialism . . . to bring to the consciousness of the now-oppressed class the conditions and nature of the act which it is its destiny to accomplish . . . "

While he reads the camera pans to other people on the trolley—an old woman, a couple of derelicts, a black man holding a bundle of rags. The streetcar passes into the night.

INT.   ROCHELLE'S BRONX KITCHEN. NIGHT. FALL '38

ROCHELLE *and her* MOTHER *in the tiny dark kitchen of their Bronx apartment. A Yahrzeit candle burns on the kitchen table.* ROCHELLE's *coat is on, she has just come in. She drops into a chair and kicks off her shoes.*

MOTHER   So late?

ROCHELLE   I had a meeting.

MOTHER   And your boy, was he at the meeting?

ROCHELLE   He's not my boy.

MOTHER   You have meetings with him. Your mother is left to rot.

ROCHELLE   Mama, would you like him to come for dinner? Even tomorrow. And the three of us can spend the evening.

MOTHER   For dinner yet. Listen to Lady Bountiful.

ROCHELLE *sighs. She takes her pay envelope out of her pocketbook and puts it on the table.*

MOTHER   When did you eat? Look at you. A girl who works and goes to school at night doesn't need meetings.

The old woman takes the envelope, withdraws the money and counts it.

Sixteen fifty this is not.

ROCHELLE   Fifty cents for my carfare. Two dollars for my allowance.

MOTHER   So? I count eleven dollars.

ROCHELLE   I gave three dollars for the Scottsboro boys.

MOTHER   *(furious)* The Scottsboro boys! And will the Scottsboro boys pay the rent?

ROCHELLE   Mama, we are trying to keep them from being lynched!

MOTHER   A cholera on them. If they are innocent God will protect them.

ROCHELLE   As God protected Papa from the sweatshops!

MOTHER   *(enraged in Yiddish)* Blasphemy! You break the Sabbath! You speak filth! You go with boys! God will strike you dead! *(clasping hands to heaven)* What have I done? What have I done to deserve such torture!

EXT.   PAINE LODGE. DAY. SUMMER '39

The dining room of Paine Lodge, a Marxist summer camp–resort. Dinner is over but everyone has remained at their tables to listen to a speaker who stands at one end of the room. The SPEAKER, *unlike anyone else, wears a jacket and tie, although the tie is open and his collar unbuttoned.*

SPEAKER   . . . and those who excused the infamous Munich betrayal are loudest in their condemnation of the nonaggression pact. And why? Because by forcing Germany to sign this pact, with one stroke of the pen the Soviet Union overturns the design of Western imperialists. Hitler's war aims are contained in the East and mankind is diverted from the abyss of darkness and destruction.

Daniel: A Screenplay | 29

At the back of the room, a group of young waiters and waitresses, listening intently. In the group are PAUL *and* ROCHELLE *and their friend* BEN COHEN.

But the reactionaries will defame the Soviet Union no matter what, my friends. Of that you may be sure. You will hear much criticism of Russia, and some of it will come disguised as sweet reasonableness . . .

Among the people sitting around the tables the camera will show us SELIG MINDISH, *a burly man with small eyes and a large nose.*

but don't be fooled! Don't be fooled, comrades. The arguments for the nonaggression pact are inescapable once you apply thought to the matter. The Soviet Union is the only socialist nation in the world, and she has done something for the world which the world will someday understand, if it doesn't already!

The SPEAKER *stares at his audience and mops his forehead with his handkerchief. Applause.*

A crowd swarms around the SPEAKER, *everyone talking at once, or trying to meet him.* SELIG MINDISH *pushes in front of someone and introduces himself.*

MINDISH   (*shaking* SPEAKER's *hand*) A great honor, a great honor. I'm Dr. Selig Mindish, the camp dentist. And this is my wife—Sadie? Where are you?

SPEAKER   How do you do.

MINDISH   And my little girl, Linda.

The SPEAKER *exchanges amenities with* MRS. MINDISH *and the child. Lots of babble makes the conversation difficult to follow. We notice the tables are being pushed to the walls.* MINDISH *is flushed and happy. We see him waving at* PAUL *and* ROCHELLE, *helping with the tables, and they make their way through the knot around the* SPEAKER *and are introduced to him by the dentist. Perhaps in the noise we hear* MINDISH *refer to* PAUL *as "brilliant."*

INT.   PAINE LODGE. NIGHT. SUMMER '39

Square dancing at Paine Lodge. Where the SPEAKER *stood are now a* CALLER, *a* VIOLINIST, *and an* ACCORDIONIST, *all with cowboy hats, plaid shirts, and string ties. The song is "Skip to My Lou."*

There are four or five sets of dancers, and one is composed of PAUL *and*

Daniel: A Screenplay

ROCHELLE, SELIG MINDISH, *and his wife,* SADIE MINDISH, *a Bess Truman kind of woman. Much merriment in the room and considerable fantasizing as these working-class urbanites struggle with the country dance steps.*

Close-ups of PAUL *and* ROCHELLE *with eyes only for each other. They dance while the Mindishes clap.*

We cut and the song is now "Old Joe Clark" with some labor union version of the words. All the dancers are in two lines facing each other and they come together, arms and hands raised, with a great whooping sound.

INT.   RUSSIAN COURT. DAY. 1900S

A foreign courtroom of some kind, a MAN *with a white beard is led to a witness box; a* JUDGE *above him leans over the bench to ask him questions. He appears to answer. All this is done in pantomime, accompanied by a commentary in a voice that will later be recognized as that of* DANIEL ISAACSON, *the son of* PAUL *and* ROCHELLE.

DANIEL   *(voice over)* Great Moments in Soviet Sports!
Accused Bukharin, Nikolaie Ivanovich, have you received a copy of the indictment?
Yes, I have.
Accused Bukharin, do you desire to have counsel for Defense?
No.
Accused Bukharin, do you plead guilty to the charges brought against you?
Yes, I plead guilty to the charges brought against me.

EXT.   SUSAN'S HOSPITAL. DAY. FALL '67

The busy intersection of two main roads at the border of a suburban city. Heavy traffic. A late-model car comes to a stop at the light and two hitchhikers (DANIEL *and* PHYLLIS) *get out, thank the driver, and scramble to the sidewalk before the traffic starts to move again.*

The hitchhikers are a young man and a young woman. The young man carries an INFANT *in a sling pouch on his chest. The young woman slings a carryall from her shoulder. Their dress suggests more or less the present: He wears a blue denim prison jacket, jeans, sandals. He sports steel-rim glasses, a scruffy beard. She wears bell-bottoms and a khaki poncho.*

They wait for the light to change.

Daniel: A Screenplay | 31

Across the road, beyond an imposing entrance gate, are the grounds and buildings of some sort of large institution. When the light changes the young couple quickly crosses to the opposite corner, where, in front of the gates, a number of oddly dressed, soiled, and derelict-looking PEOPLE *wait at a bus stop. Several carry brown paper lunchbags. As the young couple approaches, they scuttle out of the way like pigeons. One of them, a* MAN *in a ribbed undershirt and overalls, begins to run ahead of the couple, waving his arms like a windmill. They follow him through the gates onto the grounds. A sign along the driveway says* NEWTON STATE HOSPITAL.

INT. SUSAN'S HOSPITAL LOUNGE. DAY. FALL '67

The young man (DANIEL) *of the last scene is looking out a barred window. He watches his wife* (PHYLLIS) *playing with their* BABY *down on the sloping lawn in front of Newton State Hospital. At the top of the sloping lawn is a retaining wall of brick. Inside that wall a parking lot with many cars. A dark blue Chevrolet comes into the lot followed by an ambulance, driving slowly.*

GIRL'S VOICE   How's your wife?

YOUNG MAN   Fine.

GIRL'S VOICE   And your baby?

YOUNG MAN   He's fine too. They came along. They're downstairs.

The young man turns from the window and sits down next to a girl (SUSAN) *who wears a patient's robe, terry-cloth slippers on her feet. They're alone in some sort of patients' lounge. She is a dark-haired girl, about twenty, very slim. She squints, as if she needs glasses. Her wrists are taped.*

GIRL   Ah then, it's serious.

YOUNG MAN   I don't think it's so serious.

GIRL   The Lewins too?

YOUNG MAN   Their car just pulled in.

GIRL   It must be serious. My whole family is here. How supportive. The *meshpuchah.*

YOUNG MAN   Come on, Susan.

SUSAN   Oh God. Am I going to have to see them? *(She breathes deeply.)* But I have to believe no matter how bad it gets, you and I can never bring them down totally. And that's the saving grace, isn't it.

YOUNG MAN   Yes.

SUSAN   The right to do irreparable harm is a blood right.

He takes her hand. She's trying not to cry.

It just . . . I was overcome with it, with the calamity of it.

YOUNG MAN   It's OK.

SUSAN   I feel like something's torn. I forget what it is you're supposed to expect from being alive . . . I'm glad you came, Daniel. I had something to tell you . . . But I can't remember what it was.

DANIEL *now sits leaning forward, elbows on knees, head in hands.* SUSAN *reaches out and pats his shoulder.*

They're still fucking us. Goodbye, Daniel. You get the picture.

INT.   ISAACSON HOME. NIGHT. FALL '43

A party in the home of PAUL *and* ROCHELLE ISAACSON *on the occasion of* PAUL's *furlough.* PAUL *is in army uniform with T-corporal stripes. His hair is cut short and his ears protrude. He's ecstatically happy. So is* ROCHELLE, *who comes into the very modest living room–bedroom of their Bronx home with a tray of sandwiches for the guests:* DR. SELIG MINDISH *and his wife,* SADIE; BEN COHEN, *who now sports a moustache and pipe; and other friends, who continue to arrive with much hugging and kissing of the returned soldier. In the corner of the room, ignored, sits* ROCHELLE's *mother, frailer and older now. She seems oblivious to everyone but the toddler,* DANIEL, *who lurches around the room and is occasionally lifted into the air by his loving father.*

PAUL   I've got to hand it to them. Imagine making a radio technician of Paul Isaacson. But you know something? I do it well! I was first in my training. I understand the army. I get along with the men. In basic I pulled my weight. I was determined those crackers would not have the occasion to laugh at a Jew from New York. I ran with a heavy pack, I climbed ropes, I crawled under machine-gun fire with real bullets, I did the push-ups. They came to respect me. And at night in our bull sessions I told them my beliefs and they listened. And you know, those Georgia crackers living down there in the red clay, they taught *me* a few things! The dignity of ordinary men. The unsung heroism of men who work the earth with their hands. The good common sense of the masses who have not had an education.

SELIG MINDISH   And now, Paul? What now?

PAUL   Who knows? I don't have my orders yet.

SADIE MINDISH   God forbid you should end up overseas.

PAUL   Why God forbid? Should we let the Soviet Union fight our battles for us?

PAUL *has taken a record out of a 78 rpm album of the Red Army Chorus. He places it on a Victrola. The record is the martial song "Meadowland." He listens a moment.*

I would be proud to be part of the Second Front. To meet our gallant Soviet allies and link arms with them.

Everyone listens quietly, reverently, to the music. They are stirred to the soul. The camera takes the opportunity in the change of mood to examine the faces of the people in the room.

INT./EXT.   PAUL'S RADIO SHOP. DAY. SUMMER '48

PAUL ISAACSON *is at work in the back of his dingy radio repair shop in the Bronx. He works with a soldering iron.* DANIEL, *his young son, perhaps six or seven, watches intently as* PAUL *tinkers with the guts of a radio receiver.* DANIEL *has been to the grocery store for his mother and a grocery bag is on the workbench, a box of cereal protruding.*

PAUL   Did you buy everything Mommy asked for?

DANIEL   Yes.

PAUL   *(smiling)* I see you got your favorite cereal. Who's on the back?

DANIEL   Joe DiMaggio.

Daniel: A Screenplay

PAUL   Why do you suppose they put his picture on a box of cereal?

DANIEL   'Cause he's strong.

PAUL   That's right. Although it doesn't say so in so many words it puts an idea in your mind—that if you eat this cereal you'll be strong like he is. Yet . . . *(he pauses to concentrate on his work)* if you look at the nourishment this cereal contains you see you'd do better with ordinary oatmeal.

DANIEL   Oatmeal has lumps.

PAUL   So they're lying. That's what advertising is, lying.

The boy nods, watching his father's hands.

And of course not Joe DiMaggio but one or another of your baseball heroes sells his name and picture to the cereal company for money. Saying he eats their cereal. When in fact, he probably only drinks beer and smokes cigarettes!

DANIEL *laughs.*

Sure it's funny. He's putting one over on us. But he's been exploited just as we are. Because what is he but a worker like anyone who earns his bread by his labor? And the fact that he plays a game called baseball makes no difference. He's no better than the man who works in a factory. You know why?

DANIEL   *(nods, seriously interested)* Because he doesn't own the team?

PAUL   Right! You're very smart! Someone else gets rich from his labor. And when workers or baseball players get too old or sick to be good at what they do, the men who own the teams or the factories kick them out, and that's the end of them.

DANIEL   Even Joe DiMaggio?

PAUL   Yes, that will even happen to Joe DiMaggio. But at least he plays—there are Negro baseball players, marvelous athletes, who are not allowed to play because of Jim Crow. No matter how good they are.

The radio sputters to life.

There. It's working.

On an autumn day DANIEL, *same age as last scene, stands on the sidewalk in front of his house, a small frame house set back on this city street by a tiny yard. The siding of the house is green asphalt scored to look like brick.* DANIEL *is minding a baby in a baby carriage. From the front door his* GRANDMA *emerges—*ROCHELLE's *mother, white-haired and skinny. She has a shawl over her head and wears high-laced boots and a black dress. She comes down the porch steps shaking her fist at* DANIEL *and cursing him in Yiddish. He is terrified but holds his ground. She reaches the sidewalk and walks off down the street, turning every once in a while to shake her fist at him and curse and shout in Yiddish. She continues to do this till she reaches the corner and disappears from sight.*

INT.   THRUWAY RESTAURANT. DAY. FALL '67

A Howard Johnson's restaurant. At a corner table sits the young man DANIEL, *his blonde wife* PHYLLIS, *their* BABY, *an older couple,* ROBERT *and* LISE LEWIN, *and a pock-faced man named* DUBERSTEIN. *The remains of a meal on the table.*

LISE LEWIN   She was depressed. But that was nothing new.

ROBERT LEWIN   We wanted her to come home for the weekend. She said she had plans. I didn't realize . . . She was making her classes. She was doing her work.

DUBERSTEIN   Well, it's the politics. Last winter when Susan terminated therapy, I warned her not to get too involved. All that radical stuff—

A WAITRESS *comes up.*

WAITRESS   Who gets the peach ice cream soda?

DUBERSTEIN   Here.

The soda is set down, the WAITRESS *leaves.*

DUBERSTEIN   But of course she did. SDS, Resistance, who knows what? In this family dissent is traumatic. It's understandable. She bit off more than she could chew.

ROBERT LEWIN   Susan's a willfull person.

DUBERSTEIN *(looking under his napkin for a straw)* I have great faith in her.

DANIEL *(to his wife,* PHYLLIS*)* If you're not finishing your sandwich pass it over here.

DUBERSTEIN *(to* LEWINS*)* Of course, I'd be insulting your intelligence if I didn't admit this is a pretty serious business. She's been down before but this is the worst.

DANIEL What did you do, put ketchup on this?

PHYLLIS What?

DANIEL You put ketchup on a club sandwich.

PHYLLIS *is embarrassed.* LISE LEWIN, *her mother-in-law, perceives this.*

LISE LEWIN Why not ketchup?

DUBERSTEIN *(to* ROBERT LEWIN*)* On the other hand, she's got tremendous resources. We'll get her all settled and then we can go to work.

DANIEL Ketchup on a club sandwich. Yuk!

ROBERT LEWIN Would you like something else? How about ordering something?

DANIEL No thanks, Dad *(pushing the plate away)*. I'd still have to sit here and listen to this schmuck doctor talk about my sister.

Silence at the table.

LISE LEWIN Daniel, I hope you are prepared to apologize.

DANIEL What is it about Susan and me that makes anyone feel privileged to say anything at all to us? Who is this creep? Who needs him?

ROBERT LEWIN I called Dr. Duberstein because I think we need him very badly. I think Susan needs him. And I don't think you're handling yourself very well.

DANIEL She stopped going to him because he was no fucking good. And now he can't even get her out of there! He can't get her out of a public asylum for wards of the state and bums they pick up off the street!

DUBERSTEIN   One more night in what happens to be one of the best facilities in the East is not going to hurt her. The situation is under control!

But DANIEL *has left the table and is walking out of the restaurant.*

EXT.   JONES BEACH ROADWAY. DAY. SUMMER '49

*A run-down 1942 Chrysler is making its way fitfully through summer traffic.
Driving the Chrysler is* SELIG MINDISH, *the dentist. He wears a Hawaiian
print shirt, prescription sunglasses, and a white beach hat. Next to him is his
twelve-year-old daughter,* LINDA, *in two-piece bathing suit with limp halter.*
SELIG's *wife,* SADIE, *sits next to the window.*

In the rear seat, a family of four. PAUL *and* ROCHELLE ISAACSON, *their
seven-year-old son,* DANIEL, *and their two-year-old daughter,* SUSAN, *who has
just thrown up. Everyone is dressed for the beach.*

LINDA MINDISH   The smell is terrible. Open the window!

PAUL   *(laughing)* All the windows are open.

ROCHELLE   *(as she cleans the child)* Selig, maybe if the driving was
smoother, the children would not get carsick.

SADIE MINDISH   I find no fault with the driving.

SELIG MINDISH   *(blowing the horn)* Everyone had the same idea today.

ROCHELLE   If we'd gone to Orchard Beach we'd be there by now.

PAUL   Now, now, everybody. Keep calm. We want the ocean. At Jones Beach
we'll have the ocean breeze and we'll all feel better.

We see the car out on the highways of Long Island now. The traffic is still heavy.

EXT.   JONES BEACH. DAY. SUMMER '49

We see DANIEL *playing at the edge of the water. He's building bridges and
tunnels in the sand.* LINDA, *his tormentor, splashes him with water, then steps on
his constructions. He kicks sand at her then runs up to where his father and
mother and* SELIG MINDISH *are arranged on blankets.* SADIE MINDISH *sits a
few feet away under a rented umbrella.*

PAUL, *skinny and white, has just finished reading something aloud from the* Worker, *which is spread open before him.*

ROCHELLE   *(eyes closed, face in sun)* Oh, that's nonsense. Foster and Dennis are in jail, the Party is a shambles. When Browder—

MINDISH   Browder! *(He looks around to see if anyone has heard.)*

ROCHELLE   All right—but under Browder the Party was at least connected to something. Now we're alone. And what they're not destroying we're destroying ourselves.

The thought makes them all reflective.

Sometimes I wonder what's happened to our lives. *(She looks at* PAUL*)* I find it hard to remember what we've accomplished.

PAUL   *(shocked)* So things are bad at the moment. Very bad. The Party has had some effect, or there would be no reaction. What have we done for the working class? Is that nothing? And the Negroes?

ROCHELLE *gets up, brushes away the sand, walks off toward the surf. She is no longer a slim girl.* MINDISH *watches her appreciatively in her one-piece 1947 bathing suit.*

PAUL   *(noticing* DANIEL*)* Having a good time?

The boy nods.

The heat and the traffic don't matter now, do they? *(He looks out toward the water.)* The ocean is beautiful. So you see, some things are worth the effort.

INT.   DUNGEON. DAY. 1500

Some figures in shadow seem to be working over a body. A shot of the tortured face of the one on whom this work is being done. Flash of a broadsword blade. Firelight. Apparently we're in some kind of dungeon. All this is silent. Huge dogs strain at the leash.

DANIEL   *(voice over)* Drawing and quartering was a form of execution favored by the English kings. Except if he was an aristocrat, in which case he was simply beheaded, the offender was hanged and cut down before he was dead. Then he was emasculated, disemboweled, and his entrails were set on fire in front of his eyes. If the executioner was merciful the heart was then removed from the body. In any case, the ritual was completed with a hacking of the body into four parts, the quarters being thrown to the dogs. Treason was the usual crime for this punishment. It was the King who decided what treason was.

INT. ISAACSON HOME. DAY. SUMMER '49

DANIEL *is uncomfortable standing in the kitchen of the Isaacson house—in front of his* GRANDMA, *who opens her change purse of cracked leather and withdraws one penny with her thumb and forefinger. She presses the penny into his hand, pulls him toward her by the back of his neck, and kisses him on the forehead.*

GRANDMA   *(softly)* Daniel is a good boy. That is for a good boy.

DANIEL *runs out of the room. In the hall, the front door open, people stand about with blankets in arms, picnic lunches in bags, thermos bottles. Through the open door we see a yellow school bus, vintage 1946, at the curb. All these people are recognizably Isaacson friends—we saw them at an earlier age at* PAUL's *homecoming from the army. There is a hum of expectation.* DANIEL *pulls at his father's elbow, in the hall, where* PAUL *has just finished speaking on the phone.*

DANIEL   Can't I go?

Together they walk to the back end of the hall where, in the bathroom, door half closed, ROCHELLE *applies lipstick and combs her hair.*

PAUL   It's time to go.

ROCHELLE   I'm ready. The sandwiches are in the icebox.

DANIEL   Can't I go?

ROCHELLE   Your father's in charge.

PAUL   Please, Rochelle, don't start that. If there was the slightest chance of trouble do you think I'd let you go—let alone the boy? Be sensible.

.ROCHELLE   Don't talk to me of being sensible.

PAUL   There's a court order, for godssake. What can happen?

Daniel: A Screenplay

SELIG MINDISH *comes down the hall from the out-of-doors, followed by the ungainly* LINDA, *his daughter.*

MINDISH   What's the problem?

ROCHELLE   No problem.

MINDISH   We're having a meeting in the bathroom? A mobilization?

PAUL   We're deciding whether to take Daniel.

MINDISH   My Linda is coming. Why not?

As if to emphasize this, LINDA *smiles her mouthful of braces at* DANIEL, *and unseen by the adults, pokes him in the ribs.*

PAUL   Tell her, Selig—lots of children are going.

ROCHELLE *puts her lipstick in the medicine cabinet, pushes* PAUL *out of the bathroom, and closes the door on all of them.*

MINDISH   (*looking at* DANIEL) The little prince is afraid to go?

DANIEL *doesn't like this remark.*

PAUL   (*through door*) Don't you want your child to hear one of the great voices of our time? Is it such a terrible risk—if he can see Paul Robeson, a great people's artist?

Voices from the porch are calling for everyone to board the bus. MINDISH *runs off with* LINDA. *Sound of toilet flushing, water running. Door opens.* ROCHELLE *looks for a moment at* PAUL.

ROCHELLE   Danny, go get your blue jacket. And tie your shoelaces and pull up your socks. And then when you come down I want you to go to the bathroom—even if you don't have to.

EXT.   ISAACSON HOME. DAY. SUMMER '49

On the bus as the engine turns over, through the bus window, DANIEL, *sitting on his* MOTHER's *lap, sees a tall black man in overalls put down the two garbage cans he is carrying up from the alley. The black man stares at the people on the bus.*

This is WILLIAMS, *the janitor. At the same time* DANIEL'S GRANDMA *appears on the porch of the Isaacson house, her shawl around her head. In her high-laced shoes she comes down the wooden steps and sets off furiously down the street.*

DANIEL   Grandma's running away again.

ROCHELLE   I see. Don't worry.

As the bus moves off it passes WILLIAMS, *the janitor, standing and watching, and then passes* GRANDMA, *tracking her as she shakes her fist at the bus and shouts something we can't hear. People on the bus laugh and cheer.*

DANIEL   Why is Grandma crazy?

ROCHELLE   She can't stand the torment of her life.

EXT.   RALLY BUS. HIGHWAY. DAY. SUMMER '49

The bus is rolling down the highway. We hear the voices of the people on the bus as they sing, in anticpation and camaraderie, the songs identified with Robeson.

VOICES SINGING "Joe Hill" *(over)*
    "I dreamed I saw Joe Hill last night
    Alive as you and me
    But Joe, I said, you're ten years dead
    I never died says he . . ."

EXT./INT.   RALLY BUS. HIGHWAY. DAY. SUMMER '49

Interior of the moving bus. Almost everyone is singing, including PAUL *and* MINDISH.

VOICES SINGING "Peat Bog Soldiers" *(over)*
    "Far and wide as the eye can wander
    Heat and bog are everywhere
    Not a bird sings out to cheer us
    Oaks are standing gaunt and bare.
    We are the peat bog soldiers
    We're marching with our spades to the bog . . ."

ROCHELLE *does not sing. She puts her arms around* DANIEL *and settles him more firmly in her lap. We hear* PAUL's *voice louder than the others.*

Daniel: A Screenplay

INT.   THRUWAY RESTAURANT LOBBY. DAY. FALL '67

The adult DANIEL *stands in the circular lobby that provides access to the Howard Johnson's dining room, and to a gas station gift shop and to rest rooms. It is swarming with people.* DANIEL *stares at the door marked* WOMEN *and, ignoring the looks he gets, walks to a point a few feet from the door and kneels down to examine stains on the carpet; they seem to be stains of an imperfect washing of spots leading from the door.*

EXT.   THRUWAY RESTAURANT PARKING LOT. DAY. FALL '67

DANIEL *comes out of the Howard Johnson's, into the parking lot. The sky is heavy, grey, with distant lightning flashes over the turnpike.* DANIEL, *hands in his jeans, shoulders hunched, is looking for a car. He stops at an old black Volvo covered with grit. He takes some keys out of his pocket, looks at them, tries one, then another, before the door of the Volvo opens. In the car, beside the driver's seat, is a khaki backpack. Next to it, half hidden, the celluloid and cardboard packaging for a pack of Gillette Super Stainless blades. He pushes this stuff aside, sits down in the car with the door open. Sticking out of the rucksack is a cardboard mailing tube. He pulls it out, looks down inside as if he were peering through a telescope. He withdraws a poster from the tube. Unrolls it: We see the cosmetized faces of* PAUL *and* ROCHELLE ISAACSON.

SUSAN   *(voice over)* They're still fucking us. Goodbye, Daniel. You get the picture.

EXT.   SUBWAY STATION TO ISAACSON RALLY. DAY. FALL/ WINTER '53

Coming up subway steps toward the street, DANIEL, *around twelve, and* SUSAN, *perhaps seven or eight. They wear ill-fitting winter clothes—a mackinaw and wool hunter's cap for* DANIEL, *a home-knitted hat and too-thin coat for* SUSAN. *As they reach the top of the stairs gusts of wind drive soot into their eyes and newspaper against their legs.*

   Coming up behind them is ASCHER, *a middle-aged heavyset man, in a black homburg and overcoat. He is breathing heavily.*

ASCHER   I'm not going to live long.

After resting for a moment at the top of the stairs ASCHER *takes each by a hand and heads west on 42nd Street. It is a cold day.* ASCHER *gathers the children to his sides, pressing them into the bulk of his coat.*

Stay in close. That way you can walk. My God, this weather. Like the rest of our luck, like the way all of our luck is running.

They pass a Nedick's, a record store, 42nd Street movie houses. A squad of mounted police trots past. Traffic is heavy.

We are a little late. I can tell from here, a tremendous crowd. A great tribute, you should feel proud. When you're up there keep your heads up, stand straight, don't slump. So that everyone can see you, vershtey?

SUSAN   I've got something in my eye.

ASCHER   We have not time, Susan. Come.

SUSAN   *(digging in her heels)* I've *got* something in my *eye!*

DANIEL *takes his sister by the hand and leads her to the shelter of a doorway, takes off his gloves, removes a handkerchief from his back pocket, kneels in front of her.*

DANIEL   Take your glasses off. Don't rub! Look up. How can I see what it is if you don't open?

SUSAN   I can't.

DANIEL   Come on, Susyanna—you should see what a funny face you're making! Let me get it out, and when we go home I'll play with you. I'll play Monopoly with you.

ASCHER   Please, we are late. This is very important!

DANIEL   Just a minute, Mr. Ascher. She's only a little girl, you know.

As if to confirm this, SUSAN *bursts into tears. Then to everyone's relief she discovers that the irritation is gone.*

SUSAN   Will you still play Monopoly with me?

DANIEL   Yes.

ASCHER   Hurry, hurry!

Daniel: A Screenplay

A big crowd in the street, police on horseback at the edges, an impassioned and unintelligible speech over loudspeakers. Making their way through the crowd in single file, ASCHER, DANIEL, *and* SUSAN. ASCHER *is trying to get to the front of the crowd, to the speaker's platform. People are packed tight. An elbow comes up and knocks* DANIEL's *cap off. Since he is holding* ASCHER's *hand with one hand and* SUSAN's *with the other, he cannot retrieve the hat.* SUSAN *breaks his grip and dives after it.* DANIEL, *still in* ASCHER's *grip, looks behind him to see his sister disappearing between legs, behind overcoats. He in turn breaks away, goes after her.*

SUSAN   *(off camera)* Daniel! Daniel!

LOUDSPEAKER VOICE   Is this our so-called American justice? Can anyone believe that this heroic young couple, torn from their home, separated from their precious children, are being persecuted for anything more than their proudly held left-wing views? For believing in the dignity of man and the right of each and every individual to the fruits of his labor? History will record with shame the unwarranted arrest and unjustified trial and monstrous conviction of Paul and Rochelle Isaacson, this young American couple who have never been guilty of so much as jaywalking! Who can doubt that if we allow this terrible miscarriage of justice to occur that it will only be the beginning of a purge, a pogrom, the likes of which America has never known! We must say "Free them, Free the Isaacsons" to those who have vilified them and left them to languish in the shadow of the electric chair. "Free the Isaacsons! Free them! Free them! Free them!"

DANIEL *finds* SUSAN *clutching his hat with both hands. They stand, lost in the crowd, looking up at the sky over the shoulders and heads of the people around them.* ASCHER *is calling them and appears suddenly, bursting through, scolding. Once again in tow, they follow* ASCHER.

ASCHER   Please. These are the children. Let us through please, I've got the children. One side please.

Perhaps we see them from a height, their progress through the crowd like a wave of agitation that increases the closer they get to the speaker's stand.

CROWD VOICES   It's the children! The children! They've got the children!

Then DANIEL *and* SUSAN *are being raised over people's heads and passed forward like something on top of the sea. They're terrified. And when they're raised, tottering to the platform, the* SPEAKER *stands between them and says through the mike,* "Here are the children!" *and a great roar goes up from the crowd.* ASCHER *is at the foot of the platform beaming up at the children as they stand dazed, fearful, in front of the roaring crowd. The crowd chants,* "Free them, free them, free them!" *And everywhere placards go up and down in rhythm—placards with the faces of* PAUL *and* ROCHELLE ISAACSON *(same as in the poster Daniel found earlier).*

EXT.   THRUWAY RESTAURANT PARKING LOT. DAY. FALL '67

DANIEL *sitting in the Volvo in the Howard Johnson's parking lot.*

DANIEL   *(softly)* Free them.

PHYLLIS's *face peers in.*

PHYLLIS   You OK?

DANIEL *gets out of the car. Behind* PHYLLIS *are* LISE LEWIN, *holding the* BABY; ROBERT LEWIN; *and, a few feet further back, a wary* DR. DUBERSTEIN.

DANIEL   She was on her way to New York.

LISE LEWIN   Perhaps to see you?

DANIEL   I don't think so.

The family moves in closer.

ROBERT LEWIN   Dan, I see no reason why you shouldn't hold on to the car until she's better.

DANIEL   *(eyes down)* We should have spent more time. We should never have stopped talking.

DR. DUBERSTEIN *moves forward.*

DUBERSTEIN   She's a separate person, Daniel. You live separate lives.

PHYLLIS   Maybe when she's better Susan can stay with us for a while. I want her to. We would really love her? The baby would love her?

LISE LEWIN *gives the* BABY *to* PHYLLIS. *She then touches* DANIEL's *cheek to get him to look at her.*

LISE LEWIN   Daniel, this is an illness. Like any other. It will be treated.

DANIEL   Well what if she's not ill? Tell me! What if she's only . . . inconsolable?

EXT./INT.   PAUL'S RADIO SHOP. FALL '52

On a bitter grey autumn afternoon ROCHELLE *wheels a white wicker stroller carrying* SUSAN, *age four.* DANIEL, *age ten or twelve, in hunter's cap and mackinaw, walks alongside. They are going down a local shopping street in the Bronx. Suddenly something catches* ROCHELLE's *eye. Alarmed, she begins to run toward whatever it is.* DANIEL *races to keep up.*

They arrive at the edge of a crowd of people standing in front of PAUL ISAACSON's radio repair store (ISAACSON RADIO SALES AND REPAIR).

ROCHELLE   What's happened? What's the matter?

DANIEL *burrows through the crowd until he reaches the store window. In the window* PAUL ISAACSON *in shirt-sleeves and work apron adjusts the dials of the first TV set to be seen in the neighborhood, a big brown wooden console with a tiny rounded screen. He sees* DANIEL, *disappears into the store, comes out the door and walks through the gathering to* ROCHELLE, *takes her arm, and leads her a few steps apart.*

ROCHELLE   Where did you get that?

PAUL   It was on order. Listen—

DANIEL   Can we take it home?

PAUL   Just a minute, Danny. (*He lowers his voice and addresses* ROCHELLE.) Mindish has been arrested.

ROCHELLE   What?

PAUL   Keep your voice down. Early this morning while he was eating break-fast. The FBI took him downtown.

ROCHELLE   Oh my god—

PAUL   Don't say anything to anyone. Go about your business and let everything remain the same. When I get upstairs we'll talk.

ROCHELLE   How do you know this?

PAUL   Sadie Mindish called me. I can't understand the brains of some
people. She said Selig wanted me to know and he told her to call me.

ROCHELLE   (shakes her head) Oh, Paul—

DANIEL   (tugging PAUL's arm) What did he do?

PAUL   (to ROCHELLE) You've got to keep calm.

DANIEL   Why did they arrest Dr. Mindish?

PAUL   They're insane. They think he's done something. (He picks SUSAN up
out of the carriage.) How's my honey? How's my little girl? If they didn't
arrest people, they would have nothing to do . . . Do me a favor, Rochelle.
Take the groceries upstairs and close the door. I'll be home the usual time.
(He replaces SUSAN in the carriage.) It's only the coming of fascism, so why
should we be surprised?

INT.   SELIG'S DENTAL OFFICE. DAY. FALL '52

SELIG MINDISH, in dentist's white tunic, fussing in front of chair, humming a
folk song off-key. Turns to camera with drill in hand and smiles.

DANIEL   (voice over) I'm glad they arrested him.

ROCHELLE   (voice over) Danny!

DANIEL   (voice over) He likes to hurt you. And he says stupid things!

INT.   ISAACSON HOME. DAY. FALL/WINTER '52

DANIEL has just arrived home from school and is closing the front door. His
father, PAUL, is on the phone, near the door, speaking urgently, softly, with his
hand cupped over the mouthpiece. DANIEL notices the curtained glass doors to
the living room—bedroom are closed. He pushes them open cautiously, peeking
around the edge of the door just as ROCHELLE comes out of the kitchen at the
end of the hall, behind the stairs and calls out:

Daniel: A Screenplay

ROCHELLE   Danny, stay out of there!

Inside the room, sitting on the couch, TWO NEATLY DRESSED MEN (FBI AGENTS) *in overcoats, their hats on their laps.*

FIRST MAN   Hello, young fellow. Home from school?

DANIEL *nods.*

SECOND MAN   What grade are you in, son?

DANIEL *doesn't answer. His father opens the doors all the way, comes past him into the room.*

PAUL   Well, a lawyer has just advised me. I don't have to talk to you if I don't want to. That particular fact you neglected to mention.

FIRST MAN   Yes, sir, Mr. Isaacson, but we're hoping you'll cooperate. We're looking for information. You're a friend of Dr. Mindish. You could be in a position to help him.

PAUL   I will be glad to answer any questions in a court of law.

SECOND MAN   Do you deny now that you know him?

PAUL   I will answer any questions in a court of law.

EXT./INT.   PAUL'S RADIO SHOP. DAY. FALL/WINTER '52

It is morning and PAUL ISAACSON, *newspaper folded under his arm, arrives at the door of Isaacson Radio Sales and Repair, takes out his keys and opens up for business. Inside he appears startled. He stands as if he smells something or hears something strange. He goes behind the makeshift plywood counter and pushes aside the hanging curtain covering the doorway leading to the back of the store. He pulls the string of the overhead fluorescent light. He stands stock still, his eyes panning the radio tubes in their racks, the tagged radios on the repair bench, the sagging patterned ceiling, the bins of radio parts.* PAUL *is frowning, he is disturbed. He tosses his paper on the worktable, puts his hands on his hips.*

EXT. ISAACSON HOME. DAY. FALL/WINTER '52

The TWO AGENTS *sit in their sedan parked in front of the Isaacson house. The sky over the schoolyard and rooftops beyond is almost dark and the men in the car have turned on the interior light. They are writing something on clipboards.*

INT. ISAACSON HOME. DAY. FALL/WINTER '52

DANIEL *is watching them from the living-room window, holding the shade an inch or two to the side so that he can peek out.* ROCHELLE *sits in a chair,* PAUL *paces the room.*

PAUL   They don't know what they want. They're just fishing. They're dumb, clumsy, obvious people.

ROCHELLE   Polizei don't have to be smart.

PAUL   Don't worry, Mindish won't suffer from anything we've said. We've done nothing wrong. There is no reason to be afraid.

DANIEL   They're still here.

PAUL   What? Let me see. (*He takes* DANIEL's *place at the window.*) It's part of the treatment. Goddamn them! They can sit out there forever for all I care!

INT. DANIEL'S SCHOOL. DAY. FALL/WINTER '52

In the hallways of Public School 70 schoolchildren are lined up against the walls. A teacher blows a whistle and the children quickly seat themselves with their backs to the walls, their knees drawn up, their heads on their knees, their arms around their legs. Teachers walk along correcting the form of individual children. No one makes a sound. The teachers whisper. In the midst of this one of the children, DANIEL, *suddenly stands up and runs into his empty classroom. He goes to the window and hoists himself up.*

EXT. ISAACSON HOME. DAY. FALL/WINTER '52

From this vantage point he can see his house across Weeks Avenue and satisfy himself that it's still there.

Daniel: A Screenplay

INT. DANIEL'S SCHOOL. DAY. FALL/WINTER '52

A TEACHER *has followed him—a large wheezing woman in a flowered dress.*

TEACHER Just a minute, young man. What do you think *you're* doing? This is a drill! Do you know what happens to people at windows?

DANIEL Yesterday we went outside.

TEACHER That was a fire drill. For fire drill we go outside. This is atomic war drill. For atomic war drill we stay inside. And we keep away from windows!

EXT. ISAACSON HOME. DAY. WINTER '53

On a cold day, with snow on the ground, PAUL ISAACSON *and the* TWO FBI AGENTS *stand near the agents' car parked in front of the house. To a casual observer they might be three friends passing the time. One of the agents is leaning against the fender, his arms folded.*

FIRST AGENT It's no fun in weather like this.

SECOND AGENT You think he'd show some consideration.

PAUL It's your choice, gentlemen, I'm not keeping you here.

FIRST AGENT Come on, Paul, be a buddy. Give a little.

SECOND AGENT If you knew the pressures—

PAUL I commiserate, believe me.

SECOND AGENT We're under a real lot of pressure. Why don't you give us something to make our lives easier.

PAUL From whom? Pressure from whom?

FIRST AGENT Higher-ups.

PAUL And who are these higher-ups?

The TWO AGENTS *exchange a glance.*

SECOND AGENT We're supposed to ask you the questions.

PAUL   *(thoughtfully)* So, you're not getting enough out of me.

FIRST AGENT   You're a real tough nut, Paul. Next thing he'll be trying to indoctrinate us.

The TWO AGENTS *laugh.*

PAUL   Well, I'll tell you something. I've answered your questions about me. But I haven't answered questions about anyone else.

FIRST AGENT   Like Dr. Mindish.

PAUL   Anyone else. But I'm curious about you. I'm curious that reasonably intelligent men like yourselves would give their lives to this kind of work. I would like to know why you do it? Do you take pleasure in hounding all the poor exploited individuals in this country? For your Federal Bureau of Inquisition?

FIRST AGENT   *(no longer smiling)* Well now, Paul, we don't see things just the way you commies do.

INT.   ISAACSON HOME. NIGHT. WINTER '53

DANIEL *lies in his bed at night. He is awake. The door to his room is open and light comes in from the stairway. In the shadows his eyes are alert and he listens to his parents' conversation downstairs.*

ROCHELLE'S VOICE   . . . can't expect to handle this without a lawyer.

PAUL'S VOICE   Who do you recommend?

ROCHELLE'S VOICE   What's his name—the first one you called.

PAUL'S VOICE   He wants no part of it. None of them do. I live in phone booths.

Sound of ROCHELLE *saying something indistinguishable.* DANIEL *raises himself on one elbow to hear better.*

PAUL'S VOICE   Ascher. Jacob Ascher.

In the room next to DANIEL'S SUSAN *is awake too. She listens while tracing her finger over a light pattern on the wall. From below the sound of their parents' voices—urgent, troubled, unhappy.*

Daniel: A Screenplay

INT.   HAYDEN PLANETARIUM. DAY. WINTER '53

DANIEL *sits with his class in the Hayden Planetarium while the planetary music booms out and the great optical star-caster turns on its two-headed black spiny axis and with looming malevolence casts its planetary eye on him. He becomes terrified, and it is as if the planetary beam is a giant searchlight in a concentration camp. And then in fantasy silence, the incredibly bright light seems to be illuminating the inside of the Isaacson house. And while the family huddles in terror, the walls of the house begin to burn through, and flame envelops everything.*

EXT.   ISAACSON HOME. DAY. WINTER '53

DANIEL *stands on the porch of his house looking across the street to the opposite sidewalk, where, along the schoolyard fence, a crowd of children and adults looks back at him. It is early morning. In the street between* DANIEL *and the watching crowd are numbers of cars double-parked, with red turning rooflights. Their doors are open. We hear a loud police radio broadcasting its cryptic messages and static.* TWO MEN *in overcoats hold rifles loosely, casually from one hand as they stand and chat on the sidewalk in front of the house. Standing at the head of the alley, looking at these men, is* WILLIAMS, *the black janitor. He wears overalls, a sweatshirt.* ANOTHER MAN *in an overcoat comes out of the house past* DANIEL. *He carries a table radio with its cord wrapped neatly around it.*

INT.   ISAACSON HOME. DAY. WINTER '53

DANIEL *turns and runs into the house. In his parents' living room—bedroom* PAUL *sits on the edge of the hide-a-bed. He is in his underwear. He holds the warrant for his arrest. He is surrounded by* MEN *in hats and coats, including the two agents we've seen before.* ROCHELLE, *in her bathrobe, holds* SUSAN *in her arms.*

ROCHELLE   Maniacs! With guns! They think they've got John Dillinger! Haven't you hounded us enough? Can't you leave us alone!

DANIEL *runs upstairs. In his room two* AGENTS *are lifting the linoleum from the floor. They go through the blankets and sheets in the closet, flapping them and throwing them to the floor. They have ripped open* DANIEL's *mattress. One of the men riffles the pages of* DANIEL's *books, empties his cigar box of baseball cards, spilling them to the floor.*

DANIEL *looks in on* SUSAN's *room. An* AGENT *is on his knees going through an old hope chest. He removes a brownish framed picture of* DANIEL's *Grandma as a young woman, a* sidder, *a down pillow which he feels carefully, some old dresses, a lace tablecloth with fringe. Mothballs rattle on the floor.* SUSAN's *mattress is ripped open.*

DANIEL *goes back downstairs.* AGENTS *stand on line at the front door. An agent with a clipboard makes a record of what each of them has before he passes outside. The agents carry books, copies of the* Daily Worker, *a metal securities box, a toolbox, a Brownie camera, a portable record player, and so on.*

DANIEL *is still in his pajamas and with the front door open, cold winds sweep through the house and make him shiver. He stands at the door to his parents' bedroom, where* PAUL *is now finishing getting dressed:* PAUL *wears a too-large Glen plaid suit (1950 two-button) and a wide tie which he knots with a distracted thoughtful expression on his face—as if he's trying to remember something.*

When he's finished one of the two original agents lifts his arm, snaps handcuffs on his wrist and locks the other bracelet on the cuff on his arm.

As the phalanx of agents moves toward the door DANIEL *hurls himself at their legs.*

DANIEL   You leave my Pop alone! I'll kill you, I'll kill you!

He is shoved aside. The BABY *is screaming and* ROCHELLE *stands with the* BABY *in her arms, swaying with her eyes closed. Sobbing,* DANIEL *comes at the agents again, and this time one of them detaches from the group, lifts him snapping and squirming, and drops him behind the hall stairs on top of a pile of newspapers.*

On his knees, his eyes blurred with tears, DANIEL *sees his father's face for one instant as, hustled out the door, lit by flashbulbs,* PAUL *turns and yells over his shoulder.*

PAUL   Ascher!

And the door slams shut.

INT.   DANIEL'S APARTMENT. NIGHT. SUMMER '68

DANIEL *sits, lost in thought, in the kitchen of his and* PHYLLIS's *tiny apartment on the upper West Side. Supper plates still on the stable. Spaghetti. A bottle of*

Daniel: A Screenplay

Chianti. PHYLLIS *sits across the table. It is a hot summer night. The window is open.* PHYLLIS *wears a halter and shorts.* DANIEL *is shirtless.*

PHYLLIS   I think about moving out of New York.

DANIEL *doesn't answer.*

PHYLLIS   I think about it all the time. After Susan gets well. Maybe out West or the Northwest somewhere.

DANIEL   Susan won't get well.

PHYLLIS   When you finish your degree. Some small campus where you could teach and maybe I could even take a few courses. *(She registers what he's just said.)* What?

DANIEL   It's conceivable. She may not want to make it.

PHYLLIS   Omigod. Don't talk like that.

DANIEL   She's planning to die on me. It's the family tradition.

PHYLLIS   That's gross!

DANIEL   Phyllis, how can someone with such a big ass have such a small brain?

PHYLLIS *gets up, takes the dishes from the table.*

DANIEL   Listen: My sister, Susan, stopped in the ladies' room at a Holiday Inn on the Massachusetts Turnpike and slit her wrists with a stainless steel razor blade. I mean wouldn't you say something was communicated?

PHYLLIS   *(eyes downcast)* I guess.

DANIEL   Well, what happened when we found out? What did we do?

PHYLLIS   We went up there. We went to see her.

DANIEL   Yes. So it was a kind of summons, wasn't it. I mean, what she did operated on us as a kind of summons. Right?

PHYLLIS   Daniel, when you're unhappy you always take it out on me.

DANIEL   Doesn't it bother you that in Susan's mind everything I've done as an adult, including marrying you, is a waste!

A pause. He is now virtually talking to himself.

A moralist. A judge. Always taking stands. Always deciding who is right, who is wrong. What is just, what is unjust. The Isaacson gift. You see what it is? *(He makes a fist.)* It enrages me that anyone, let alone my kid sister, can find in my life enough of a pattern—to make a confident moral judgment.

INT.   LEWIN'S HOME. DAY. FALL/WINTER '66

In the living room of DANIEL'S *foster parents* ROBERT *and* LISE LEWIN, *Brookline Mass. (It is Thanksgiving, some six months before* SUSAN'S *suicide attempt.)* DANIEL *is here, and his wife* PHYLLIS, *who is heavy with child. Everyone, including* SUSAN, *is having a glass of sherry.* SUSAN *looks elegant for the holiday: she's dressed in an old clothes–boutique way, and she wears granny glasses that enlarge her blue eyes. She unbuttons her sleeves and silently displays her wrists and forearms, which are black and blue.*

PHYLLIS   How horrible!

SUSAN   What they aim for is your crotch.

LISE LEWIN   I don't want to think about police today. I want to have a nice holiday dinner. The turkey is cooling, and Robert, you will mentally prepare yourself to carve in just a few minutes.

She leaves. SUSAN *rebuttons her sleeves.*

SUSAN   So. To get back to the subject.

DANIEL   A foundation.

SUSAN   Right. The Paul and Rochelle Isaacson Foundation for Revolutionary Studies.

DANIEL   *(to* ROBERT LEWIN*)* You know anything about this?

ROBERT LEWIN   Well, Susan's been thinking about it and talking to some people here and in New York, and she asked me if it's technically feasible, which it is. This is the year you come into equal possession of the trust. As Ascher drew it up, there are no conditions.

SUSAN   It's our legacy, Daniel. What the Movement *needs* is money. We can do great things!

DANIEL   Suppose I happen to feel demonstrating in front of draft boards and getting busted is not the way to do great things.

SUSAN   All right, that's fair. Resistance is one alternative. But other things are going on, new things at Columbia too, right? Not just up here. Everywhere. I'm going through changes—so is everyone. The proper stance is not to criticize from the outside, but to get inside and create.

DANIEL   Susan, how is it whenever you present me with an idea or ask me to do something it's in a way calculated to turn me off?

Pause.

SUSAN   Maybe because not much is required to turn you off.

ROBERT LEWIN   Let's try to keep the discussion on a reasonably high plane.

SUSAN   I try to, Daddy. But anything that comes from me is automatically suspect. Right, Daniel?

DANIEL   No, it's just that I hear about it almost as a privilege, after the decisions are made.

SUSAN   But nothing's happened yet. We're just talking!

DANIEL   Who's just talking.

SUSAN   You're unbelievable. You and me. Us!

DANIEL   Dad said you're talking to people in New York.

SUSAN   I talk to lots of people. All the time. I talk to whoever listens.

DANIEL   Who?

Pause.

SUSAN   Forget it. Forget I said a thing. (*to* ROBERT LEWIN) It makes me sad, it really does. We're in this horrible imperialist war, we're burning people in Vietnam, and the issue is how I happen to talk.

DANIEL   No, I'll tell you what the issue is. The issue is if you want to give away your money, why not just do it—why do you have to put the family tag on it. Why do you have to advertise?

SUSAN   The name Isaacson has meaning. It's important! What happened to the Isaacsons is history!

DANIEL   The Isaacsons! You hear that? She fucking calls her own mother and father the Isaacsons.

ROBERT LEWIN   Listen you two, if you can't conduct a civil discussion—

SUSAN   I'm not ashamed of the name. I'm proud of who I am! If you could only see the schmucky way you come on in this world!

DANIEL   That may be—but I don't think a foundation is necessarily a good idea just because it has the name Isaacson. How will it work? Who is it for? What will it do?

SUSAN   WHY NOT LET'S TRY IT AND SEE! You cop out with this phony cynicism. Maybe you have a better idea what to do with that blood money?

DANIEL   That blood money earned you a college education. It straightened your teeth!

SUSAN   Why don't you just admit you're a selfish prick!

DANIEL   I don't want the bread. I thought we'd give it to our parents.

ROBERT LEWIN   That's the one alternative that, as guardian, I won't permit.

DANIEL   Well, you ought to reconsider. Your just due for all the bullshit you've put up with the last dozen years.

SUSAN   Don't worry, Daniel. You can forget the foundation. It doesn't need you. Go back to your life. (*She gestures toward* PHYLLIS) Take this milk cow of yours and go home.

LISE LEWIN   (*in doorway*) If this doesn't stop right now, I'm not serving.

SUSAN   Go back to the stacks, Daniel. The world needs another graduate student.

DANIEL   Well, I don't have to go out and get clubbed to justify my existence.

SUSAN   No, you'd rather jerk off behind a book.

LISE LEWIN   Stop, you two!

ROBERT LEWIN   Susan, you're not handling this very well.

DANIEL   Yes she is! She's a revolutionary! She's got all the answers. She's been to the barricades!

SUSAN   *(breaking down)* Oh, Jesus.

DANIEL   Once it was acid. Acid was gonna do it, right? And before that it was sex. Remember that, Susyanna? And before sex it was God. You knew all about God.

SUSAN   Oh shit—

DANIEL   Now it's revolution. But I thought we did that! I thought we've been through that!

SUSAN *is leaving.*

ROBERT LEWIN   Susan—

SUSAN   Let go, Daddy! He thinks they were guilty! That's why he's like this! Can't you see? I mean what did they die for—this piece of shit?

ROBERT LEWIN   Now calm down—

SUSAN   My father and mother were murdered! Why do you let him sit here and do it again!

INT.   ISAACSON HOME. DAY. WINTER '53

The lawyer, ASCHER, heavyset, is seated in a chair, his overcoat on, open, his homburg tilted back on his head. ROCHELLE sits on the sofa. Her ankles are crossed, her hands in her lap. She looks pale, drawn.

ASCHER   I suppose I'm a religious man. For many years now, when I've had the time, I've been working on a book showing the contributions of the Old Testament to American law. What is happening today in this country is paganism. That's the only word for it. *(sighs ... a pause)* He's been indicted along with Selig Mindish and unnamed others for conspiring to violate the Espionage Act of 1917. Bail has been set at one hundred thousand dollars.

ROCHELLE   On the basis of what evidence?

ASCHER   Well, a conspiracy charge usually requires evidence like a confession. Somebody in the conspiracy has to say it existed.

ROCHELLE   What conspiracy?

ASCHER   In legal terms it means simply an agreement among people to do something. That they intended to do something.

ROCHELLE   Paul is not accused of stealing atomic secrets?

ASCHER   That is correct.

ROCHELLE   He's accused of conspiring to steal secrets.

ASCHER   That is correct.

ROCHELLE   With Selig Mindish.

ASCHER   That is correct.

ROCHELLE   That doesn't sound as serious.

ASCHER   It's as serious as it can be.

ROCHELLE   But if they don't charge espionage, but only what, intending to do espionage, that means they have no evidence that anything was done.

ASCHER   That is correct.

ROCHELLE   Isn't that weaker? What evidence can you provide of what was in someone's head? Tell me. I don't understand.

ASCHER   As I said. A conspiracy is by nature secretive. Only the people in it can prove its existence. That's why I think they have forced a confession.

ROCHELLE   Who? How can they?

ASCHER   I think they have Selig Mindish.

ROCHELLE *is stunned.*

ASCHER   *(standing)* Are you all right? Where is the boy? Daniel!

ROCHELLE   I'm all right.

DANIEL *comes in.*

ASCHER   Bring your mother a glass of water. Quickly!

ROCHELLE   My God. My God. Oh my God.

ROCHELLE *and her* CHILDREN *are entertaining a guest,* BEN COHEN, *the old family friend from City College days. They're in the kitchen having tea. The two children are eating chocolate cake and showing signs of it around their mouths.* BEN COHEN, *bald, moustached, smokes his pipe—a quiet contemplative man.*

ROCHELLE   The cake is a big success.

BEN COHEN   I'm glad.

ROCHELLE   It's not smart to come here, Ben. You're a foolish man.

COHEN *lifts his hand deprecatingly.*

ROCHELLE   These days we have only the police for company. Police and photographers. The Party in its wisdom has decided we don't exist. Would you like more tea?

BEN COHEN   Don't fuss.

ROCHELLE   It's all right, I like to have things to do. *(She goes to the stove.)* I've been keeping the store open since the FBI unsealed it. I thought Paul's customers would want their property back. We need every dollar. But nobody comes. We're contaminated, you see.

She pours tea, returns the kettle to the stove, comes back to the table, sits down. Silence.

What possessed him to do it? Can you tell me? All these years . . . I just can't understand what possesses a man to do something so terrible. To ruin a family, the lives of children.

BEN, *mute, shakes his head.*

And I can't forgive his wife either. There's never been any love lost between Sadie Mindish and me. God knows what they've concocted between them.

BEN COHEN   I want you to tell your lawyer that I will make myself useful in any way I can. I will testify as your witness. Anything.

ROCHELLE   Paul discussed this with Ascher: Anyone who associates with us is suspect. He says he couldn't bear the responsibility. Neither could I, Ben. It's enough to know you've offered it.

ROCHELLE's *regal composure is about to crack.*

BEN COHEN   Some financial help—

ROCHELLE   *(wiping the tears from her eyes)* I miss him so. Ascher says he's fine. His letter says he's fine. But how can a man in jail be fine? He's locked up like some common criminal.

EXT.   PAUL'S RADIO SHOP. DAY. WINTER '53

On a grey afternoon, cold and wintry, ROCHELLE *comes out of Isaacson Radio Sales and Repair carrying two boxes tied with twine. Behind her* DANIEL *emerges pushing the baby carriage filled with electronic junk. Behind* DANIEL *comes* SUSAN *carrying radio parts in her pudgy hands.*

    We see the family, like some bedraggled line of refugees, walking down the street. Behind them, bringing up the rear, is WILLIAMS, *the black janitor in his faded overalls and sweatshirt. He is pushing the TV console on a dolly. Behind* WILLIAMS, *we see the landlord directing a painter, who is blanking out the sign* ISAACSON RADIO.

INT.   ISAACSON HOME. DAY. WINTER/SPRING '53

DANIEL *comes down the stairs, hair combed, neatly dressed for school, a school notebook in his hand. We track him around the bottom of stairs into the kitchen.*

    In the kitchen a stout grey-haired woman wearing an apron stands over SUSAN, *who's eating breakfast. The woman smiles at* DANIEL. *He turns and leaves the kitchen.*

    DANIEL *goes to the living room—bedroom of his parents. Standing at the wardrobe mirror,* ROCHELLE *is fitting a small pillbox hat on her head and arranging a tiny veil. She wears a below knee-length dress with a high collar.*

ROCHELLE   *(with forced cheerfulness)* Good morning, Daniel. You remember Mrs. Bittleman. She was a friend of your Grandma's. She's sitting with Susan.

DANIEL   Where are you going?

ROCHELLE   I have to go downtown to testify before the Grand Jury. Thank God for Mrs. Bittleman. She lost her son, Jerome, in the war. For her, misery has no politics. How does this look?

DANIEL   Good.

ROCHELLE *withdraws a tiny wristwatch from the bureau drawer.*

ROCHELLE   Do you want to shut the clasp for me?

DANIEL *goes to her, turns her wrist palm up, and with effort closes the clasp of the watchband.*

ROCHELLE   Your father gave this to me before we were married. This I won't pawn, no matter what.

DANIEL *holds her arm in both his hands and lays his face against it.*

ROCHELLE   *(with a laugh)* Danny!

DANIEL   Don't go. I don't want you to go.

ROCHELLE   But I have to! The government lawyers want to question me about your father. I'll be able to tell them what a terrible thing they're doing.

She withdraws her arm, kneels down in front of the boy and holds his face in her hands.

I always forget how young you are. You're such a big brave boy. *(She kisses him.)* You take such good care of Susan, I forget you're a baby too.

DANIEL   I'm not a baby.

ROCHELLE   You're my baby. *(She kisses him.)*

She stands, gets her overcoat from the wardrobe closet, puts it on, buttons it in front of the mirror. She picks up her pocketbook and gloves.

I should be back before you're out of school. But in case I'm not, have a snack and take Susan to the park. For lunch I left you a peanut butter sandwich, and an apple, in the icebox.

INT.   ISAACSON HOME. DAY. WINTER/SPRING '53 (SEQUENCE)

We see a wind-up alarm clock on top of the old icebox in the Issacson kitchen. The time is four o'clock. The clock ticks loudly.

DANIEL *and* SUSAN *are at the table with coloring books.* DANIEL *stops coloring to look up at the clock.*

The children, their crayons abandoned, are simply sitting at the kitchen table. MRS. BITTLEMAN *goes to the front door and looks out. She closes the door, comes back to the kitchen, sits down. Sighs.*

MRS. BITTLEMAN *puts on her coat and a kerchief on her head. She stands at the doorway.*

MRS. BITTLEMAN   People must eat. Come with me and I'll make a nice
meal at my house. In my kitchen where I know everything.

DANIEL   You go. We'll wait for my mother.

SUSAN   I want Mommy. I don't want you.

MRS. BITTLEMAN   Vey iss mir, vey iss mir.

She leaves and a moment later the front door closes softly. The clock ticks.

SUSAN *is asleep at the kitchen table, her arm sprawled on the table, her head on her arm.* DANIEL *sits straight in his chair—almost at attention. He shivers. He hears the distant sound of a radio. He goes to the kitchen door leading to the basement, puts his ear against the door, listens. His eyes widen. Someone is coming up the basement stairs. He steps back. There is a heavy knock on the door, and then it shakes and the doorknob rattles.* DANIEL *twists the key in the door and run back to his chair.* SUSAN *starts awake. The door opens:* WILLIAMS, *the black man, towers in the doorway. We hear a radio more loudly now—it is in the basement.* WILLIAMS *seems almost to reach to the ceiling. He stands there looking at the children in his menacing, red-eyed way.*

WILLIAMS   Your momma leave you here alone?

DANIEL   Mrs. Bittleman is here. But she went home to make us dinner.

WILLIAMS   *(He studies the children.)* Ain't no one told you?

DANIEL   What?

WILLIAMS   Dear Jesus. It on the radio.

At that moment the phone in the front hall begins to ring.

EXT.   E. SIXTH STREET. DAY. SPRING '68

The adult DANIEL *coming up the subway steps at 14th Street and Union Square. He carries the cardboard mailing tube. It's early evening, summer. He walks*

Daniel: A Screenplay

past the buzzing neon of S. Klein, past the cheap goods stores, the Spanish movie house, the porno bookstore. Lots of people out this hot summer night—blacks, Puerto Ricans, street people.

DANIEL *(voice over)* What could she mean? She could mean the government checks me out once or twice a year. Not an assignment to excite your average FBI man. Nevertheless, they keep my file current. My file. She could mean my file . . .

DANIEL *walking through Tompkins Square Park. Old women in babushkas on the benches. Old men with small dogs on leashes. Men and girls playing handball. Shouting in Spanish. Lots of dogs running loose.*

DANIEL *(voice over)* Nothing I could do would surprise them. If I took a shot at the President the genetic criminality of my family would be established. She could mean they're not worried . . . She could mean I live in continuous and degrading relationship to the society that destroyed my mother and father . . .

DANIEL *walks along Avenue B. He looks at the house number on the tenements. Rock music, Afro music, mambo music, coming from open windows.*

DANIEL *(voice over)* They're still fucking us. Goodbye, Daniel. You get the picture.

INT.   ARTIE'S PAD. DAY. SPRING '68

A room with mattresses on the floor, piles of books and newspapers. An NLF flag hangs on the wall. Only one piece of formal furniture stands out: a color TV console. STERNLICHT *is shirtless, barefoot. He wears cutoff jeans. He wears a headband for his long hair, which makes him look Indian. He's muscular, short. He sits with his back against the wall, his arm around* BABY, *a skinny sexy girl in halter and shorts. They are facing* DANIEL, *who sits crosslegged in the middle of the floor.*

STERNLICHT   You want to know what was wrong with the old American Communists? They wore ties. They held down jobs. They put people up for President. They thought politics is something you do at a meeting. Shit. Russia? All Stalin ever wanted was steel up everyone's ass.

He looks at DANIEL.

The American Communist Party set the Left back fifty years. They were invented by J. Edgar Hoover. The man's a genius.

DANIEL   How do you know Susan?

STERNLICHT   Baby, how do we know Susan? I think we met her in Cambridge when I went up there to rap.

BABY   That's when it was.

STERNLICHT   She was into this thing about your parents.

DANIEL   Right.

STERNLICHT *is appraising* DANIEL.

STERNLICHT   Can I tell it to you straight? I mean how sensitive are you?

DANIEL   Go ahead.

STERNLICHT   *(leaning forward)* Your folks didn't know shit. Instead of standing up and saying, "fuck you, do what you want, I can't get an honest trial anyway with you fuckers," they made motions. They pleaded innocent. They spoke when spoken to. The whole frame of reference brought them down because they acted like defendants at a trial. *(pause)* I mean, it was a tremendous opportunity. Someday, when the Feds wake up and see it's not some maniac acid head Artie Sternlicht, but a whole *movement* of freaks, then I'll have my turn. I will have a beautiful trial, man. What I say and do in that courtroom will go out on the wire and make headlines. And kids all over the world will say, "Man, who is that dude? Dig the way he's got his shit together!!" And I will judge the judges, and if they find me guilty, I will find them guilty. And if they find me innocent, I will still find them guilty. And they will be on trial, not me. You see? (STERNLICHT *slumps against wall.*) They blew the whole gaddamn thing.

DANIEL   And Susan disagreed.

STERNLICHT   Yeah.

BABY   She said they were martyrs.

STERNLICHT   Sure they were. The revolution has more martyrs than it knows what to do with. Like spades you never heard of murdered in their beds. Like the population of Vietnam.

BABY   *(smiling)* You can't disagree with Artie.

Pause. DANIEL *holds out the cardboard mailing tube.*

DANIEL   Has your name and address on it. She was bringing you this to hang on your wall.

STERNLICHT *accepts the tube.*

Did she ever talk to you about her trust money?

STERNLICHT *appears to ignore the question. He is removing the poster from the tube. He unrolls it.*

STERNLICHT   "Free Them." Far out . . . What?

DANIEL   Did Susan ever say anything about her trust money?

STERNLICHT   I suppose she did.

DANIEL   What do you think of the idea?

STERNLICHT   I'll tell you man, I think it's a fantastic idea. Fuck me if I'm consistent. I told your sister if she had all that bread to pass on for a bail fund or a free school or any good shit like that, I would retract everything I said about your parents. Not only that, I would actually change my opinion. I would think differently. OK?

DANIEL   OK.

STERNLICHT *discards the poster.*

STERNLICHT   That's the one question you shouldn't have asked.

DANIEL   Maybe so.

STERNLICHT   And I've been pretty easy on you, too. Susan never mentioned you. Except once. She said she had a brother who was politically undeveloped. She made it sound like undescended testicles.

BABY   Come on, Artie.

STERNLICHT *gets up, turns on the television, squats in front of it.*

STERNLICHT   What time is it? On the late news they should have that kid in Los Angeles who set fire to himself. See, that's the kind of action that came into being because of *television.*

He brings in a picture. Perhaps his face is lit by the screen.

Listen, man. Next month we're having a thing in Washington. We're going to levitate the Pentagon with spells and incantations. We're gonna wear flowers in our hair, burn flags, dance in circles! Think about it, man. You'll be on the tube. We're going to overthrow the United States of America with images!

INT. ISAACSON HOME. DAY. WINTER/SPRING '53

In the living room, ASCHER *stands in his overcoat, his homburg pushed back on his head like a cowboy hat.* FRIEDA COHN, PAUL ISAACSON's *sister, sits on the sofa bed. She too wears a coat. She's weeping. She is a very plain middle-aged lady with orthopedic shoes and heavy-gauge stockings.*

FRIEDA   I'm a widow, I have no one. I stand on my feet twelve hours a day. How can I afford to do what you're asking?

ASCHER   Mrs. Cohn, I'm not asking you to do anything. Paul is your brother, not mine.

FRIEDA   God help me, I was always the responsible one. From the time we were children. If you didn't put the food in front of him, he wouldn't eat. If you didn't hold his money, he would lose it. It was Frieda *(she pokes herself in the chest)*, the good-natured slob, who always got him out of trouble. And when my father followed my mother to the grave, I was the mother *and* father. My life was never my own.

Sitting on the floor watching television (the set from the window of Isaacson Radio) are DANIEL *and* SUSAN. *They sit very close, watching* Hopalong Cassidy.

ASCHER   They seem to enjoy the television. Do you have a television, Mrs. Cohn?

FRIEDA   What? No—who can afford it.

ASCHER   It's an expensive item. When the dealer comes to assess the belongings, I'll tell him not to include the television.

FRIEDA *opens her pocketbook, brings out a handkerchief, takes off her glasses, wipes her eyes.*

FRIEDA   Can there be a greater tragedy? To turn into a Red. My Pauly, a *Commonist*—and worse!

ASCHER   What do you mean worse?

FRIEDA   God only knows. I will be lucky to keep my store. If someone should make the connection. If my neighbors should find out?

ASCHER   What are you saying?

FRIEDA   How do I explain who these children are? How do I explain where their parents are?

ASCHER   Their parents are in jail. They're in jail because their bail bond is prohibitive. It helps the government establish how dangerous they must be. If the shame of that is too much for you, you can say they are in Florida.

FRIEDA *puts her handkerchief away, snaps shut her shiny black pocketbook.*

FRIEDA   I don't blame him. He couldn't help himself. I blame her. She's his ruination. In school he had a ninety-six average. In Townsend Harris High School, which was nothing but brilliant children. And then to get these crazy ideas—all right, so you join a radical club in CCNY, it's the thing to do. He would have outgrown all that craziness. But she drove him. It is she who did this!

ASCHER   Mrs. Cohn.

FRIEDA   That he never even finished college, a mind like that. I will never forgive her for what she has done to Pauly. To all of us.

ASCHER   Mrs. Cohn, do you really want the children to hear this?

FRIEDA   Vey iss mir, vey iss mir.

ASCHER   So what do I understand from your answer? They can't stay here. There's no money. The black man can't take them. The neighbor can't take them. I can't take them.

FRIEDA *moans, her hand to her mouth.*

FRIEDA   Babies! What do I know from babies! Where will I put them? What do they eat!

ASCHER   *(shouts)* Lady! They are not animals from the zoo! Vas is der mair mit dein kopf? Have you no pity? Don't you know what trouble is? Don't you know what terrible trouble these people are in?

EXT.   ISAACSON HOME. DAY. SPRING '53

In front of the Isaacson house a taxi stands at the curb, the motor running. It's a big yellow DeSoto, limousine size, circa 1950. The passenger door is open. Coming down the porch steps are DANIEL, SUSAN, FRIEDA COHN, *and* ASCHER. *The children carry shapeless packages wrapped in brown paper and tied with string.* ASCHER *carries a small beat-up suitcase, which he places in the cab.* FRIEDA *gets into the cab, followed by* SUSAN *and then* DANIEL. *It's a cold, wintery day. The wind blows.* ASCHER *closes the door, takes a money clip out of his pocket, unfolds a five and a couple of ones, and bending to the window, hands the money through to* FRIEDA.

ASCHER   Go ahead. Take it.

FRIEDA *accepts the cab fare.*

FRIEDA   I'm not making any promises. I'll do my best, but that's all.

As the taxi moves off, FRIEDA *and the two children are snapped back in their seats. Quickly both* DANIEL *and* SUSAN *scramble to look out the rear window: their house is receding.* ASCHER, *wiping his nose with his handkerchief, stands looking after them. Behind* ASCHER, WILLIAMS, *the janitor, staring after them from the head of the alley.*

EXT.   MACARTHUR D.C. PARADE (STOCK SHOT). DAY

General MacArthur rides up Pennsylvania Avenue, which is lined with waving crowds . . . General MacArthur strides up in the center aisle in Congress, the joint session on its feet and applauding . . . General Mac-Arthur addresses Congress, his hair slicked down on his head. These shots are silent.

Daniel: A Screenplay

ROCHELLE   *(voice over)* Hi, my dearest Danny, what do you think of Brooklyn? Is it interesting? Have you made any friends yet? I know it's boring for
you to be out of school, my honey, but all of this is only temporary.

DANIEL *and* SUSAN *are watching General MacArthur on TV in* FRIEDA
COHN's *stuffy, overfurnished Brooklyn tenement apartment.* DANIEL *suddenly
jumps up and turns off the set. He and* SUSAN *attempt to straighten the room.
This is silent, too.*

   *Down a short dark hall from the living room is the front door. We watch it
and then it opens.* FRIEDA *comes in carrying a bag of groceries. Laboriously
locks the door. Comes into the living room, says something to the children now
sitting guiltily on the couch. She goes over to the TV, feels the top of the console,
and screams something at them. (Silent.)*

ROCHELLE   *(voice over)* In the meantime, you should get Aunt Frieda to
take you to the library and get lots of books. Mr. Ascher, Uncle Jacob, is
trying to get you into the public school there, but that may take a few more
days. My beloved little Susan will go to nursery school.

INT.   FRIEDA'S APARTMENT. DAY. SPRING '53

ASCHER, *in his coat, is seen trying to raise a window in the dark airless living
room. It won't budge. He shakes his head. He turns on a lamp, which glows
weakly with a low wattage bulb.*

ROCHELLE   *(voice over)* Listen, my dear sweetheart, Uncle Jacob will be
bringing a present for each of you from us. I hope you enjoy it. Your father
and I discussed what we would get you in our letters (since we are in
different jails), and we have asked him to purchase it from the store and
bring it to you.

ASCHER *goes to children who sit on the floor listlessly examining their presents—an erector set, a tin tea set. He bends down, tilts* DANIEL's *chin upward to
the light and sees a frowning pale child who looks bad.*

ROCHELLE   *(voice over)* That is to make you feel not so lonely, because it is
from us—and also so that you'll have the best possible time!

Daniel: A Screenplay

INT./EXT.   FRIEDA'S CANDY STORE. DAY. SUMMER '53

DANIEL, *dressed for outdoors, sits at the counter of a beat-up neighborhood candy store. He is looking at newspapers stacked on the counter. The* News *headline:* ISAACSONS MASTERSPIES SAYS FBI. *The* Times *headline:* NEW IN-DICTMENTS DRAWN FOR ATOMIC SPY RING. *Separate pictures of* PAUL *and* ROCHELLE *side by side in the papers—they are recognizable as the source of the famous poster.* DANIEL *turns the page of the* News, *looks up:* FRIEDA *coming along behind the counter, wearing proprietor's smock; she waves him away violently.* DANIEL *retreats and* FRIEDA, *still talking, lines papers up and straightens the display. (Silent.)*

ROCHELLE   *(voice over)* By the way, I am writing this for your father, too. He wants to tell you not to worry about us because we are fine and every-thing is all right with us. Even though we miss you very much!

INT.   FRIEDA'S APARTMENT. DAY. SUMMER '53

DANIEL *and* SUSAN *using* FRIEDA's *bed as a trampoline. Up and down they jump, with solemn faces. As if they are performing some kind of stomping ritual. (Silent.)*

Now they're doing acrobatics on the messed-up bed. DANIEL *is on his back, his knees drawn up, and* SUSAN *lies prone on his legs, and she holds her arms out as if she is flying.* DANIEL *puts his hands under* SUSAN's *arms and lifts her to an upside-down position over the edge of the bed. Her dress falls over her head. (Silent.)*

ROCHELLE   *(voice over)* Please write me again, my sweet angel boy—I enjoyed your letter so much. Tell me what is on your mind. You are such a comfort to me. Please cooperate with your aunt and take care of your sister—I know you do that without my even asking—and before you know it, we'll all be together again. With lots and lots of love. Your Mom.

INT.   FRIEDA'S APARTMENT. NIGHT. SUMMER '53

AUNT FRIEDA *is telling* ASCHER *off, expostulating, carrying on while the pa-tient, grim, weary lawyer stands with his hands under his coat behind his back. They are in* AUNT FRIEDA's *apartment. On she raves while the two children sit, dressed, beside their belongings, the broken-down suitcase, the packages*

Daniel: A Screenplay

wrapped in string. SUSAN *traces the lock on the suitcase with the tips of her fingers.* DANIEL *yawns. (Silent.)*

INT.   SHELTER DORM. NIGHT. SUMMER '53

A boy's dormitory. Army bunk beds in crowded rows. Small windows covered with wire-mesh grates. Thirty or so boys just before lights out are raising hell— beds pushed together to create a kind of ring, where various wrestling matches are going on. Some kids are smoking cigarettes. Others chasing each other across beds. At the door, a heavyset man, the boys' SUPERVISOR, *appears and blows a whistle. Immediately the boys scatter to their beds, push them back in place. Giggling can be heard in the sudden quiet.*

SUPERVISOR   Awright, settle down. What is this, some fuckin' zoo?

Sitting on one of the beds is a BOY, *clearly retarded or autistic, lost in reverie.*

Someone get El Stupido down on his bed or he'll sit like that all night.

Sound of laughter. DANIEL *gets up from his cot, goes to the slack-jawed* BOY, *gently pushes him down, puts his feet up on the bed, goes back to his own bed.*

Awright, that's it for the night. Anymore trouble with you guys, I'm gonna whip your ass. And if I catch anyone jerkin' off, I'm gonna tie it in knots.

Catcalls, laughter. The SUPERVISOR *turns the lights off with a key in a wall switch. The door closes. Immediately a lot of whispering and moving around in the shadows.*

INT.   SHELTER DORM. NIGHT. SUMMER '53

Same scene, now quiet, everyone asleep. Camera travels down a row of beds, passes over EL STUPIDO *sleeping on his back with his eyes open. In the next bed* DANIEL *lies awake. We study his face. He appears to be listening. We hear the faint screams of a child, perhaps someone on another floor of the building.*

INT.   SHELTER LUNCHROOM. DAY. FALL '53

An institutional lunchroom. DANIEL *stands in a long line of boys. He holds a plastic tray. He moves along the steam table as one attendant spears a frank-*

Daniel: A Screenplay | 73

furter from a vat of water covered with slick and drops it on his tray; as another ladles a portion of creamed corn onto the compartmented tray; as a third deposits a half-pint container of milk and slice of white bread.

At the far end of the lunchroom, at a girls' table, SUSAN *stands on the bench searching for something. She ses* DANIEL *and reacts. She jumps down, runs in his direction.*

FEMALE ATTENDANT   Hey, get back here—hey!

We see SUSAN *clutching* DANIEL's *arm and hanging on as the* ATTENDANT *pries her hands loose.*

How many—times—do I have to—tell you—to stay with—your group!

SUSAN *hangs on grimly.* DANIEL *holding his tray, tries to keep food from spilling.* SUSAN *bites the* ATTENDANT *on the hand.*

Ow! You little bitch!

She slaps SUSAN's *face.* SUSAN *cries.* DANIEL *throws the tray in the* ATTEN-DANT's *face. Pandemonium.*

INT.   SHELTER SUPERVISOR'S OFFICE. FALL '53

In a bare institutional office DANIEL *sits in front of a desk talking to* MR. GUGLIELMI, *a balding man in his thirties who wears a coat and tie.*

MR. GUGLIELMI   My job isn't to yell at people but to find out why things go wrong. So let's forget about your throwing the tray. I would probably do the same thing if it was my sister.

DANIEL, *who has been staring at the floor, looks at the man.*

It's Susan who worries me. We're trying to make her feel at home. We're trying to make friends with her. But she's giving us a very hard time. She doesn't eat. She keeps the other kids awake. She won't cooperate in anything.

DANIEL *smiles.*

Do you have any ideas? I mean, what do you think the problem is?

DANIEL   She thinks this is jail.

GUGLIELMI   Jail! Why?

DANIEL   In jail people are kept apart from each other.

GUGLIELMI   Well, we have rules here. The boys are in one section, the girls in another. Those are the rules.

DANIEL   So—that's like a jail.

GUGLIELMI   Daniel, this is not jail. This is the East Bronx Children's Shelter. Hey—look at me when I talk to you. Did I make you come here?

DANIEL   No.

GUGLIELMI   No! Did I force Susan to come here?

DANIEL   No.

GUGLIELMI   NO! Then how can it be jail?

DANIEL   *(shrugging)* I don't know.

GUGLIELMI   I don't know! You're here because your parents asked the City if you could stay here. Are you saying your own parents would put you in jail?

DANIEL *shrugs.*

Children don't get put in jail. In this country nobody gets put in jail without a trial.

DANIEL   My mother and father haven't had a trial.

GUGLIELMI   Well, that's a technicality. They're waiting for their trial.

DANIEL   Why can't they wait home with us?

GUGLIELMI   I don't know, Dan. I'm not a lawyer. Maybe the government is afraid they'd try to run away.

DANIEL   Well, they wouldn't be afraid of that unless they were going to kill them.

Pause.

GUGLIELMI   Have you discussed this with Susan?

DANIEL   No.

GUGLIELMI   Does Susan think this is a jail? Where children are killed?

DANIEL *doesn't answer.* MR. GUGLIELMI *turns away, becomes lost in thought; his brow contracts, he closes his eyes.*

EXT.   SHELTER PLAY YARD. DAY. FALL/WINTER '53

A cold windy morning, clouds racing across the sky. DANIEL *stands near the cyclone fence (reminding us, perhaps, of the schoolyard fence opposite his home) as far from the Shelter building as he can be. He wears his mackinaw and hunter's cap. Nearby is the boy called* EL STUPIDO *examining with a smile the conformations of his own hand.* DANIEL *glances at the threatening sky.*

The yard is filled with children in unsupervised play. One adult at the door leading into the Shelter. From this door we see SUSAN *emerge.* DANIEL *raises his arm. She sees him and comes running across the yard. She wears a snow jacket with hood. Her legs are bare. She wears her shiny black ankle-strap shoes.*

DANIEL   *(not looking at her but around the yard)* All right—do you have to go to the bathroom?

SUSAN   No.

DANIEL   I don't know where to find any bathroom, so you better go now just to make sure. I'll wait for you.

SUSAN   I don't.

DANIEL *surveys the yard.*

DANIEL   All right. Now the most important thing is to listen to me carefully and do what I tell you and don't argue. Say you promise.

SUSAN   I promise.

DANIEL   All right. Get ready!

SUSAN *sits behind* EL STUPIDO, *waits expectantly.* DANIEL *moves over next to the boy, waits, sees the* ATTENDANT *at the far end of the yard occupied in breaking up a fight.*

DANIEL   Now!

Daniel: A Screenplay

SUSAN *stretches out on the ground behind the cover of* DANIEL *and* EL STUPIDO. DANIEL *reaches behind him, lifts the slack bottom edge of the fence.* SUSAN *rolls under, scrambles to her feet, runs behind the battery of garbage cans.* DANIEL *looks once more around the yard, quickly lies down, and slips under the fence, which he holds above his head.*

EXT.   TREMONT AVENUE. DAY. FALL/WINTER '53

We see DANIEL *and* SUSAN *running hand in hand down Tremont Avenue, a busy curving cobblestone street lined with stores and delicatessens, movies and automobile showrooms, bars, Chinese restaurants. A heavy-traffic street, lots of shoppers on the sidewalks.* DANIEL *and* SUSAN *disappear in the masses of people.*

EXT.   BUS STOP. DAY. FALL/WINTER '53

We see the children at a bus stop. DANIEL *allows a couple of buses to go by as he studies their designation signs. We understand he's not sure of his direction.*

EXT.   MORNINGSIDE HEIGHTS. DAY. FALL/WINTER '53

No longer running, the children hurry along, the little girl pulled by her brother.

SUSAN   Not so fast. You're going to make me fall!

She stops to pull her socks off her heels. Her white cotton socks slip down into her shoes and she has to tug them up.

EXT.   THIRD AVENUE. DAY. FALL/WINTER '53

Now they stand at a corner under the Third Avenue Bronx El. The steel beams supporting the old tracks shimmy as a train rumbles overhead and the children look up fearfully. They hurry on under the El.

SUSAN   How much more? Are we going to be there soon?

DANIEL   Be quiet.

EXT.   TENEMENT STREET. DAY. FALL/WINTER '53

Hand in hand they are walking down a tenement street. OTHER CHILDREN *whose turf this is look at them. They pass a string of ramshackle houses with asphalt siding that suggests their own house.* DANIEL's *eyes are ever alert for street signs, traffic, other kids, adults who might stop them. He hears a soft hiss-hiss, like a signal of some sort. It is repeated. The sound becomes synchronous with* SUSAN's *snifflings-in of her runny nose. She draws a sleeve across her face. Realizing she is the source of the sound,* DANIEL *stops.*

DANIEL   What are you crying about?

SUSAN   I'm not.

DANIEL   Are you tired?

SUSAN   Yes.

He leads her to the front stoop of a tenement, sits her down on the bottom steps, takes up a position of guard alongside, his eyes ranging up and down the street.

EXT.   BATHGATE AVENUE. DAY. FALL/WINTER '53

Now we are looking down the teeming open-air market of Bathgate Avenue. Vegetable and fruit stalls. Merchants in dirty white aprons over outer clothes crying out their wares to passersby. Along the curb pushcart vendors selling notions, factory-second shoes, ladies underwear. DANIEL *and* SUSAN *drift along in the current of shoppers. In the street trucks and cars inch along slowly, horns blowing. The sense of all this is of dangerous passage for* DANIEL *and* SUSAN. SUSAN *is very disturbed by the pressing crowds.* DANIEL *becomes exhilarated.*

DANIEL   I know where we are! We're not far now, Suzyo!

EXT.   WEBSTER AVENUE. DAY. FALL/WINTER '53

DANIEL *and* SUSAN *negotiating their way across Webster Avenue, a doubly wide street of buses and cars and trucks going two ways. The grinding of gears, bleating of horns. Islanded between the two directions of traffic, they wait to make their move. Then they run. A screech of brakes, a loud horn, and they appear breathless on the opposite sidewalk, a driver's curses following them.*

Daniel: A Screenplay

EXT.   CLAREMONT PARK STEPS. DAY. FALL/WINTER '53

They are climbing the steep stone steps leading up from Webster Avenue to Claremont Park. Perhaps we watch this through a long-distance lens so that their progress seems to be minimal in terms of the effort they are putting out.

They reach the top of the great stone steps. SUSAN *sits down to yank her socks out of her shoes.* DANIEL *surveys the distance they've come. From the heights of these steps, he sees the roofs and streets of the East Bronx—the territory he and* SUSAN *have traveled to reach this point. The wind is blowing and it's very cold.*

EXT.   CLAREMONT PARK. DAY. FALL/WINTER '53

DANIEL *and* SUSAN *running through empty Claremont Park. A bitter wind blows through the bare trees, blows leaves around their feet, blows newspaper against their legs.*

ASCHER   *(voice over)* Mamaneu! If you children knew what you were doing to me. I can't tell your mother and father. But how can I not tell them? What can I do? I'm not going to live long.

EXT.   ISAACSON HOME. DAY. FALL/WINTER '53

DANIEL *and* SUSAN *stand in front of the schoolyard fence looking across the street at their house. Now that they're here, they appear almost reluctant to take the last few steps. Slowly they cross the street, climb up on the porch. They press their faces against the dark window. We hear their breathing.*

Through the window we see what they see: in the grey, wintry afternoon light, bare floorboards, bare walls, an empty, unused room.

EXT.   ISAACSON HOME. DAY. FALL/WINTER '53

DANIEL *tries the front door. It is locked. He rattles the doorknob. He moves to the second window on the porch, cups his eyes, looks in. He runs down the steps, around to the alley. He bangs on* WILLIAMS' *cellar door. He tries it. It is locked. He hoists himself up against the door, sees his own reflection in the window panes.*

DANIEL *runs back to the porch. He and* SUSAN *stand on the porch silhouetted against the silver light in the sky over the schoolyard. We hear the wind and*

Daniel: A Screenplay

their breathing. SUSAN *suddenly spreads her legs, stands like an "A," and watches a dark stain growing in the wood under her foot. They both watch the stain spreading in all directions around* SUSAN's *shoes on the wooden porch.*

ASCHER   *(voice over)* What can I tell you? Some people are singled out. The world lacks civilization. Men do not respect God. You're only children and you can't understand. It's natural. I would run away too.

INT./EXT.   TAXI. DAY. FALL/WINTER '53

ASCHER *and the two* CHILDREN *in a cab. He sits between them hugging them to his sides. They look frightful—dirty, tearstained. Each holds a plastic jack-o'-lantern and a cardboard skeleton hanging on a rubber band.*

ASCHER   I would run away too. Thank God, I knew where to look. Will you enjoy these Halloween presents? . . . This family has given me itself as a present . . . Oh my children, what can I tell you? Soon, soon we will be in court. We shall have our trial.

EXT.   CZARIST FIELD KNOUTING. DAY. 1830S

In an open field a man is bound to a wooden block by his arms and neck and knees. A crowd is watching. The man's shirt is ripped from his back and a stout executioner steps up with a leather thonged whip knotted at the tip. He applies the knout to the man's back. Blood is drawn. The whip is applied again and again and again, till the back is bloody and the sound of the thong on the back is a splash. This procedure continues.

DANIEL   *(voice over)* Knouting was the primary means of punishment for capital offenses in Czarist Russia. It was used exclusively on serfs just as drawing and quartering was reserved for the lower classes of England. The institution of serfdom depended on the use of savage corporal punishment. Knouting was also popular in the military services of Europe and on plantations in the American South. Always it expressed the same class principles.

EXT.   TIMES SQUARE BAR. DAY. FALL '68

A police car, sirens blaring, tears down Broadway, and pedestrians including DANIEL *(adult) stop for a moment to watch it. It's early autumn.* DANIEL

Daniel: A Screenplay

wears his denim jacket. Off Times Square he checks out a restaurant, looks at it, goes in.

INT.　TIMES SQUARE BAR. DAY. FALL '68

DANIEL *sits at a table in the rear. Across the table is a bald, robust middle-aged man with white sideburns. This is* JACK P. FEIN, *a reporter for the* New York Times. *Glasses of beer in front of each of them.* FEIN, *in addition, is eating lunch. The restaurant is crowded, noisy.*

FEIN　You remember the trial?

DANIEL　We weren't allowed to go.

FEIN　The government had no case. All they had was Mindish. The testimony of an accomplice. You had to believe it's possible for a radio repairman without training or education to draw plans of the most sophisticated technology, and then reduce them to fit on dental x-ray film. I still don't know why anyone would want to do that. It was too much. And that this stuff was valuable to the Russians! Insane! The Russians had everything they needed. They had their own men right on the spot! (FEIN *enjoys his meal.*) You sure you don't want anything? The *New York Times* is a big spender.

DANIEL　No thanks.

FEIN　Anyway, the day after the *Times* ran my tenth-anniversary reassessment piece on the case I was having lunch downtown and just as I'm leaving the restaurant Red Feuerman walks up behind me, the chief prosecuting attorney? He's now Judge Feuerman of the Southern District—it was a career-making case, baby, everybody did well. Feuerman grabs me by the elbow, like it was a tit or something, and he says, "Jack, you let the wrong guys get to you, I can't believe you'd buy their story." "What story, Red, you're not gonna stand there and tell me without smiling that you had a case!" "Someday when you have the time," he says, "come up to my office and I'll show you some things."

DANIEL　What things?

FEIN　Oh, it's bullshit. It's the way they all talk. Even before the execution, when the heat was on to commute the sentence, they dropped these hints about evidence they couldn't use because of national security. Like there's supposed to be this big report in the Justice Department. But a friend of mine in Justice told me if the report had evidence like that they'd have released it. There's a report all right and the reason it's classified is it favors the defense. Shit, between the FBI and the CP, your folks never had a chance. (FEIN *takes a swig of beer.*) I'm glad you popped up. I'm glad you're alive and kicking. What's the name of your foundation?

DANIEL   The Isaacson Foundation for Revolutionary Studies.

FEIN   What's it gonna do?

DANIEL   Fund community action programs. Start a magazine maybe. Raise revolutionary consciousness. Everything.

FEIN   Great! You want to tell me where you're getting the money?

DANIEL   It's no secret. It's our trust money.

FEIN   That the old lawyer put together? From the defense committee?

DANIEL   Right.

FEIN   How much?

DANIEL   I can find out for you. I haven't been counting.

FEIN   Beautiful! You're all right. Where's your sister? I'd like to talk to her.

DANIEL   Well, see I don't think she wants to talk to anyone right now. She's recovering from the trial.

Pause.

FEIN   Yeah. Yeah, I heard something like that. How old is she now?

DANIEL   Susan is twenty.

FEIN   And where is she?

DANIEL   Out of state, that's all I can tell you.

FEIN   Well, how about your foster parents? Could I talk to them?

Pause.

Daniel: A Screenplay

DANIEL   Look, I don't care about blowing our cover. I don't think any of us cares anymore. Whoever's interested could have traced us up to Boston. But I mean, there are certain family things to be settled by all of us, not me acting alone. We've got responsibilities to each other.

FEIN   Kid, you called me!

DANIEL   Right. But I mean, I'm trying to lay the foundation on you. Not the family.

FEIN   It's the same story isn't it? I mean, I don't fuck around, don't worry. But what you're trying to do isn't possible.

DANIEL   What—

FEIN   Clear their name.

DANIEL   That's not what we're trying to do.

FEIN   Sure, sure. But I want to tell you something. A radical's no better than his analysis. You ought to know that. Your folks were put away on a bad rap. But that doesn't mean they were innocent babes. I don't believe they were a dangerous conspiracy that passed defense secrets. But I don't believe either there was a conspiracy in Washington against *them*.

DANIEL   I thought you said the evidence was phony.

FEIN   That's right. Those guys had to bring in a conviction. That was their job. But in this country people don't get picked out of a hat to be put on trial for their lives. Your parents were up to something. They had to be. They were little neighborhood commies probably with some kind of third rate operation that meant *bupkis*. Maybe what they were doing was worth five years. Maybe ten. But that would have been in the best of times, and in the best of times nobody would have cared enough to falsify evidence. No one would have been afraid enough to throw a switch.

EXT. FANNY ASCHER'S APARTMENT/STREET. DAY. WINTER '69

DANIEL *coming down West End Avenue checking apartment house numbers against a slip in his hand. He wears a jacket and tie. His hair is longer than it has been and he sports a new beard. He finds the address he's looking for and disappears inside a house.*

DANIEL *sits with some discomfort in an expensively furnished living room with wall-to-wall carpeting, antique chairs, heavy drapes, etc. A baby grand piano is in the room and on the piano, in a leather and glass frame, is a picture of* JACOB ASCHER *as a somewhat younger man than we have seen.*

A thin woman with very fair, finely wrinkled skin, grey jeweled eyeglasses, and hair tinted blue sits on the edge of the sofa, facing DANIEL. *This is* JAKE ASCHER's *widow,* FANNY. *Her hands are folded in her lap and her ankles are crossed.*

FANNY ASCHER   You are a student still?

DANIEL   Yes.

FANNY   And married with a baby?

DANIEL   Yes.

She shakes her head.

FANNY   And your sister?

DANIEL   She's getting better.

FANNY   Still?

DANIEL   Yes.

The woman's eyes are fixed on him.

I don't want to take up a lot of your time, Mrs. Ascher.

FANNY   My time? What do you think I do with my time?

DANIEL   Well, I only came to ask if there were any papers, any letters you know about. Files.

FANNY   There are none. Robert Lewin has all the files. I gave him everything.

DANIEL   I see. I thought there might be more.

FANNY   When Jacob died, when I sold the practice and closed the office, I had to first clean up the garbage of thirty-five years. He threw away

Daniel: A Screenplay

nothing. For months I went through papers. It was very difficult for me. I made myself ill.

DANIEL   Yes.

FANNY   Robert Lewin did not want the practice . . . Would you like something, a glass of milk? There was a point Jacob and I seriously discussed adopting you ourselves.

DANIEL   I didn't know that.

FANNY   Well, it's true. How we would have managed at our age, I can't tell you. It was his idea of course, not mine. I held my breath and he talked himself out of it. Only after he died did I think maybe he knew he hadn't long and that was why he decided he couldn't. Otherwise, who knows.

DANIEL   He was very kind to us.

FANNY   Your parents should have been so kind.

DANIEL *stands up to leave.*

I don't know what to tell you. I have no love for the memory of your parents. They were Communists and they destroyed everything they touched.

DANIEL   You don't think they were innocent?

FANNY ASCHER *rises from the sofa.*

FANNY   They were not innocent of permitting themselves to be used. And of using other people in their fanaticism. Innocent. The case ruined Jacob's health.

She leads DANIEL *through the living room to the foyer.*

They were difficult to deal with. They were very stubborn. He would come home furious, he would want to do something and they wouldn't let him. He would want to do something for their sake and they wouldn't allow it.

DANIEL   Like what?

FANNY   He wanted to call certain people as witnesses and they wouldn't let him. All sorts of things like that.

DANIEL *now faces* FANNY ASCHER *at the door.*

DANIEL   Who? Who did he want to call for a witness?

FANNY   Who knows? Jacob was a brilliant lawyer. And today when people talk about the case, it is Jacob they criticize. He should have done this, he shouldn't have done that. Do they know what he had to put up with?

Her hand goes to the doorknob.

INT.   SUSAN'S HOSPITAL ROOM. DAY. WINTER '69

DANIEL *sits in* SUSAN's *sanitarium room. His beard is grown out, hair long. The heel of his boot is on the edge of the chair and his arms are wrapped around his raised knee.*

SUSAN *lies on her bed. It is clear her condition has deteriorated. She is dressed in a blue gown ridden up about her knees. She lies supine, grasping the edges of the mattress with her hands, and her feet are hooked into the crevice of mattress and spring—so that she appears to be holding onto the bed for stability, even though she's on her back. She stares at the ceiling directly above her head. She does not seem to be aware that* DANIEL *is in the room.*

DANIEL *gets up, looks out of the window.*

EXT.   FROM SUSAN'S HOSPITAL ROOM. DAY. WINTER '69

The plants and trees outside indicate autumn. The trees are half-stripped, leaves blow about the ground, winter is coming.

INT.   SUSAN'S HOSPITAL ROOM. DAY. WINTER '69

DANIEL *goes to* SUSAN's *bedside, gently lifts her under the knees and shoulder, picks her up, hugs her like a baby. She weighs next to nothing. She is very, very thin. Her legs hang down like sticks, her head lolls back as if her neck is broken. Her open eyes see nothing.* DANIEL *kisses her eyes. He whispers her name in her ear. There is no response. He lowers her gently back down to the bed. He watches as her legs slowly spread, her feet hook the sides of the mattress, her arms reach out, her hands curl over the mattress, her head moves back and forth to recover its former position. She writhes gently on her back, like some underwater creature. And then, finally, she is still.*

DANIEL *moves from the bed, picks up a cardboard tube near the door, with-*

Daniel: A Screenplay

draws a poster, tapes it on the wall at the foot of SUSAN's *bed. It's a poster of himself—a black and white grainy photograph of himself, bearded, tough, scruffy, militant, with arm raised, fingers making the peace sign. He has put the poster up next to the famous poster of his parents.* DANIEL *goes out the door.*

EXT. LEWINS' HOME/STREET. DAY. WINTER '69

SUSAN's *Volvo coming down Winthrop Road in Brookline, Massachusetts. It screeches to a stop in front of the Lewins' home, a large frame house in a neighborhood of old large two- and three-story frame houses.* DANIEL *gets out of the car, he wears the same dungarees and sheepskin jacket he wore in the last scene, walks quickly up to the front door, the door opening just as he reaches it,* ROBERT LEWIN *standing there to greet him.*

INT. LEWINS' HOME. DAY. WINTER '69

DANIEL *sits at the dining-room table in his foster parents' home. In his hand, an ancient memo. Spread over the table are papers, memoranda, yellow legal-size sheets, file folders, etc.* ROBERT LEWIN *stands nearby,* LISE LEWIN *in the doorway to the kitchen.*

ROBERT LEWIN   You sure you're up to this?

DANIEL   I'm sure. Listen . . . do you know of anything my parents did to hurt the case Ascher was putting together?

ROBERT LEWIN   What do you mean?

DANIEL   Testimony, evidence, they wouldn't let him use.

LISE LEWIN   Who have you been talking to now? Fanny Ascher?

DANIEL   Yes.

LISE LEWIN   Of course.

ROBERT LEWIN   *(clearing his throat)* You've got to understand Fanny. Jake was in poor health and she blames his death on the case. That means she blames the Isaacsons. Of course she's going to resent any criticism of the way he handled the defense.

DANIEL   She wanted you to take over Ascher's practice.

ROBERT LEWIN   My father and Jake Ascher were law partners in the forties. I was the heir apparent. Fanny never forgave me for wanting to teach law.

He goes to the sideboard, pours himself a scotch.

Anyway, I don't remember Jake ever saying anything along those lines. Of course, I didn't really get involved until the appeals. And who knows? Your parents were Party members and possibly they felt they had to handle their defense with an eye out for the Party. Maybe there's something to it, maybe they did hold back. I don't know. But if they did, the Party didn't show any gratitude, did it? They were no help until after the sentence, when the propaganda value of the case was too good to be ignored.

INT.   LEWINS' HOME. NIGHT. WINTER '69

DANIEL *and the* LEWINS *having dinner in the kitchen of the Lewin home.*

ROBERT LEWIN   In those days it was fashionable to downgrade Russian technology. Before *Sputnik.* The joke was how they copied everything and claimed it for their own. So of course when they got the bomb it was our bomb and that meant we were betrayed. This is good, Lise.

DANIEL   *(not hungry)* Yeah, great.

LISE LEWIN   If I had more notice, I could have made something special. We never know when to expect you. We never hear from you.

ROBERT LEWIN   *(continuing train of thought)* After the war we built our whole foreign policy on a bomb. On our having the bomb and the Soviets not having it. A terrible mistake. It militarized the world. And when they got it, the only alternative to admitting our bankrupt policy was to find conspiracies. It was one or the other.

LISE LEWIN   You stopped at Susan's?

DANIEL *nods.*

LISE LEWIN   I washed her hair this morning. I bought her a lovely robe, but it's too big. I'll have to get the smaller size.

Daniel: A Screenplay

DANIEL *looks at her. He looks at his plate, a heavy roast beef dinner, baked potato, the works. He doesn't want to eat. His foster parents are obviously suffering* SUSAN's *decline; he sees now they look tired, dragged out, old.*

DANIEL   I used to think about the odds against it.

ROBERT LEWIN   What?

DANIEL   That it would be laid on us. A particular family out of millions.

ROBERT LEWIN   Well, if you're the FBI and you know you have to bring in something, what do you do? You go to your files. You have a file of known left-wing activists. And if you find someone who gives off a sense of his own vulnerability, you go to work on that.

DANIEL   Selig Mindish.

ROBERT LEWIN   They questioned him for weeks before they arrested him. And for weeks afterwards. And Mindish became their case.

LISE LEWIS   Robert, I wish we wouldn't talk about this.

ROBERT LEWIN   He became their case because he named your parents. And if they had named other people, they could have become prosecution witnesses, like Mindish. But they didn't. So they became the defendants.

LISE LEWIN   *(laying down knife and fork)* What is this family's continuing desire for punishment?

ROBERT LEWIN   Lise, the boy is asking questions.

LISE LEWIN   I know what this is leading to. You're going to tell him how you would have conducted the defense. With the Isaacsons a dozen years now in their graves. How comforting.

DANIEL   Hey, Mom, did I ask for comfort? Did I say I needed comfort?

ROBERT LEWIN   *(quietly)* Lise, you'll forgive me: I never thought it was a good idea to talk to Susan about the case.

The family abandons all pretense of continuing to eat dinner.

We are up at the bench where ASCHER, *the* U.S. ATTORNEY, *and the* JUDGE *are engaged in argument. The jury is not in the courtroom. Looking on from the defense table some distance away are* PAUL *and* ROCHELLE ISAACSON—*again dressed in* DANIEL's *vision of them, ill-fitting Glen plaid suit, black dress with white collar. They strain to hear what is going on.*

ASCHER   If you admit this line of questioning, their political beliefs, their political affiliations, that is what the trial rests on. Do we try people for their beliefs, now, in America?

U.S. ATTORNEY   Your Honor, we simply want to establish motivation for what they stand accused of.

JUDGE   Defense counsel is concerned that if his clients are forced to answer questions concerning their political affiliations, presumably the, er, unpopularity of those affiliations will prejudice the minds of the jury.

ASCHER   That's part of it, Your Honor.

U.S. ATTORNEY   If I may cite precedent—

ASCHER   I see nowhere in the bill a charge that they belong to a political party. If their politics is to be answered for, why is it not written in the indictment?

U.S. ATTORNEY   In the U.S. versus Schmidt, 1942, the political affiliation of the defendant was admitted as establishing motive. People commit crimes for reasons and sometimes those reasons are political reasons.

JUDGE   That seems reasonable, Mr. Ascher. *(laughs)*

ASCHER   Pardon me, Your Honor, I don't see the humor in this situation. Schmidt was a Nazi and he was indicted as a traitor. Treason is defined in the Constitution as levying war against the United States or in adhering to their enemies in war and giving them aid and comfort.

U.S. ATTORNEY   I'm grateful to Mr. Ascher for keeping us up on things.

ASCHER   If you want to put my clients on trial for treason that's fine with me. Then the uncorroborated testimony of one witness will not be admit-

Daniel: A Screenplay

ted as evidence as it is under the present conspiracy charge. Then you will have to prove that they *did* something, as you do not now.

JUDGE   Mr. Ascher, surely you're not saying a Nazi's politics should be in the record, but a Communist's should not.

ASCHER   Of course not, Your Honor.

JUDGE   These are momentous times. We're not technically at war with the Reds, but we are at war, wouldn't you agree, Mr. Ascher? I'm going to go ahead and rule for the prosecution on the grounds that the politics of your clients are crucial to the argument of this trial.

ASCHER   Over my strenuous objections, Your Honor. You are granting prosecution the right to turn my clients into devils in the eyes of the jury. You continue to try my clients under one law as if they had broken another.

JUDGE   (*to* OFFICER) Recall the jury.

INT.   LEWINS' HOME. NIGHT. WINTER '69

DANIEL *and* ROBERT LEWIN *late at night at the Lewins' dining-room table. The only light is a desk lamp moved to the center of the table. Papers, files spread all over the tabletop.* ROBERT LEWIN *is in his shirt-sleeves.*

ROBERT LEWIN   Today Jake wouldn't have the same problems to contend with. If they were on trial today the prosecution couldn't pull the stuff it pulled. Like, for instance, this fellow. (*He hands* DANIEL *a page from a file.*) The FBI nabbed him as another spy in the ring and said he would corroborate Selig Mindish's testimony. Big headlines. They never put him on the stand. He was never brought to trial. (*He cleans and fills his pipe.*) Poor old Jake. What he was up against. The whole temper of the time. It was . . . medieval. A few years later it came out the Secretary of State, Dean Acheson, gives testimony to a closed committee of the Senate, that even after they had the bomb the Soviets weren't regarded as a serious military threat. (*He lights his pipe.*) How could one tired, aging lawyer be expected to know that?

INT. ISAACSON COURTROOM. DAY. WINTER '54

The JURY *sitting.* PAUL *and* ROCHELLE ISAACSON *at the defense table.* ASCHER, *pacing in front of the jury box, is delivering his summation.*

ASCHER   Selig Mindish needed no one else to commit his crime. The dentist working in the darkness of his dental laboratory to steal the formula for atomic fission—there is your spy. The prosecution witness! And only his word condemns my clients. Shall you believe the word of such a man? A man whose own punishment will be in inverse ratio to the punishment he can dispense to my clients? He took them under his wing, a guide, a mentor—closer than family!—and watched over them and used them and held them in readiness for the time when, to escape with his own skin, he would point the accusing finger at this young couple, Paul and Rochelle. Is this beyond belief? There are such things, Horatio, says Shakespeare's Hamlet, never dreamed of in your philosophies . . .

The summation continues, the sound fades. ASCHER *points his finger in the air and pantomimes the words we hear in* ROBERT LEWIN's *voice.*

ROBERT LEWIN   *(voice over)* Selig Mindish, ladies and gentlemen of the jury. He is your spy. He and he alone is responsible.

INT. LEWINS' HOME. DINING ROOM. NIGHT. WINTER '69

DANIEL *and* ROBERT LEWIN *sit close together in the late night.*

ROBERT LEWIN   God knows the pressure was enormous. At the time I couldn't have come up with anything better. Maybe no one could.

DANIEL   I don't understand.

ROBERT LEWIN   The strategy was to turn everything back on Mindish. Show him guiltier than he himself confessed to being. Show his self-interest in testifying against the Isaacsons. To save himself. He is your spy. He and he alone.

DANIEL   Well?

ROBERT LEWIN   *(leaning forward)* But you see the terrible flaw—it admits there was a crime! Your parents and Ascher granted the prosecution the one premise they shouldn't have—that any crime was committed at all!

Daniel: A Screenplay

DANIEL   But Mindish confessed. Why would he confess if no crime was committed?

ROBERT LEWIN   Why indeed. *(He gets up and begins to pace.)* I don't know how well you remember Selig Mindish. An ignorant man. Never properly naturalized. A dubious degree from some third-rate dental college. A very ordinary man perfectly capable of joining the Communist Party for no more than an exalted sense of himself. So you ask what is the motivation for a man to do what he did: Well one motivation is to believe, or to have been persuaded to believe, in his own guilt. And to live in mortal fear of the consequences. Another is to believe, or to have been persuaded to believe, in the guilt of his friends. And to live in mortal fear of the consequences . . . But there's a third possibility. Don't you remember what their lives were like? They believed! Your father had the faith! He suffered the passion of his faith.

DANIEL *is stunned. As if he has been struck.*

EXT.   ROBESON "CLIP" (STOCK SHOT). DAY. SUMMER '49

A clip of Paul Robeson singing "Peat Bog Soldiers."

EXT.   PEEKSKILL. DAY. SUMMER '49

A sustained rush of applause and suddenly people begin to stream into an open meadow used as a parking lot for buses at the Lakeland Picnic Grounds in Peekskill, 1949.

The applause is over and masses of people move to the buses. We find the ISAACSONS, SELIG MINDISH, *and their friends in the crowd.* ROCHELLE, *her head up, alert to danger, takes her seven-year-old son,* DANIEL, *by the hand and hurries him on.*

The Isaacson's bus, with DANIEL's *face at the window, moves off in a line of buses and cars.*

Sound over: Paul Robeson singing "Peat Bog Soldiers"

> *"Up and down the guards are pacing*
> *No one, no one, can go through*

Flight would mean a sure death facing
Guns and barbed wire greet our view.
We are the peat bog soldiers
Marching with our spaces to the bog."

INT.   BUS. DAY. SUMMER '49

From inside the Isaacsons' bus we see a local policeman waving the traffic onto a narrow road that winds through some woods. The bus follows another just like it.

"But for us there is no complaining
Winter will in time be past
One day we shall cry rejoicing
Homeland, dear, you're mine at last.
Then will the peat bog soldiers
March no more with their spades to the bog."

At song's end sound is cut back in: the buses proceeding in slow gear, a grinding painful sound. MINDISH, *behind* PAUL, *on the aisle, leans forward and says quietly:*

MINDISH   This isn't the way we came.

PAUL *half rises from his seat and looks down the aisle.*

DANIEL, *his face at the window, notices through the streaked dirty glass four men running along the edge of the woods and actually running faster than the bus is going. He presses his face to see more clearly the almost ghostly figures— many more now—coming out of the woods and running along with the bus. One of them stops to throw something.*

DANIEL   Look out!

The bus jerks to a stop, stalling in gear, and everyone is thrown forward. Windows shatter. Screams. PAUL, *shaken, sits back down holding the rail of the seat in front of him. The bus* DRIVER *stands up, turns to the passengers, hands covering his eyes, blood streaming between his fingers. Passengers duck, go down like dominoes, as the windows of the bus shatter.*

ROCHELLE *presses* DANIEL *to the floor. They kneel between the seats.* ROCHELLE's *arms cover* DANIEL *protectively. Rocks pound against the side of the bus.*

Daniel: A Screenplay

VOICES   *(outside)* We'll teach you commie kike bastards! Reds! Nigger lovers! Kikes! Jew bastards!

With each shout, each splatter of breaking glass, ROCHELLE *presses* DANIEL *further under her until his head rests on her folded legs and her breasts and arms cover the curve of his back. The bus begins to rock.*

ROCHELLE   *(softly)* Scum! Nazi pigs!

PAUL *has slipped out of his seat and now crouches in the aisle. He begins to make his way to the front of the bus, stepping over people and squeezing past them.*

PAUL   *(shouting)* Officer! Officer!

ROCHELLE   Pauly! Get down—what are you doing!

PAUL   This mustn't be permitted. *(He reaches the front of the bus.)* Open the door! We cannot permit this outrage!

MINDISH *has followed* PAUL *forward. The dentist has a peculiar smile on his face—a smile of embarrassment for the plight they find themselves in.*

MINDISH   Get down, Paul. What are you doing?

PAUL *has again sighted the* POLICE OFFICER *outside. He steps into the stairwell at the front and tries to pry open the double doors, struggling to fold them back.*

PAUL   Officer! Why do you permit this?

We see the OFFICER *standing out there, arms folded, smiling.*

MINDISH   Paul, he's in on it! Get back!

A cheer from the patriots outside as PAUL's *entire left arm is suddenly yanked through the partially opened doors. The bus stops rocking.* PAUL *is now pulled up to the door.*

The men outside are doing something to his arm. Calmly, with his right hand he removes his eyeglasses, folds them against his chest and hands the glasses up to MINDISH. *In his naked eyes is the angry decision to suffer this pain and become a revolutionary sacrifice.*

ROCHELLE *struggles to her feet, pushes* DANIEL *aside, pushes down the aisle.*

ROCHELLE   Stop them! Stop them before they break him in half!

PAUL's *face is popping with sweat and contorting as he silently experiences the breaking of his arm. Two men in the bus are holding him, trying to pull him back.* MINDISH, *holding* PAUL's *glasses, leans over the driver's seat, pulls the handle that opens the bus doors. A hiss, the doors open, and* PAUL *and the men holding him disappear, and a roar goes up outside.*

INT. ARTIE'S PAD. NIGHT. SUMMER '69

DANIEL *and* PHYLLIS *at a party in* ARTIE STERNLICHT's *Lower East Side apartment. A crowded scene, very cool. Students, literary and media people, poets, freaks, and so forth. Rock and roll music on the record player.* DANIEL *walks through the rooms, between bodies.* PHYLLIS *tries to keep up, gets left behind.* DANIEL *is very drunk. He is shouting something, or singing, and by and large people ignore him. One or two, those closest, react, turning their heads to look at him as he sidles by.*

DANIEL   The verdict is guilty! The Isaacsons are guilty! Of conspiracy to give the Soviet Union the secret of the atom bomb. No—the secret of the hydrogen bomb.

He whispers into a girl's ear.

Or is it the cobalt bomb?

GIRL   What?

DANIEL   Or the neutron bomb. *(screaming)* OR NAPALM! *(softly)* Something like that.

We see the faces looking at him, some amused, some put off. And our point of view of the party has quietly become DANIEL's: *Calmly and without fuss these faces are among those who turn toward him a moment and turn away as he makes his way through the party:* GRANDMA, JACOB ASCHER, *a* JUDGE *in his robes,* SELIG MINDISH, WILLIAMS, AUNT FRIEDA, PAUL ISAACSON, ROCHELLE ISAACSON. *They are not dream distortions but guests at the party, drinking and chatting. However, the sound has faded. We are in the silence of* DANIEL's *mind.*

EXT./INT.   CAR TO PRISON. DAY. SUMMER '54

A 1953 Buick going north on the Saw Mill River Parkway, in New York State, on a grey winter morning. Grey snow piled in banks along the side of the road.

In the back seat of the car the children, DANIEL *and* SUSAN, *with* ASCHER *sitting between them. A young* ROBERT LEWIN *is driving. The children are dressed for an occasion;* DANIEL's *hair is combed,* SUSAN *has a ribbon in her black hair.*

DANIEL   Is this the right day?

ASCHER   Yes, Daniel.

DANIEL   Do they know we're coming?

ASCHER   I told you, yes.

DANIEL *stares out the window.*

SUSAN   They're dead.

ASCHER   No, my little girl, that is not true. They are alive.

SUSAN   Not anymore. They were killed. It was in the newspaper.

DANIEL   How do you know, you can't read.

SUSAN   *(solemnly)* I can, I have learned how to read.

EXT.   PRISON COMPLEX. DAY. SUMMER '54

Outside the walls of state prison ASCHER *guides the children toward the gate. The walls rise up in yellow brick.* DANIEL, *looking up, sees a tower topped with a glass booth. He starts as a light flashes in his face. Walking backward in front of them a photographer with a Speed Graphic. The children hold their arms up to shield their eyes against the flashes.*

ASCHER *and the children follow a uniformed* GUARD *through an outer prison yard to one of the buildings of the prison compound. No prisoners are in sight here, but trucks move in and out and from all the buildings a hum of machinery, as if this is a factory complex rather than a prison.*

Daniel: A Screenplay

INT. PRISON COMPLEX. DAY. SUMMER '54

They follow a GUARD *down a long concrete hallway. Their footsteps echo. At the end of the hall the* GUARD *unlocks a steel door, they all pass through.*

ASCHER *and the children with* GUARD *in an elevator grinding noisily as it slowly rises. It comes to a stop, the* GUARD *pulls back the gate door, they follow him out.*

Now they have their first glimpse of cells: they stare through a barred window that looks down on a vast quiet cellblock. ASCHER *has to hustle them on. They continue down another concrete passage, and here we become aware that the constant hum of machinery which we have been hearing is gone. The sense that they've come to the heart of the prison.*

INT. VISITORS' CELL. DAY. SUMMER '54

In the visiting room of the Death House, a room bare except for a wooden table and some chairs. The children and ASCHER *wait in this room, their coats still on.* ASCHER *sits down, pushes his homburg back on his head, puts his hands on his knees.*

After a moment a GUARD *comes in, closes the door softly, and stands against the wall with arms folded.* DANIEL *goes over to the* GUARD *and raises his hands.*

ASCHER   What's this?

DANIEL   He has to frisk me.

GUARD   'Ats all right, kid.

DANIEL   No, go ahead and search me. I might have a gun.

GUARD   'Ats OK, kid, I'm satisfied you don't have a gun.

Now SUSAN *as well as* DANIEL *stands, arms raised in front of the* GUARD.

ASCHER   They haven't seen their parents in over a year.

GUARD   Yeah, well they're here.

DANIEL   *(enraged)* SEARCH ME!

The GUARD *looks at* ASCHER, *who nods. The* GUARD *touches* DANIEL's *sides.*

DANIEL   Now her!

Daniel: A Screenplay

The GUARD *touches the hem of* SUSAN's *coat. Then he straightens up, folds his arms, and looks straight ahead.*

INT.   VISITORS' CELL. DAY. SUMMER '54

Time has passed. SUSAN *walks around the edge of the room, measuring each wall with her footsteps. When she comes to the* GUARD *she goes around him as if he's part of the wall.* DANIEL *stands at the barred window looking out:*

EXT.   PRISON COMPLEX. DAY. SUMMER '54

The view is of a woods and, in the distance downhill through the trees, the silver strip of a river.

INT.   VISITORS' CELL. DAY. SUMMER '54

Suddenly DANIEL *feels* SUSAN's *hand in his. He turns. His mother is watching him from the door.* ROCHELLE *looks small. She wears a grey sack dress and house slippers. She's pale, almost waxen, and she's put red lipstick on her mouth, which gives her a burning look. Her eyes blaze brightly. She looks ghastly, nothing like the* ROCHELLE *of the recent courtroom scenes.*

ROCHELLE   Look at you two. You're so big I don't recognize you.

DANIEL   We sent you pictures.

ROCHELLE   Not the same. *(She presses her fingers to her temples as if containing the tears.)* Aren't you going to give me a hug?

DANIEL *and* SUSAN *shuffle across the room and suffer themselves to stand before* ROCHELLE *as she kneels and hugs each of them. They are stiff, uncomfortable.*

ROCHELLE   You're so big. You're beautiful. You're my beautiful children.

SUSAN   When are they going to kill you?

ROCHELLE   Oh, they're not going to do that. It's just their way of talking. I'm sure Uncle Jake told you about appeals, about other judges who have to reexamine the trial. That takes time. We're in no danger right now.

SUSAN   But what if they kill you anyway? How will they do it?

ROCHELLE   Well, darling, what they do is called electrocution and it's very painless. But let's not talk about that. Aren't you warm? Take your coats off and let me look at you.

She helps them off with their coats.

You're very nicely dressed. How lovely you look. Here, I have a little surprise.

From her pockets she offers them Milky Way candy bars.
The children sit with their mother and self-consciously nibble their candy bars while she looks at them with her starved strange look.

And how's school?

DANIEL   Fine. I'm going to be a lawyer. Then I can get you free.

ASCHER   So? This I hadn't heard before.

ROCHELLE   You'll make a good lawyer. Won't he, Jake?

DANIEL   I won't let them kill you. I'll kill them first!

ROCHELLE *takes a Kleenex from her pocket and wipes the chocolate from the corner of his mouth.*

ROCHELLE   Oh now. Where did you get that expression?

SUSAN   Where's my daddy?

ROCHELLE   First I get a visit with you, then it's his turn.

SUSAN   Why not together?

Pause.

ROCHELLE   Look how long your hair has gotten. It's so pretty.

SUSAN   Do you see my daddy?

ROCHELLE   Oh yes. I talk to him once a week through a screen.

SUSAN *begins to walk around the table, her fingers lightly touching her brother, the chairs, her mother,* ASCHER's *sleeve. She walks in a methodical circle that widens until she traces, once again, the wall of the room.*

SUSAN   We went home. But it was gone.

ROCHELLE *tracks* SUSAN *with her eyes.* DANIEL *in turn is looking at her and when their eyes meet, he turns away and she keeps looking at him.*

ROCHELLE   It's hard to make up for all the lost time. A strange feeling, isn't it?

DANIEL *nods. She touches his face.*

DANIEL   We're living with a family.

ROCHELLE   I know.

DANIEL   It's closer to here than the Shelter.

ROCHELLE   *(smiling)* I know.

DANIEL   The Judge made us. When this term is over.

ROCHELLE   Danny, you don't understand. I chose the Lewins from all the people. I wanted that for you. It will be some time before this is over and that's too long to live in the Shelter.

The GUARD *near the door looks at his watch. At the same time the door opens and a* MATRON *looks in.*

ROCHELLE   Already?

The MATRON *nods.* SUSAN *interrupts her race around the room and comes back to the table.* ROCHELLE *hugs her, hugs* DANIEL.

ROCHELLE   You'll come back soon, won't you?

DANIEL   Yes.

ROCHELLE   I love you, my sweetest angels. I love your letters. I love your pictures. I'm so proud of you, do you know that?

ROCHELLE *is on one knee, her hand on the back of each child. She presses them to her.*

Soon this will all be over and we'll have peace. It's a terrible thing to do to people, isn't it? But don't worry. We'll get out of here. We'll have fun again.

ROCHELLE *smiles through her tears, rises, leaves quickly. The door closes, the children stare at the closed door. They are dry-eyed.* ASCHER, *clearing his throat, comes over and stands behind them with his hands on their shoulders.*

PAUL ISAACSON *looks different: his hair is short, his ears prominent. He wears glasses with colorless plastic frames. He wears grey pants and a grey shirt too big for him. Slippers and no belt. He looks young. He is effusive, manic.*

PAUL   How are the two best children in the world! How are my favorite children! Look at them, Jake! A million dollars! A million dollars!

He holds out a cigar box tied with a rubber band.

Do you know what I have here? Do you?

DANIEL   No.

PAUL   Well, I'm going to show you. Watch carefully.

With a flourish he removes the rubber band, places the cigar box on the table and slowly lifts the lid. The children move closer and look into the box.

My collection!

In the box are dead moths, roaches, spiders, beetles, flies, and an enormous brown water bug with its legs curled up.

DANIEL   How did you catch them?

PAUL   With a paper cup. I can't keep them from drying out. They won't let me have pins or preservative. But the insect world is truly amazing. Look at this moth—isn't it beautiful?

He holds up a large moth on a piece of paper. His hand trembles and it seems as if the dead moth is trying to fly.

SUSAN   I hate it. I hate dead things.

PAUL   Now these are roaches—I can usually find all the specimens I need. *(He laughs.)* But you have to trick them. Sometimes it takes hours!

PAUL *in a delayed reaction to what* SUSAN *has said suddenly closes the box; flustered, he doesn't know what to say. He sits down and holds his head in his hands. When he looks up again he has composed himself.*

You know, I figured it out—I'm not more than twenty feet from your mother as the crow flies. I'm one floor below and one block over. Of course,

Daniel: A Screenplay

there's a lot of stone between us. Poor Mommy, she's all alone up there, the only woman. I at least have murderers to talk to!

He laughs, frowns, stands up, walks around the room. He lights a Camel with a practiced con gesture. The children stare at him. He sits down again.

Are you still a baseball fan?

DANIEL *shrugs.*

They put the Giant games on the loudspeaker. They'll make a fan of me yet! Also, I play chess with the other inmates. We make our boards and chessmen out of paper and we shout the moves. I always thought chess was a waste of time. It is! It's a terrible waste of time . . . Time which is so valuable. In jail you've got to kill it. (*He grabs* DANIEL *by the shoulder.*) They can put a person in jail but not his mind. What's wrong, did I burn you?

DANIEL *is shy of the cigarette in* PAUL's *hand.*

Look here, it didn't fall, the ash is still here, you see? Don't worry. I wouldn't hurt my boy . . . They're the ones with minds in jail. But you can't put innocent people to death in this country. It can't be done. You'll see, public opinion will get behind us. You'll see, my handsome boy. Am I right, Jake?

ASCHER   Of course. But calm yourself.

PAUL   Before our trial even started we were convicted by the paid hirelings of the kept press. It was not a fair trial. On that ground alone!

ASCHER   (*looking at the* GUARD) Paul, I don't think now is the time or place.

PAUL   It's all right. I want my son to know we're not alone, the Isaacsons. Soon the whole world will be behind us in our fight to regain our freedom. And he can help! You want to help, don't you?

DANIEL   Yes.

PAUL   That's my boy, my wonderful brilliant boy.

He holds DANIEL's *face in his hands.*

You know, you're getting to look like me?

SUSAN   Am I?

PAUL   Ah, you're luckier. You're the image of your mother. A beauty like your mother.

He pulls SUSAN *to him.*

Jake, isn't that an ideal situation? What could a father ask for but that his son take after him and his daughter after his wife. Is that not ideal?

ASCHER   Absolutely.

PAUL   We're an ideal family!

EXT.   BURNING STAKE. DAY. 1800S

A woman is burning at the stake. Horribly. Her hair is gone, her skin is rupturing, she screams silently through the smoke made by her own flesh.

DANIEL   *(voice over)* Burning at the stake. Known to all European nations through the nineteenth century. Used into the twentieth century in the American South, together with castration. Always, in whatever country, used on the lower classes. Like the knout, like drawing and quartering. No accident Joan of Arc was a peasant.

EXT.   LOS ANGELES INTERNATIONAL AIRPORT (STOCK SHOT). DAY. FALL '69

An American Airlines 707 coming in for a landing.

INT.   LOS ANGELES INTERNATIONAL TERMINAL. DAY. FALL '69

DANIEL *coming into the terminal: he wears prison shirt and pants, sandals. His beard is full, his long hair tied with a headband of red cloth. Carries a small duffle bag slung from his shoulder. Also, his fleece-lined jacket, coming as he does from a colder climate.*

EXT. SAN DIEGO FREEWAY ACCESS. DAY. FALL '69

DANIEL *stands at Century Boulevard at the corner of the feed onto the San Diego Freeway. A map in his hand. A battered VW van pulls up, a shirtless blond California kid with long hair behind the wheel.*

EXT. VW VAN. SAN DIEGO FREEWAY. DAY. FALL '69

We follow the battered VW down the Freeway, south. Past oil refineries, billboards, power plants, industrial parks, storage tanks, ramps, cloverleafs, tract housing, the pennants flying. Power lines strung across the highway, military convoys in the right-hand lane. Smoke over the flatlands, the sight of military jets high overhead. The VW gets lost in the heavy stream of traffic.

EXT. DR. LINDA'S OFFICES. DAY. FALL '69

The VW camper coming up the drive of a huge luxurious shopping center (possibly Fashion Island at Newport Beach). It stops for a moment in front of a professional high-rise office building in the shopping center, and when it pulls away, DANIEL *is standing on the sidewalk. He waves to the van, turns, regards the spotlessly clean, aseptic, sleek professional building in front of him.*

INT. DR. LINDA'S OFFICES. DAY. FALL '69

DANIEL *getting out of the elevator, walking down a carpeted hall, checking the professional names on each door. Muzak in the air. Stops at a door with the discreet shingle, Dr. L. Minton, DDS, Dr. S. Minton, DDS. Goes in.*

DANIEL *sitting in the waiting room of the Doctors Minton office. A patient comes out of the inner office; leaves; the door to the inner office opens again, a woman stands with hand on doorknob, looks at* DANIEL. *A woman in her late twenties or early thirties. Wears a white doctor's jacket.*

DANIEL   Hi, Linda.

DR. MINTON   *(looking at card in her hand)* Mr.——?

DANIEL   *(standing)* Come on, Linda. It's me, Danny Isaacson. From Weeks Avenue.

The Doctor walks over to her RECEPTIONIST, *talks softly to her for a moment, waves* DANIEL *to the inner office. She follows him, closes the door behind her.*

In the dentist's office, white, gleaming, modern, DANIEL *sits down in the chair, swings around to face* LINDA.

DANIEL   *(smiling)* Pretty nice. I bet you're a very good dentist. You always had strong hands. I can still feel those pokes in the ribs. You were good at bending fingers back too.

Pause.

LINDA   What do you want? What are you doing here?

DANIEL   I happened to be in the neighborhood.

LINDA   If you think I'm afraid of you, you're wrong.

DANIEL   I don't think you're afraid of me.

LINDA   We have friends here. Loyal friends who know who we are. We don't have anything to hide, so don't think you can threaten me.

DANIEL   I just want to talk to your father. Where is he?

LINDA MINDISH *stands behind a small desk. She's very pale, very tense.*

LINDA   He's retired. He no longer practices.

DANIEL   That right?

LINDA   He's an old man and he's sick.

DANIEL   I just want to pay my respects.

LINDA   There's a law against bothering people!

DANIEL   Linda, be civilized.

LINDA   How dare you come here! How dare you!

DANIEL   I recognize in you the same look I see in the mirror. The look of the same memories . . . We were all hurt, OK? It happened to all of us. I feel the need to see you people. Is that so hard to understand?

INT.   DR. LINDA'S OFFICES. DAY. FALL '69

DANIEL *sits, legs outstretched, in* LINDA's *waiting room. It is decorated in southern California dentist decor of the phony modern painting, the textured wallpaper, the driftwood lamp.* DANIEL *yawns, folds his arms. Same Muzak we heard in the halls. Two people, a* MAN *and a* WOMAN *sit on the chrome and vinyl chairs opposite. The inner door opens; a* CHILD *comes out. The* WOMAN *rises, takes the* CHILD'S *hand, speaks to the* RECEPTIONIST, *leaves. At the same time,* LINDA *comes to the open inner door.*

DANIEL *waits for the* MAN *to go into the inner office. Instead,* LINDA MIND-ISH *comes out, taking off her white jacket. She bids goodbye to the receptionist, who leaves; she locks the front door after the* RECEPTIONIST *and she sits down next to the man opposite* DANIEL.

LINDA   This is Dale. He's a lawyer.

The man opposite nods at DANIEL. *He has a crew cut, is in his late thirties, beginning to get fat. He leans forward, hands* DANIEL *his card.* DANIEL *takes the card, smiling.*

DALE   What can we do for you?

DANIEL   (*to* LINDA) Pretty good.

DALE   Linda did the right thing. You can't barge in on people like this and expect them to put out the welcome mat. She has no way of even knowing you're who you say you are.

LINDA   No, it's him. It's Danny Isaacson.

DALE   Linda's a big girl and I can only advise her what to do. She and her family have nothing to fear. They're not obliged to discuss that case or see you at all. Do you need money? What's your problem?

DANIEL   Why don't you shut up for a fucking minute, Dale.

DALE   (*standing*) I'm going to warn you as a lawyer—on intimidation, threatened or implied, obscene language or slander in the state of California.

DANIEL *sighs, crosses his legs, extends his arms over the back of the couch on which he sits. The lawyer sits back down and glares at him.*

DANIEL   (*to* LINDA) I'm hoping your father can help settle some questions.

LINDA   Are there still questions? As far as I know all questions were settled a long time ago.

DANIEL   Do you really want me to talk in front of this guy?

LINDA   (*Her hand meets* DALE'S) Dale and I are going to be married.

Pause.

DANIEL   I'm interested to know how you and your mother supported your-selves after your father went to jail.

DALE   Linda, it's none of his business.

DANIEL   You were fourteen or fifteen. Your mother's not the kind of woman who could go out and get a job. And when you moved here you went to college and dental school.

DALE   Linda, you're not obliged—

LINDA   It's all right. When my father went to prison, my mother and I suffered terribly. But something good happened too—I discovered resources in myself that I otherwise might not have. From what I understand, neither you nor your sister have been that fortunate.

LINDA MINDISH *sits up on the ledge of the chair with her hands folded in her lap and ankles primly together.*

In many ways it's been worse for me than for you. Your parents after all, were heroes in some circles. But Selig Mindish is a hero to no one. To say the least. We lost our honor, our friends. And the years he spent in jail ruined his health. I'll tell you something: I often dreamed that if we could change places, the Isaacsons and the Mindishes, I would be glad to stand in your shoes just so that you could stand in mine. Let me have your hanky, Dale.

DANIEL   Well, it's a nice thought, Linda. A nice thought.

LINDA   I owe you nothing. Your family was full of high ideals except when it came to other people. Except when it came to ruining the lives of friends.

DANIEL   What does that mean?

LINDA   They led Papa down the garden path. He chauffeured them where they wanted to go, he fixed their teeth, he turned into a spy for them.

DALE   Linda honey, calm yourself.

DANIEL   *(standing)* Well, the awful Isaacsons are dead, Linda. All you have
to worry about is me. And what can I do? Tell people your real name? But
this is Southern California. Orange County. I mean, after all, Selig helped
bust a commie spy ring.

DALE   His testimony is a matter of record.

DANIEL   Yes, it is. But things that seemed clear then are not clear now. For
instance, have you ever asked him why he confessed?

Pause.

LINDA   That's a naive question.

DANIEL   Why? Because he was caught and had no choice? Or because he
was sorry for what he'd done? Or because he wanted to save himself? That's
what Jake Ascher thought—that Selig fingered my parents to save himself.
As for my parents I don't know what they thought. It's all very puzzling.

LINDA   What are you talking about?

DANIEL   Nobody knows what happened. Nobody seems to know what really
happened! Even the government! They were never satisfied they had the
criminal masterminds they'd gotten a death sentence for. They only arrested my mother to get my father to talk, to try to break my father. Right
up to the end they were ready to deal. They had a damn phone in the death
chamber in case my father wanted to confess. Confess to what! Didn't they
have him? They sat him in the electric chair where he could see the fucking
phone! There were ready to commute the death sentence if he told them
who really ran the atomic spy ring!

Pause. DANIEL *goes to the window, looks out.*

There was another couple in the Bronx membership who'd dropped out of
the Party some years before. Everyone believed they'd gone underground.
To do dangerous work. Even I heard that. Did your father ever mention
them? Their name or anything?

LINDA   No, Danny.

DANIEL   Nobody ever mentioned them without lowering their voice. The
daredevil heroes of the Bronx. After all the Party was falling apart, people
needed to feel good about something. This other couple was supposed to

live just a few blocks from us. They were supposed to have had two children. But who knows where they lived. Or how many children there were.

DANIEL *turns to* LINDA *for her reaction.*

LINDA   You poor tormented boy.

DANIEL   Yeah, well, it's hard to get it down, I know.

DALE   I'm not sure I understand.

LINDA   (*to* DANIEL) Of course you have no proof of this.

DANIEL   Of course. That's why I want to talk to Selig.

LINDA   Stop calling my father *Selig.*

DANIEL   (*palms up*) I've still got his fillings in my mouth!

DALE   Let me see if I understand this.

LINDA   Oh Dale, it's insane.

DALE   You're saying Dr. Mindish lied about your parents in deference to another couple who looked like them?

DANIEL   I don't know if they looked like them. To protect another couple everyone thought was working undercover. To keep the FBI away from people of real value. They were closing in. To get the heat off.

DALE   And that this mythical couple, these other people, were the ones who actually stole the secrets.

DANIEL   Well, not necessarily, because it's never been proven any secrets were stolen. It isn't what really happened or was going to happen. It was what Selig and/or some of the others thought had happened. Or what was going to happen. It was as much fantasy as what the FBI thought had happened.

DALE   And your parents lent themselves to this deception?

DANIEL   My father. I think my father would have figured it out. And gambled. I don't think my mother would have known anything about it.

LINDA   I feel sorry for you. (*to* DALE) I knew that's what he wanted. Some way of squirming out of it. My God! That's pathetic. My God, the more I think about it! Papa didn't tell the half of it! They were into all sorts of things that never even came up at the trial. Missiles. Germ warfare. Gas. Everything. They ran the show. They planned things and paid people off. Lasers—years before anybody heard of lasers! So don't tell me my father sacrificed them. Or anybody! Another couple—my God that's pitiful.

DANIEL   Linda, I didn't come three thousand miles to hear the family line.

LINDA   I've wasted enough time. I'm sorry, we can't do anything for you.

DANIEL   Ah, you're not the little hipster I used to know. Now your Dale with his dacron suit and tie and his haircut, if they were his parents, he'd want it to be another couple. But look at me—do I look like Dale?

Indeed, DANIEL *with his long hair and red bandanna and steel-frame glasses and beard, suddenly confronting* LINDA *here with his mysterious presence, embodies nothing if not a revolutionary. She is unable to remove her gaze from him.*

Whatever it is, I can live with it. *(looking around office)* Jesus. This could be another planet.

LINDA   There's something wrong with you.

DANIEL   Linda, don't you want to come back to the world? Don't you want your life on earth? . . . Whatever it is, Linda, I *want* to live with it. Let Selig tell me. Let Selig tell me what you just told me. I want to know the guys he put the finger on were the guys who did it. Or didn't do it. I want to hear it from him. That's all.

LINDA *and* DANIEL *stare at each other.*

LINDA   Take us to Selig now, Dale.

EXT.   SELIG'S CALIFORNIA RETIREMENT. DAY. FALL '69

An Oldsmobile 98 moves slowly down the wide street of a southern California retirement village. Rows and rows of garden-apartment condominiums and small ranch houses, decorated with clusters of palm trees and watered by automatic sprinklers.

    DANIEL *in the car regards with narrow eyes the scene that* LINDA *makes no attempt to explain. The only people visible are old people. On oversized tri-*

cycles. Strolling in aluminum walkers tipped with rubber feet. Sitting on corner benches. No stores, no traffic, no visible weather.

The car pulls into the driveway of a large pillared mansion in stucco. At the entrance gate, a sign: CORONA DEL MAR RETIREMENT HOME.

INT. SELIG'S CALIFORNIA RETIREMENT. PAINT CLASS/HALL. DAY. FALL '69

DANIEL *sits at a small round metal patio table on a terrace. Quiet old people sit on benches or yard chairs and regard him. From within the sounds of an angry woman and at one point* SADIE MINDISH, *an old woman now, appears inside the back screen door, a gauzy figure of* DANIEL's *past, and glares at him for a moment.*

DANIEL *waits patiently, his arms folded. The back screen door swings open and* LINDA MINDISH *emerges, leading her father,* SELIG. SELIG MINDISH *wears a Hawaiian shirt. He is incredibly old. White haired. His jaw moves up and down, his lips make the sound of a faucet dripping as they meet and separate. Palsied, with brown spots all over his skin, and white of eyes discolored in age sockets of fat and skin. But still a large man with remnants of rude strength.*

LINDA *seats him facing* DANIEL. *From the doorway now open,* SADIE MIND-ISH *glares;* DALE *stands with his hand on her arm.* LINDA *kneels down beside* SELIG MINDISH, *her knees blanching in her sheer stockings.*

LINDA   Papa? You remember Danny Isaacson?

The old man's head stirs and he struggles through his senility to understand what is being said.

LINDA   (*to* DANIEL) You see? Ask him anything you want, Danny.

She is both bitter and triumphant as she says this.

DANIEL *leans forward, hands on his knees, so that he is directly in* SELIG MINDISH's *line of sight.*

DANIEL   Hello, Dr. Mindish. I'm Daniel Isaacson. I'm Paul and Rochelle's son. Danny?

MINDISH's *head stirs like a turtle's head coming out of its shell. He smiles and nods. Then as he continues to look at* DANIEL, *he gradually becomes still, and his facial palsy ceases. He no longer smiles. Water wells from the congested yellow corners of his eyes. Tears track down his face.*

MINDISH   Denny?

LINDA *pats his hand. She has begun to weep.*

LINDA   It's all right, Papa. It's all right.

MINDISH   It's Denny?

For one moment of recognition, MINDISH *is restored to life. He leans forward, raises his hand, touches* DANIEL's *face. He finds the back of* DANIEL's *neck, pulls him forward, and touches the top of* DANIEL's *head with his palsied lips. Then he slumps back into his senility.*

    DANIEL *smiles, shakes his head.*

DANIEL   *(softly)* OK, Selig. I was hoping. But it's all locked up, isn't it? I wanted it for my sister. I wanted to give her something. You remember Susan? You remember the little girl? No?

Silence.

There's such a thing as too much hope.

INT.   EXECUTION CHAMBER. DAY. SUMMER '54

PAUL ISAACSON *is led into the execution chamber. He has to be held up. His eyes are red, but dry. He wears slippers, grey slacks, and a loose shirt with the sleeves rolled. A round area on the top of his head has been shaved. His right pants leg is slit up to the knee.*

DANIEL   *(voice over)* Electricity is a form of energy. It is generated by power sources driven by water, steam, or atomic fission. The two leading electric power—producing countries in the world are the United States of America and the Union of Soviet Socialist Republics.

In the chamber are REPORTERS, *a* RABBI, GUARDS, *the* WARDEN, *and the* EXECUTIONER. PAUL *is helped into the wooden electric chair, lowered gently, like an invalid. Seated, he breathes rapidly. He bites his lip. He clenches his hands in his lap. He does not look at anyone.*

A red phone specially hooked up sits on a shelf, very prominent. It is in PAUL's *line of sight.*

DANIEL   *(voice over)* The theory of electricity is that atoms gain or lose electrons and thus become positively or negatively charged. In this way a current is produced. The current is designed to flow through a circuit. In 1889 the first electric chair was put into use by the State of New York. It was hailed as the most humane means of putting someone to death. For his electrocution the condemned individual is simply made part of the circuit.

PAUL *closes his eyes. His hands are raised, separated, his arms strapped at the wrists to the arms of the chair. His ankles are strapped to the chair. Another strap across his lap, another across his chest, and another, like a phylactery, around his forehead. A guard gently removes his eyeglasses, folds them, puts them aside. Another guard fixes the electrodes in place.*

The guard looks at the warden, who waits a moment, shakes his head. PAUL *sucks in his breath as the guard puts a black leather hood over his head.*

DANIEL   *(voice over)* Ah, Pauly. Ah, my Pop. Nothing has gone right. The gamble has failed. The world has not flamed to revolution. And your chance for life seems to have turned on the gentility, the manners, of the people fighting for you. There is a grand fusion of guilt—you are confirmed in guilt because of who campaigned for your freedom, and your supporters are discredited because it is you they campaigned for.

PAUL's *hands grip the arms of the chair. The executioner takes his place in a glass-paneled cove. He looks at the warden. The witnesses lean forward. The warden closes his eyes, nods, the executioner throws a large-handled fork switch.*

PAUL *smashes into his straps as if hit by a train. He snaps back and forth, crackling like a whip. The leather straps groan and creak. Smoke rises from his head. The witnesses have turned away. The switch is thrown back and the body of* PAUL ISAACSON *slumps in the chair. Underneath the chair a pool of urine has collected on the cement floor. This is mopped away as efficiently as the body is released and carried off.*

INT.   EXECUTION CHAMBER. DAY. SUMMER '54

ROCHELLE *walks toward the execution chamber with the knowledge that her husband is already dead. She wears her grey shapeless prison dress and terry-*

cloth slippers. On her face is a carefully composed ironic smile. A prison MA-TRON *walks beside her.*

Coming into the chamber she stops and calmly appraises each witness—the three REPORTERS, *none of whom can meet her gaze. Then she sees the prison* RABBI *in yarmulke and tallis.*

ROCHELLE   I will not have him here.

There is some confusion and the RABBI *leaves.*

Let my son be bar mitzvahed today. Let our death be his bar mitzvah.

Disdaining any helping hand, ROCHELLE *turns her back to the chair. She hugs the* MATRON *who has accompanied her and who runs out of the room now, weeping into a handkerchief.*

ROCHELLE *sits down in the electric chair and observes the strapping in of herself like a passenger getting ready for a plane journey.*

DANIEL   *(voice over)* Oh Rochelle, you never had any doubts, did you? Through every appeal. Through every stay. You knew it would come to this. You knew they would give back to you in comparable intensity the voltage of your hatred for them.

When the hood goes over ROCHELLE's *eyes, they are open.*

The EXECUTIONER *throws the switch.* ROCHELLE's *body bucks and arcs in the chair. Then it slumps. A* DOCTOR *comes over to her figure and listens for a moment with a stethoscope. He looks up, alarmed, goes quickly to the warden.*

DOCTOR   You'll have to do it again.

EXT.   JEWISH CEMETERY. DAY. SUMMER '54

A vast funeral cortege slowly moving into a Jewish cemetery. Police direct traffic. Police stand at the entrance to the gates of the cemetery. It is a hot, sultry day and the sky is grey. The headlights glow on each car turning into the cemetery. An endless number of cars. They make virtually no sound.

In a 1954 Cadillac limousine, the first behind the hearse, sit the two children, DANIEL *and* SUSAN. *In the jump seats, a young couple,* ROBERT *and* LISE LEWIN. *Sitting up front, next to the driver,* JACOB ASCHER. *The children sit toward the center of the wide seat, and their hands are entwined. Their legs touch.*

In the narrow cemetery road, faces loom at the window and peer in at them as the car moves slowly after the hearse.

EXT. JEWISH CEMETERY. DAY. WINTER '70

In a 1967 Cadillac limousine following a hearse into the same Jewish cemetery, the adult DANIEL, *his wife,* PHYLLIS, *his foster parents* ROBERT *and* LISE LEWIN. *The* LEWINS *look old, exhausted, demolished.* PHYLLIS's *eyes red with crying.* DANIEL *tight-lipped, grim. The day is cold, clear blue sky, possible old snow on the ground. The Cadillac follows the hearse into the cemetery; it is the only car behind the hearse.*

EXT. JEWISH CEMETERY. DAY. SUMMER '54

The children DANIEL *and* SUSAN *stand in front of the open graves of their parents. A* RABBI *chants kaddish. An enormous crowd presses behind them. Many people weep. The day is grey, people are in black.* DANIEL *has on a jacket and tie.* SUSAN *is neat and trim in a sleeveless black dress. A black lace hand-kerchief rests on her head. Her hair is parted in the middle and combed over her ears and tied at her neck in a grown-up way. She is dry-eyed, as is* DANIEL. *He holds her hand, looks at her calm, serene face, her lovely eyes cast down at the open earth at their feet.*

EXT. JEWISH CEMETERY. DAY. WINTER '70

DANIEL, *his wife,* PHYLLIS, *and* ROBERT *and* LISE LEWIN *stand in front of an open grave. At a discreet distance grouped around a yellow trench digger, three cemetery* WORKERS *observe them with mild curiosity. Near the open grave are two gravestones of matching size. The air is crisp, wind blows the winter debris along the ground. The* FUNERAL DIRECTOR *looks put out at these four people standing numbly here.*

FUNERAL DIRECTOR   (*to* DANIEL) We're ready for the service. You wanted your own rabbi.

DANIEL *rouses himself, looks around. A few yards away stands a shabby bearded man in black, one of those who hang around cemeteries to pick up a few dollars saying prayers less devout Jews don't know.* DANIEL *beckons to him.*

Daniel: A Screenplay

Coming down the cemetery street another such man, and DANIEL *walks out to meet him. Soon,* DANIEL *is peeling bills off a roll of bills, looking angry, is directing an increasing number of these old shamuses to the gravesite.*

DANIEL   In the name of Susan. Susan Isaacson. And when you're through in the name Paul. In the name Rochelle. In the name of all of them.

DANIEL *gazes into the grave, his foster parents and wife beside him as the old shamuses pray, each going through the characteristic singsong prayers, oblivious of the others, rocking back and forth on their heels. Perhaps here, the camera will detect tears streaming down* DANIEL's *face—before it rises over the cemetery, a city of stones, a city for the dead in the middle of the city.*

EXT.   NEW YORK CITY RALLY. DAY. SUMMER '70

A huge antinuclear demonstration. Hundreds of thousands of people flow up the avenues. A festive massive demonstration—flags, balloons, children on shoulders of parents, bands, oversized puppets, nuts, creeps, freaks, young people, old people, people in wheelchairs. DANIEL *and* PHYLLIS *are standing to the side, watching it go by.* DANIEL *hoists his* BABY BOY *on his shoulders,* PHYLLIS *takes his arm, and together the young family joins the march. The camera pans back, loses them in the immense crowd flowing through the city.*

END

Interview with Sidney Lumet

PAUL LEVINE   There are three recurring themes in your films that are all connected with *Daniel*: social justice, urban life in New York, and Jewish experience in America. Could you comment on the significance of these themes for you?

SIDNEY LUMET   The funny thing is I have never consciously approached it from a thematic point of view because the response to material is completely instinctive. Usually, in fact, if I have to read a script more than once, I'm going to say no. The ones that I really want to do with all of my being have invariably been accepted on the first reading. And obviously with *Daniel* all three themes fell into place. Talk about the unconscious working! If I'd ever been a writer, it's the novel I would want to have written, number one. Number two, when I read the screenplay, I thought it was close to perfect and my response was immediate. And I think it was seven years between the time I first read Edgar's screenplay and when we got the picture done. But it was always just laying there as something that I was hoping I would get done in my life.

It added a fourth element and in that sense was a sort of watershed experience for me. I was at that point in my life, again without knowing it, very ready for anything to do with family. My children were growing up and, like all people who have been, well, obsessive about work, I started wondering what damage I had caused. Who was paying for my obsessiveness? Had my kids paid for my obsessiveness? And from a thematic point of view that to me is the largest single element in *Daniel*. To me, it is a book about who pays for your passion. Because passion is such a part of one's life.

So, aside from the three thematic lines that you've mentioned, it opened up a new one for me. It's interesting because I have gone on with it. I went on trying to work on that part of the thematic line: the cost of obsessiveness on the next generation. I then did a picture called *Running on Empty*, which had the exact same thematic line but a much more sentimental version, much simpler. I thought, maybe *Daniel* was too complex, maybe it was too hard for an audience to take in and identify with. So let's do a simpler one to grasp. That didn't work either. I then went on to do a comedy called *Family Business*, about a family of thieves—hoping that maybe if we did it in a light way something of that idea would get through—which also failed. I'm going to keep working on it until I get it right.

I was so hurt by the failure of *Daniel*—not commercially, but I was hurt at the obscuring of what I thought that piece was about, the refusal of people to look at it past the word *Communist*. There was, I felt, a conspiracy of silence about the movie. It was the first time that a major American novelist had written a screenplay of his own work, and there wasn't even an article in the Sunday *New York Times* "Arts and Leisure" section the week before we opened. Obviously a picture like that was going to need support from the press.

I felt *Daniel* was a wonderful movie. There aren't many pieces of mine that I think are good when I look at them again (and I very rarely do). But I did look at *Daniel* again a few years ago, which was the first time I had looked at it since we did it because the rejection was that painful, and it's a fine piece of work. It's a brilliant screenplay. I succeeded in a lot of it. I failed in certain critical instances. But, what a good movie!

The other elements—the three themes that you mention—were all givens. Edgar and I would go around on interviews; we went to eleven cities (Paramount Pictures was very good about the release of it. They really tried. There's no blaming the studio for its failure.) We went to eleven cities—Edgar would join me for at least six of them, as he had other work to do—and we would sit with interviewers and theoretically intelligent people and we would both talk about this thematic line in it—the cost of passion on the next generation—and people thought we were being disingenuous. They thought we were denying the politics of the picture, which is ridiculous. You can hardly deny the politics of a picture based on the lives of the Rosenbergs. It was not out of embarrassment or to try to make it something else. We were telling the truth. That is, in my view, the heart and soul of that book and that movie. These two children are asked to pay a price that nobody could have anticipated. And it's a profound question. There is a cost, a generational cost that in a way accounts for history. Because most accomplishment happens because of obsessive people and they are not necessarily the ones who pay.

PL   You have made films adapted from many books ranging from Agatha Christie and Peter Maas to Edward Lewis Wallant and E. L. Doctorow. Are there any special problems connected with adapting a literary work for the screen?

SL   One of the most fascinating things to me about working on *Daniel* was that it went against a basic tenet that I'd had about the adaptation of literary works. In my view, *Daniel* is possibly a great book, and I've always felt that one cannot adapt great novels into movies. I felt that bringing them to the screen basically reduces them. Even though the image may be forty feet or what have you, the very fact that you will never be able to portray the inner life of a character with the depth that a novelist can makes working on a great book a pursuit of futility. The failure is built in.

Agatha Christie is easy because it's plot, and plot is wonderful for movies. Edward Lewis Wallant was easier because, though he was a magnificent writer, it was all potential. *The Pawnbroker* is a flawed book. It's oversymbolized. It's sentimentalized. The picture was much tougher than the book. Peter Maas, that's reportage. So again that translates itself more easily because you're not dealing with a literary quality that you have to find an equivalent for.

Daniel, for a director, presented nightmarish problems because, first of all, you must find out how to make that internal life clear, and find the visual equivalent of Edgar's poetry, of Edgar's nonreality. How do you make a picture *seem* real? But you can't use reality because it's not a realistic novel. The time fracturing that Edgar did was the only way to tell the story; you could not do that story linearly: here they are at four, here they are at seven. It would have become rather prosaic if you had told it in sequence, and predictable, because certainly a majority of the audience knew the outcome. So how to find the stylistic equivalent of the almost pointillistic approach that Edgar used in the novel? I felt that I succeeded in some cases, did not succeed in others.

PL   Would you like to give an example?

SL   I think the sequence when the children leave the home and Paul Robeson is singing "This Little Light of Mine": I found it there. That is the equivalent of what Edgar wrote. The rally, when the children are handed up over the heads of the crowd: we found it in that sequence. Through the sheer brilliance of performance we found it in both scenes in which Daniel comes to visit his sister in the hospital. When he carries her around in his arms when she is catatonic and in the first meeting when she winds up saying, "They're fucking us, Daniel." There it was the actors doing it and I just got out of the way.

We failed in the ending. I failed in the ending. I don't think we ever got the feeling that Daniel is reborn. The book, after all, is Daniel's search for his own reincarnation. He's trying to come back to life. He's trying to struggle his way up out of a grave because he buried himself with his parents. How to get out of that grave again: I don't think I ever found that. I think I was depending on, or at least jumped at the crutch of, a political rally. Not that that was a bad idea; it's just that somehow or other I should have been able to find a simpler, more beautiful way.

And then there is an important area that Edgar and I struggled with endlessly. In the book there's this extraordinary chapter in which Daniel comes to see Abby Hoffman and Hoffman trashes the Old Left and says, "Your parents were shits and dopes and tools of Stalin and what you're after is laughable. Don't bother me with your sister. So she cut her wrists, big deal." We had a scene like that in the movie. I don't know to this day whether the problem was in Edgar's writing of the scene, my direction of the scene, the performance, or some combination of all three. We did it once. We looked at it in rushes. We were dissatisfied with it in rushes. We went back and reshot it—which, in a budget like ours, was a Herculean thing to do; we didn't have the money to do such things. I reshot it, cut it in. No help, no improvement. I completely changed the way I directed the scene. What had been complex and fancy, at the time I thought justifiably so, I did dead simple and just let the words come out. It didn't help. And yet it's a crucial scene, at the heart of one of the things that Edgar is talking about in that book, which is: This is why we have no American Left today, because it cut itself off from its roots. It was an important thing to say and we never got that right. So that was missing from the movie.

PL   Once you discovered that you couldn't use this scene and that it was structurally as well as thematically important for you, how did you go about compensating for its absence?

SL   Because of the nature of the scene we couldn't. There was no other moment in the movie that dealt with that. So it's a perfect illustration that when you take a magnificent or, as I said before, possibly a great novel, you reduce it. Movies of great novels are always a reduction of the great novel. And there was an instance in which we lost some of the majesty of the novel in the movie.

In Daniel's soliloquies, the ones that he addressed directly to the camera, we wound up with something that was very, very good, but, you know, movies are enormously literal, people somehow don't understand that: a picture is a picture. The first thing I wanted to try—and Edgar was very much in favor of this—was illustrations, drawn illustrations. We both thought Paul Davis would be marvelous for it. Paul would draw up the whip and the knout and all of the literal things that Daniel was talking about. And even though they were drawings and completely unliteral interpretations, they still came through totally literally. It was as if we were taking "Jane and John Meet Rover." You know: Here, Rover, here! It was babyish.

There we were able to salvage something because what finally occurred to me was that what Daniel is really talking about in all of this is his parents' execution. He's not talking about the knout and the Russians and the Cossacks. He's talking about Paul and Rochelle. And so I got this idea of taking snippets, two and three frames, of the execution and intercutting them in such a way that you could not identify it, you didn't know what they were. But when you saw the execution you had seen snippets all during the film leading up to it. So in that instance we were able to salvage an element in the novel, perhaps not brilliantly, but certainly with some impact and certainly with meaning.

PL   You've mentioned the question of the powerful narrative voice. But a second problem you had in dealing with this film is the abrupt time shifts in the novel, from the radical thirties to the McCarthy period in the fifties to the revolutionary sixties. How do you feel now about the method you developed to deal with that, which was to change the color to project different times in the film?

SL   I thought that was a very good way of handling it. Obviously, since Daniel is spiritually dead, I literally made his face blue. Technically, it's very simple. For shooting out of doors, because of the nature of light on film, you have a corrective filter, what we call an 84, so that the skin tones become what we look like. We simply pulled the 84; we did them without the 84 so that the skin tones went blue. As the picture went on, the golden time became less golden and closer and closer to realistic photography and the blue also changed. As Daniel started coming back to life, we began adding the 84s in greater and gentler stages, first a tiny amount, what we call a quarter 84, then in a certain section a half 84, then a three quarter 84, and then into a full 84. So that by the end of the movie, past and present had met visually and we were now into today. This is the way it looks when you're not in the same pain any more, when you've come back to life.

PL   In what scene did that happen?

SL   It happened very slowly throughout the entire movie. Not until the children went to visit their parents at Sing Sing were we in natural color. That memory and that revelation releases Daniel into the present. His dealing with their death is what brings him back to life.

PL   Because it's been denial and suppression up until that point. How did you go about casting the film? In what ways did the casting end up determining the film?

SL   The most difficult part was Daniel. I thought that Timothy Hutton was wonderful, I think it's a beautiful performance. But I wish I could have found a more Jewish-looking person because I felt that a big part of the book and a great part of the historical reality is that these were the only two people who were killed in peacetime for espionage. That they were Jewish and that the judge was Jewish was no coincidence. The historical line of German Jew versus Russian Jew—what that meant in the history of New York City and American Jewish life—was a texture I would love to have gotten into the movie. So from that point of view, I would have loved a very tightly curly haired Daniel. I would have loved a slightly hooked nose. I wanted him beautiful but I wanted him Jewish-beautiful. I couldn't find him. So we opted, and Edgar was integrally involved in the casting, completely for beauty and what we both thought was a wonderful actor—Timothy read many, many times—and a passionate desire on his part to play the part. He camped out on my steps, literally, he wanted to do it so badly. That was the tough part.

The man who put up the money was a very good and honorable man named John Heyman. Even though it was very little money, Heyman needed to insure the people he was getting the money from and Paramount Pictures; he needed somebody who would hopefully guarantee us a television sale. This is a common thing in most movies. That's where Ed Asner came in. I think Ed gave a good performance. I think we could have gotten somebody better but Ed was a tremendous financial help to us and that's a perfectly good reason to cast somebody for a movie like *Daniel*.

Mandy Patinkin and Lindsay Crouse were pure thrilling choice. I think Patinkin's performance is phenomenal, a great screen performance. Lindsay was brilliant and willing to do something that not many actresses would do. I don't know whether Edgar agrees, but for myself, emotionally, I always felt more censorious about Rochelle than I did about Paul as a character. (This may come out of my own background, I don't know.) I did little things about it but I think they were true things. Like when she's leaving to go downtown and the kids are having breakfast, and she's putting on her hat, and she's trying to explain to Daniel what happened. As she leaves, she hugs Daniel and kisses him. And she never hugs the girl. There had to be a difference in the parental treatment of them, so in my view there had to be an element of difference in the way these two children simply related to their parents as parents. Parents, most of the time, love one child more than another. And I chose to make it that Rochelle loved Daniel more. I don't know Edgar's feelings about that. He certainly never objected to it.

By the way, one of the interesting things is that I promised Edgar that he would be in on every stage of the production. I have something that is very difficult to achieve in movies: I have final cut. In those days it was even more difficult to achieve. One day Sam Cohn, Edgar's agent, came over and said, "Will you share the final cut with Edgar?" I had to say no and I explained why. This was a contract achievement that was unbelievably difficult, that had come as a result of twenty-five years of work. One of the most important things in movie contracts is precedent, and if I'd shared this final cut with Edgar, Paramount Pictures would know, and that meant the entire industry would know, and from then on in I would be asked to do that constantly. I pointed out I had had the same thing with Paddy Chayevsky when I did

Network. Paddy asked for a share of the final cut and I had to say no. But I did promise Edgar, "Nothing will wind up on that screen that you do not want up there." And that held true.

PL How closely did you work with Doctorow on both the revision of the screenplay and the making of the film?

SL There wasn't that much to revise. I loved the screenplay. I don't know that we did three days of work. Certainly nothing radical. I was not afraid of the things that would terrify most directors. When the newspaperman makes a four-page speech at Daniel: that doesn't faze me. I'm never concerned with those movie clichés, that a speech mustn't be too long. The only thing is that a speech mustn't be too bad. As long as it's good, I don't care. If I've got a good actor to play it, and, God knows, I had a good one with Lee Richardson, there was no fear of any of that. So there was little to do on the screenplay. On the casting, Edgar was in on the selection of *all* of the principals. He got to trust me very rapidly on it. He knew most of the actors I was thinking of for the smaller parts. But everything was checked with him.

He was present at the shooting. One of the things that moved me most was the first day of shooting, the scene of the passing of the children over the heads of the crowd scene with five thousand extras. (I did it with six cameras; I was through in three hours. Nobody can quite believe it but we just didn't have any money. I had those extras for just that time. I did that and the Union Square rally in the same day.) They were all in place. I had explained to the crowd what was going to happen. It was one of those magical days because it had been raining up until 6:55 and then at 7 o'clock it stopped raining and we got just the light we wanted. I was running around—it was now about 8— giving a final check to the six cameras, and they were over a block apart and so there were enormous distances to cover, and at one point I looked over at Edgar as I was checking the next-to-last camera and he was weeping. I was so touched because I felt that the way I had staged the scene was what he had in mind, that that was the way he had seen it and that he was enormously moved at seeing this "coming to life" on the screen.

And then, once I had done the first cut, he was in the cutting room every day. The discussions were endless when we felt we had trouble. We did have problems with time fragmentation. We tried certain variations. We had a certain amount of freedom in that, obviously. But from there on in, not a step of the film's completion was done without him being physically present.

PL   Had you ever done that before?

SL   Never. Paddy to some extent. But Chayevsky was also the producer of the film. I had never done that before. But I felt I owed it to Edgar—I had promised it to him. And we had only one disagreement. And that was about the choice of music at the end. I wanted a reprise of Robeson singing "This Little Light of Mine." Edgar felt that it should be a complete break and something very, very modern. We went through many things. There was a thrilling Odetta recording of a militant leftist song. We tried that and, from a dramatic point of view, it worked. And at one point, it was fascinating. I think at that time I was plunking for the Odetta and Edgar was simply plunking for a modern rock song. And Quincy Jones was in town. Quincy was a dear friend. I had given him his first movie assignment, writing music for *The Pawn-broker*. We ran the movie for Quincy and asked, "What do you think should be the end music here?" And he said, "It should be a rock thing, Edgar's right." That still dissatisfied me, but when you're facing talent like that you had better listen! And then, of course, it occurred to me to take "This Little Light of Mine" and have it sung in sixties rock style. Which is how it wound up and which I always found thrilling.

PL   Could you give me a little bit of the chronology of your involvement with this project?

SL   I'm terrible on years; I just don't remember them. I know that I read the script initially seven years before we actually did the movie. Edgar and I had had one or two or three meetings over those years. Whenever I had a hit, the company always wanted me to do another picture for them and this is the first thing I would submit. I'm a great believer in *Annie Get Your Gun* when the character of Sitting Bull says, "Never put money in show business." And so I didn't want to take an option on the material myself. I didn't want to spend my own money, it's as simple as that. And I couldn't see anyone picking up the rights and grabbing it. At one point, I think somebody did have it under option for two years.

Then I met John Heyman, who was a fascinating guy. He's one of those powers on the inside of movies that we never know anything about because he arranges financing for the studios, not for an individual picture. I'd known him earlier, in London, when he was an agent. He had a script he wanted me to do about a right-wing candidate emerging from a fundamentalist religious movement. We're talking a lot of years ago, none of that had even begun to happen! I said, "John, I would love to do it but before we go into that, read this and see if you love it as much as I do. If you like it, let's do a two-picture deal. I would like to do this first because the season is coming up for it." *Daniel* had to be done either in the fall or the spring because, for instance, I needed leaves on trees, leaves in transition, and no leaves. I needed the feeling of different seasons. John read it, loved it, and agreed. And that's how it got done. And once John said yes, bang, we went right into production. I was free and there wasn't that much work to do on the script. So all credit and power to Mr. Heyman.

P L   If you were to remake *Daniel*, is there anything you would do differently?

S L   It's a hard question, Paul. Interestingly enough, there's one thing that I might do now, structurally, that I could have done in the cutting but didn't do at the time. We didn't do it because the suggestion came from John Heyman and we were both suspicious of the money-man's suggestion. (I know that was what my resistance was. Maybe Edgar had another reason.) But in retrospect I think he may have been right. The suggestion was to start the movie with the children being lifted over the heads of the people. And that the next scene be the scene around the dinner table, when Susan accuses Daniel of being ashamed and trying to hide and live down his parents' and their past. That terrible fight between the two kids.

I think it may have been a good idea now that I look back on it because it would have been a bracket. It would have told the audience many things: we're going to fracture time, folks; their parents were brutally killed, none of which you knew. It would have set up in parentheses everything that slowly developed in the movie. It would have said, This is the beginning of our lives, this is the end of our lives. Now this movie is going to be my, Daniel's, attempt to bridge the gap and in doing that resuscitate myself. I don't know whether it would have made the picture better because I think you would have finally got to that anyway. It might have made it more accessible without compromising its content one iota.

P L   A last question. How would you define the relationship between the screenwriter and the director?

S L   It depends completely on the director. The director is the power. But we are the power for one simple reason: with all of the cooperation between

Edgar and myself I was still the one who said: *Print.* That's the magic word. One of the reasons I'm in movies, one of the reasons I love movies, one of the reasons it has been a deeply satisfying life, is that I love the communal experience. So the idea of working with a writer and not involving him is stupid to me. There are those who can't wait to get rid of the writer. I think that's crazy. I want the writer there at rehearsals and he or she is always welcome at postproduction. And my greatest tension is when the writer sees the first cut of a movie.

Revising *Ragtime*

Ragtime was published in 1975, the year before the United States celebrated its two hundredth anniversary, but the novel did not owe its extraordinary success to the bicentennial celebration. Rather, *Ragtime*'s critical and popular acclaim were products of both its innovative style and its special historical circumstances. The concatenation of political events beginning with the Kennedy assassination and culminating in the Watergate scandal created a cultural climate more hospitable to a skeptical reading of the American past. "History was no longer a pattern of factually and philosophically analyzable causes," observed Leo Braudy; "it was a nightmare, an allegory of good and evil, a metaphysical comic book."[1]

The new skepticism was part of a growing heterodoxy about the meaning of history in general and American history in particular. In the 1960s, a new generation of "revisionist" historians had already begun to attack the traditional view of American history, which stressed consensus, assimilation, and progress. In the process they opened up new areas in the social history of previously "silent" groups like blacks, immigrants, women, and the working class. At the same time, critics like Hayden White and Roland Barthes challenged the traditional distinctions between the writing of history and fiction by noting the similarity between the linguistic structures and rhetorical strategies of historical and imaginative writing. There seemed no longer to be a privileged view of the past, no such thing as "objective" history. Facts did not speak for themselves but were selected and organized according to the particular narrative vision employed by the historian.

This breakdown of the traditional distinction between history and fiction was also noted by novelists. In 1960 E. L. Doctorow published his first novel, a revisionist version of frontier history entitled *Welcome to Hard Times*. During the sixties writers like John Barth, Thomas Berger, and William Styron also began imaginatively to reinvent aspects of the American past. But the publication of *Ragtime* announced to a wider public the arrival of a different kind of historical novel. Doctorow's blending of fact and fiction challenged conventional ideas of historical objectivity and undermined the assumption that there is a single ascertainable order of history. In *A Poetics of Postmodernism*, Linda Hutcheon argues that the new historical fiction "reinstalls historical contexts as significant and even determining, but in so doing, it problematizes the entire notion of historical knowledge." Hutcheon calls these new novels, in a tongue-twisting phrase, "historiographic metafiction."[2]

The new metafiction not only challenged historiographic practice but subverted social precept as well by inscribing into history the experiences of marginalized social groups. *Ragtime* is a panoramic novel that mixes fiction and history in telling the story of three families—WASP, immigrant, and black—whose separate fates become intertwined until they finally become, like the nation, one large family. In the process, Doctorow shows how American popular culture was created by those "silent" groups that mainstream society had banished to its margins. Like the "revisionist" historians, Doctorow imaginatively rewrites the American past from the perspective of its outsiders.

In *Ragtime*, Doctorow takes up the conventional view of turn-of-the-century America and turns it inside out. As the narrator tells us on the first page:

Patriotism was a reliable sentiment in the early 1900's. Teddy Roosevelt was President. The population customarily gathered in great numbers either out of doors for parades, public concerts, fish fries, political picnics, social outings, or indoors in meeting halls, vaudeville theatres, operas, ballrooms. There seemed to be no entertainment that did not involve great swarms of people. Trains and steamers and trolleys moved them from one place to another. That was the style, that was the way people lived. Women were stouter then. They visited the fleet carrying white parasols. Everyone wore white in the summer. Tennis racquets were hefty and the racquet faces elliptical. There was a lot of sexual fainting. There were no Negroes. There were no immigrants.[3]

From the beginning, the detached narrative voice, so different from the first-person narrative of *The Book of Daniel,* distances us from the events of *Ragtime* as it rewrites American history. *Ragtime* begins with the traditional view of the turn of the century as an age of innocence but then deconstructs the surface calm to reveal the social and economic conflicts that lurked beneath. "Apparently there *were* Negroes. There *were* immigrants."[4] If American history had traditionally been written from the vantage point of the dominant culture, then in *Ragtime* Doctorow rewrites it "from the bottom up."

Doctorow's novel was both a critical success and a media event. *Ragtime* won the first National Book Critics Circle Award for fiction and was the bestselling novel of the year. In contrast to the uncritical bicentennial hoopla, *Ragtime*'s fusion of highbrow and popular elements and its blend of revisionist history and cool irony caught the imagination of post-Watergate America in much the same way as did Robert Altman's contemporaneous film, *Nashville.* When the film rights to *Ragtime* were purchased, it seemed inevitable that Altman would be asked to direct the movie.

Doctorow was pleased with the choice of director but wary of Altman's reputation for discarding screenplays and remaking films in his own image. In order to protect his work, Doctorow set about writing an adaptation that would contain his entire novel. He told Altman: "I want to make sure that no matter what you do and how you take off, you are still in my book." Based on this proposition one would imagine that Doctorow's screenplay would be a carbon copy of the novel. But it is not.

In writing *Ragtime,* Doctorow claims he was inspired by the story *Michael Kohlhaas,* by the nineteenth-century German writer Heinrich von Kleist. "I had always wanted to rework the circumstances of Kleist's story," he said. "I felt the premise was obviously relevant, appropriate—the idea of a man who cannot find justice from a society that claims to be just."[5] Kleist's tale, itself based on a historical chronicle, recounts the efforts of an honest horse dealer to obtain justice from the corrupt feudal German society he had respected. In Doctorow's version, Kohlhaas becomes Coalhouse Walker and Kohlhaas's disputed horses are transformed into Coalhouse's ruined car. Both are proud men who are willing to create social chaos in their pursuit of social justice.

In an appreciative essay, Doctorow describes the striking modernity of the German writer. "Perhaps the most stunning feature of Kleist's work is its faculty of narrative advance," he observes. "Typically, some sort of infernal proposition launches the work, some disorder of the world's logic: It powers its way through the lives of the characters as a demonic animation that possesses them and . . . appropriates their very being."[6] A similar principle informs *Ragtime*, in which characters like Morgan, Houdini, Tateh, and Coalhouse become possessed by "some disorder of the world's logic." So Doctorow writes of Coalhouse's rage: "Or is injustice, once suffered, a mirror universe, with laws of logic and principles of reason the opposite of civilization's?"[7]

Doctorow notes that "in Kleist things change and they change fast."[8] In the novel, "it appeared nothing was immune to the principle of volatility, not even language."[9] The novel describes the modern world's celebration of speed, wherein Peary plays the Minute Waltz in fifty-eight seconds and Ford wants to produce an automobile in under five and a half minutes. The narrative begins with Harry Houdini's automobile accident and unannounced visit to the house in New Rochelle. The immigrant Houdini feels claustrophobic in this closed world of American Victorian respectability, which is about to implode. Part Two begins with Father returning to the New Rochelle house after his sojourn at the North Pole. Now everything has come apart. Father feels like a derelict in his own home as he views with incomprehension the new black baby, his wife's new independence, even the new-fangled vacuum cleaner run by the Irish maid: all harbingers of the changes that will irrevocably destroy his world.

The book's kaleidoscopic quality is reproduced in the panoramic style of the screenplay, whose episodic action moves rhythmically within a repetitive narrative pattern of arrivals and departures. The opening scenes swiftly introduce us to all the major characters, except Coalhouse Walker. Part One begins with Freud debarking from a ship in New York and ends with Tateh and the Little Girl departing Lawrence on a train. Part Two begins with J. P. Morgan entering his Daimler on Wall Street and ends with Houdini being hoisted above Times Square wrapped in a straitjacket. In between we encounter Houdini's airplane, Coalhouse's automobile, Father's polar sled, the immigrant ship that transports Tateh to America, and the luxury steamer that takes Morgan up the Nile. Doctorow emphasizes the principle of repetition in the

Revising *Ragtime*

screenplay when he films the mechanical birth of the Model T Ford. Morgan tells Ford that "there are universal patterns of order and repetition that give meaning to the activity on this planet," and Ford proves him right by reproducing identical automobiles every six and a half minutes.

Compared to *Daniel*, there is little dialogue and a great deal of narrative description in the *Ragtime* script. Doctorow often directs the reader's attention to visual details that illuminate the novel. For instance, in the novel Archduke Franz Ferdinand congratulates Houdini on the invention of the airplane, but in the screenplay, we also get Houdini's reaction: "We see on his face an expression of dismay or resignation—it is hard to tell which." At other moments, the screenplay goes beyond the novel in drawing explicit parallels. In the script Doctorow compares the Morgan Library with a prison, the Tombs, and Tateh's beautiful daughter with sex goddess Evelyn Nesbit; he notes that Morgan and the Archduke drive matching Daimlers, symbols of their imperial status, and he even suggests that Henry Ford, like the mummy of the Egyptian Pharaoh which he resembles, has the face of a despot.

In this fashion, Doctorow wrote his encyclopedic script to preserve the spirit of his novel. But Altman's plans to shoot all of Doctorow's screenplay in a six-hour film ran afoul of the conventions of American filmmaking, and he was fired by producer Dino De Laurentiis. Instead, Milos Forman was hired to make *Ragtime*. The result was a film far different from the one that Doctorow and Altman had envisioned.

ONE METHOD of fulfilling audience expectations in film is through a series of formalistic conventions which critics refer to as *genre*. Speaking of the power of cinema, Joseph Reed says, "I believe we all lead lives that take their cue from film genre, and that we lead generic lives because we're Americans." Of course, Reed knows that Plymouth Rock came before Hollywood. "But even at the beginning there was a sense of script. How else could the Puritans so surely have persuaded their fellow inhabitants of this wild new land that the imaginary landscape they saw was what mattered—and not the real one."[10] In *American Scenarios*, Reed sees American literature from Michael Wigglesworth to Mark Twain following and amending this script with its various elements of success, failure, democracy, and racism. In the twentieth century, however, film has taken over the burden of creating the American script: "Ever since 1903 or 1893 (or whenever one wants to date the dawn of the movie) most everyone's been living a movie."[11]

By the American script, Reed means the complex of generic conventions and ideological assumptions by which Americans individually and collectively live their lives. In *Ragtime*, as we have seen, Doctorow takes up these conventions and transforms them. At the same time he subverts historical clichés, Doctorow also exploits generic conventions in the style of Kleist's historical chronicles. "In *Ragtime* it was the historical imagery and the mock-historical tone which most interested me," he observed. "And the idea of composition at a fixed narrative distance to the subject, neither as remote as history writing—which is very, very distant from what is being described—nor as close as modern fiction, which is very intimate with the subject."[12] In adapting his novel, Doctorow remained truer to the spirit of the historical chronicle than to the conventions of the historical film, in which, as a producer famously remarked, someone is always writing with a feather.

The "mock historical" novel like *Ragtime* interweaves history and fiction to depict America's uneasy transition into modernity at the beginning of the twentieth century. Its cast of characters includes such historical figures as Sigmund Freud and J. P. Morgan as well as invented characters like the black ragtime pianist Coalhouse Walker and the immigrant filmmaker Tateh. The generic historical film typically blends fact with fiction but with different emphasis. Reed says that these films are less interested in historical reality than in historical appearance, so it is more important that the buttons on Napoleon's jacket be authentic than that his characterization be accurate. Yet period films traditionally appeal to authority. They are based on official history, confirming what we already know about, say, Lincoln or Disraeli. But Doctorow's subversion of what we already know is at the heart of *Ragtime*. He shows us how fiction can revise our understanding of history by revisioning the world of facts. "If you ask me whether some things in this book 'really' happened," he explains, "I can only say, 'They have now.'"[13]

We can see how Doctorow sought to preserve the integrity of the novel in his adaptation by examining the beginning and ending of the book and the script. The novel begins with a sly description of the times: "That was the style, that was the way people lived." Doctorow's screenplay begins with a scene at the Port of New York in 1906. In a clever conflation of incidents from chapters 3 and 6 of the novel, Doctorow juxtaposes Sigmund Freud's arrival in America with Stanford White's unloading of European architectural artifacts. "Quite extraordinary," observes one of Freud's disciples. "All of Europe is

Revising *Ragtime*

flowing into America." Both Frued and White represent the European disdain of an American vernacular culture identified with immigrants, blacks, and proletarians. The opening scenes swiftly depict Freud's comic discomfort in brash New York, with its noisy streets, rude waiters, and paucity of public toilets, culminating in his witnessing Stanford White's spectacular murder in Madison Square Garden. In the novel, Freud returns happily to Europe, concluding that "America is a mistake, a gigantic mistake."[14] In the script, his departure is more abrupt. "I am glad to leave," he explains. "I have lectured to a heedless nation. Now I go home. America is a mistake. A gigantic mistake." Both versions underscore Doctorow's portrait of the undercurrents beneath the orderly surface of turn-of-the-century American life.

The novel closes with the end of World War One, the deportation of Emma Goldman, the decline of Evelyn Nesbit, the merging of the three fictional families, Tateh's vision of the interracial "Our Gang" movies, and Harry K. Thaw's release from the insane asylum in time for the first Armistice Day parade. "And by that time the era of Ragtime had run out, with the heavy breath of the machine, as if history were no more than a tune on a player piano."[15] Doctorow's screenplay follows the novel closely here, ending with a newsreel montage of World War One, the Mexican Revolution, Younger Brother's death, and Harry K. Thaw marching on Armistice Day. It is the end of an epoch. In the script Doctorow writes: "At this point the audience should realize that the color of the film has gradually been leaching out—something that has been going on since the death of Coalhouse Walker, by this point everything is in black and white and continues so to the end—the picture becoming flickier and more rudimentary as in early silent film."

Whereas the novel ends with Thaw marching, the screenplay ends with a fitting image from the movies. Tateh is describing his vision of the "Our Gang" comedies to Mother and we see the three children marching jerkily in a parody of the Armistice Day parade, waving a toy flag. They get smaller and smaller, then the screen goes black and all we hear is "the rinky-tink ragtime music of a player piano." The final black-and-white images are a commentary on Hollywood's technicolor version of American history. In *City of God*, Doctorow echoes *Ragtime* when he describes how Hollywood created idealized "social archetypes," including "darling children with chocolate cake smeared over their faces," to demonstrate "that movies were a form of life to which life must aspire, as it has now shown every sign of doing."[16]

Postscript

SINCE Doctorow wrote his screenplay, two other versions of *Ragtime* have appeared: the 1984 film version directed by Milos Forman and the 1998 staged musical version written by Terence McNally. Since Forman's film is not based on Doctorow's screenplay but on a quite different script by Michael Weller, it need not detain us for long. In his memoir, *Turnaround*, Forman recounts the story of how he replaced Robert Altman on the *Ragtime* project. While Altman was committed to filming all of Doctorow's six-hour screenplay, Forman had more modest ambitions. "The one narrative strand of the novel that gripped me immediately was the story of the piano player," he recalls. "I had a gut knowledge of Walker's dilemma from the old country: in the everyday life of Communist Czechoslovakia, you constantly found yourself before ignorant, powerful people who didn't mind casually humiliating you, and you risked your livelihood and maybe your life by defying them."[17]

Forman's brief account in *Turnaround* illuminates problematic aspects of adapting *Ragtime* for the screen. Whereas Doctorow's expansive screenplay retains the kaleidoscopic design of the novel, Forman chose to make a linear film about a single hero. In the process, significant events, like the Lawrence strike, and important characters, like Freud, Ford, and Emma Goldman, were deleted. By simplifying the narrative and eliminating key historical figures, Forman's film undermines the complex interplay between history and imagination and underplays Doctorow's subversive revisioning of history.

The most radical change is in the character of Tateh. In the novel, he is a mature working-class radical whose decision to discard the European dream of socialism for the American dream of success is treated as a complex act of betrayal and rejuvenation. In the film, he is a virile young man, devoid of political awareness, whose success as a pioneer movie director is unblemished by any ambivalence. Though Forman's *Ragtime* does not follow the generic conventions of historical movies (nobody writes with a quill), it does adhere to the imperatives of classical film narrative. Finally, Forman's film reminds us of Jean Mitry's aphorism: "The novel is a narrative that organizes itself in the world, while the cinema is a world that organizes itself into a narrative."[18]

The musical *Ragtime* stays closer to the spirit of Doctorow's novel. Playwright Terrence McNally retains all three strands of the plot and cleverly weaves them into a tapestry of turn-of-the-century Americana. The show opens with the country viewed through a stereopticon and ends a decade later with a changed nation viewed through a movie projector. McNally retains

Revising *Ragtime*

enough of the historical ballast to give the show its texture. Here Ford and Morgan are more cheerful villains than in the novel, but Emma Goldman is as feisty as Doctorow had imagined her.

The staging of *Ragtime* is spectacular, combining music, dance, rear-screen projection, and digital techniques on the largest stage on Broadway. The high point of the musical is a sequence depicting the immigrants coming to America and being absorbed into the melting pot as they are exploited by capitalists like Ford and Morgan. In the scene ironically entitled "Success," we see Morgan bestriding a platform that slowly descends on the heads of the workers. After that, the show becomes less original and the music and lyrics less individual as *Ragtime* conforms more strictly to the conventions of American musical comedy.

Ragtime succeeds brilliantly as musical theater, but it does not finally transcend its generic roots. In song after song, we are compelled to admire Coalhouse Walker's nobility, Mother's feminism, and Younger Brother's idealism because they are conventional musical comedy figures. In the novel, however, the tone is more objective, the character's motives are more complex, and the treatment of Coalhouse Walker's violent rebellion is less celebratory.

There is also a certain amount of flag-waving in the play that is not in the book, in which Doctorow instead playfully describes the family business of manufacturing flags. Put simply, the three versions of *Ragtime* not only reveal variations in generic forms but also reflect the different times in which they were produced. Doctorow's novel, published at the end of the Vietnam War, mirrors the revisionist sympathies of the times; Forman's film, made during the Reagan years, is less politically engaged and more conventionally constructed; while McNally's musical play, produced in the Clinton era of centrist politics, is both politically correct and patriotically upbeat.

NOTES

1. Leo Braudy, "Realists, Naturalists, and Novelists of Manners," in *Harvard Guide to Contemporary American Writing*, ed. Daniel Hoffman (Cambridge: Harvard Univ. Press, 1979), 116.

2. Linda Hutcheon, *A Poetics of Postmodernism* (New York: Routledge, 1988), 89, 5.

3. E. L. Doctorow, *Ragtime* (New York: Random House, 1975), 3, 4.

4. Ibid., 5.

5. *E. L. Doctorow: Essays and Conversations*, ed. Richard Trenner (Princeton: Ontario Review Press, 1983), 34.

6. Foreword to Heinrich von Kleist, *Plays*, ed. Walter Hinderer (New York: Continuum, 1982), vii–viii.

7. Doctorow, *Ragtime*, 225.

8. Foreword to Kleist, *Plays*, vii.

9. Doctorow, *Ragtime*, 97.

10. Joseph W. Reed, *American Scenarios: The Uses of Film Genre* (Middletown, Conn.: Wesleyan Univ. Press, 1989), 3.

11. Ibid., 5.

12. Trenner, ed., *E. L. Doctorow*, 39.

13. Walter Clemons, "Houdini, Meet Ferdinand," *Newsweek*, July 14, 1975, 73.

14. Doctorow, *Ragtime*, 3, 33.

15. Ibid., 270.

16. E. L. Doctorow, *City of God* (New York: Random House, 2001), 238.

17. Milos Forman, *Turnaround: A Memoir* (New York: Villard Books, 1994), 246.

18. Quoted in Gore Vidal, "Who Makes the Movies?" in *The Second American Revolution and Other Essays* (New York: Random House, 1982), 134.

- 1975 novel
Film (1984)?
Milos Forman, director
Michael Weller, screenplay

RAGTIME

A Screenplay

Part One

EXT. PIER, PORT OF NEW YORK. DAY. 1906

Passengers are debarking from the Lloyd Liner George Washington. *All the noise, confusion, excitement of a ship's arrival. Coming down the gangplank is* SIGMUND FREUD. *He is greeted at the foot of the gangplank by* DR. A. A. BRILL *and* ERNEST JONES.

FREUD *is bumped by other arriving passengers unceremoniously, and a shock goes through his followers and he himself is startled and affronted.* BRILL *is attempting to tell him all the wonderful things they are going to show him.*

BRILL   Much to see, Dr. Freud . . . the Greek vase collection at the Metropolitan Museum . . . the beautiful Central Park . . . and the marvelous neighborhoods, the Lower East Side, Chinatown . . .

But FREUD *can't hear him. It is too noisy. The horns of the ocean liners, the shouts of teamsters, the ever-present cacophony of New York City traffic.*

EXT. ANOTHER SECTION OF THE PIER. DAY

From another ship sharing the same pier, TEAMSTERS *are unloading piles of architectural furnishings. The dock is filling with numbered marble pieces of Florentine palaces and Athenian Etria. Overseeing the unloading is a well-dressed, robust, burly man. He is* STANFORD WHITE. *He carries a rolled-up umbrella. He raps a teamster across the back with his umbrella.*

143

WHITE   (*to* TEAMSTERS) Careful you fools!

The debarking passengers from the liner George Washington *drift through the monumental obstructions of* STANFORD WHITE's *cargo.*

As FREUD *and his party come by,* ERNEST JONES *leans over to* FREUD *and says something in his ear.*

FREUD   What? What?

JONES   Quite extraordinary. All of Europe is flowing into America.

EXT.   WEST SIDE STREET AT ENTRANCE TO DOCKS. DAY

FREUD *and his* PARTY *are boarding an open touring car (a Marmon), which is being driven by* BRILL. *Horses and wagons clatter by on the cobblestones. Policemen blow their whistles. Cars and taxicabs, horns, etc. A trolley car goes by with its bell clanging.*
   FREUD *holds his palms over his ears, oppressed by the hideous noise.*
   His hosts BRILL *and* JUNG *notice this uneasily.*

EXT.   THE MARMON DRIVING DOWN FIFTH AVENUE. DAY

FREUD *perched in the high backseat of the car as it puts its way through the unending noisy traffic. There are no traffic lights, but policemen hold long poles with discs at the top on one side of which is the word* Stop *and on the other the word* Go.

FREUD   I am to speak of my ideas here in America. But how will they ever hear me?

The traffic is stalled. The Marmon is adjacent to a double-decker bus of the period. FREUD, *with cigar stuck in his mouth and his homburg on his head, looks up and sees from the second open deck children leaning over, pointing at him, and laughing.*

EXT.   ROOF GARDEN RESTAURANT. NIGHT

This is the famous roof garden atop Madison Square Garden designed by STANFORD WHITE. *Diners face the stage at one end of the restaurant, where a revue is being performed*—Mamzelle Champagne. *Nightlife circa 1906. Sexuality is definitely in the air.* FREUD *and his party at one of the tables are inevitably out of place. At another table the man we recognize as having overseen the unloading of architectural furnishings at the dock,* STANFORD WHITE, *dressed for the evening in white tie and gazing fiercely at the stage, a bird of prey. Two or three gentlemen are at his table along with* MRS. STUYVESANT FISH, *a mature woman, dressed with all sorts of feathers and pearls.* WHITE *leans to a man at his right, points to one of the chorus girls, a particularly buxom one, says something, they both laugh heartily.*

MRS. STUYVESANT FISH   May we expect now, Stanford, to see in your work a *penchant* for the flying buttress?

At another smaller table somewhat behind STANFORD WHITE's *sit* EVELYN NESBIT *and her husband* HARRY K. THAW. EVELYN *is dressed in white and wears a broad-brimmed hat of the period. She is extremely beautiful, a slim animal, very cool and self-possessed.*

THAW *is quite mad-looking, with a broad doll-like face. Man and wife are watching* STANFORD WHITE *at his table.*

HARRY   The bastard. The old bastard. He's laughing at me.

EVELYN   Oh, Harry, don't be silly. He doesn't even know you're here.

HARRY   Who do you love?

EVELYN   I love my Harry.

HARRY   (*continuing to stare toward* WHITE's *table*) Who's the best you ever had?

EVELYN   My own Harry.

HARRY   I'm going to kill him.

He removes a pistol from his pocket and lays it on the tablecloth. EVELYN *giggles. She touches the barrel of the pistol with her index finger.*

EVELYN   Oh, you're the wildest man! You're such a crazy devil I believe you would!

EVELYN *becomes aware that she is being looked at. She glances over her shoulder to the benches behind the table, where sits a quiet young man,* YOUNGER

BROTHER, *with blonde moustaches, his hat in his hand. He is gazing at her adoringly but blushes and looks away when she glances at him.* EVELYN *smiles to herself.*

The song being sung and played now is "I Could Love a Million Girls." It is the hit number of the show and represents a high point in the evening's excitement.

Perhaps we see from a height the design made from the tables and the audience, the palms, the lights. And from this POV one man, THAW, *makes his way between the tables. He reaches the table of* STANFORD WHITE *and, holding the pistol with arm outstretched, touches the barrel to the back of the jaw of* WHITE *and fires three times. Screams. Music stops abruptly. People on stage are in shock. A moment of silence in which just one voice is heard.*

EVELYN   Oh my God! Harry!

Pandemonium. Reaction shots. FREUD *closes his eyes, hits his head with the heel of his hand.* YOUNGER BROTHER's *reaction is to stand and never lose sight of* EVELYN.

EXT.   THIRD AVENUE UNDER THE EL. NIGHT

A NEWSBOY *hawks his papers. "Stanford White shot to death. Wuxtry, Wuxtry." A wagon comes up and a* NEWSBOY *with competing papers jumps off the wagon. The wagon leaves, and in seconds they drop their papers and fight for the corner.*

We see them wrestling on the ground. A pair of strong hands roughly pulls them apart and yanks them to their feet. The hands belong to a short sturdy woman with a large jaw, severe hairdo, and glasses. She is EMMA GOLDMAN.

GOLDMAN   Boys! Boys! Don't you see what you're doing? You're fighting each other when you should join forces and strike against your employer, who is keeping you in poverty.

The newsboys are anxious to get away from her. They pick up their papers and run off in different directions.

GOLDMAN   *(calling after them)* Solidarity, Boys! Solidarity of the working class!

We see now that GOLDMAN *isn't alone but is accompanied by a tall, shabby, dirty-looking but nevertheless charming man with bad teeth,* GOLDMAN's *lover,*

BEN REITMAN. *He is used to* EMMA's *speeches and has occupied himself reading one of the newspapers he has picked up from the ground.*

REITMAN   Look, Emma . . . an assassination! "The Crime of the Century!"

Insert close-up of New York World *with steel-engraved portraits of* EVELYN NESBIT, HARRY K. THAW, *and* STANFORD WHITE. *Big black banner headline reads:* CRIME OF THE CENTURY!

GOLDMAN   How can they be sure, Ben? It is 1906. We have ninety-four years to go.

INT.   WEST 113TH STREET BROWNSTONE. HARRY HOUDINI'S BEDROOM. DAY

HARRY, *combed and washed in silk pajamas, sits up in bed happily anticipating his breakfast. He is blue-eyed and has coarse wiry hair parted in the middle. His face lights up, the door opens and an old frail lady brings in his breakfast tray:* CECILIA WEIS, *his mother, with whom he lives.*

CECILIA WEIS   This morning shirred eggs for my boy. Oatmeal, the juice of three oranges, lots of nice toast, and a big glass of milk.

HARRY   Mamaleh! Mamaleh! You'll make me fat! I'll be too fat to escape!

CECILIA WEIS   *(sitting down on the bed and tucking a napkin under his chin)* No, no, you will never be fat. You will only be strong.

He grabs her, hugs her, as she laughs and protests. She squirms away.

HARRY   *(laughing)* From you, Mama, I never want to escape.

And the old woman leaves. HARRY *opens the newspaper on the breakfast tray and briefly looks at the front page while he drinks his orange juice. He clucks his tongue disapprovingly.*

INT.   NEW ROCHELLE. BROADVIEW AVENUE HOUSE. DINING ROOM. DAY

The family is having Sunday dinner. FATHER, *at the head of the table, carves a roast and dispenses it. At the other end of the table* MOTHER *adds vegetables.* BRIGIT, *the servant girl, stands behind her. Sitting on one side of the table is*

GRANDFATHER *and* MOTHER's YOUNGER BROTHER, *whom we recognize as the young man who was watching* EVELYN NESBIT *at the Roof garden.*

On the side of the table opposite MOTHER's YOUNGER BROTHER *and* GRANDFATHER *sits the* LITTLE BOY, *an extremely handsome, tow-headed youth whose age might be anything between eight and ten.*

The furnishings are heavy turn of the century.

MOTHER *is a beautiful blonde-haired woman with high cheekbones and hair upswept. Our sense of the family and their dress might be that they have returned from church and are now meeting for the most formal meal of the week.*

MOTHER   It is a tragedy.

FATHER   Stanford White was a profligate. He associated with demimondes and the worst sort of low life.

MOTHER   He was our greatest architect.

FATHER   And now that he is commemorated in the most lurid of newspaper accounts, they are not talking about his architecture, are they? They are talking about this what-ever-her-name-is, Nesbit woman.

YOUNGER BROTHER's *reaction is to stare at his plate and say nothing.*

FATHER   At the North Pole all this will be as nothing. The great barrenness of ice, the winds. It is at the edges of the world that man tests his true purpose and finds his nobility.

YOUNGER BROTHER *looks at him.*

FATHER   Didn't you hear? Commander Peary has chosen two of us from the Explorer's Club. And I am one.

YOUNGER BROTHER   Excuse me.

He puts his napkin on the table and leaves.

INT.   BROADVIEW AVENUE HOUSE. FRONT HALL. DAY

YOUNGER BROTHER *walks upstairs.*

Ragtime: A Screenplay

INT.   YOUNGER BROTHER'S ROOM. DAY

A very neat room. A little table with a machine for stringing tennis racquets. Scull oars crossed on the walls. A very neatly made single bed. A bureau with two hairbrushes on top. A small oval mirror.

YOUNGER BROTHER *stares at a reproduction he has pinned on the wall of the Charles Dana Gibson drawing entitled "The Eternal Question." It is a line drawing of* EVELYN NESBIT *in profile with a profusion of hair. One black strand, undone and falling in the configuration of a question mark.*

EXT.   FRONT PORCH, BROADVIEW AVENUE HOUSE. DAY

The LITTLE BOY *sits at a rocking chair and uses it as a swing. Our sense on this porch of a lazy afternoon at the turn of the century. There is not a sound on the street.* YOUNGER BROTHER *comes out of the front door. He wears a straw boater and the same white linen suit of the previous scene. The* BOY *watches him leave.*

INT.   BROADVIEW AVENUE HOUSE. PARLOR. DAY

GRANDFATHER *naps on the divan, his hands crossed over his stomach.*

INT.   MOTHER'S BEDROOM, UPSTAIRS. DAY

MOTHER *and* FATHER *sit fully dressed on the edge of the bed.* FATHER *is in his vest and has sleeve garters on.* FATHER *is awkwardly holding* MOTHER's *hands. Her face is turned away from him.*

FATHER   My dear, by next Sunday I shall be on the high seas. Thereafter, I shall be icebound in the arctic for several months.

MOTHER *rises abruptly, freeing her hands. Walks to her dressing table. Stands with her back to* FATHER. *She is quite nervous. The cuff of her sleeve knocks over an atomizer.*

She stands at the window, a filtered curtained light making her very beautiful. She turns, begins to remove her things. FATHER, *seated on the bed, studies her shamelessly.*

EXT. FRONT PORCH, BROADVIEW AVENUE HOUSE. DAY

A car is coming up the Broadview Avenue hill. It is a black 45-horsepower Pope-Toledo Runabout with brass headlamps and wood-spoked wheels. The LITTLE BOY *runs down the porch and stands at the front steps. The car comes past the house, makes a loud backfiring noise, and swerves into a telephone pole. The* LITTLE BOY *runs into the house.*

INT. BROADVIEW AVENUE HOUSE. FRONT HALL. DAY

LITTLE BOY   Mother! Father!

INT. PARLOR

GRANDFATHER *wakes from his nap with a start.*

EXT. BROADVIEW AVENUE. DAY

The DRIVER *stands in the street looking at the car. It does not appear to be damaged. The* DRIVER *is in livery. He folds back the hood and a geyser of white steam shoots up with a hiss. The* LITTLE BOY *stands nearby gazing intently at the owner of the car.*

  FATHER *is hurrying down the front steps putting on his jacket.*

  The owner of the car is HARRY HOUDINI, *whom we have seen previously being served breakfast in bed by his mother.* HOUDINI *introduces himself to* FATHER, *who asks him if he can be of assistance.*

  HOUDINI *is escorted into the house by* FATHER. *The* BOY *follows.*

INT. BROADVIEW AVENUE HOUSE. PARLOR. DAY

MOTHER *and* FATHER *and the* BOY *entertain* MR. HOUDINI. *Lemonade is served.* HOUDINI *is dressed inappropriately in a rumpled winter suit. He is very respectful to* MOTHER *and* FATHER *and speaks of his profession with diffidence.*

HOUDINI   Yes, I escape for a living. That's what I do. I'm a headliner in the top circuits. I get a cross section of people, poor and rich, young and old, and they all come to see Houdini break out. I accept all kinds of bondage and I escape. For instance, I'm roped to a chair . . .

LITTLE BOY (*to* MOTHER *and* FATHER) He escapes.

HOUDINI I'm chained to a ladder . . .

LITTLE BOY He escapes.

HOUDINI (*acting out his description*) I'm handcuffed, my legs are put in irons, I'm tied in a straitjacket, and I'm put in a locked cabinet.

LITTLE BOY (*enthusiastically*) He escapes!

HOUDINI Yes, Sonny, I escape. I have escaped from bank vaults, barrels, iron boilers, sealed milk cans filled with water. All over the world people have tried to contain me. I have escaped underwater from manacles and from diving suits. There's nothing I haven't escaped from. (*He sighs.*)

FATHER (*patronizingly*) Those are considerable feats.

HOUDINI (*modestly*) Ah yes, but you are going with Peary to the Pole. The Pole! Think of it! Now that's something. You must be pretty good to get picked for that.

FATHER (*lighting a cigar, nods*) I am fortunate.

HOUDINI (*He turns his blue eyes on* MOTHER) . . . and keeping the home fires burning ain't so easy either. That's real life. Yes, that's real life.

EXT.   POPE-TOLEDO, BROADVIEW AVENUE. DAY

HOUDINI *getting into his car. He waves to the family back on the porch. The* LITTLE BOY, *however, has followed into the street and stands gazing at his own reflection, distorted and macrocephalic in the shiny brass fitting of the head-light.*

HOUDINI *studies the* BOY *a moment, leans over the side door and holds out his hand.*

HOUDINI Goodbye, Sonny.

LITTLE BOY (*The* LITTLE BOY *does not take his hand but gazes up at him.*) Warn the Duke.

HOUDINI *is startled. The* BOY *runs up the steps to his house.*

INT.   FATHER'S FLAG AND FIREWORKS FACTORY. DAY

Seamstresses are rising from their machines, and other workers from the fire-works assembly tables, and coming down the aisles toward FATHER's *glass-partitioned office.* FATHER *stands at the door of his office looking pleased but embarrassed, too.*

   YOUNGER BROTHER *comes out of a smaller office off to the side in his shirt-sleeves and stands apart from the crowd and watches.*

FOREMAN   Sir, we your employees have taken this liberty to wish you Bon Voyage and have, using our best hands and minds, made this special flag for you and Mr. Peary in the Great Expedition.

The folded flag is passed forward from the crowd.

FATHER   *(examining the stitching)* I am very moved and touched by this and I'm sure Commander Peary will be grateful for the fine workmanship. It is light and folds compactly but has body nonetheless. I will do my best to see that your American flag will be planted at the North Pole.

The workers cheer.

EXT.   NEW ROCHELLE. RAILROAD STATION. EARLY MORNING

FATHER *standing beside the train is being seen off by his family.* MOTHER *has a handkerchief and dabs at her eye.* FATHER *shakes* YOUNGER BROTHER*'s hand.*

FATHER   While I'm gone the firm is in your hands. I know I can rely on you. I have your sister's assurances that my judgment is not ill-placed.

YOUNGER BROTHER   You may rest assured.

And to MOTHER *who stands between them and holds each by the arm . . .*

FATHER   She's the best judge of character I know.

MOTHER   Don't worry, my dear.

The LITTLE BOY *stands by the great wheels of the train engine and watches closely while the* WIPER, *with his oil can, checks the brass drive pistons. He feels a hand on his shoulder, turns, and looks into the face of his smiling* FATHER.

Ragtime: A Screenplay

FATHER   Goodbye, young man. Take care of your mother. I'll bring you something from the Arctic.

A moment later FATHER *and* MOTHER *hug in a restrained manner. A gentle embrace. He kisses her on the cheek.*

EXT.   EAST RIVER, DECK OF THE S.S. *ROOSEVELT.* DAY

PEARY *and his* MEN *aboard the sturdy little ship that will take them to the Arctic Ocean. Members of the press and assorted guests come to their farewell. On the dock adjacent to the ship a marine band plays "Hail to the Chief" as* COMMANDER PEARY *and his* MEN, *including* FATHER, *receive the President of the United States,* THEODORE ROOSEVELT.

ROOSEVELT *is expansive and very happy to be seeing the great explorer off on a ship named after himself.*

ROOSEVELT   Commander, I've dispatched some great American ships around the world, battleships the likes of which this world has never seen, but I'll tell you now, this little exploration vessel says more about the American spirit than anything else. I'm honored by your having named it after me. Godspeed all of you. (*He shakes* PEARY's *hand as a cheer goes up.*)

INT.   ELLIS ISLAND. DAY

This great shed we see as kind of a human warehouse which processes immigrant families by the hundreds. They are shown standing in lines, sitting on benches, queued up in front of customs immigration officials' desks.

We come upon a small dignified family, TATEH, MAMEH, *and their* LITTLE GIRL. *Like the others they stand with big cards with identifying numbers hanging from strings looped around their necks. They are poor but neat. The* LITTLE GIRL *is astonishingly beautiful. She wears a pinafore. She is anywhere between seven and ten. Her large black eyes take in everything.*

INT.   LOWER EAST SIDE. TENEMENT FLAT. DAY

A pathetically small room, one window giving onto an air shaft. MAMEH *and the* LITTLE GIRL *sit across a table from each other and sew knee pants by hand. Their fingers are quite nimble. The* LITTLE GIRL *is only slightly slower than her mother. There is a bed in the corner of the room. A cupboard with some dishes. Candles. Stacks of unsewn knee pants wait on the bed.*

EXT. LOWER EAST SIDE. STANTON STREET. DAY

Peddlers with pushcarts stand at the curbs and engage in intricate and vociferous commerce with passersby. One of the many itinerant peddlers is TATEH. *He stands on a corner with a display cart of framed silhouette portraits pinned to a piece of black velvet cloth. He makes his art with a scissors and pieces of black and white paper. He calls to passersby to have a portrait done in seconds, a framed silhouette for fifteen cents. He is ignored by the stream of shoppers.*

INT. LOWER EAST SIDE SWEATSHOP. DAY

MAMEH *and the* LITTLE GIRL *carry in string bundles of their work and deposit it on a table in front of the* BOSS. *He is a tall man with wavy dark hair. Well-dressed. He looks at* MAMEH *appreciatively. She stares at the floor as he turns his attention to the work and deftly counts off the numbers of sewn knee pants.*

INT. TENEMENT FLAT. MORNING

TATEH *is preparing to leave for the day.* MAMEH *and the* LITTLE GIRL *are setting up their work. There is a rapping at the door.*

Standing in the door is a POLICE OFFICER *and a* WOMAN *from the Board of Education.* WOMAN *holds a clipboard.* MAMEH *and* TATEH *are finally made to understand that the* LITTLE GIRL *has to be enrolled in school.*

WOMAN   The child must go to school. This is America.

TATEH   For the whole day?

WOMAN   Yes.

MAMEH *gasps and bites her thumb.*

TATEH   (*to the* WOMAN) With her labor (*pointing to the* LITTLE GIRL) we buy the bread for our mouths. What will we do when she can no longer help us?

WOMAN   You want this life too, for your child? Or you want her to *be* somebody?

INT.   SWEATSHOP. DAY

MAMEH *is again presenting her work to the* BOSS.

BOSS   So little?

Takes a big bankroll out of his pocket, counts off a few dollars, and puts the dollars into her hand. She does not look at him. He touches her hair. She shuts her eyes but does not move.

BOSS   Such an attractive woman. I'll give you extra because you are so lovely.

He takes another dollar and presses it in her hand. He touches her breast.

EXT.   LOWER EAST SIDE. STANTON STREET. DAY

TATEH *stands on his corner awaiting customers. Seeing that there is no business for him here he folds up his display case and walks off.*

INT.   TENEMENT FLAT. EARLY MORNING

MAMEH *sits alone sewing at the window. She sings softly to herself with a high sweet thin voice. Her song has no words.*

INT.   SWEATSHOP. DAY

MAMEH *walks through the aisles of men and women at their sewing machines and when she goes into the* BOSS's *office he closes the door. There is a cutting table in his office. He pays her for her work and then, pawing and kissing and offering her money, stuffs dollar bills in her hand as he slowly forces her down on the table. Through all this* MAMEH's *head is averted and her eyes are closed.*

INT.   DRAWING ROOM IN A SMALL RESIDENTIAL HOTEL. DAY

EVELYN NESBIT *is having a dress-fitting. She stands before a mirror while the* DRESSMAKER, *pins in mouth, kneels on the floor behind her. Sitting stiffly in a straight chair by the door is a distinguished woman of great class,* MRS. THAW, HARRY's *mother. She is attended by a* LAWYER. *She is under considerable strain but nevertheless carries herself with dignity.*

EVELYN   You find it difficult? Being in the same room with me, I mean?

MRS. THAW   You have ruined his life. You have destroyed my son. What he married was something from the alleys of McKeesport, Pennsylvania. Something made of coal dust.

EVELYN   That may be, dear Mother Thaw. But it's not my blood Harry has in his veins. I did not teach him to drink laudanum or to inject things into himself. He did not learn from me how to drive his automobile on the sidewalk or to make scenes in restaurants.

MRS. THAW   You will memorize the testimony prepared for you by the lawyers.

EVELYN   Did I ever tell you what he did to me on the honeymoon?

MRS. THAW   You shall testify as a good wife, and comport yourself with restraint outside the trial courtroom.

EVELYN   *(to* DRESSMAKER*)* It's a bit snug about the fanny, don't you think?

MRS. THAW   I have your word then.

EVELYN   And I have yours: two hundred thousand simoleons.

MRS. THAW *stands abruptly. She turns on her heel and walks out. The* LAWYER *follows.*

EVELYN   *(calling after her)* And a car with a chauffeur! *(to the closed door)* Thank you, I'm sure.

She starts.

EVELYN   *(to* DRESSMAKER*)* Ow! Goddammit, Maddie, you stuck me in the ass.

INT.   THE TOMBS. HARRY THAW'S CELL ON MURDERER'S ROW.
DUSK

The cell is outfitted rather luxuriously. Two GUARDS *are bringing* THAW *his dinner. It is on a wheeled table in linen in the manner of hotel service.*

GUARD TWO   Dinner, Mr. Thaw.

They make a fuss about setting things up and arranging his chairs, etc. THAW *removes a money clip from his pocket. He drops a couple of twenty dollar bills at his feet. The* GUARDS *scurry to pick up the money. Lock the cell.*

THAW   Swine!

INT.   CELLBLOCK PROMENADE. DUSK

The GUARDS *leaving.*

GUARD   The man's got class.

INT.   THE TOMBS. WARDEN'S OFFICE. DAY

Something of an occasion. A PHOTOGRAPHER *shooting the* WARDEN *shaking the hand of the magician* HARRY HOUDINI. REPORTERS *are present, and* UNIFORMED PRISON GUARDS. HOUDINI *holding a pair of handcuffs.*

HOUDINI   (*to* REPORTERS) The warden here and his men have fashioned what they take to be the latest in handcuffs. (*looking at the cuffs*) They're good all right. I accept the challenge.

The REPORTERS *are excited. "When, Harry?" etc.*

HOUDINI   I will attempt to escape from these irons tomorrow night at the Keith Hippodrome. Let me give you boys some tickets. You too, Warden.

HOUDINI *is very much in charge of this scene.*

HOUDINI   (*appearing to get an inspiration*) Say, I've got an idea! Warden, where do you keep your most dangerous prisoners? Where you *know* a man can't get away?

WARDEN   That would be the top tier, Murderer's Row.

HOUDINI   OK. I challenge you to lock me up on Murderer's Row right now.

I'll submit to a search. I'll take off my clothes if you like and I'll break out of that cell in five minutes.

The WARDEN *is discomfited. He finds excuses.*

Come on, Warden. I accepted your challenge. Or isn't your jail all that escape-proof?

The reporters are on HOUDINI's *side. The* WARDEN *is cowed. He picks up a telephone and makes a call.*

INT.   CELLBLOCK PROMENADE. MURDERER'S ROW. DAY

A procession of GUARDS, WARDEN, *and* REPORTERS, HOUDINI *in their midst, solemnly march to the cell.* HOUDINI *is naked.*

INT.   HOUDINI'S CELL. DAY

HOUDINI *steps inside. Door is locked:* GUARDS *and* REPORTERS *withdraw after great show of checking their watches. One of the* GUARDS *has placed* HOUDINI's *clothes beyond reach on the promenade.*

HOUDINI *runs his fingers through his thick, wiry hair and withdraws a piece of stiff wire, fingers a callus on his heel and extracts a strip of metal. He fits the metal and the wire together, inserts the makeshift key in the lock, and twists it slowly clockwise.*

The cell door swings open.

HOUDINI *realizes he is being observed from across the gloomy vault of the prison. A cell directly opposite is furnished as a room. The* INMATE (THAW) *stands and waves with a stately gesture.*

Cut back and forth, HOUDINI *dressing,* THAW *undressing.* HOUDINI *rushes fully dressed from the promenade to the exit door almost in a panic.* THAW, *now naked, is laughing and making obscene gestures.*

EXT.   BRIDGE OF SIGHS, THE IRON CATWALK CONNECTING THE TOMBS WITH THE CRIMINAL COURTS BUILDING. DAY

HARRY THAW *and* EVELYN NESBIT *walk back and forth. He weeps.* EVELYN *holds his arm and pats his hand.*

Ragtime: A Screenplay

INT.   THAW'S CELL. DAY

EVELYN *is on her knees on the cell floor. Her broad-brimmed hat, topped with dried flowers, is askew. She removes a handkerchief from her purse and dabs at her mouth.* HARRY *assists her to her feet and brushes the sawdust from the front of her skirt. She repins her hat. Smirking, he gives her some bills from his money clip.*

EXT.   STEPS OUTSIDE THE TOMBS. DAY

Emerging from the Tombs EVELYN *is besieged by a flock of* REPORTERS. *She stands at the curb, where an electric hansom waits, a* CHAUFFEUR *in grey livery attending.*

EVELYN   Harry is very cheerful. He is serene and at peace with himself. My husband Harry K. Thaw is innocent. That is all I'm going to say.

She ducks into the car.

INT.   DETROIT ELECTRIC. DAY

EVELYN *turns and looks through the rear-view window. She sees the last of the reporters giving up the chase. She slumps back in the seat and sighs. Tears course down her cheek. The* CHAUFFEUR *unhooks the speaking tube from the dashboard.*

CHAUFFEUR   And where does Madame wish to motor today?

EXT.   LOWER EAST SIDE. STANTON STREET. DAY

EVELYN NESBIT's *Detroit Electric, with its hard rubber tires, hums slowly through the crowded tenement street.*

INT.   DETROIT ELECTRIC. DAY

From EVELYN's *point of view we see dark-eyed faces peering into the car, street workers fanning themselves with their debris, boys in knickers running alongside.* EVELYN *gazes at stores with Hebrew signs in the windows.*

The CHAUFFEUR *is nervous. He noses the car through the narrow, crowded, filthy street.* EVELYN *sees something, raps on the window.*

EVELYN   Stop the car.

EXT.   STANTON STREET. DAY

The CHAUFFEUR *opens the door.* EVELYN *steps into the street and kneels. What she has seen is the* LITTLE GIRL *in a pinafore, sitting on the curb and playing in the muck along the curbstone, a piece of clothesline tied around her wrist.* EVELYN *stands and follows the clothesline and finds herself looking into the face of an old man with a closely cropped grey beard. It is* TATEH. *The end of the clothesline is tied around his waist. He is standing beside his display cart of framed silhouette portraits.*

TATEH   I do your portrait, Lady, with a piece paper and a scissor. Fifteen cents, Lady.

EVELYN   Why do you have this child tied with a rope?

TATEH *gazes at her finery, shakes his head. He begins to talk to himself in Yiddish. A small crowd has collected. A tall* WORKINGMAN *steps forward from the crowd, removes his hat with respect and addresses himself to* EVELYN. *He will be the intermediary.*

WORKINGMAN   Please, Missus, so the Little Girl is not stolen from him. (*looking at* TATEH *and listening as the old man laughs bitterly and thrusts his chin in* EVELYN's *direction*) He says the rich lady may not be aware that little girls are stolen everyday from their parents and sold into slavery.

EVELYN   (*shocked*) This child can't be more than ten.

TATEH *waves his arms, begins to shout in Yiddish.*

WORKINGMAN   Please, Missus, married women, children, anyone they can get their hands on. They defile them and then in shame the female gives her life to vagrancy.

EVELYN   Where are the child's parents?

Ragtime: A Screenplay

TATEH *is now talking strictly to the crowd, beating his breast and pointing his finger in the air. Two or three women in black shawls groan in sympathy.* TATEH *takes off his cap and pulls at his grey hair.*

WORKINGMAN   Please, Missus, the man himself is the child's father. (*He points to* TATEH's *torn sleeve.*) His own wife to feed them gave herself to the boss and now he has driven her from his house and mourns her as we mourn the dead, with a rent in his garment. His hair has turned white. He is thirty-two years old.

TATEH *is weeping and biting his lip.* EVELYN *too is moved. For a moment everyone standing on the corner shares* TATEH's *misfortune. Then one person walks away, then another.* EVELYN *goes back to the* LITTLE GIRL *at the end of the rope, kneels down, looks into the face of the child, her eyes dewy.*

EVELYN   Hey, pumpkin.

EXT.   DIRT ROAD AT THE EDGES OF THE CITY. DAY

The FREUDIANS *in their open car going down the road.* FREUD *leans forward and shouts over the noise of the engine to* BRILL *in the driver's seat.*

FREUD   And the place to which we go?

BRILL   (*yelling back over shoulder*) Coney Island, Herr Doctor. Where the people take their amusement.

INT.   CONEY ISLAND. TUNNEL OF LOVE. DAY

Little boats in the underground river with smooching lovers of the period. And then the stiff shapes of men sitting upright, FREUD *and party are sitting upright, and uncomfortable.*

EXT.   ENTRANCE TO TUNNEL OF LOVE. EVENING

JONES *and* BRILL *assisting* FREUD *out of the boat. They come out on the boardwalk. We hear the sounds of a calliope and a hawker. The sound of Coney Island excitement somehow grows more intense.* ERNEST JONES *looks up, reacts.*

JONES   Look, Herr Doctor!

EXT. CONEY ISLAND. VAUDEVILLE THEATER FACADE. NIGHT

A responsive and noisy crowd watching HARRY HOUDINI *raised by the ankles into the air high above the boardwalk.* HOUDINI *wrapped in a straitjacket.* WORKMEN *on the theater roof are cranking the winch.*

The FREUDIANS *are standing at the edge of the crowd, looking up like everyone else.*

FREUD   *(sways again and seems to totter)* I am beginning to understand this country.

INT. DETROIT ELECTRIC. DAY

EVELYN *commands the* DRIVER *to stop. She removes her hat, jacket, and takes from the seat beside her a rather old-looking shawl, which she wraps around her head in the fashion of the immigrant women. She steps out of the car.*

EVELYN   Wait here.

CHAUFFEUR   *(smirking)* Will Madame be long?

EVELYN   *(She takes a bill out of her purse.)* Today and always, mum's the word, right Charles?

CHAUFFEUR   *(accepting the bill and looking straight ahead)* Absolutely, Madame.

EVELYN   My husband taught me that.

EXT. STANTON STREET. DAY

EVELYN *comes around the corner to find* TATEH *at his stall and the* LITTLE GIRL *still attached by the rope.* EVELYN *looks at the child with total adoration. She removes a package from a satchel she carries.*

TATEH   *(in Yiddish)* What do you wish?

EVELYN   I have something for her.

TATEH   *(in English)* Nay, no charity. Go away.

The child regards this exchange impassively. EVELYN *replaces the gift in her bag and stands up defiantly in front of the display of silhouettes.*

EVELYN   Very well then. I want my portrait.

TATEH   I have done your portrait.

EVELYN   I want a dozen more. I want my left side. I want my right side. (*taking the* LITTLE GIRL's *hand*) I want us together like this. Fifteen cents each.

Reluctantly, TATEH *begins his work.*

We discover across the street YOUNGER BROTHER, *standing at the curb and watching* EVELYN *as she has her portrait done.*

INT.   BROADVIEW AVENUE HOUSE. FRONT HALL. DAY

MOTHER, *in some distress, talks on the wall phone.*

MOTHER   (*speaking loudly*) Why are you calling me? That is a matter for my brother to take care of. (*pause*) I see. Send the letter round to me and when my brother returns please have him call.

She hangs up. She stands for a moment in place. The LITTLE BOY *is coming down the stairs.*

When did you last see your uncle?

BOY   I don't know.

MOTHER *goes up the stairs and he turns and follows her.*

INT.   YOUNGER BROTHER'S BEDROOM. DAY

MOTHER *walks in. The bed is made, the room is neat and does not look as if it has been slept in.*

MOTHER *walks over to the wall where, on the flowered wallpaper, is the pinup of the* EVELYN NESBIT *drawing by Charles Dana Gibson. She is appalled.*

MOTHER   (*to* BOY) At my behest your father entrusted him with the business. And now a letter from the Republican Committee invites us to bid on the fireworks and decoration for the Inaugural Ball next year, when Mr. Taft is to succeed Mr. Roosevelt. What am I to do now?

INT. STAIRWELL. DAY

MOTHER *is marching down the stairs followed by the* LITTLE BOY.

MOTHER   I am deserted by the race of males. I live with children, lazy housemaids (*here she reaches the ground floor and for a moment faces* GRANDFATHER, *who gives her an amiable wave from the doorway of the parlor*), . . . and old men!

She exits down the hall to the kitchen. LITTLE BOY *remains with his* GRAND-FATHER. *He has a book in his hand. He looks idly after* MOTHER.

GRANDFATHER   (*tiding over a bad moment*) Come my boy. I'll read to you from Ovid. He tells marvelous stories of the instability of things and people. Women turn into flowers, bats, birds, spiders. Men become snakes, pigs, stones. They even turn into thin air.

BOY   Are they true stories?

GRANDFATHER   Absolutely.

EXT. THE ARCTIC. TWILIGHT

There is a howling wind. The camera discovers in the darkness of an arctic storm the S.S. Roosevelt *frozen solid in its berth of winter floes.*
    But there's a strange incongruous music coming through the sound of the wind.

INT. PEARY'S STATEROOM ABOARD THE S.S. *ROOSEVELT.*
TWILIGHT

The Commander, PEARY, *is pumping away at a player piano as fast as he can: Chopin's Minute Waltz. He stares at the keys, which appear to be played by invisible fingers.*
    The piece is over and the piano role flaps.

PEARY   What was my time?

MATTHEW HENSON, *who is black, checks the stopwatch in his hand.*

HENSON   Fifty-eight seconds, Commodore.

The MEN *in the room, including* FATHER, *applaud* PEARY *for having played the Minute Waltz on the player piano in under a minute.*

There is a commotion outside the stateroom door. The door opens. An ESKIMO *comes in talking very fast, loudly.*

PEARY   (*to* HENSON) What is this?

There are other ESKIMOS *in the doorway, all chattering.*

PEARY   (*rising*) Take care of this, Henson. Get these Wogs out of here.

HENSON *herds the* ESKIMOS *out and goes with them.* FATHER *follows.*

INT.   S.S. *ROOSEVELT.* FO'C'SLE TWILIGHT

THREE ESKIMOS *carrying an* ESKIMO WOMAN *down the ladder. A blanket is wrapped around her. She moans.* TWO ESKIMO WOMEN *put her on a table and begin to rub snow on her hands and feet.* HENSON *orders someone to bring hot tea.*

FATHER   What is wrong with her?

HENSON   This is a fairly common sickness. The women tear off their clothes and run into the storm and scream. They don't know there is another world, as we do. They don't know there are places where there's no wind and no dark. They think this is all there is.

FATHER *is disturbed.*

EXT.   BROADVIEW AVENUE. AUTUMN. DAY

MOTHER *in a shawl walks among the flowers in her yard. The leaves have turned and some have already begun to fall.*

INT.   BROADVIEW AVENUE HOUSE. LITTLE BOY'S BEDROOM. DAY

The BOY *watching his mother walk in the yard. He is extremely attentive. He sees from his upstairs window that she has stopped her walk for a moment as if listening to something. She slowly drops to her knees in the flower bed, then she begins to paw the ground.*

INT.   STAIRWELL. DAY

The BOY racing downstairs.

INT.   KITCHEN. DAY

The BOY follows BRIGIT, the housemaid, out the back door.

EXT.   YARD. DAY

MOTHER *has dug something up. She is brushing the dirt from a bundle which she holds in her lap.* BRIGIT *screams.*

BRIGIT   Holy Mary Mother of God! *(She crosses herself.)*

The BOY kneels beside his mother. She holds an INFANT. Dirt is in its eyes and mouth. It is small and wrinkled. Its eyes are closed. It is a brown baby bound tight in a cotton blanket.
    MOTHER *is sobbing. She frees its arms. It makes a weak cry.*
    They all three hurry into the house, the women in terrible distress, MOTHER *holding the INFANT.*

INT.   KITCHEN. DAY

The WOMEN are washing the little BABY in a basin on the kitchen table. It is a bloody unwashed newborn boy.

BRIGIT   The cord was *bitten!*

They swaddle the child in towels. MOTHER *dries her hands, runs out.*

MOTHER   Oh, where is he? Where is he?

INT.   KITCHEN. DAY

The DOCTOR is examining the CHILD.

MOTHER   I heard a cry coming from the earth. The moment I'd heard it I
    was sure I'd only imagined it. And what if I had walked on?

The DOCTOR *removes his stethoscope, straightens up.*

DOCTOR   These people. *(He shakes his head. He is looking for something in
    his bag.)* Bring me some hot water.

EXT.   LOWER EAST SIDE. STANTON STREET. DAY

EVELYN, *a shawl around her head, hurries down the street, looking for* TATEH,
the LITTLE GIRL. *Alarmed, she comes to a decision and moves on hurriedly
around the corner.*

EXT.   LOWER EAST SIDE. HESTER STREET. DAY

EVELYN *comes to a flight of iron stairs leading up to a brownstone. She takes a
deep breath and rushes up the steps.*

INT.   TENEMENT STAIRWELL. DAY

EVELYN *coming to the top floor and in the dimness of the hallway finds the door
and knocks. She knocks again. The door opens a crack. There is a chain latch in
place.*

EVELYN   What is the matter? What's wrong? Let me in.

INT.   TATEH'S FLAT. DAY

TATEH *lets* EVELYN *in and leaves the door open. He is scandalized to see her
here. He is only in his pants held up by suspenders. He wears house slippers. He
quickly puts on a jacket and shoes.*
    The room is lit by a candle, a tiny room, but as EVELYN *looks about, one that
is obviously clean.*
    *The candle sits on a stand by a small bed. From some pillows and a quilt the
dark eyes of the* LITTLE GIRL *shine.* EVELYN *feels the child's forehead.*

EVELYN   *(to* TATEH*)* What is the matter with her?

TATEH   I don't know.

EVELYN   She has a fever. I will stay with the child while you go to work.

INT.   TATEH'S FLAT. DAY

EVELYN *lifts a pot of water from the coal stove and pours the heated water into a galvanized tin tub beside the bed.*

   The LITTLE GIRL *clutches the covers.* EVELYN *gently removes the covers, sits her up on the edge of the bed, and lifts her nightgown over her head.*

EVELYN   Come stand a moment in the tub.

EVELYN *kneels in front of the* LITTLE GIRL *and bathes her in the warm water. Then she takes a towel, pats her dry, and dresses her afresh. She has found in the bureau drawer a thin cotton gown, much larger than the other one, so funny that the* LITTLE GIRL *for the first time laughs.*

   EVELYN *settles the* LITTLE GIRL *back in bed, plumping up the pillows and feeling her forehead.*

EVELYN   There, isn't that better?

The LITTLE GIRL's *dark eyes shine in the dim light.* EVELYN *touches her face and leans over her and the* LITTLE GIRL's *arms go around* EVELYN's *neck and she kisses her on the lips.*

EXT.   FRONT PORCH, BROADVIEW AVENUE HOUSE. DAY

MOTHER *stands holding the little brown* BABY *in her arms, listening to the* POLICE OFFICER.

POLICE OFFICER   We knew she couldn't be far. She works on the next block. She's a washwoman there and we found her in the cellar.

EXT.   BROADVIEW AVENUE HOUSE. DAY

MOTHER *follows the* POLICE OFFICER *to the Police truck,* MOTHER *looks grim.*

INT.   POLICE TRUCK. DAY

When the door opens the light of day falls upon a beautiful black girl, SARAH. *We should be shocked by her youth. She has a child's face, guileless. Her hair looks chopped and uncared for. She's exhausted, wiped out.* MOTHER *mounts the step at the back of the van and comes into the truck and sits down next to her and hands her her* BABY. *Holding her* BABY *the black girl begins to cry.*

EXT.   BROADVIEW AVENUE. DAY

MOTHER *coming out of the van, where the* POLICE OFFICER *is talking to the* DOCTOR. POLICE OFFICER *is writing something in a book.*

MOTHER   (*to* DOCTOR) Where will you take her?

DOCTOR   To the charity ward. Eventually she will have to stand charges.

MOTHER   What charges?

DOCTOR   (*primly*) Well, attempted murder, I should think.

MOTHER   Does she have family?

POLICE OFFICER   No, Ma'am, not so's we know.

MOTHER *is thoughtful, intense. She takes a deep breath.*

MOTHER   I will take the responsibility. (*to the* OFFICER) Please bring her inside.

EXT.   FRONT STEPS. BROADVIEW AVENUE HOUSE. DAY

The NURSE *and the* OFFICER *are helping the young* BLACK GIRL *holding her* BABY *as they go up the steps.* MOTHER *follows, her hands clasped in front of her.*
    Standing on the porch in the shadows BRIGIT, *the maid, frowning with displeasure and disapproval.*

INT.   BROADVIEW AVENUE HOUSE. PARLOR. DAY

MOTHER *in a state of agitation paces the parlor.* GRANDFATHER *sits on the sofa. The* LITTLE BOY *is in the room, too, and does not take his eyes off her.*

MOTHER   I put her on third floor in the room next to Brigit. She didn't even know to give the baby suck. She's barely more than a child herself.

GRANDFATHER   You did the right thing.

MOTHER *glances upward as if to see through the ceiling.*

MOTHER   At this moment I feel my husband's absence keenly. I shouldn't have so readily agreed to this trip.

GRANDFATHER   You did the right thing.

MOTHER   This girl has brought sadness into the house.

MOTHER *hugs herself, walks to the front window. She stares out.*

Every morning these Negro washwomen walk up from town and distribute themselves to the neighborhood. And the Italian gardeners come round to keep our lawns trim. And the icemen on the wagons drive their horses up the hill. These are the people who serve us, and we know nothing about them. How do we live so well in the midst of such agony?

GRANDFATHER   It's not hard.

EXT.   THE ARCTIC. S.S. *ROOSEVELT*. TWILIGHT

From the igloo camp built alongside the icebound ship the sound of eskimo chanting is heard.

INT.   FATHER'S CABIN. TWILIGHT

There is an excited rapping on his door. It is MATTHEW HENSON.

HENSON   You really ought to see this!

FATHER *dons his caribou fur jacket and follows* HENSON *out.*

EXT.   AFTERDECK. TWILIGHT

FATHER *and* HENSON *come up on deck, where* PEARY *and the* OTHER WHITE MEMBERS *of the expedition are standing and pointing to the south. There is a thin ray of light in the southern sky.*

HENSON   Spring!

The men stand awestruck as the sky gradually lightens. There rises above the horizon a blurred and blood-red sun elliptically misshapen. The men congratulate each other.

FATHER   (*softly, to* HENSON) Henson, Who's going to make the final run to the Pole? That last leg—with the Commodore to the Pole itself?

HENSON   (*exhilarated*) Well, sir, to tell you the truth, I don't think you or any of the other gentlemen. The Commodore will take me and a couple of the best boys.

FATHER   How do you know, Henson?

At this moment with the risen sun the entire earth seems to flash like a mirror and everything is brilliantly white.

HENSON   Well, sir, I just know.

INT.   LOWER EAST SIDE. WORKINGMEN'S HALL. NIGHT

EMMA GOLDMAN *speaking to an audience of perhaps a hundred people.*
As she speaks the camera examines the members of the audience: They sit on benches, or stand against the walls. The camera also finds members of the New York City Police Department stationed at the doors. A SERGEANT, *after consultation with two or three of his men, steps forward, holds his hand up, and calls for* EMMA *to stop her speech.*

SERGEANT   (*to* GOLDMAN) I have to warn you, your permit is for a lecture on the drama. You will not be permitted to speak unless you stick to the subject of drama instead of this whatshisname, Ibsen.

Jeers and catcalls greet the SERGEANT's *earnest warning.*

GOLDMAN   My friends, an embarrassed police force can be dangerous. We must not laugh because a member of our class, a working man like ourselves, a police officer, does not realize Henrik Ibsen is one of the greatest dramatists of the western world. When our revolution comes his sons, his grandsons, will know who Ibsen is and Shakespeare and Cervantes.

Applause.

The camera finds TATEH *and the* LITTLE GIRL *and* EVELYN NESBIT *sitting in the audience.* NESBIT *wears a shawl over her head and a moth-eaten sweater. She is engrossed by the occasion.*

She finds the room warm and removes the shawl from her head and folds it in her lap and gives her hair a shake. This movement and the sudden visibility of her beauty attracts GOLDMAN'S *eye.*

GOLDMAN   Those who, like Mrs. Alving, have paid with blood and tears for their spiritual awakening repudiate marriage as a shallow, empty mockery.

Some of the audience disagrees and shouts "No!"

GOLDMAN   Comrades and brothers, can you socialists ignore the double bondage of one half of the human race? Do you think the society that plunders your labor has no interest in the way you live with women? Not through freedom but through bondage? Is there no connection between the institution of marriage and the institution of the brothel?

At the mention of this word cries of "Shame! Shame!" fill the hall. TATEH *puts his hand over his daughter's ear and presses her head to his side. A man stands and shouts.* GOLDMAN *holds her hand up for quiet.*

GOLDMAN   Comrades, let us disagree without losing our decorum. We do not want the police to have an excuse to interrupt our meeting. *(speaking urgently now but more softly)* The truth is, Comrades, women may not vote, they may not love whom they want, they may not develop their minds and their spirits, and why not, Comrades? Is our genius only in our wombs? Can we not write books and perform music and provide philosophical models for the betterment of mankind? Must our fate always be physical? *(Again she glances at* NESBIT.) There sits among us this evening one of the most brilliant women in America, a woman forced by this capitalist society to find her genius in the exercise of her sexual attraction—and she has done that, Comrades, to an extent that a Pierpont Morgan and a John D. Rockefeller could envy. Yet her name is scandal and their names are intoned with reverence by the toadying legislators of this society.

EVELYN *is stunned. She bows her head and begins to put her shawl back on but is afraid to draw attention to herself.*

Ragtime: A Screenplay

People in the audience are standing and craning their necks trying to locate the object of GOLDMAN's *remarks.*

At this moment there is a shout from the back of the hall and a phalanx of blue-coated POLICEMEN *jams through the doors. There is a scream and suddenly the hall is pandemonium.*

POLICEMEN *pour down the center aisle and begin to break up the meeting as violently as they possibly can. Behind the speaker's table* EMMA GOLDMAN *calmly puts her papers in her briefcase.*

In the chaos and confusion EVELYN *finds* TATEH's *eyes upon her. He is looking at her with terrible judgment in his eyes.*

TATEH   *(whispering)* My life is fouled by whores.

TATEH *runs off through the crowd pulling the* LITTLE GIRL *behind him.* EVELYN *stands staring after them. She is faint. A strong hand grabs her arm. It is* EMMA GOLDMAN *herself.*

GOLDMAN   This way. Come with me.

GOLDMAN *leads* EVELYN NESBIT *to a small door behind the speaker's table.*

GOLDMAN   Don't worry. I'm an old hand at this. This is just an ordinary evening in the life of Emma Goldman.

She opens the door and EVELYN, *turning and looking back, sees, fighting his way furiously through the crowd, her silent admirer,* MOTHER's YOUNGER BROTHER, *trying to reach her.* GOLDMAN *pulls her through the door and it closes on the chaotic scene in the hall.*

EXT.   LOWER EAST SIDE. SIDE STREET DOOR, WORKINGMEN'S HALL. NIGHT

MOTHER's YOUNGER BROTHER *staggers out of this door, panting. He looks up and down the street to get his bearings. Sees a block away two* FEMALE FIGURES *crossing under a streetlight. He hurries in that direction.*

EXT.   LOWER EAST SIDE STREETS. NIGHT

YOUNGER BROTHER *follows the* TWO WOMEN *at a distance.*

INT. ROOMING HOUSE. ENTRANCE HALLWAY. NIGHT

YOUNGER BROTHER *comes in the door stealthily. Looks around. Quickly walks up the flight of stairs.*

INT. ROOMING HOUSE. SECOND FLOOR LANDING. NIGHT

YOUNGER BROTHER *ducks into the shadows.* GOLDMAN *passes carrying a basin. He does not move. A moment later he hears the sound of water running and tiptoes down the corridor. Finds the open door to* GOLDMAN's *room. He peeks around the door.*

INT. EMMA GOLDMAN'S ROOM. NIGHT

It is a modest rented room, lit by a single bedside lamp. EVELYN NESBIT *sits at the side of the bed. Sobs shake her body.* YOUNGER BROTHER, *hearing the returning footsteps of* GOLDMAN, *soundlessly darts into the room, slips into the closet, leaves the door slightly ajar.*

GOLDMAN *reappears. Places the basin of water on the bed table and shakes out a thin starched face towel.*

GOLDMAN   Poor girl, poor girl. I followed your case in the newspapers. From the beginning I found myself admiring you. I couldn't understand why.

She kneels and unlaces EVELYN's *high-top shoes and slips them off.*

GOLDMAN   Put your feet up.

EVELYN *lies down on the bed, rubbing her eyes with the heels of her hand. She takes the towel.*

EVELYN   Oh, I hate to cry. Crying makes me ugly.

GOLDMAN   *(continuing her thought)* After all, you're nothing more than a clever prostitute. You accepted the life given to you and you triumphed. But what kind of a victory has it been? (GOLDMAN *begins pacing back and forth in front of the bed.*) You are a creature of capitalism, the ethics of which are so totally corrupt and hypocritical that your beauty is no more than the beauty of gold, which is to say false and cold and useless.

EVELYN *is so spellbound she has forgotten to cry. She sits up in the bed, the towel lowered from her face.*

GOLDMAN   So why should I have felt such strong bonds of sisterhood between us? When I saw you at my meeting I was ready to accept the mystical rule of all experience. You came because in such ways as the universe works your life was destined to interact with my own. Through the vile depths of your own existence your heart has directed you to the anarchist movement.

EVELYN   *(shaking her head)* You don't understand. I came with my Little Girl. I found them on the street and now I've lost them. I have lost my urchin.

She begins to weep again. GOLDMAN *pulls a straight-back chair up to the bed, places her hands on her knees, and leans forward.*

GOLDMAN   What do you mean? Who? What urchin?

INT.   GOLDMAN'S ROOM. CLOSET. NIGHT

YOUNGER BROTHER *listening solemnly, a pencil line of light coming through the door. As we study him we hear* EVELYN's *voice but cannot make out the words.*

INT.   GOLDMAN'S ROOM. NIGHT

GOLDMAN   All right. If I had not pointed you out your Tateh wouldn't have run off. But what of it? Don't worry. Truth is better than lies. When you find them again you will be able to confront them as the person you really are. And if you don't find them perhaps that will be for the best.

GOLDMAN *suddenly notices something about* EVELYN.

GOLDMAN   Are you wearing a corset? You ought to be ashamed of yourself. *(She stands.)* Look at me, even with my figure I have not one foundation garment. I wear everything loose and free-flowing. That's what I mean. You are a creature of their making. Stand up a minute. (EVELYN *obeys.*) My God, your waist is pinched tighter than a purse string.

GOLDMAN *unbuttons* EVELYN's *shirtwaist and removes it. She unclasps* EVELYN's *skirt and has her step out of it. She removes* EVELYN's *petticoat. She unlaces* EVELYN's *corset.*

GOLDMAN   It is ironic that you are thought of in homes all over America as a shameless wanton. Step out of this. Raise your arms. Stretch your legs and breathe.

EVELYN *does as she is bidden.* GOLDMAN *lifts the undershift over her head and then she kneels and removes* EVELYN's *lace-trimmed underdrawers.* EVELYN *is now standing nude in the lamplight, holding her hands over her breasts.*

GOLDMAN   Look at that. It's amazing you have any circulation at all. Women kill themselves. A superb body like this and look what you do to it. Lie down.

GOLDMAN *goes over to the bureau, where there is a small black doctor's bag.*

I'm a professional nurse you know. That is how I support myself.

She removes a bottle from the bag.

This is an astringent. The first thing is to restore circulation.

INT.   GOLDMAN'S ROOM. CLOSET. NIGHT

From YOUNGER BROTHER's *point of view through the crack in the door:* GOLDMAN's *hand pouring a bit of the liquid over* EVELYN's *back and buttocks and her other hand beginning the massage.*

EVELYN'S VOICE   Ow! It stings!

INT.   GOLDMAN'S ROOM. NIGHT

GOLDMAN *is giving* EVELYN *a vigorous professional rubdown.* EVELYN *has responded to the massage. Her eyes are closed, her hair is all undone about the pillow, and her mouth is fixed in an involuntary smile.*

GOLDMAN   You must have the courage to live.

At this moment a phone begins to ring.

Ah, that will be Reitman with the report of how many from the meeting have been jailed. Wait just a moment.

When GOLDMAN *leaves the room, she closes the door behind her.* EVELYN, *left alone on the bed, continues to move as if in response to a massaging hand. Intercut with* YOUNGER BROTHER's *responses in the closet, until, with a strangled cry,* YOUNGER BROTHER *comes stumbling out the door and falls into the room clutching himself, his face in a paroxysm of mortification.*

Eventually YOUNGER BROTHER *looks up from his position on the floor:* EVELYN's *face peers down at him from the edge of the bed. They stare at each other.*

INT.   TATEH'S FLAT. NIGHT

TATEH *is packing his things in a musty suitcase with a rotting strap. He is in an ill temper. The* LITTLE GIRL *stands and watches him.*

TATEH   And what are you standing? Bring me your things quickly. I cannot bear it here another moment.

EXT.   LOWER EAST SIDE STREET. NIGHT

TATEH *and the* LITTLE GIRL *are boarding a streetcar.*

INT.   STREETCAR. NIGHT

The trolley is crowded. TATEH *and the* LITTLE GIRL *sit in one of the empty, hard rush seats. He looks straight ahead. She gazes out an open window.*

INT.   STREETCAR. NIGHT

The trolley, empty except for TATEH *and the* LITTLE GIRL, *is moving quickly along a wide moonlit street in the North Bronx. The scene is almost countrified, with grassy lots interspersed with an occasional block of rowhouses under construction.*

LITTLE GIRL   Where are we going, Tateh?

TATEH   Sha, close your eyes. Lean against me. We're leaving New York.

TATEH *takes out his change purse and counts, not for the first time, a pitifully few crumpled bills and coins.*

EXT.   THE ARCTIC. DAY

The PEARY *expedition has set out for the Pole. Point of view from a height: separate parties consisting of a white man or two, a group of eskimos, a pack of dogs, and four or five sledges.*

EXT.   THE ARCTIC. DAY

The arduous effort of crossing the Polar ice with the lead party, the trail-breakers.

Nowhere in sight at this point is PEARY, *except as the camera pans back to the sledges well in the rear. Here the going is easy over the trail pounded out of the ice by the lead parties. Camera finds* PEARY *wrapped snugly in furs, sitting aboard a sled driven by the ever-industrious, competent, and energetic* MATTHEW HENSON.

EXT.   STREETCAR STOP. DAY

TATEH *and the* LITTLE GIRL *board a spanking new red and yellow trolley car. The* DRIVER *is changing the destination cards in the window. The new card says* NEW ROCHELLE. *The* CONDUCTOR *greets* TATEH *and the* LITTLE GIRL *and accepts their coins.*

The CONDUCTOR *pulls a cord. The trolley bell rings and the car lurches forward into motion.*

INT.   TROLLEY CAR. DAY

The trolley is crowded now with the morning well along in downtown New Rochelle, New York. People get on and off. The CONDUCTOR *explains to* TATEH *and the* LITTLE GIRL *what he thinks they ought to know.*

CONDUCTOR   These are transfer tickets. You understand? At North Avenue we turn around and you get off and you wait for the Number Six and you can ride all the way to New Haven, Connecticut.

TATEH   *(nodding)* Good.

EXT. INTERSECTION, NEW ROCHELLE. DAY

TATEH *and* GIRL *wait for the Number Six. Two or three Model T Fords pass. Pedestrians. A busy, bustling intersection in a thriving town, circa 1910.*

EXT. DEPARTMENT STORE ENTRANCE. DAY

MOTHER *and the* LITTLE BOY *emerge from a department store, whose window display is of things for outfitting babies and nurseries.* MOTHER *is carrying packages.*

EXT. STREET. DAY

MOTHER *and* BOY *are walking purposefully. He sees something ahead of him and stops in his tracks.*

MOTHER   Come along. What's the matter?

EXT. INTERSECTION, NEW ROCHELLE. DAY

The LITTLE GIRL *and* TATEH *are running into the street to board the arriving streetcar. The* LITTLE GIRL *turns, looks over her shoulder, and becomes rapt with what she sees.*

TATEH   *(pulling her arm)* Come, come.

He pulls her aboard the streetcar while she stares behind her.

EXT. INTERSECTION. DAY

The LITTLE BOY *and the* LITTLE GIRL *regard each other, he standing on the sidewalk and she on the trolley platform. As the trolley moves off the intensity of their eye contact is indicated by close-ups of their faces.*

INT. TROLLEY CAR. DAY

From the LITTLE GIRL'*s vantage point we see the* BOY *receding as the trolley moves on down the street and her journey with* TATEH *continues.*

EXT. ARCTIC. DAY

The wind is howling and the members of the expedition move along painfully behind the yapping dogs. The beard of FATHER *is crystallized with ice. His eyebrows are encrusted.*

FATHER's *party is trailbreaking for the expedition.*

EXT. PIER, PORT OF NEW YORK. DAY

A great liner is soon to sail. At the foot of the gangplank HARRY HOUDINI *is passionately kissing his* MOTHER *goodbye. There is a great basso toot of the ship's horn.* HOUDINI's MANAGER *urges him to hurry. Reluctantly,* HOUDINI *parts from his mother.*

HOUDINI   Mamaleh, I'll send you cables from Germany. I'll buy you pretty things and bring them home for you.

CELIA WEIS   You're a good boy. The audiences of Europe are entitled to see you perform. They need magic too.

HOUDINI *runs up the gangplank, runs back down and kisses her again, holding her face in his hands and kissing her eyes. She nods and pats him. The horn blows. He runs up the gangplank. On the deck he takes off his cap and waves.*
On the dock, FREUD *and his* PARTY *with baggage, porters, etc.*

FREUD   I am glad to leave. I have lectured to a heedless nation. Now I go home. America is a mistake. A gigantic mistake.

EXT./INT. TROLLEY CAR SEQUENCE. DAY AND NIGHT

The journey into New England by interurban trolley of TATEH *and the* LITTLE GIRL. *Inside the trolleys the* OTHER PASSENGERS *change from dissolve to dissolve. Through the windows we see first city, then country.*

EXT. LOWER EAST SIDE STREET SEQUENCE. DAY

A sequence of scenes showing EVELYN *looking for* TATEH *and the* LITTLE GIRL. *She is accompanied by* YOUNGER BROTHER. *She stops people on the street, runs up behind someone who might be* TATEH, *goes into stores and comes out dis-*

Ragtime: A Screenplay

appointed. She becomes increasingly discouraged, holds YOUNGER BROTHER's *arm as they walk along.*

They arrive at the front steps of the tenement where TATEH *lived. They are followed at a discreet distance by a burly, moustached* MAN IN A DERBY, *who takes up a position across the street with a newspaper. After the couple has disappeared into the house he checks the time on his pocket watch and he writes something in a notebook.*

INT.   TATEH'S FLAT. DAY

EVELYN *and* MOTHER's YOUNGER BROTHER *camp out here. He sits quietly in a chair, his eyes on her constantly as she moves about in her sadness touching things: the coverlet on the bed, the plates in the cabinets, like a blind person trying to read with her fingers.*

A knock at the door. YOUNGER BROTHER *opens it. Standing there is the tenement* LANDLORD.

LANDLORD   So? You still want to pay the rent for that bum, that thief?

YOUNGER BROTHER *looks back into the room to* EVELYN, *who is lost in thought.*

YOUNGER BROTHER   (*to* LANDLORD) Yes, we're paying his rent.

LANDLORD   Fine with me. Twelve dollars.

YOUNGER BROTHER   Last week it was eight. I see now why the poor stay poor.

LANDLORD   Listen, Mister, no one's twisting your arm. So leave and I'll have a tenant in here by tomorrow. Besides (*he looks past* YOUNGER BROTHER *to* EVELYN), you ain't so poor.

YOUNGER BROTHER *removes some bills from his pocket, thrusts them into the landlord's hand. Closes the door on him.*

YOUNGER BROTHER *finds* EVELYN *lying prone across the* LITTLE GIRL's *bed. She's sobbing. He sits down beside her, gently rubs her back, smoothes her hair. He turns her on her back and with his fingers wipes the tears from her face. She clutches him about the neck and gradually, from his tenderness and her desolation, they proceed to lovemaking.*

EXT. THE ARCTIC. DAY

PEARY *stands by his igloo staring through the whirling snow as* FATHER's *sled comes into camp.* FATHER *is limping behind the sled.*

INT. IGLOO. DAY

HENSON *is attending to* FATHER's *left leg, the trousers of which have been rolled above the knee.*

HENSON   (*to* PEARY) It's his knee again and his heel.

He inspects FATHER's *arm and hands, his left arm under his elbow.*

FATHER   I freeze in the oddest places. (*looking apprehensively at* PEARY) It's all right. This has happened for several nights. It thaws out soon enough.

PEARY   I said the identical words in 1898, right, Henson? And that was the expedition that cost me three toes. You'll have to go back. (FATHER *is shaken by this news.*) There's nothing to be done for it. Some people have a disposition to freezing. If you don't go back to the ship more and more of you will freeze each day.

FATHER   I wouldn't appeal your order, commander, but I really do think I am physically able.

PEARY   You were the last in this evening. You're slowing us up. There, there, don't look so sad. The New York Explorer's Club has after all got their man to . . .

PEARY *looks for help from one of the* OTHER MEN, *who has been working with a protractor and a notebook.*

OTHER MAN   Seventy two degrees, forty six minutes.

PEARY   (*to* FATHER) A very respectable way, Sir, very respectable.

EXT. LAWRENCE, MASSACHUSETTS. MILL STREET. DAY

A trolley car is coming along the street. This is a mill town and the trolley car passes a huge block-long textile mill of red brick. It is early morning and

Ragtime: A Screenplay

men are streaming through the gates of the mill on their way to work. A sign says LAWRENCE TEXTILE COMPANY and another sign, less permanent, says MEN WANTED.

INT.   TROLLEY CAR. DAY

TATEH *holding his suitcase tied with clothesline half stands up in the seat and stares at this possibility of employment. When the trolley car stops and several workingmen at the mill get off,* TATEH, *clutching the* LITTLE GIRL's *hand, disembarks too.*

INT.   TEXTILE MILL. DAY

TATEH *stands in front of a loom, one of dozens in a long line of clacking, clattering looms in the vast, badly lit textile mill.* TATEH *has the look of weariness of the other men in the line. The din is incredible.*

INT.   TEXTILE MILL OFFICE. DAY

TATEH *on the payline. Comes to the window and receives his first weekly check. He stands to one side, opens his envelope and finds a five-dollar bill, a one-dollar bill, and change. His face falls.*

EXT.   LAWRENCE, MASSACHUSETTS. HILL STREET. DAY

TATEH *is climbing a hill of wooden tenements. He goes into one of them.*

INT.   FURNISHED TENEMENT ROOM. DAY

The LITTLE GIRL *sits at the window and gazes out over a backyard of clotheslines.*

The door opens and she rises and turns suddenly with anticipation. But her FATHER *entering is too exhausted and desolate to do more than barely greet her. He falls across the bed and is almost immediately asleep. She finds a thin blanket and puts it over him.*

EXT. THE ARCTIC. DAY

The sky is bright blue. The sun shines brightly. The wind is fierce as PEARY *and* HENSON *and their party of* ESKIMOS *and their two sledges—all that remains from the original expedition—make their way across the floes.*

EXT. THE ARCTIC. LATER IN THE DAY

The party is pushing along. We examine PEARY *in close-up and see his chin raised, his nose tilted in the air above his moustache. He is like a hound on the scent. He calls a halt.*

PEARY *(shouting into the wind)* Henson! Build me a snow shield! I want to take my observations! This may be it!

EXT. CLOSE-UP OF PEARY. LATER

PEARY *is lying prone behind a wall of snow. In front of him is a pan of mercury with a needle in it. He holds a sextant and is writing his figures in a book with his pencil. His calculations do not satisfy him. He sits up and looks over the snow wall at the waiting* ESKIMOS. *He beckons to them.*

EXT. THE ARCTIC. LATER

The ESKIMOS *carrying* PEARY's *equipment follow him across the trackless ice. They are bewildered that he would find one place in all this vast, incredibly cold wilderness more meaningful than another place.*

INT. IGLOO. LATER

PEARY *clutches a cup of hot tea in both hands and studies the figures in his book. Only* HENSON *is with him.*

PEARY It's the goddamnedest thing! I can't find the Pole! You walk a few steps due North and you find yourself going due South. This goddamn planet is made of water! But all the sitings together tell me that we're here, Matthew! We must be! We're here at the goddamn North Pole!

Ragtime: A Screenplay

HENSON   *(holds out his hand and smiles)* Congratulations, Commander Peary.

Taking his cue from HENSON, PEARY *struggles to his feet. Stands straight and tall.*

PEARY   Thank you, Henson. Where's that flag? And my camera? Get me my camera.

EXT.   THE ARCTIC. LATER

HENSON *and* THREE ESKIMOS *stand in front of the flag, which is set on a pole in a snow peak behind them. They are frozen and impassive. In front of them* PEARY *stands behind a camera on a tripod arranging everything to his satisfaction.*

PEARY   *(shouting into the wind)* All right! Look alive! Look alive! Wave your hands! Do something! Cheer!

He sticks his head under the black cloth of the camera as HENSON *and the* ESKIMOS *obey. They wave shyly at the camera and we see their mouths opening. But the wind blowing the snow across their faces leaves them soundless, and in this light and gusting snow-filled wind even their faces are hard to see. Perhaps their faces freeze as in stop action.*

INT.   LAWRENCE, MASSACHUSETTS. FURNISHED TENEMENT
ROOM. DAWN

Now TATEH *is at the window with a shawl on his shoulders and the* LITTLE GIRL *is asleep under the blankets on the bed. The sun is coming up. As the light comes into the room the girl wakes with a start and sits up. The coverlet falls from her and reveals her fully dressed as in the previous scene.* TATEH *gets up. There is a coal stove, a kettle with water boiling. He pours hot water into two cups and dunks a tea ball into each cup from a little chain.*

TATEH   Again you slept in your clothes, but I didn't know what else to do. You're a growing young woman. I watch you sleeping and I see the future of you. At this time in a girl's life she needs a mother to instruct her. What can I do? If I find someone and court someone how would you take to her? Tell me. What do you think of the idea?

LITTLE GIRL   *(thoughtfully)* I don't know.

INT.   TEXTILE PLANT. DAY

TATEH *at his loom becomes aware of a commotion down the line. Someone is shouting in Italian and English. The* WORKERS *step away from their machines and peer down the line.*

INT.   TEXTILE PLANT (ANOTHER VIEW). DAY

The cause of the commotion seems to be a small knot of MEN *talking volubly in Italian. One of the men walks over to his loom, shuts it down with a grand gesture, and encourages the others to do the same. The crowd increases in size.*

People on the edge want to know what the problem is. The SPEAKER *yells out in English.*

SPEAKER   Short pay! They give us short pay!

MEN *begin to shut their looms and gather.*

INT.   TEXTILE MILL (ANOTHER VIEW). DAY

MEN *are streaming down the aisles. Some grab chunks of coal from the coal buckets standing along the wall and begin to heave chunks through the dusty windows of the mill.* TATEH *shuts off his loom, grabs his coat and hat, joins the throng. The camera can pull back and up and we see* TATEH *become part of the crowd with the cries of "Strike! Strike!" coming up out of the clamor.*

EXT.   STREET IN FRONT OF THE LAWRENCE WOOLEN MILL. DAY

PICKETS *are walking in the snow in front of the mill. The camera finds* TATEH *and the* LITTLE GIRL *walking in the great line. They pass the mill gates, where the* MILITIAMEN *stand guard with rifles.* TATEH *points to the* MILITIAMEN.

TATEH (*to* LITTLE GIRL) I thought we'd starve to death, or freeze to death. But maybe with luck we'll be shot to death. *(He points.)* You'll notice the militia, how they have overcoats.

They huddle down into themselves, pushing through the snow and disappearing behind the backs of the other workers following them.

INT.   NEW YORK CITY. RESIDENTIAL HOTEL. DRAWING ROOM. DAY

A man we recognize as MRS. THAW's LAWYER *is talking to* EVELYN NESBIT. *With him is the* MAN IN THE DERBY *who followed* EVELYN *and* YOUNGER BROTHER *when they walked together in the street and went up the steps to* TATEH's *flat.*

LAWYER A million dollars? Come, come, Miss Nesbit. You are not the heroine in a fairy tale.

EVELYN I am Mrs. Harry K. Thaw and you will address me by my proper name.

LAWYER But my dear lady that is exactly the point. It is my client's contention that you have never been Mrs. Harry K. Thaw in the strict sense of the word: a loyal, faithful, and modest wife.

EVELYN Why you unctuous legalistic little twirp.

The LAWYER *sighs and affects a weariness or boredom. He addresses the other man.*

LAWYER Would you be so kind as to continue reading from your log?

MAN IN DERBY At 3 P.M. on Friday last the subject was seen entering the Hester Street tenement accompanied again by the same young male. They emerged from the building at 5:30 P.M. On Saturday last the subject was seen in the company of a large, older man at Louis Sherry's restaurant until past twelve midnight. The following night the subject was seen . . .

EVELYN *is really enraged. She paces the room, her face is flushed.*

EVELYN Get out of here. Both of you, get out. I've changed my mind. I'm going to contest this divorce. You and your client can take a flying fuck at the moon. I'll go see Harry. I'll visit him at Matteawan and I'll wrap him around my little finger the way I always did.

The LAWYER *motions to the* MAN IN THE DERBY, *who leaves. The* LAWYER *takes his hat and gloves and prepares to follow*

LAWYER   Now my dear, you may do that. But if you contest it's going to cost you and you don't have the money. You can't compete with the Thaws when it comes to money, you know. Besides which, Harry has put all his affairs into the hands of his mother. She has his power of attorney. He can love you all he wants from the insane asylum but it's us you have to contend with.

EVELYN   Get out. Get out.

LAWYER   We will pay twenty-five thousand. Please give this your most careful consideration.

He leaves.
   EVELYN *stares at the door. She finds a chair and sits down slowly.*
   YOUNGER BROTHER *comes out of another room of the suite.*

YOUNGER BROTHER   How could you have gotten involved with that man? Any of them, how could you have anything to do with any of them?

EVELYN   *(aroused from her revery)* You're not feeling possessive, are you?

YOUNGER BROTHER   I don't like to hide behind doors when you have visitors.

EVELYN   I thought that's what you did.

She goes to the mirror over the mantle and looks at herself, closely touching her face and making judgments about the skin under her eyes and her mouth and under her chin.

   I am finished. My life is over. *(to image in mirror)* You're a whore past your prime.

YOUNGER BROTHER   Please stop it. I love you.

EVELYN   What fun is love?

YOUNGER BROTHER   I will devote my life to you.

EVELYN   *(Suddenly sympathetic, goes to him and embraces him. Then she holds him at arm's length and looks at him.)* Ah, you poor boy. *(She walks away from him and becomes thoughtful and ruminative.)* I really miss old Stanny. I try not to think of him with his face shot away. He was a lusty old fuck. I could wrap him around my finger. I could wrap Harry Thaw around my finger. But Harry was difficult. He had nothing to do *but* love me. At least Stanny White would go off somewhere and put up a building. And now they're both gone. Everyone I love is gone. *(to* YOUNGER BROTHER*)* Do you have any money?

YOUNGER BROTHER   No.

EVELYN   Well, I can see now the end of mine. It is a finite sum.

YOUNGER BROTHER   *(apologetically)* The detective who was with that lawyer. He said you were seen in the company of a man at Louis Sherry's on Saturday. That was the day you told me you were ill.

Evelyn sits in a chair, removes her shoe, holds it.

EVELYN   A finite sum.

EXT.   LAWRENCE, MASSACHUSETTS. RAILROAD PLATFORM. DAY

The famous Wobbly, BIG BILL HAYWARD, *has arrived to lead the striking mill workers. A big crowd on hand including* TATEH *and the* LITTLE GIRL.
    HAYWARD *stands on a luggage cart waving his hat to shouts and applause.*

HAYWARD   This is going to be a peaceful strike. There is going to be no violence. I'm here to say we're all going to work to break the back of these damn mill owners.

Cheers.

All of us: Jews, Eyetalians, Poles, Belgians, Whatall. Solidarity, my brothers. There is no foreigners here except the capitalists.

Massive cheer. The crowd goes wild. He plunges into it.

INT.   TATEH'S FLAT. EVENING

TATEH *is just coming in the door. He has under his arm scraps of oak tag, cardboard. Carries pens and bottles of india ink. He puts these things on the table.*

The LITTLE GIRL *has been looking in a mirror seeing how her hair looks tied in the back.*

TATEH   For the strike display committee. To draw some posters for them.

He takes from his pocket a homemade book of drawings tied with a string and hands it to her. He takes off his coat and stands by the little coal stove to warm his hands. He looks at his daughter.

TATEH   But really to make things for you. To make things for your eyes so that you can see beyond this room. Beyond Lawrence, Massachusetts, and the strike. So that your Tateh can give you at least a little joy.

LITTLE GIRL *with her thumb governs the flipping pages. Close-up:* TATEH *has drawn a girl on ice skates. She skates away, becoming smaller, skates back, becoming larger. She does a figure eight, returning, pirouetting and making a lovely bow to her audience.*

The LITTLE GIRL *is ecstatic. She rushes to him and hugs him.*

TATEH   *(on his knees hugging her)* Ah, poor *Kind*, whose father can do nothing more than make pictures.

INT.   GERMANY. STAGE OF THEATER.

HARRY HOUDINI *stands in bathing trunks before a large forty-quart milk can. As the* ANNOUNCER *points and speaks in German an* ASSISTANT *handcuffs* HOUDINI's *hands behind his back and then puts leg-irons on* HOUDINI's *ankles.*

Orchestra music is heard. TWO MEN *in fireman's uniforms turn a hose into the milk can until it brims over with water.* HOUDINI *motions to his assistants, takes a deep breath, and is picked up and deposited upside down in the milk can, which is then sealed with a great metal lid. The audience oohs and ahs. A screen is pulled in front of the milk can and the music begins. The music mounts in intensity and the German* ANNOUNCER, *holding a stopwatch in his hand, reads off the time every ten seconds. The* ASSISTANT *in front of the curtain begins to look worried.*

He beckons and a German FIREMAN *with an axe appears ready to break open the milk can. Finally the screen is pulled away and the* ASSISTANTS *feverishly begin to unscrew the lid of the milk can. They open it and it is empty. At this point the* FIREMAN *takes off his helmet and reveals himself to be* HARRY HOUDINI. *The crowd goes wild.*

INT. DRESSING ROOM. EVENING

HOUDINI *is tying his bow tie before a dressing-table mirror. Something is bothering him. His* MANAGER *paces the little dressing room happily.*

MANAGER   You were a smash, Harry. They love you. Hansa wants to extend the engagement three more weeks. Let's face it Harry, your act is the best there is. It's the top act in the whole world.

HOUDINI *is unimpressed. He points to the newspaper on his dressing table. Close-up: a picture of* PEARY'S *assistants, the* ESKIMOS, *and* HENSON *standing in front of a snow peak with an American flag on it.*

HOUDINI   *(tapping the newspaper)* See that? They made it. They reached the North Pole. And that, my friend, is the kind of real world act that gets into the history books.

EXT. GERMANY. WOODEN STANDS, MILITARY PARADE GROUND. DAY

HARRY HOUDINI *and his* MANAGER *sit among a crowd of people on this wintry day. Their coat collars are up. Their breath is visible.*

MANAGER   I don't know what's gotten into you, Harry. I wish you'd tell me. Is it your mother? We could have her over here in a week.

HOUDINI   No, no. She's too frail . . . I'll tell you what it is. It's that I'm a magician and that's all I am.

MANAGER   Goddamnit, Harry. I wish you'd stop this.

HOUDINI   Peary discovers the Pole. A man like Roosevelt runs at the Spanish on San Juan Hill and gets to be president. You see what I mean? Look at that.

They both look into the sky.

EXT. SKY. DAY

A primitive biplane is slowly circling over the parade grounds. It is a Voison, a construction of wood and fabric. The PILOT *can be seen sitting between the wings. The plane is not more than a couple of hundred feet off the ground.*

HOUDINI'S VOICE   Pound for pound I'm as strong as any man in the world. I can escape from any kind of restraint. But I work on stages. You get what I mean? There's this real world out here where things are happening!

HOUDINI'*s face mirrors the passing of the airplane overhead and we hear the engine quite nearby.*

EXT.   AUTOMOBILE GARAGE AND MILITARY PARADE GROUND. DAWN

The sun is just coming up over the edge of the field. Slowly from the darkness of the garage emerges the awesome contraption of a biplane that we have seen flying in the previous scene. Two men are pushing it. One of them is a ME-CHANIC. *The other is* HARRY HOUDINI.
   The MECHANIC *talks with a French accent.*

MECHANIC   The wind is good. Have you the conviction?

HOUDINI   I'm ready.

MECHANIC *in his jumpsuit shrugs and puts his cigarette in the corner of his mouth.*

MECHANIC   Bien. You will please to remember all my instruction.

HOUDINI   *(covering his nervousness)* Listen, Raoul, this baby cost me five thousand dollars American. You can bet I'll remember.

He climbs into the pilot's seat. It is a little perch between the two wings.
   The mechanic spins the wooden propeller. The engine fires. HOUDINI *throttles the engine. The craft slowly moves forward.* HOUDINI *breathes faster and faster as the plane bumps along and picks up speed.*
   Finally it lifts off. HOUDINI *is practically crying with joy. His feet work the pedals. He clasps the control wheel and gently the rudder in front of him tilts down and the machine climbs into the sky. Painted in block letters on the fuselage:* HOUDINI.

Ragtime: A Screenplay

EXT. FLYING DISSOLVES. DAY

A sequence of flying shots showing the growing confidence of HOUDINI *as a pilot. He waggles the wings for what we can see now is a small crowd of men below him.*

EXT. PARADE GROUND. DAY

We are with a small group of MEN *watching the biplane bank over the field and then come in for a landing. We see that some of the men are* YOUNG OFFICERS *of the German army.*

EXT. PARADE GROUND. FRONT OF AUTO GARAGE. MID MORNING

It is another day and HOUDINI *is standing in front of his plane pointing to the foot controls and lecturing the group of* YOUNG OFFICERS *now somewhat larger than before. The camera is just far enough away so that we can't hear* HOU-DINI's *actual words. It pulls back farther to reveal a Mercedes staff car entering the parade grounds. The staff car carries general officers of the Imperial German Army, two elderly men, heavily medaled, in the rear.*

The young officers and HOUDINI *spring to attention the minute they see the car and offer a salute as the car comes to a stop. The old* GENERALS *do not move. The* COMMANDANT *stands up in the car and formally addresses* HOUDINI.

COMMANDANT *(in loud voice)* Herr Houdini, our caserne is privileged this morning by the visit of our superiors. May I impose upon you to give them the pleasure of a demonstration in the air?

EXT. ROAD LEADING INTO PARADE GROUND. MID MORNING

An enormous white Daimler landau now turns into the parade ground and slowly cruises toward the group. It is a glorious car with brass fittings polished to a brilliance and white wooden wheel spokes. A gold-fringed flag of rank flies from the right front fender.

The passenger's cab is enclosed and HOUDINI *peering at it cannot see who is inside. The windows reflect the sky.*

HOUDINI   My pleasure, Commandant. (*calling to his* MECHANIC) Raoul! I
need a fillup.

EXT. SKY. DAY

Shots of HOUDINI, *cocky and happy doing some lumbering aviation stunts
flying over the parade ground.*

EXT. PARADE GROUND. DAY

The biplane lands and rolls up to the cars. HOUDINI *jumps down and approaches them with the same triumphant expression on his face as when he
produces a feat for his audiences. The* COMMANDANT *walks* HOUDINI *over to
the Daimler. The* CHAUFFEUR *runs around to the rear door of the Daimler. He
opens the door and stands at attention.* HOUDINI *reacts to what he sees.*

INT. CAB OF DAIMLER LANDAU. DAY

*Sitting in state inside the car is a man in the uniform of a field marshal of the
Austrian Army. He has large, waxed moustaches, which curl up, and he gazes
at* HOUDINI *with stupid heavy-lidded eyes. He is the* HEIR *to the Austro-
Hungarian throne. Sitting next to him is his* WIFE, *a stately matron yawning
delicately behind a gloved hand.*

COMMANDANT   (*in German, standing at attention*) Your highnesses, May I
present the American aviator and performer, Herr Harry Houdini. (*to*
HOUDINI, *in English*) Herr Houdini, May I here present you to the Archduke Franz Ferdinand, Heir Apparent to the Austro-Hungarian empire.
And the Countess Sophie.

HOUDINI   (*wide-eyed, trying to maintain his calm, whispering to himself*)
Oh, Mama, wait till you hear this.

THE ARCHDUKE FRANZ FERDINAND   (*in a very thick German accent*) We
congratulate you, Herr Hoodooni, on ze invention of ze aeroplane.

HOUDINI's *face falls and we see on his face an expression of dismay or resignation—it is hard to tell which.*

Ragtime: A Screenplay

INT.   RESIDENTIAL HOTEL. EVELYN'S DRAWING ROOM. DAY

EMMA GOLDMAN *paces the room. Her hat and coat are on. A small valise stands near the door.* EVELYN *is in a robe.*

GOLDMAN   I want you to see. I want you to perceive. I want to instill in you the revolutionary consciousness that will allow you to live your life in pride and hope.

EVELYN   That's hard to do when you're broke.

GOLDMAN   And if you had gotten your million? It still would have been only as much as Thaw wanted to give you. You understand?

GOLDMAN *looks at* EVELYN *and appears to make some judgment of her. She walks over to her and touches her face.*

Money is the character of rich people. It's not for the likes of you or me. Besides, whatever money you have some man will come along and steal from you. He will pretend to love you and break your heart.

EVELYN   *(nods)* I know.

EXT.   LAWRENCE, MASSACHUSETTS. STOREFRONT, STREET. DAY

More snow is falling. There is a LINE *along the sidewalk two or three deep but it is not a picket line. It leads to a storefront.* TATEH *and the* LITTLE GIRL *are on the line. In the window is a poster of workers marching together with the word* SOLIDARITY *in large letters over the heads of the marchers. This poster is in sharp contrast to the wornout, defeated-looking families in the line.*

TATEH   *(to another man next to him)* I don't know if this is the right thing.

SECOND PICKET   It is the fathers who are the weak link. What strike is worth a child? If nothing is done for the men with families the strike will be broken and the damn mill owners will again have us by the balls.

There are several lines of workers and children leading to the back of the storefront, where well-dressed women in hats sit behind the tables with benches interviewing workers and their children who come up to them.

A big sign on the wall says CHILDREN'S CRUSADE.

The camera finds TATEH *at the front talking to one of the interviewers. She is a large friendly* WOMAN *who wears a hat—not one of the working class.*

WOMAN   Listen, Comrade, we have more good working-class families who have volunteered to board the children than we know what to do with. Our strike is famous. Reporters are here from all over the country and families in Boston, New York, and Philadelphia are offering their homes.

TATEH   Jewish?

WOMAN   You name it, we got it.

TATEH *is sitting at the table across from the* WOMAN *and in front of him are some papers. He looks at them dubiously.*

WOMAN   Listen, our families are investigated. Could we be careless about such things?

TATEH   I've been a socialist all my life.

WOMAN   Of course. The Doctor will listen to her chest. For that alone it's worthwhile. We give each child a new outfit of clothes. She'll be with a good family and eat hot meals and know that her father has friends in the world. But I'm not pushing you. Look, look behind you, plenty of customers.

TATEH *looks and the anxiety-ridden parents behind him waiting for their turn to sign up impresses him. He turns back to the woman who holds out a pen for him to sign the papers.*

He takes the pen. He mutters.

TATEH   *Ach, mein Kind.* What happens to us in our lives.

He signs.

EXT. LAWRENCE, MASSACHUSETTS. RAILROAD STATION PLATFORM. DAY

The platform is filled with MOTHERS *and* CHILDREN. TATEH *is practically the only man in sight. He holds by the hand his* LITTLE GIRL, *who is wearing a new cloak and a hat that keeps her ears warm. She is excited, her bright eyes darting here and there as she measures herself against the other children.*

Someone shouts "Here it comes!" as the crowd surges forward, and a moment later a train slides into the station chuffing and hissing great clouds of steam.

Women wearing armbands that read PHILADELPHIA WOMEN'S COMMIT-TEE *come along getting everyone in line.*

The line of mothers and children begins to move slowly toward the end of the platform, where a special car awaits them.

TATEH   Don't forget your manners. When people ask you a question answer them. Speak up so they can hear you. You have nothing to be ashamed of.

LITTLE GIRL   I am not ashamed, Tateh.

TATEH   You will see Philadelphia. A great city. This is where freedom began. You will live with a good family and be warm through the winter so don't feel sad.

LITTLE GIRL   I don't feel sad, Tateh.

TATEH   After a few days you won't even miss your Tateh.

He glances at her waiting for her denial, which does not come.

EXT. STREET ALONGSIDE RAILROAD TRACKS. DAY

A line of MILITIAMEN *in close file with their blocked hats and their rifles held across their chests stand with their backs to the station platform.*

EXT. STATION PLATFORM. DAY

The procession stops, backs up on itself. There seems to be some sort of commotion in front of the line. A scream is heard, POLICE *are everywhere and suddenly the crowd is in a terrible turmoil.*

EXT. PASSENGER CAR. DAY

Passengers within the train look through a glass window with astonishment.

EXT. STATION PLATFORM. DAY

The POLICE *are roughly separating mothers from children. They drag off the mothers kicking and screaming to trucks.*

EXT. STATION PLATFORM. HEAD OF PROCESSION. DAY

A DIGNIFIED WOMAN, *the head of the Philadelphia Women's Committee, wearing a white armband is shouting at a* POLICE OFFICIAL.

DIGNIFIED WOMAN   What is this? What are you doing? By what right or authority are you doing this?

POLICE OFFICIAL   I have an order from the city marshal prohibiting all children from leaving Lawrence.

DIGNIFIED WOMAN   You're maniacs! You're insane!

EXT. STATION PLATFORM. DAY

The scene is terror. The POLICE *swing away with their clubs.* WOMEN *are bloodied.* CHILDREN *are crying and scattering in all directions. Steam from the engine drifts back along the platform like fog.*

The camera finds TATEH *clutching the* LITTLE GIRL *protectively. A* WOMAN *appears in front of them. She tries to say something. She holds her stomach. She falls.*

TATEH *lifts the* LITTLE GIRL *bodily and swings her up on the platform of the nearest car, out of harm's way. He picks up the fallen woman under the shoulders and drags her through the crowd to a bench. A* POLICEMAN *sees him and cracks him on his shoulders and head with his stick.*

TATEH *retreats with his hand on his head as the policeman follows him back into the crowd, beating him about the arm and shoulders.* TATEH *falls.*

EXT. STATION PLATFORM. DAY

In the aftermath of the police action the train is gone. Only a few sobbing, battered adults and children are to be seen on the platform. Everything is quiet. TATEH is leaning against a pillar to regain his strength. He is groggy. His eyes squint in the light of the day, the station platform no longer in the shadow of the train.

LITTLE GIRL'S VOICE Tateh, Tateh!

He lifts his head. From somewhere he has heard the LITTLE GIRL's *voice.*

LITTLE GIRL'S VOICE Tateh, Tateh!

It seems to be in his head. He looks and there is nobody. He hears the voice again. Suddenly he is completely alert and realizes what has happened. He looks down the tracks.

EXT. RAILROAD TRACKS. DAY

The last car of the train is seen some yards beyond the end of the station. It is not moving.

EXT. STATION PLATFORM. DAY

TATEH *starts to run along the platform. He hears the* LITTLE GIRL's *voice again.*

EXT. RAILROAD TRACKS. DAY

The train slowly begins to move.

EXT. STATION PLATFORM. DAY

TATEH *jumps off the platform and runs down the tracks.*

EXT. TRACKS. DAY

TATEH *is hatless and has an ugly wound. The train is picking up speed. It appears as if he will not catch it. His arms and his fingers outstretched as he stumbles after the train.* TATEH's *hands catch the guardrail of the observation platform. The train begins to pick up more speed and his feet come off the ground. Finally, hoisting his knees to the platform overhang he clings there with his head pressed against the bars.*

EXT.   REAR OBSERVATION PLATFORM. DAY

TWO CONDUCTORS *are pulling* TATEH *over the rail onto the rear observation platform.* TATEH *does not realize that his hands are bleeding from clutching the railing. He stumbles into the railroad car.*

INT.   TRAIN CAR. DAY

TATEH *finds his daughter. He goes down on his knees and hugs the* LITTLE GIRL. *Sobbing with relief he notices that her new cloak is bloody. He sees that she is smeared with blood and he becomes hysterical.*

TATEH   Where are you hurt! Where did they hurt you!

She shakes her head and points to him. The blood all over her is his own.
    A man with a little black bag pushes through the small group of conductors and passengers watching this scene. A DOCTOR.

DOCTOR   Let's have a look.

INT.   PASSENGER CAR. DAY

TATEH *is asleep in the empty car, curled up on a double seat using his arm for a pillow. His head is bandaged and his face cleaned up. In the seat facing him and riding backwards is the* LITTLE GIRL. *She looks out the window. She watches the hills of snow going past.*

EXT.   TRAIN. DAY

The train with TATEH *and the* LITTLE GIRL *disappears around the bend.*

END PART ONE

Part Two

EXT. FACADE, 23 WALL STREET. DAY

A brass plaque polished to a high shine reads J. P. MORGAN CO.

EXT. STEPS, 23 WALL STREET. DAY

The camera pulling back; discovers J. P. MORGAN *himself emerging, surrounded by his retinue. The effect of this is of a flurry. He is a vigorous, burly man in his seventies. One of* MORGAN'S ASSISTANTS, *uncoated, follows him with a sheaf of papers.*

MORGAN   No, no. I can't be bothered with that now.

A POLICEMAN *standing at the bottom of the steps salutes him.*

POLICEMAN   Morning, Mr. Morgan.

MORGAN *grunts. At the curb in front of the building is a large shiny black limousine.* MORGAN *bends to go into the car as the* CHAUFFEUR *stands at attention with the door open.*

INT. LIMOUSINE. DAY

MORGAN *is seated in the car and an elderly female bank* EMPLOYEE, *who wears no coat, covers his knees and legs with a luxurious car robe.*

MORGAN   Go back. That's enough. Close the door. Leave.

EXT.   WALL STREET. LIMOUSINE. DAY

CHAUFFEUR *runs around to the wheel. Starts the engine. Turns for instructions. He is separated from* MORGAN *by a glass partition. The old man grasps the flexible speaking tube.*

MORGAN'S VOICE   My library, Charles.

EXT.   FINANCIAL AREA. LIMOUSINE. DAY

We watch from a height the stately car moving along the street.

MORGAN'S VOICE   Damn it, Charles. I'm in a hurry. If you can't get some speed on this thing I'll find someone who can.

The car picks up speed.

EXT.   THIRTY-SIXTH STREET. MORGAN LIBRARY. DAY

The stately black limousine pulls up in front of the white marble Morgan Library. A tall, thin man, MORGAN'S CURATOR (MACLEAN), *wearing a morning coat and striped pants, awaits him on the front steps of the library.*

INT.   MORGAN LIBRARY. ENTRANCE HALL. DAY

MORGAN *enters through the great brass doors. His footsteps resound on the marble floor. He flings open his coat, which is caught by a* BUTLER *just before it reaches the floor.*

MORGAN   (*over his shoulder to the* CURATOR) *Come along. Come along. Where is it?*

He walks through the door from the hall leading to the East Room, the CURATOR *following.*

INT. EAST ROOM. DAY

Here the high walls are covered with tiers of bookshelves having promenades of frosted glass, and polished brass balustrades.

MORGAN *walks up to one of the bookshelves alongside the fireplace and presses the spine of a certain book and the shelving swings back to reveal a passageway. He disappears within, the* CURATOR *following.*

INT. SECRET ROOM. DAY

A small modest room, sparsely furnished, very simple. TWO MEN (ARCHEOLO-GISTS) *are standing at either end of a large covered object at rest on a four-wheeled cart. The draped object is roughly in the shape of a coffin but somewhat larger.*

MORGAN   So, it's here.

CURATOR   Yes, sir.

MORGAN   Took long enough.

CURATOR   Mr. Morgan, sir. The utmost precautions had to be taken.

FIRST ARCHEOLOGIST   You must remember, sir, the Egyptian government and the entire archeological community has no idea of this loan.

MORGAN   *(impatiently)* Yes, yes.

FIRST ARCHEOLOGIST   Were your possession of it known, there would be an international uproar.

MORGAN   Yes, well I paid enough, didn't I? Come along, come along.

SECOND ARCHEOLOGIST *removes the quiltlike covering. We see a glass case sealed with lead. As the camera moves in we see that inside the case is a sarcophagus.*

For the first time since MORGAN's *appearance we see him relax. He exhales with admiration and bends over the sarcophagus with a transformed expression on his face.*

MORGAN   *(close to a whisper)* Yes. That's it all right. My God. It's magnificent.

We look closely at the sarcophagus as we listen to MORGAN's *harsh panting breath. The sarcophagus is made of alabaster. Topping it is a wooden effigy of a Pharaoh. The effigy is painted in gold leaf, red ochre, and blue.*

MORGAN'S VOICE   Is it—complete?

CURATOR'S VOICE   Yes, sir. Under that effigy is the mummy of the great nineteenth-dynasty Pharaoh, Seti the First.

MORGAN   Yes.

He straightens and addresses the TWO ARCHEOLOGISTS.

You may rest assured, sirs, that my temporary stewardship of this great treasure will be effected by me with the deepest respect. Your government shall not be embarrassed.

They turn off all but a small dim reddish light. The ARCHEOLOGISTS *proceed to open the sarcophagus, and the headstone lid, and with great effort, place the lid on the floor. The top of the exposed crypt is covered by a sheet of glass set in the stone like a window pane.*

MORGAN   It's too dark. I can't see.

SECOND ARCHEOLOGIST   I'm sorry, sir. Light is very damaging. We can't have any more than this.

MORGAN   Ah, there it is. My eyes . . . Ah, yes. Ah, yes.

The camera peers over MORGAN's *shoulder and comes in on the* MUMMIFIED FACE *in the coffin: It is of a middle-aged man three or four thousand years dead but with a shrewd human face, prominently boned and long jawed, with closed eyes that nevertheless give the impression of a shrewd judge of character and a canny mind. But the face, also, of a despot.*

MORGAN   Good. Cover it up.

He storms out of the room, heedless of the sharp light that suddenly darts from the open door and not hearing the protestations of the archeologists behind him.

Ragtime: A Screenplay

INT. EAST ROOM. DAY

MORGAN *walking briskly through the room.*

MORGAN   Maclean!

The CURATOR *running after him.*

MACLEAN   Sir?

MORGAN *walks along. He has taken a cigar from a case in his pocket and is nipping one end of it with a special device from his waistcoat.*

MORGAN   Call the bank and tell them to get busy. I want to meet that tinkering fellow, whatshisname . . . the motorcar mechanic, Ford.

EXT.   AUTOMOBILE ASSEMBLY SHED. DAY

Camera should explore the great length of the automobile assembly shed, a block-long, tin-roofed structure by a dirt road in the country. We look at the open end of the automobile assembly shed, which is set well above ground level. The doors are open and a ramp leads to the ground.

We zoom back now and frame the figure, from behind, of a thin MAN *with a tight-fitting black coat and black derby. He holds a stopwatch. He's waiting. Suddenly there appears in the open doors of the shed a black and ungainly machine which crests the doorsill, points at the sky, and then lurches down the ramp, coming to rest in the grass. It is a Model T automobile. The* MAN *whose back is to us presses the mechanism of his stopwatch and tilts his derby back on his head. He waits. Perhaps he can pull from the ground a piece of grass and begin to chew on it.*

EXT.   CLOSE-UP POCKETWATCH

We observe the watch and the hand ticking.

EXT.   MOUTH OF AUTOMOBILE SHED. DAY

Another Model T appears in the doorway as if being born. It too points for a moment at the sky and then rolls down the long ramp and bangs into the rear of the first car.

There is a cheer and several men rush into the scene, congregating around the MAN *in black. They are* EXECUTIVES *and* ENGINEERS *and they are all very happy. They congratulate the* MAN *in the black coat and black derby. But he studies his watch.*

MEN   Beautiful, Mr. Ford. You've done it. Classic . . . Historic . . . Earth-shaking . . .

FORD   *(his back still to us)* Six minutes thirty seconds. We make a car now in six minutes thirty seconds. That ain't enough.

The MEN *grow silent.*

FORD   *(turning)* Webster?

WEBSTER   Yes, sir?

FORD   The man who puts on a bolt does not put on the nut. The man who puts on the nut does not tighten it. I want to speed up those moving belts another turn. The Kraut or Pollack in there who ain't keepin' up—you get rid of him.

WEBSTER   Yes, sir.

FORD   Dang it. I want a Ford car coming out of that shed in under five and a half minutes. You hear me?

EXT.   LONG VIEW. DAY

Down the road alongside the shed comes a Model T raising some dust behind it. It pulls to a stop in front of a small group of people. A MAN *jumps down with a cable in his hand. Comes running up to* FORD.

FORD   *(to group)* All right. Everybody back to work.

Chastened ENGINEERS *and* EXECUTIVES *disperse.*

MESSENGER   From J. P. Morgan, Sir.

FORD   Morgan? *(He begins to open the cable.)* Now what in tarnation does he want?

For the first time now we see FORD's *face: It is, of course, virtually identical to the face of the mummy Seti the First seen in the Morgan Library.*

EXT.   FRONT PORCH, BROADVIEW AVENUE HOUSE. DAY

LITTLE BOY *stands alertly at the top of the porch stairs. He's looking down the Broadview Avenue hill.*

EXT.   BROADVIEW AVENUE HILL. DAY

A black Model T is coming up the hill. It is identical to the cars in the park of the prior scene except that it has a customized grey canvas roof and brass headlamps. We zoom in on the driver of the car, who is a black man and wears an impeccably correct driving costume. This is COALHOUSE WALKER JR. *As he drives up the hill he peers left and right as if looking for a particular number.*

EXT.   BROADVIEW AVENUE HOUSE. DAY

From COALHOUSE'S *point of view behind the wheel we can see the house on Broadview Avenue as it goes by, the* LITTLE BOY *coming down the steps toward the street.*

EXT.   BROADVIEW AVENUE. DAY

COALHOUSE WALKER *puts the Ford into a strenuous* U-*turn and pulls up in front of the Broadview Avenue home. He switches off the engine, lifts the goggles from his eyes and leans over the passenger side of the front seat and addresses the* LITTLE BOY, *now standing on the sidewalk gazing up at him.*

COALHOUSE   I'm looking for a young woman of color. She goes by the name Sarah. She is said to reside in one of these houses here.

BOY   She's here.

COALHOUSE WALKER *steps down from the car, but instead of approaching the porch steps, walks around the side of the house and disappears from sight.*
    The BOY *watches him go and then turns his attention to the car. Brass headlamps sparkle and the windshield flashes the rays of the afternoon sun.*

INT.   BROADVIEW AVENUE HOUSE. KITCHEN. DAY

BRIGIT *is washing dishes and* MOTHER *is busy with something we can't quite make out when there is a knock on the kitchen door, the top half of which is glass and curtained.*

MOTHER *goes to open it and sees* COALHOUSE WALKER.

MOTHER   Yes?

COALHOUSE   Pardon me, Madame. May I please speak with Sarah?

MOTHER *gazes at him a moment, somewhat startled.* COALHOUSE *has removed his hat respectfully. He is a fairly stocky man of indeterminate age.*

MOTHER   Wait one moment please.

She closes the door on him.

INT.   KITCHEN. DAY

MOTHER *strides through the kitchen and out into the hall.*

INT.   HALL. DAY

MOTHER *comes from the back of the house, turns, and walks up the stairs.*

INT.   SARAH'S ROOM, THIRD FLOOR. DAY

The black girl, SARAH, *stands tensely at the open door listening to* MOTHER's *footsteps coming up the stairs.* MOTHER *appears on the landing, catches her breath for a moment, her hand on her chest.*

MOTHER   *(with some excitement)* Sarah, there's someone here to see you. You have a caller.

SARAH *says nothing. She stares at the ground and clasps her hands in front of her tightly.*

MOTHER   Will you come to the kitchen?

SARAH *shakes her head no.*

Ragtime: A Screenplay

MOTHER   *(taken aback)* You don't want to see him?

SARAH   *(softly, after a pause)* No, Ma'am. Send him away please.

The girl is in torment. MOTHER *is about to say something. She thinks better of it. Leaves.*

INT.   KITCHEN. DAY

MOTHER *comes into the kitchen. Sees* BRIGIT *standing with a furious expression on her face and finds the black man not outside at the back door but in the kitchen near the cookstove, which is where a wicker carriage stands, in which* SARAH's *little brown* BABY *lies sleeping.*

   COALHOUSE *is on one knee beside the carriage staring at the child.* MOTHER, *suddenly outraged and not thinking clearly, goes to the back door, opens it, and holds it open.*

MOTHER   Sarah is unable to see you.

COALHOUSE WALKER *takes another glance at the* BABY, *rises, and goes to the back door.*

COALHOUSE   Thank you kindly.

MOTHER *slams the door after him, which wakes the* BABY, *who begins to cry. She picks the* BABY *up, comforting him and staring out the back door. Her point of view: The black man, as he walks away, jumps up and clicks his heels.*

EXT.   DOWNTOWN STREET, PHILADELPHIA. DAY

Cars and trucks going by. Lots of Model T's. TATEH *and the* LITTLE GIRL *walk along. He carries a pasteboard valise tied with a rope, she a little satchel. His head has a bandage on it. They walk more slowly than the other pedestrians. They stare in the windows of the shops.*

   At a corner TATEH *picks a newspaper out of a trash basket. He opens the paper. Close-up: The* Philadelphia Evening Bulletin. *The headline says* CALL FOR INDICTMENTS IN LAWRENCE POLICE RIOTS. *Subheadlines say* MOTHERS BEATEN, CHILDREN TORN FROM THEIR ARMS. *There is a picture of two policemen clubbing a woman on the ground.*

TATEH   That's it. The strike is won.

He throws the newspaper back into the trash basket. They continue to walk. TATEH *hums the "Internationale."*

Now I will get a pay envelope of seven dollars and change.

EXT.   ANOTHER STREET. DAY

They walk past iron-front buildings where trucks pull up to warehouse platforms.

TATEH   The workers have won. But what? A few more pennies in wages? Will we now own the mills?

He stops and looks around.

This is Philadelphia?

LITTLE GIRL   Yes, Tateh.

He turns to her and crouches in front of her and holds her arms.

TATEH   Listen. Seven dollars and change. We would still live in that wretched room. In that terrible town.

LITTLE GIRL   Yes, Tateh.

TATEH   There is nothing there for us. Our belongings? Our rags? The landlord may have them. I bequeath them.

He stands and takes her by the hand over to a warehouse platform, which is about chest high.

This country does not let you breathe. What do you have with you? Let me see what you have in the satchel.

He puts the bag on the platform and goes through it; he finds the flip book he had made for her of the skater.

You brought this?

LITTLE GIRL *nods.*

EXT.   PHILADELPHIA STREET, SHOP WINDOW. DAY

TATEH *and the* LITTLE GIRL *are looking in a store window.*

TATEH   Give me the little book of the skater.

The LITTLE GIRL *brings the flipbook out of her satchel. They go into the store. The name on the door is* THE FRANKLIN NOVELTY COMPANY.

The camera sees them through the glass in pantomime: TATEH *introducing himself to the* PROPRIETOR, *a man in a striped shirt with sleeve garters, and showing him how the flipbook works. The* PROPRIETOR's *obvious interest as he works the book for himself.*

TATEH *and the* PROPRIETOR *in animated conversation. The* LITTLE GIRL *drifts away, comes back into the street, and stares at the objects in the window.*

The Franklin Novelty Company deals in practical jokes and parlor magic tricks. In the window are exploding cigars, rubber roses for the lapel that squirt water, a pamphlet entitled "An Eastern Fakir's Eternal Wisdom," and so on.

Close-up of LITTLE GIRL *in profile as she studies the window. This turns into a silhouette.*

INT.   EVELYN NESBIT'S HOTEL SUITE. DAY

MOTHER's YOUNGER BROTHER *holds the silhouette of the* LITTLE GIRL. *There is an open desk drawer with a stack of silhouettes, of the* LITTLE GIRL, *of* NESBIT, *of the two of them.*

YOUNGER BROTHER *looks around the room. It is the room of someone who has left it forever. Armoire doors open, empty clothes hangers, bureau drawers askew, trash in the middle of the floor.* YOUNGER BROTHER *is devastated. In the trash he finds one satin shoe, picks it up, holds it to his chest.*

FLASH SHOT: NESBIT ON BED REMOVING HER SHOES AND SMILING SEDUCTIVELY AT CAMERA

A sob escapes from YOUNGER BROTHER's *throat as he stands there with his eyes closed, a pack of silhouettes in one arm, the peach-colored satin shoe in the other.*

EXT. BROADVIEW AVENUE. DAY

FATHER *stands at the curb amid the wicker trunks and baggage from his journey. The sound of a car driving off. He turns and gazes at his home. It is a blustery day in March and snow is in the yard. As he watches the front door opens and the* BOY *runs out abruptly, sees him, and stops at the steps of the porch. Father and son are stunned to see each other and make no move to decrease the distance between them.*

From the BOY's *point of view* FATHER *looks shrunken and thin, nothing remotely like the confident, burly man who left the previous summer.*

INT. BROADVIEW AVENUE HOUSE. PARLOR. DAY

FATHER *is on his knees with his open bags around him and he is chattering almost hysterically as he distributes the gifts up over his head without noting the responses of the members of the* FAMILY.

FATHER   This I bought from an eskimo for three .36 caliber shells. This tea is worth its weight in gold. This is polar bear fur. This is my hood of caribou.

As he chatters the FAMILY *stares at him, each holding some item or other, incredible treasures from the North, but here in the parlor, the embarrassing possessions of a savage.*

They stare at the strange man FATHER *has become.*

INT. MOTHER'S BEDROOM. NIGHT

MOTHER *is at her dressing table brushing out her blonde hair.* FATHER *sits at the edge of the double bed. He is in his nightshirt, and although he is not looking at* MOTHER, *he listens very carefully to what she is saying.*

MOTHER   Oh, and I thought it would be better to adopt some new billing procedures. It makes everything a lot clearer. Every credit and every debit is entered twice. Also I hired four new sales agents in California and Oregon and their volume of business now justifies the cost of shipping. I think in a year or less we'll begin to show very good profits from the western coast.

FATHER's *eye notices a pamphlet on the bedside table. As* MOTHER *talks he picks it up. The title is* Family Limitation *and the author is* EMMA GOLDMAN.

Ragtime: A Screenplay

The bed jostles and he turns and sees MOTHER *on the other side. She is quite lovely in her nightdress and unbound hair and she is looking at him with great affection.*

MOTHER   I do hope you will approve of the decisions I have made.

FATHER   *(nodding dumbly)* I'm sure I will.

MOTHER   I have ideas too about inventory and the kind of advertising you've done, but that can wait.

She turns off the light and there is a rustling as they get under the covers.

MOTHER   Oh, you're so thin! You're all bones and so cold. My poor darling!

INT.   PARLOR. DAY

BRIGIT *the maid pushes an electric suction cleaner across the rug. The camera finds* FATHER *in the door staring at it as if he hears from it the wind of the Arctic.*

INT.   HALL. DAY

FATHER *wanders back toward the kitchen.*

INT.   KITCHEN. DAY

FATHER *stands in the door.* MOTHER *holding the little brown* BABY *turns and smiles at him.*

INT.   BOY'S ROOM. DAY

Standing in the door here, FATHER *sees the* BOY *sitting at his own new desk. The sense here should be of a child who has grown up somewhat and now appears to us as a young student. The* BOY *reading at his desk turns and looks at his father.*

INT.   SARAH'S ROOM. DAY

FATHER *walks by and stops for a moment at the half-open door and looks in on* SARAH, *who sits at the window and ignores him.*

INT. DINING ROOM. DAY

The FAMILY *is sitting down for Sunday dinner. They are dressed for it.* FATHER*'s clothes seem too big for him and there is a sense, perhaps, that they are treating him with such courtesy as to make him feel almost like a convalescent.*

BRIGIT *brings in a roast of beef and appears not to know where to place it.* FATHER *perceives this.*

FATHER   Put it here, Brigit. *(He looks around the table.)* I want you all to stop treating me with such solicitude. I'm not an invalid.

YOUNGER BROTHER *stares at his plate.* MOTHER *smiles.*

GRANDFATHER   I'm the invalid around here and don't anyone forget it.

FATHER *standing with carving utensils suddenly perceives another change that he had not previously noticed. He looks around the room. The old Victorian dining room with its heavy furnishings and floral wallpaper is gone. On the walls is a paper with an elegant pattern in an ancient Egyptian motif. He looks at the furnishings, the table and the chairs, and sees that it too is in a simple elegance of Egyptian style.*

MOTHER   Do you like it? It's the latest thing you know.

Behind the Egyptian figures on the wall are sand-colored pyramids and temples.

BOY   *(deadpan)* Beware the mummy's curse.

INT. DINING ROOM. DAY

Later: the FAMILY *is rising from the table.* BRIGIT *is clearing the dishes.* FATHER *goes to the window and reacts to what he sees.*

EXT. BROADVIEW AVENUE. DAY

In front of the house a Model T Ford at the curb is being polished assiduously by a BLACK MAN.

INT.   BROADVIEW AVENUE HOUSE. DINING ROOM. DAY

FATHER *turns to* MOTHER *and the* BOY, *who are still in the room.*

FATHER   I wish whoever it is entertaining the people whose car and chauffeur that is would have them park in front of their own home.

BOY   That's not a chauffeur. That's Coalhouse Walker Jr.

MOTHER   He's a suitor of Sarah's. He comes every Sunday.

FATHER   What the devil is he doing?

MOTHER   She won't see him. (*She smiles, goes to* FATHER, *takes his arm.*) I think I ought to tell you that we are privileged to be witnessing a courtship of the most stubborn Christian kind.

INT.   HALL. DAY

The FAMILY *is leaving the dining room.* SARAH *appears in the hallway carrying the little brown* BABY *from the kitchen. She ignores the family and walks slowly upstairs with the child.*

FATHER   (*addressing* MOTHER) Do you call it a courtship that has already produced a child?

MOTHER   I find that an unkind remark.

INT.   PARLOR. DAY

MOTHER, FATHER, *the* BOY, *and* GRANDFATHER *take their ease in the parlor after Sunday dinner.*

MOTHER   I had no hope for Sarah before this man appeared. Now she has the possibility of a future.

FATHER   Who is he?

MOTHER   We're not sure. Sarah won't speak of him. But from the looks of him he has income. He's quite well dressed. He keeps his car impeccably.

FATHER *goes to the window.*

EXT.   BROADVIEW AVENUE. DAY

COALHOUSE WALKER *stands gazing at the upper story of the house.*

INT.   BROADVIEW AVENUE HOUSE. PARLOR. DAY

FATHER   Yes. He dresses in that affectation of wealth to which colored people lend themselves.

MOTHER   I don't see why you would dislike someone you don't know.

FATHER   They never take responsibility for their behavior.

MOTHER   But he's here you see. He keeps coming back. There's been suffering and now there's penitence. It's very grand and I'm sorry for you that you don't see it.

INT.   SARAH'S ROOM. DAY

Holding her BABY, SARAH *peeks out the window. From her point of view we see* COALHOUSE *getting behind the wheel of his car and driving off. The* BABY *gurgles and captures her attention. She places her cheek against his cheek and hugs him.*

INT.   YOUNGER BROTHER'S ROOM. DAY

YOUNGER BROTHER *is pacing his room. He holds against his chest a silhouette of* EVELYN. *He is distraught and a low moan escapes from his throat. His suffering seems to come to a climax and with a kind of strangled cry he grabs his derby and a cardboard box in which the silhouettes and the peach satin shoes are kept and rushes out of the room.*

INT.   PARLOR. DAY

LITTLE BOY, *hearing* YOUNGER BROTHER's *footsteps coming down the stairs, stations himself at the doorway.* YOUNGER BROTHER *rushes out the back with the box. The* BOY *slowly follows.*

EXT. BACKYARD, BROADVIEW AVENUE. DAY

YOUNGER BROTHER *with his two hands heaves the box of silhouettes and the shoes into a trash bin. Under his arm is a long scarf, which he now throws around his neck, his only concession to the cold, and rushes off. After a moment the* LITTLE BOY *retrieves the box with the silhouettes and shoes. He discards the shoes and goes back into the house.*

INT. LITTLE BOY'S ROOM. AFTERNOON

The BOY *is going through the colletion of silhouettes. One in particular strikes him. It is a silhouette of the* LITTLE GIRL. *With thumbtacks, he pins this silhouette to the inside of his wardrobe door. The remainder of the collection he secrets in a drawer.*

INT. COOPER UNION MEETING HALL. NIGHT

The hall is hot and crowded. A generally immigrant-looking CROWD. EMMA GOLDMAN *is making a speech about the revolution in Mexico of the peons. On the platform behind her stand two or three* MEN *in Mexican share-farmers' bleached pajama coats and flopping trousers and sombreros. Bandoliers criss-cross their chests.*

GOLDMAN (*pointing to* MEN *on platform with her*) My Comrades, this is not a foreign costume. There are no foreign lands. There is only one struggle throughout the world. There is only the flame of freedom trying to light the hideous darkness of life on earth.

The applause is deafening.

My friends, the Mexican revolution needs arms. The men and women marching in the army of the South behind Emiliano Zapata—need guns and ammunition.

People are rushing up to the platform with fistfuls of dollars and change in their hands. There is exhilaration and great clamor.

GOLDMAN (*over this*) Who will deny our brothers our comradeship in this profound struggle for freedom and justice?

*She raises the arms of the Zapatistas beside her and the place goes wild. In the
turmoil* GOLDMAN *glances down and sees at the foot of the platform the head of
a blondish young man,* YOUNGER BROTHER, *the eyes turned upward.* GOLD-
MAN, *recognizing him, laughs.*

INT.   GOLDMAN'S BOARDINGHOUSE ROOM. NIGHT

YOUNGER BROTHER *sits Indian style at the bottom of the bed. He is staring at
nothing.* GOLDMAN *and* REITMAN *are in the room with him.*

YOUNGER BROTHER   (*to* EMMA) I didn't know if you'd remember me.

GOLDMAN   (*smiling*) But how could I forget? Could anyone forget a sight
such as that, my pagan? (*She touches his cheek with her thumb and mashes
away a tear.*) So tragic. So tragic. Is that all you want from your life?

YOUNGER BROTHER   I don't want to live without her. I have to find her.

GOLDMAN   She has run off with a Ragtime dancer. She wants to dance on
the stage. But where she is I don't know. And if I could tell you what good
would that do? Suppose you got her to come back to you? She would only
stay awhile. She would stay until someone else wanted her and then she
would go with him. Don't you know that?

YOUNGER BROTHER   (*downcast*) Yes. (*a whisper*)

GOLDMAN   Believe me, you are better off this way.

YOUNGER BROTHER *is crying. He kisses her hand.*

YOUNGER BROTHER   You're right. Of course, you're right. I have no memories of her. It was something I dreamed.

GOLDMAN   (*unappeased*) I'll tell you something. Here is Reitman, my lover.
But in the meeting tonight you saw also two of my former lovers. (*to*
REITMAN) Is that right, Ben?

REITMAN   Absolutely, my darling.

GOLDMAN   And we are all good friends. Friendship is what endures, shared
ideals, respect for the whole character of a human being. Why can't you
accept your own freedom? Why do you have to cling to someone in order
to live?

REITMAN   (*peering at* YOUNGER BROTHER) He reminds me of Czolgosz.

GOLDMAN   (*nodding*) Yes. The same poor boy around the eyes. The same poor dangerous boy.

YOUNGER BROTHER   (*drying his cheeks with his hand*) Who is Czolgosz?

GOLDMAN   You don't remember the assassination of McKinley? He walked up to the President and he shot him.

EXT.   EMPTY FIELD OF TALL MARSH GRASSES ALONG NEW ROCHELLE SHORELINE. DAY

Two men in black overcoats and derbies are coming through the grass. The first is YOUNGER BROTHER, *the second is* FATHER. *Gulls hover overhead. The two men reach a slight rise, a bare spot. They stop.*

YOUNGER BROTHER   (*reaches into his left coat pocket*) Now these are our standard three-inch crackers. When I hold up my left hand it will be to indicate that I'm firing one of these. (*He reaches into his right-hand coat pocket.*) And this is my new spherical design.

CLOSE-UP OF YOUNGER BROTHER'S HAND WITH CHERRY BOMB. DAY

FATHER'S VOICE   It looks like a crab apple or a cherry.

YOUNGER BROTHER   It contains no more powder than the standard model, yet because of the design of my packing it goes a lot farther, as you'll see. Wait here, please.

With FATHER *we watch* YOUNGER BROTHER *walk some yards away through the grass. We see him raise his left hand, bend down and crouch over the firecracker. He straightens up. There is a distant popping sound and the barest wisp of smoke quickly blown away by the breeze.*

He pauses dramatically, crouches again but steps back this time holding up his right hand and waving. There is an explosion so loud that FATHER *starts. The sea gulls above are suddenly wheeling through the air.*

EXT. MUD FLAT. DAY

FATHER *is approaching* YOUNGER BROTHER, *who stands awaiting his opinion with face flushed and eyes glistening.*

FATHER   Very impressive.

YOUNGER BROTHER   I have a new rocket too. I have all sorts of designs on the drawing table.

FATHER   (*putting his hand on* YOUNGER BROTHER's *shoulder*) I never hoped you would take to the business.

YOUNGER BROTHER   Just this part. The ordnance. *(He laughs.)*

FATHER   Perhaps the charge is too powerful. I don't want to produce something that might put a child's eye out.

YOUNGER BROTHER *laughs and withdraws just a few yards, takes another silvered cherry bomb from his pocket, lights the fuse and puts it on the ground at his feet and does not step back but holds out his arms and looks up at the sky. There is an enormous report. Again he bends down and lights another bomb. Another bang.* FATHER *holds his hands over his ears but* YOUNGER BROTHER *is laughing, and above him the alarmed seabirds are turning in widening circles.*

Somewhere in this scene, the sound of a Ragtime piano is heard, becoming louder and more vigorous as the scene plays out. The music is the "Maple Leaf Rag" and bridges into the next scene.

INT. BROADVIEW AVENUE HOUSE. PARLOR. DAY

The piano making the music is the family's own parlor upright, and the hands on the piano are black.

COALHOUSE WALKER JR. *is the pianist and* MOTHER, FATHER, GRAND-FATHER, *and the* BOY *are listening.* YOUNGER BROTHER *appears in the doorway to listen. He is in his shirt-sleeves. They are all stirred by the music. As he plays* COALHOUSE WALKER *might glance at the ceiling speculatively.*

INT. SARAH'S ROOM. DAY

Holding her BABY, SARAH *stands by her open door listening to the brilliant music as it comes up the stairwell.*

Ragtime: A Screenplay

INT. PARLOR. DAY

COALHOUSE WALKER *brings the piece to a rousing conclusion. The family applauds.* COALHOUSE *swings around on the piano stool to face* YOUNGER BROTHER.

YOUNGER BROTHER   *(cheerfully amazed)* That's Ragtime!

COALHOUSE   *(nodding)* "Maple Leaf Rag" by the great Scott Joplin.

YOUNGER BROTHER   *(laughing)* I never thought I would hear Ragtime in this house.

COALHOUSE   You know the music? I'm not at my best on this piano. I'm not used to playing instruments so out of tune.

FATHER's *face reddens.*

MOTHER   Oh yes. We're terrible about that.

FATHER   Where did you say that you played?

COALHOUSE   I'm with the Jim Europe Clef Club Orchestra at the Manhattan Casino on 155th Street.

MOTHER   Won't you have some more tea, Mr. Walker?

COALHOUSE   Thank you.

FATHER *observes the black man handling a tea cup without any difficulty and patting his lips with a cloth napkin.* FATHER *clears his throat.*

FATHER   Is that a good position, the Jim Europe orchestra?

COALHOUSE   It is very good. It's a permanent place. I am through traveling. I am through going on the road.

As he speaks COALHOUSE *glances upward as if addressing these last words through the walls and ceiling to* SARAH.

FATHER   *(clearing throat)* Do you know any coon-songs?

The pianist sips his tea, places the cup and saucer down on the tray, pats his mouth.

COALHOUSE   Coon-songs, Sir, are made for minstrel shows. They are made for white men who sing them in blackface.

There is an embarrassed silence. COALHOUSE *stands.*

Well, it appears as if Miss Sarah will not be able to receive me this afternoon.

He turns abruptly and walks out.

INT.   HALL. DAY

MOTHER, FATHER, *the* BOY, *and* YOUNGER BROTHER *follow* COALHOUSE WALKER *to the kitchen.*

INT.   KITCHEN. DAY

COALHOUSE, *ignoring the maid,* BRIGIT, *who stands by a cupboard folding tea towels, takes his coat from a kitchen chair, puts it on. He takes up his cap and driving goggles.*

COALHOUSE   Goodbye to you all. Thank you for a most excellent tea.

YOUNGER BROTHER   *(stepping forward, extending his hand)* Thank you for the most excellent music.

COALHOUSE *glances at* YOUNGER BROTHER *and after a pause shakes his hand. He leaves.*

FATHER   I question the propriety of this.

YOUNGER BROTHER *leaves into the hall.*

MOTHER   I see nothing wrong with it. He has been coming here week after week, driving all the way from Harlem, and I felt bad leaving him outside. When Mr. Roosevelt was in the White House he gave dinner to Booker T. Washington. Surely we can serve tea to Coalhouse Walker.

FATHER *looks at the rear door.*

FATHER   He doesn't act or talk like a colored man. He doesn't ingratiate himself. Even Matthew Henson knew his place.

INT. PARLOR. NIGHT

BRIGIT, *the maid, without her cap, puts a record on the Victrola and sits down to John McCormack singing "I Hear You Calling Me."* BRIGIT *lies down on the couch and lights a cigarette and with a cavalier gesture blows out the match and tosses the matchstick onto the floor.*

INT. MOTHER'S BEDROOM. NIGHT

FATHER *raises his head from the pillow suddenly awake.*

FATHER Something's burning.

MOTHER *(who has been awake)* No. It's Brigit. She's smoking cigarettes again.

The distant sound of John McCormack's voice can be heard.

MOTHER She's doing what she can to lose her place. She's no longer efficient or respectful. It's because of Sarah. It's because we have a colored girl in the house.

FATHER It's the collapse of civilization, that's what it is. There is talk among the seamstresses in the flag department that they want to join a New York union. A union!

EXT. THIRTY-SIXTH STREET. MORGAN LIBRARY. DAY

The Morgan limousine pulls up to the curb. CHAUFFEUR *runs around, opens the door, and out steps* HENRY FORD.
   FORD *glances at library facade, turns and takes a hard look at the huge car he's just been carried in.*
   The CURATOR *is coming down the front steps of the library.*

INT. MORGAN LIBRARY. WEST ROOM. DAY

In the great West Room of the library, MORGAN *and* FORD *are lunching with two of* MORGAN'S HOUSE STAFF *providing impeccable service.* FORD *eats lightly but does not touch either of the wines set before him.* MORGAN *consumes food in great amounts.*

As MORGAN *talks and eats* FORD *fingers the gold plate, picking up a knife or a fork and examining it.*

MORGAN   Ford, Mr. Ford, I have no interest in acquiring your business or sharing its profits. Nor am I associated with any of your competitors.

FORD   I have to allow that is good news.

MORGAN   Nevertheless I admire what you have done, and while I have qualms about the thought of a motorcar in the hands of every mongoloid who happens to have a few hundred dollars to spend, I recognize that the future is yours. You're still a young man. Fifty or thereabouts?

FORD   Thereabouts.

MORGAN   I control 741 directorships and 112 corporations. I have had the privilege of arranging a loan to the U.S. government that saved it from bankruptcy. I have spent my life in the coordination of capital resources and the harmonious combination of industries. And this has had the effect of isolating me from my fellow man. There are very few people to whom I feel I can talk. Do you have that feeling?

FORD   Only all the time. Them that ain't fools is thieves. The thing about my assembly line is that it don't tax the mental capacity of the workers.

MORGAN   Exactly.

FORD   The man who puts on the bolt don't put on the nut and the man who puts on the nut don't tighten it.

MORGAN   My dear Ford. That's exactly what I want to talk about. I see in your use of men a reincarnation of Pharaohism. Let me ask you a question. Has it occurred to you that your assembly line is not merely a stroke of industrial genius, but a projection of organic truth? After all, the interchangeability of parts is a rule of nature. This is not to say all mammals have interchangeable parts as do your automobiles. But shared design is what allows taxonomists to classify mammals as mammals and within a species. Man for example. Our individual differences are measured on the basis of our similarity. So that individuation may be compared to a pyramid in that it is only achieved by the placement of the top stone.

FORD   *(after a moment of pondering)* Exceptin' the Jews.

MORGAN   I beg your pardon?

FORD   The Jews. They ain't like anyone else I know. There goes your theory up shit's creek.

MORGAN *does not entirely understand what has happened to the conversation. He covers this by drinking some wine and waving his arm for the next course.*

INT.   WEST ROOM. DAY

The WAITERS *are wheeling away the luncheon table.* MORGAN *and* FORD *take chairs on opposite sides of the great fireplace. A* WAITER *appears with a leather-covered humidor on a tray.* FORD *declines a cigar.*

MORGAN   From time to time I have retained scholars and scientists to assist me in my philosophical investigations in hopes of reaching some conclusions about this life that are not within the reach of the masses of men. I do not think you can be so insolent as to believe your achievements are the result only of your own efforts.

FORD   Well now, Mr. Morgan, I always know to look for ways to get things cheaper than the next man.

INT.   CENTER HALL. DAY

The TWO MEN *are coming out of the West Room.*

MORGAN   You may need me more than you think. Suppose I could prove to you that there are universal patterns of order and repetition that give meaning to the activity on this planet?

INT.   EAST ROOM. DAY

The TWO MEN *are coming in from the Center Hall.*

MORGAN   Suppose I could demonstrate that you yourself are an instrumentation in our modern age of trends in human identity that affirm the oldest wisdom in the world?

FORD *stands in the center of the great East Room and gazes about him. He gazes at the tiers of books, this vast repository of incalculable intellectual wealth. He shakes his head.*

FORD   That's a considerable stack of books.

MORGAN   Yes. I have spent years of my life investigating the previous civilizations of mankind. I have spent millions. And do you know the idea that comes through in each and every era but our own? It is this: that there are special people born in each age who have a secret wisdom, which they use to manage the world for the benefit of mankind. Why do you suppose an idea which has had currency in every age of mankind disappears in modern times?

MORGAN *walks over to the secret panel and presses the binding of a particular book. A side of the wall swings open.*

MORGAN   I'll tell you why: The rise of mechanistic science was a great conspiracy. A great devilish conspiracy to destroy our awareness of the transcendentally gifted among us. But they are with us today, nevertheless, they are with us in every age. They come back, you see! They come back!

He beckons to FORD, *who is still standing in the middle of the room, and disappears into the passageway.*

INT.   SECRET ROOM. DAY

The TWO MEN *hover over the mummy's crypt, the dim light glowing on their faces, which should at this moment have a grotesque cast.* MORGAN *glances at* FORD *with a kind of fierce proprietary triumph.* FORD's *face continues to be impassive and give no indication of being impressed by what he sees.* MORGAN *is breathing heavily.*

MORGAN   The great Pharaoh Seti the First, Mr. Ford, recovered from the temple of Karnak, where he was buried three thousand years ago. Why should we not satisfy ourselves of the truth of who we are and the eternal beneficent force which we incarnate?

FORD   I get you. Close her up.

Ragtime: A Screenplay

The two men replace the lid on the crypt and MORGAN *turns on some more lights and the two men sit down.* MORGAN *pats his forehead with a handkerchief and attempts to recover his composure.* FORD *sits slightly hunched.*

FORD   Let me tell you something, Mr. Morgan. As a youth I was faced with an awful crisis in my mental life when it came over me that I had no call to know what I knew. I had grit, all right, but I was an ordinary country boy. Yet I knew how everything worked. I could look at something and tell you how it worked and probably show you how to make it work better. But I was no intellectual, you see, and I had no patience with the two-dollar words.

MORGAN *leans forward—as attentive as he has ever been to anyone in his entire life.*

FORD   *(continuing)* Well, then I happened to pick up a little book. It was called "An Eastern Fakir's Eternal Wisdom," published by the Franklin Novelty Company of Philadelphia, Pennsylvania. And in this book, which cost me just twenty-five cents, I found everything I needed to set my mind at rest. Reincarnation is the only belief I hold, Mr. Morgan. I explain my genius this way—some of us have just lived more times than others. And I'll tell you something, in thanks for the eats, I'm going to lend that book to you. *(waving his hand)* Why, you don't have to fuss with all these things, you don't have to muck around in some poor old mummy's grave just to prove something that you can get in the mail order for two bits!

The two men stare at each other. MORGAN *sits back in his chair the blood draining through his face.*

MORGAN   *(weakly)* Mr. Ford, if my ideas can survive their attachment to you, they will have met their ultimate test.

INT.   BROADVIEW AVENUE HOUSE. PARLOR. DAY

The MAID *in a starched uniform who is dusting the furniture is now the black girl,* SARAH. *She goes about her cleaning very energetically, dusting, polishing, etc., while* YOUNGER BROTHER, *with his arms folded, leans against the door jamb and talks to her.*

YOUNGER BROTHER   *(smiling)* No one in the family believes you anymore. You'll give in because you want to.

SARAH   *(stopping for a moment and looking up)* No, sir. Never.

YOUNGER BROTHER   Oh, you will, Sarah. When people love it's like the heart had a flaw of tenderness in that part of the body. Just like rickets in the bones, or congestion in the lungs, some people are affected with love in the heart and there's no cure. *(He swallows and clears his throat.)*

She looks at him.

INT.   SARAH'S ROOM. DAY

MOTHER is helping SARAH dress in a pink shirtwaist and a black skirt and jacket. She is happy and chattering, soothing SARAH, who is nervous and looking at herself in the mirror. We understand that these are MOTHER's clothes that are being adapted for SARAH. She steps back and admires the young woman's beauty. The crowning touch is a broad-brimmed hat, which MOTHER places on her head.

MOTHER   Oh, Sarah. You're absolutely beautiful.

The young black woman nervously holds her fist up to her face and bites her knuckles.

MOTHER   Take your hand down. Everything is just fine. Mr. Coalhouse Walker is waiting for you. Let's go down now and you and the baby will go for a ride in his fine automobile.

INT.   STAIRWELL. DAY

Preceded by MOTHER, SARAH comes down the stairs into the front hall almost as a bride might make her entrance. By the open front door stands COALHOUSE WALKER, his hat in his hand. Also standing there gazing at the young woman are FATHER, GRANDFATHER, and the BOY. GRANDFATHER holds the little brown BABY and Sarah takes him from GRANDFATHER's arms.

EXT.   FRONT PORCH, BROADVIEW AVENUE HOUSE. DAY

With the FAMILY standing in assembly on the porch COALHOUSE WALKER and his family descend to the street. He helps MOTHER and CHILD into the car, takes his place behind the wheel, and with a wave to the people on the porch, he drives off for a Sunday afternoon excursion.

EXT. ROAD SHOTS. DAY

A sequence here of the shining black Ford as it proceeds through streets and roads, which become progressively more countrified. Perhaps there is some indication of the end of SARAH*'s shame, given by the briefest of smiles, tentatively shy as* COALHOUSE *glances at her while he proudly drives the Model T.*

EXT. OPEN FIELD. DAY

Car is parked along the road. COALHOUSE *and* SARAH *sit under a tree, their hats removed.* SARAH *sits, incredibly graceful, watching her* BABY *play in the grass.*

COALHOUSE   I want to make good by you, Miss Sarah. In the time I was away, never a minute passed I didn't think about you. I'm asking you to marry me so that we can make our fate together. For the rest of my life I will show you the honor and respect you deserve.

SARAH *is crying. She picks up her baby passionately and as* COALHOUSE *leans toward her she settles into his arms still crying while he kisses her face and holds his large hand around the* BABY*'s shoulders.*

INT. FRONT HALL. DAY

MOTHER *welcomes* SARAH *and the* BABY. SARAH *extends her hand, a modest diamond ring now on the fourth finger.* MOTHER *embraces her, both crying happily.*

EXT. BROADVIEW AVENUE. DAY

Shadows of the trees lay over the street. COALHOUSE WALKER *gets up into his Ford and with a wave back to the house drives off down the Broadview Avenue hill.*

EXT. FRONT PORCH, BROADVIEW AVENUE HOUSE. DAY

SARAH *is waving goodbye. She waves the* BABY*'s hand. She is smiling, happy, and very beautiful.*

EXT. NEW ROCHELLE STREETS. DAY

A short sequence of COALHOUSE *making his way south through the pleasant streets of New Rochelle. He turns right onto a narrower lane. The street sign here says* FIREHOUSE LANE.

EXT. FIREHOUSE LANE. DAY

Firehouse Lane goes along a field; a gentle slope, at the bottom of which is a pond. This is on his right. On his left is a clapboard station house belonging to the Emerald Isle Engine, a volunteer fire company.

As COALHOUSE *approaches he has to brake sharply: A team of three matching grey engine horses has cantered out of the firehouse into the road pulling behind them a big brass steam pumper. The horses are reined and the entire equipage blocks* COALHOUSE's *path. The driver of the pumper, a* VOLUNTEER FIREMAN, *looks at the Negro in his car and yawns ostentatiously. Two more* VOLUNTEERS *come out of the building to gaze at* COALHOUSE. *All the* FIREMEN *wear blue workshirts with green handkerchief ties, dark blue trousers, and boots.*

COALHOUSE WALKER *pulls on the handbrake and climbs down to crank his car, which has stalled.*

FIRST VOLUNTEER   Are you a resident of this city?

COALHOUSE   I beg your pardon?

SECOND VOLUNTEER   You're on a private toll road and if you're not a resident there's a toll of twenty-five dollars.

COALHOUSE   This is a public thoroughfare. I've traveled it dozens of times and no one has ever said anything about a toll.

He cranks the engine, it sputters and starts. He gets back up behind the wheel.

COALHOUSE *presses the reverse drive pedal and turns in his seat as if to back up to the corner and go another way. At this moment two other firemen carrying a twenty-foot ladder between them come into the street behind the car. Soon other members of the Emerald Isle Volunteers are bringing out from the firehouse all the equipment they possess and piling it in the street behind the car— carts of coiled hose, buckets, axes, hooks, etc.*

COALHOUSE *sighs and switches off the motor. He folds his arms and sits behind the wheel waiting for the next development.*

Ragtime: A Screenplay

EXT.   POND.   DAY

TWO BLACK BOYS *ten or twelve years old are diverted in their play here by the sight up the slope on the road of a black man in his car surrounded by the members of the Emerald Isle Engine Company. Their curiosity gets the best of them and they drift up toward the road.*

EXT.   FIREHOUSE.   DAY

The CHIEF *of the Company, somewhat older than the rest, stands beside* COAL-HOUSE's *car. He wears a white garrison cap at a cocky angle. He is a beefy man with a big belly and thick arms. His name is* WILLIE CONKLIN.

CONKLIN   Well, sir, we know you've come this way before. We've seen you. But as of now, we're enforcing the law and if you do not pay, you don't pass. It's as simple as that.

With his two hands CONKLIN *lifts his hat from his head and resets his hat so that the visor covers his eyes. He tilts his chin up in a pugnacious manner.*

That's a fine machine you have there. A lovely machine. You see, we need the money for a firetruck so we can drive to fires, just like you drive to whorehouses.

COALHOUSE *considers his situation. He glances at the sloping field, as if he might be able to turn around in the grass. He sees the two Negro* BOYS *standing at the edge of the road. Close but not too close.* COALHOUSE *jumps down from the car, walks around to the two little boys. Seeing him coming they begin to run.*

COALHOUSE   Hey! Come on over here!

They stop and allow him to approach.

EXT.   FIELD.   DAY

COALHOUSE *talks to the two* BOYS *off the road in the grass out of hearing of the* VOLUNTEERS. *Perhaps as he addresses them he gazes back at the road, where the three matched grey horses stand restlessly switching their tails.*

COALHOUSE   Would you like a ride in that automobile?

BOYS   Yes, sir!

COALHOUSE   Well I'll give you a ride if you just help me out for a minute. I've got to go somewhere and leave this car just as it is, all blocked in by these white folks. I want you to keep your eye on that car. Don't stop looking at it and when I come back you tell me if anyone touched it, hear?

BOYS   Yes, sir.

COALHOUSE *strides off through the field back the way he came, toward the corner of Firehouse Lane. The* VOLUNTEERS *are watching him as he goes.*

EXT.   INTERSECTION, NEW ROCHELLE. LATE AFTERNOON (SEE P. 179)

(SEE P. 179)

At this busy downtown intersection we see COALHOUSE *talking to the* POLICE-MAN *on duty. The* POLICEMAN *is operating a stop-and-go signal and shakes his head. At this moment the* POLICEMAN *sees a patrol wagon going by and he flags it.*

EXT.   INTERSECTION. LATE AFTERNOON

TRAFFIC POLICEMAN *is talking to the* DRIVER *of patrol wagon with* COAL-HOUSE *standing by.*

POLICEMAN   . . . and they told him it was a toll road.

DRIVER   *(laughing)* Those boys don't mean no harm. I know them all. (*to* COALHOUSE) Come on, I'll take you back now. They're probably tired of the sport.

INT.   POLICE WAGON. LATE AFTERNOON

COALHOUSE *is sitting up beside* DRIVER *as the wagon moves through New Rochelle.*

DRIVER   Who do you drive for?

COALHOUSE   I drive for myself. It's my car. I own it.

DRIVER *looks at him, noticing his tailoring.*

EXT. FIREHOUSE LANE. LATE AFTERNOON

The police wagon turns on to Firehouse Lane.

EXT. FIREHOUSE. LATE AFTERNOON

The road is clear. COALHOUSE *and the* POLICEMAN *are looking around. The light is dimming now. The evening is definitely coming on.* COALHOUSE *sees no boys, no firemen, no steam pumper or horses in the street. But down the slope his car is standing in the field well off the road.*

EXT. FIELD. LATE AFTERNOON

COALHOUSE *approaches the car. It is spattered with mud. There is a huge tear in the custom pantasote top. Deposited in the back seat is a mound of fresh human excrement.*

EXT. FIREHOUSE. LATE AFTERNOON

COALHOUSE *and the* POLICEMAN *are coming across the road toward the firehouse doors. The* CHIEF *stands there with his arms folded, leaning against the door jamb.*

COALHOUSE   The Police Department advises me there is no toll road anywhere in this city.

CONKLIN   That's right. Anyone is free to come and go on this road anytime he thinks he has to.

COALHOUSE   I want my car cleaned and the damage paid for.

The CHIEF *begins to laugh and a couple of his men come out to join the fun. At this moment another police van drives up and two more officers join the group. One of them is the* TRAFFIC POLICEMAN COALHOUSE *originally spoke to and the other is a* SERGEANT.

EXT. FIELD

The group swollen now by several more of the VOLUNTEERS *stands near* COALHOUSE's *car.*

SERGEANT   Willie, did you or your boys do this desecratin'?

CONKLIN   Pat, I'll tell you exactly what happened. The nigger here pulled his damn car in the middle of the road right in front of the firehouse. So we had to move it. It's a serious business, blocking a fire station. Ain't that so, boys?

The VOLUNTEERS *agree righteously. The* POLICEMAN *looks at the car, looks again at* CONKLIN. *Sighs. Takes* COALHOUSE'S *arm and walks him a short distance away.*

SERGEANT   (*to* COALHOUSE) *Listen. We'll push your tin lizzie back on the road and you be on your way.*

COALHOUSE   I was on my way when they stopped me. I didn't park my car there. They stopped me.

SERGEANT   Well, it was just a prank. Scrape off the shit and forget the whole thing.

COALHOUSE   I'm sorry. They put filth in my car and tore a hole in the top. I want the car cleaned and the damage paid for. I don't think you would condone this prank, as you call it, if I was a white man.

SERGEANT   You don't?

COALHOUSE   Not for a minute.

CHIEF CONKLIN, *the traffic* POLICEMAN, *and the* DRIVER *of the van are drifting toward the two to hear their conversation better. The* SERGEANT, *at the same time, has begun to appreciate* COALHOUSE'S *style of speech. He looks him up and down. He grows angrier.*

SERGEANT   If you don't take your automobile and get along out of here I'm going to charge you with driving off the road, drunkenness, and making an unsightly nuisance.

COALHOUSE   I do not drink. I did not drive my car off the road, or slash the roof, or defecate in it. I want the damage paid for and I want an apology.

CHIEF CONKLIN *and the others are grinning at the* SERGEANT'S *discomfiture so that the issue for the* SERGEANT *is now his own authority.*

Ragtime: A Screenplay

SERGEANT (*to* COALHOUSE) I'm placing you under arrest. You'll come with
   me in the wagon.

The group moves off toward the road, the SERGEANT *holding* COALHOUSE'*s
arm, the car left where it is in the grass.*

INT.   BROADVIEW AVENUE HOUSE. PARLOR. EVENING

MOTHER *is reading the evening paper.* FATHER, *having just concluded a phone
call, appears in the doorway.*

FATHER   Coalhouse Walker has been arrested. He's asked me to put up his
   bail so he can get to the city and not miss his job this evening. Fifty dollars.

MOTHER   Arrested for what?

FATHER   It's not clear. *(He begins to unbelt his jacket.)* I'll go immediately.

INT.   PARLOR. LATE AFTERNOON

MOTHER, FATHER, *and* YOUNGER BROTHER *are receiving* COALHOUSE
WALKER, *who sits with his arms folded looking quite calm.*

MOTHER   Mr. Walker, I feel this must be a Sunday if you are here. *(She
   smiles.)*

COALHOUSE'*s expression remains impassive.*

   I'm ashamed that this community is represented in your mind by that
   bunch of toughs.

FATHER   They have a bad reputation. The other volunteer engines are not
   that way at all.

YOUNGER BROTHER *sits on the piano stool with his legs crossed. He leans
forward.*

YOUNGER BROTHER   Where's the car now? And what about those two boys?
   They are witnesses for you.

COALHOUSE   I have found the boys but their parents refuse to have them
   involved in the matter. I'm a stranger to the Negros here. They have to live
   here and they want no trouble.

INT. HALLWAY. LATE AFTERNOON

SARAH *stands just out of sight of the parlor door, listening to the conversation. She holds her* BABY *on her hip.*

COALHOUSE'S VOICE   As for the car I have not looked at it again and I won't until it's returned to me as it was when I drove away from this house last Sunday.

A look of terrible distress comes over SARAH's *face.*

INT. PARLOR. LATE AFTERNOON

FATHER   If you intend to pursue your claim you should engage a lawyer. There is such a thing as the power of subpoena for witnesses.

COALHOUSE   Are there any colored lawyers here?

FATHER   I don't know of one. But any lawyer who loves justice will do I should think. *(He pauses. Clears his throat.)* I will underwrite the expense.

COALHOUSE   That won't be necessary. I thank you for the loan. *(He removes from his breast pocket an envelope and puts it down on the sidetable.)* I'll just say good night to Miss Sarah.

COALHOUSE MONTAGE

Here are several scenes showing COALHOUSE *in interview with two or three* WHITE LAWYERS *or their* RECEPTIONISTS, *always with discouraging results. Over this should be a fairly slow, somewhat stately rag, a piano with an orchestra sound track.*

EXT. POND SITE. MORNING

YOUNGER BROTHER *stands down the slope from Firehouse Lane beside the pond. He is gazing at the Model T, which sits with its front end in the tall weeds at the edge of the pond. The wheels are sunk in the mud. The headlamps and the windshield are shattered. The rear tires are flattened. The tufted upholstery has been gutted and the custom top has been slashed to ribbons.*

Ragtime: A Screenplay

YOUNGER BROTHER *stares at the ravaged machine. We hear the lapping of the pond water against the front fenders.*

INT.   HARLEM LAW OFFICE. DAY

COALHOUSE *and a* BLACK ATTORNEY, *a grey-haired man, sit across the desk from each other. The* ATTORNEY's *office is modest and the furniture old.*

COALHOUSE   Every attorney I spoke to up there told me to forget the matter. I found out from one of them that the fire chief, Willie Conklin, is a stepbrother of the judge of the city court and a nephew of a county alderman in White Plains.

ATTORNEY   Well, Mr. Walker. There are ways to divert the case to other jurisdictions, but they're time-consuming and expensive and you don't know what the outcome would be. Do you have the money for that?

COALHOUSE   I am soon to be married.

ATTORNEY   That is an expensive proposition. Surely your responsibility to your intended is more important than your need to redress a slight on the part of white folks.

COALHOUSE *looks for a moment at his hands.*

COALHOUSE   I didn't suppose they let you hang your shingle up without knowing you was safe.

ATTORNEY   *(standing)* Mr. Walker, I'll thank you to leave. I have charity cases you know nothing of. I want justice for our people so bad I can taste it. But if you think I would go to Westchester County to plead on a colored man's behalf that someone deposited a bucket of slops in his car you are very much mistaken.

INT.   NEW ROCHELLE ATTORNEY'S OFFICE. DAY

Here FATHER *and a* WHITE ATTORNEY *sit across a desk from each other.*

WHITE ATTORNEY   I'll have the papers for you by the end of the week.

FATHER   *(standing)* Fine. *(He goes to door.)* Oh, there's one other matter.

WHITE ATTORNEY   The colored man?

FATHER   Yes.

WHITE ATTORNEY   You don't need me for that. When a property owner in this city walks into court with a Negro they usually dismiss the charge.

FATHER   But he's not interested in the charge. He wants to sue.

The attorney's SECRETARY *at this moment comes through the open door past* FATHER *with some papers in her hand.*

WHITE ATTORNEY   *(Smiling, he accepts the papers, his mind already diverted.)* Glad to be of help.

INT.   BROADVIEW AVENUE HOUSE. DINING ROOM. EVENING

FAMILY *is at the evening meal.* SARAH *is serving.*

FATHER   It is such a foolish thing to have happened. *(to* SARAH*)* Your fiancé would have done better after all to drive away his car when he could and forget the matter. Now it's rotting away down there by the firehouse. Of what use is that?

YOUNGER BROTHER   *(angry, to* FATHER*)* You speak like a man who has never been tested in his principles.

The two men begin arguing. SARAH *drops a serving tray. She runs out of the room sobbing.* MOTHER *quickly follows her.* FATHER *stands, flings his napkin on the table and storms out to the parlor.* GRANDFATHER *remains the only person eating.*

INT.   CITY CLERK'S OFFICE. DAY

COALHOUSE *stands at the counter behind which an impatient* CLERK *attempts to dismiss him.* CLERK *is in shirt-sleeves with sleeve garters, cuff guards, and a green eyeshade. He is white.*

CLERK   This is something that a lawyer attends to. Who is your lawyer?

COALHOUSE   I'm acting as my own attorney. I have filed a complaint and would like to know how to go about getting a place on the court calendar.

CLERK   *(sighing)* This is a busy office and today is a busy day. Why don't you come back when things aren't so hectic?

COALHOUSE *looks around the office. He is the only visitor, and the two or three people at their desks seem barely alive.*

COALHOUSE   I'd like to know, please, what steps have to be taken in order for me to get a hearing.

CLERK   Your complaint isn't on file. We'll need several weeks to trace it. Come back then.

COALHOUSE   I think it would be quicker to simply write out another complaint.

CLERK   Do as you wish. Right down the hall. But I'll tell you something: you might as well take it easy on yourself.

COALHOUSE   Why is that?

CLERK   *(blandly)* Well, the Volunteer Fire Companies are not municipal employees. So, you see, they don't come under the jurisdiction of the city.

EXT.   FRONT PORCH, BROADVIEW AVENUE HOUSE. DAY

FATHER   I can't even sit in my own parlor when I want to.

MOTHER   Oh, tush. It's very lovely out here this afternoon. Why should you want to sit in a stuffy old house?

FATHER   *(restless, begins to pace)* Are we to go on entertaining Coalhouse Walker every Sunday for the rest of my life?

MOTHER   I wish instead of grumbling you would come to a decision about the Republican Victory dinner this evening.

FATHER   Well, I bought the tickets.

MOTHER   And so we are going?

FATHER   I think not. If it were Mr. Taft himself the evening would be bearable, but it's Vice-President Sherman, Sunny Jim, and I've been listening to that hack since Hector was a pup.

Ragtime: A Screenplay

INT. PARLOR. DAY

COALHOUSE *and* SARAH *sit together on the sofa.* SARAH *is again dressed in her Sunday clothes.*

COALHOUSE   I saved my money to buy that automobile. Just as I've been saving for our marriage. Everything I have, the shoes on my feet, the clothes I wear, I earned with my labor.

SARAH *says nothing. Gazes at her hands in her lap.*

But beyond that. If I do as you ask, if I accept what has been done to me, how can I offer you and my son the strength and shelter of my manhood? There will be none left.

SARAH   It don't mean nothin' if you don't want it to.

COALHOUSE   That's true, Miss Sarah. *(He stands.)* And if you don't care what man you marry, go down there to coon-town and you can find a dozen.

He puts on his straw boater and leaves without another word.

EXT. PORCH. DAY

COALHOUSE *comes out the front door, tips his hat, walks down the steps, and goes off down the street. As* MOTHER *and* FATHER *are reacting, the front door opens again and the* LITTLE BOY *steps out.*

BOY   Sarah's crying.

INT. HALL. DAY

MOTHER *is coming down the stairs from* SARAH'S *room.* FATHER *meets her at the foot of the stairs.*

MOTHER   Coalhouse has told her that they cannot marry until his car's been returned to him in its original condition.

FATHER *throws up his arms.*

FATHER   That's it! I'm fed up! It's ridiculous to allow a motorcar to take over our lives. Tomorrow morning I'm going to the firehouse.

MOTHER   What will you do?

FATHER   I will make them see that they are dealing not with Coalhouse
Walker but with a property owner in this city. And if that doesn't work I
will quite simply bribe them to repair the car and return it to my door. I'll
pay the money. I'll buy them off.

MOTHER   Mr. Walker would not like that.

FATHER   Nevertheless that's what I'm going to do. Just to have an end to
this! Those volunteers are the town dregs. They'll respect money.

INT.   SARAH'S ROOM. NIGHT

SARAH *has rocked the* BABY *to sleep. She tucks a light covering over him and gets
a shawl from the closet. She opens the room door and listens.*

INT.   STAIRWELL. NIGHT

*She steps out into the hall and closes the door quietly. She walks down the stairs
so as not to make a sound. She is wearing her Sunday clothes but her feet are
bare. As she passes the second floor landing and continues down, the door to the*
LITTLE BOY'S *room is open and he peeks out.*

INT.   FRONT HALL. NIGHT

SARAH *stands at the foot of the stairs. The sound of* MOTHER'S *and* FATHER'S
voices can be heard from the parlor.
    SARAH *goes back along the hall into the kitchen.*

INT.   KITCHEN. NIGHT

SARAH *puts a shawl over her head and steps out the back door and closes the
door quietly behind her.*

EXT.   BROADVIEW AVENUE. NIGHT

SARAH *is running down Broadview Avenue. She runs as swiftly as a child. Dark
night clouds pass over the moon and we see* SARAH *as a shadow going down the
street as fast as she can.*

EXT.   NORTH AVENUE INTERSECTION. NIGHT

SARAH *is running across this main thoroughfare just as a trolley car comes along, its interior lights flickering in the night. She runs in front of the streetcar just before the driver stops. She pays the fare and the streetcar goes off tolling its bell.*

EXT.   NEW ROCHELLE. TIDEWATERS HOTEL. NIGHT

A small crowd, which includes SARAH, *is on hand to watch the fancy cars drive up for the Republican victory dinner. A stir in the crowd as a Panhard auto-mobile comes to the curb and* MILITIAMEN *snap to attention as the local* POLICE *open the door and welcome the* VICE-PRESIDENT, SUNNY JIM SHERMAN. *He is a short bald man and he comes out of the car to smile and wave at the crowd.*

At this moment, in great agitation, SARAH *begins to push through the people around her.*

SARAH   President! President!

She breaks through the lines and runs toward the VICE-PRESIDENT *with arm outstretched. The* MILITIAMEN, *seeing the advancing black woman with her hand extended, step in front of the* VICE-PRESIDENT, *who instinctively has backed away, and one of them butts* SARAH's *chest with his Springfield rifle. She falls. Two of the policemen fall on top of her. In the confusion the* VICE-PRESIDENT *is hustled into the hotel.*

The police begin to disperse the alarmed crowd and a police van, its bell tolling, comes into the scene.

INT.   POLICE VAN. NIGHT

The door is opened and SARAH, *half-conscious, is unceremoniously thrown to the floor of the van. She moans and the light picks up her face of pain.*

SARAH   *(mumbling)* President. President.

INT.   NEW ROCHELLE HOSPITAL CORRIDOR. NIGHT

MOTHER *and* YOUNGER BROTHER *sit on a bench outside a closed door. A* POLICEMAN *lounges against the door jamb. A* POLICE SERGEANT *arrives.*

SERGEANT   (*to* POLICE GUARD) Go on back to the station house. (*to* MOTHER *and* YOUNGER BROTHER) The charge against her has been reduced from attempted assassination to disturbing the peace.

YOUNGER BROTHER   How kind.

SERGEANT   Yes sir. But you have to remember the militiamen thought she had a gun in her hand. Everywhere anarchists are walking up to people and shooting them. They shot President McKinley. They shot Mayor Gaynor. We still don't know what she thought she was doing.

YOUNGER BROTHER   She was petitioning the United States.

A DOCTOR *comes out of the room.*

DOCTOR   (*to* MOTHER) Her sternum was crushed. She has incurred several rib fractures. It appears as if one of her lungs is punctured.

MOTHER   Oh my God.

DOCTOR   She's in the gravest condition. If a pneumonia develops I don't hold out much hope.

INT.   HOSPITAL ROOM. NIGHT

SARAH *lies asleep in her bed. Her breath is raspy and a bubble of blood on the corner of her mouth inflates and deflates with each breath. Sitting beside the bed with his head bowed is* COALHOUSE WALKER. *His shoulders heave: the sepulchral sounds of a grown man's grief.*

EXT.   CEMETERY. DAY

The camera finds the BLACK MOURNERS *in a small section inside ceremonial lodge gates, the scrollwork of which says* NEGRO MUSICIANS BENEVOLENT ASSOCIATION.

At the graveside a PREACHER *with his Bible.* MOURNERS, *with cornets, trombone, clarinet, and bass drum, play a mournful slow drag.*

COALHOUSE WALKER *stares into the grave. Behind him, negro men in tightly buttoned dark suits.* WOMEN *in dresses that come to the tops of their shoes, wide-brimmed hats, and small furs over their shoulders.*

The camera shocks us with a spattering of white faces: MOTHER, FATHER, YOUNGER BROTHER, *and the* BOY.

EXT.   ANOTHER CEMETERY. DAY

The headstones here grander and more elaborate. It is a cemetery for white people and we see just one figure, a man on his knees, beside a well-tended grave: HARRY HOUDINI. *He is weeping and piling small stones and pebbles in the form of a pyramid at the graveside. Behind him stands his patient manager,* JACK.

He sobs and sinks to his knees and lays across the grave. JACK *sighs.*

INT.   VAUDEVILLE STAGE

HOUDINI *is doing his act. In this and all future sequences of* HOUDINI *performing there should be a rising level of intensity.*

Here we see coins pouring from his fingers and doves appearing to fly from his ears. Shots of the audience applauding. He slips into a packing case that is nailed shut and tied with a stout rope. The orchestra plays suspense music. TWO BURLY MEN *come out in full view of the audience with great axes and begin to smash the packing case to bits. People scream. One man comes running down the aisle shouting Stop! Stop! He leaps up on the stage. It is* HOUDINI *himself. The audience goes wild.*

INT.   BACKSTAGE. NIGHT

HARRY *comes into the wings. The sounds of applause behind him. He is sweating profusely and terribly preoccupied. He rushes past* JACK *and two or three of the* REPORTERS *standing there.*

FIRST REPORTER   What's the matter? He doesn't talk to us anymore.

JACK   I don't know. I don't know. He scares me.

SECOND REPORTER   What do you mean?

JACK   Well, you saw. He's supposed to do two or three major tricks in a show. He's doing six or eight.

THIRD REPORTER   He's never been better. Where are you tomorrow?

JACK   At the Pantages. In New Rochelle.

INT.   STAGE

HOUDINI *is doing his famous milk can escape; he is handcuffed and his ankles are padlocked, he is submerged in a forty-quart milk can filled with water. A drape on a wheeled frame is placed in front of the can. Suspense music. Shots of audience agitation as music mounts in intensity. Finally the drape is pulled away and there is* HOUDINI *thoroughly soaked standing by the milk can holding the padlocks and handcuffs over his head. The audience applauds as much in relief as delight. We see the physical strain on* HOUDINI's *face. He is panting heavily.*

INT.   BACKSTAGE. NIGHT

HOUDINI *comes into the wings as the music plays.* JACK *is with him. Five or six* REPORTERS *in background.*

JACK   Harry, tonight do me a favor and go easy. (*indicating* REPORTERS) They're waiting for something to happen to you.

HOUDINI *rubs his forehead. He is exhausted and distracted. He waits for the next cue as onstage a line of chorus girls dance to some bright music.*

HOUDINI   What town is this?

JACK   New Rochelle, Harry.

HOUDINI   New Rochelle. I once looked for a house here. I was going to buy a house for my Mama in New Rochelle.

EXT.   NEW ROCHELLE. FIREHOUSE LANE. NIGHT

A large black touring car turning onto Firehouse Lane. It comes abreast of the Emerald Isle Engine Company and pulls off the road across the way into the field. The motor goes off. The car has been traveling without lights.

INT. EMERALD ISLE FIREHOUSE. NIGHT

The grey horses are in their stalls. The steam pumper beside them ready for fast hitching. One of the VOLUNTEERS *tends a small coal fire under the big brass boiler. Four other volunteers are sitting in a corner playing poker. They are smoking, drinking beer, and having a good time.*

EXT. FIREHOUSE LANE. NIGHT

The door on the far side of the touring car opens and we see MEN *in derbies emerging but we can't see them clearly.*

INT. NEW ROCHELLE THEATER

HOUDINI *onstage is telling a rapt audience that his next trick requires such concentration and such an expense of his physical energies that it is quite dangerous. He asks for their hopes and best wishes. Points to the* CONDUCTOR *in the pit and the music for the trick begins.*

EXT. FIREHOUSE LANE. NIGHT

The SHADOWY FIGURES *hovering around the car are carrying weapons. One runs to a tree and takes position there. Another comes and kneels beside the bumper of the car. Across the street the glass panes of the firehouse doors are glowing with the interior lights.*

INT. NEW ROCHELLE THEATER

As the suspense music plays HOUDINI *appears to be levitating, standing with his eyes closed and his arms tightly at his sides at least six inches above the stage. The audience is standing open-mouthed. A child begins to cry.*

EXT. FIREHOUSE LANE. NIGHT

A figure emerges from the back of the touring car and stands for a moment on the running board with no thought of concealment. The camera closes on this figure: COALHOUSE WALKER JR. *He stares directly across the road at the firehouse.*

Ragtime: A Screenplay

INT. NEW ROCHELLE THEATER

An ASSISTANT *passes his arm under* HOUDINI's *feet and over his head to show that he is indeed unsupported. A moment later* HOUDINI *collapses on the stage. The audience stands with a gasp.* HOUDINI *is helped to his feet and there is a rush of applause but the audience is quite anxious now, and a current of distraction and worry runs through it.*

EXT. FIREHOUSE LANE. NIGHT

COALHOUSE WALKER *takes a pocket watch from his vest and checks the time by the light, striking a wooden match on the sole of his shoe and crouching as he holds the match to the watch face. He quickly blows out the light.*

INT. STAGE

HOUDINI, *wearing only his swim trunks, is lying in a glass coffin, entirely visible. On his chest is a small candle, the flame flickering. The flame goes out, indicating there is no more oxygen in the airtight glass tank. An* ASSISTANT *holding a watch begins to announce the number of minutes in which* HOUDINI *has been in there. "One minute!" He calls. The orchestra plays. Back to the assistant on stage. "Two minutes!" he calls.*

INT. EMERALD ISLE FIREHOUSE. NIGHT

The phone begins to ring and the VOLUNTEER *who's been tending the boiler runs to it. It is an old-fashioned wall phone, and as he picks it up the* CARD PLAYERS *look up from their game.*

INT. NEW ROCHELLE THEATER

"Four minutes!" the ASSISTANT *shouts as* HOUDINI *lies in his coffin. A* WOMAN *in the audience rushes her* CHILDREN *out of the theater.* MEN *are shouting to stage personnel to let* HOUDINI *out. Some people close their eyes and put their hands over their ears. Finally the* ASSISTANTS *lift off the fitted top of the glass coffin.*

    HOUDINI *is helped to his feet somewhat dazed. He is glistening with sweat, his hair is in spirals.*

The VOLUNTEERS *are efficiently hitching the horses to the steam pumper, grabbing their firehats and jackets. One of the men opens the great double doors of the firehouse. A* DRIVER *gets up behind the horses and grabs the reins.*

EXT.   FIREHOUSE LANE. NIGHT

The light coming through the open doors picks up the THREE BLACK-DERBIED FIGURES, *including* COALHOUSE WALKER, *as they raise shotguns to their shoulders, standing beside the dark car like a firing squad.*

INT.   NEW ROCHELLE THEATER

The AUDIENCE *is standing and silent. A* CLERGYMAN *in a clerical collar calls out.*

CLERGYMAN   Houdini, you are experimenting with damnation!

A number of people are so agitated by the display they have seen that they begin to leave the theater. HOUDINI, *realizing that his trick has backfired, holds his hands up.*

HOUDINI   Ladies and Gentlemen! Please forgive me! My feats look far more dangerous than they really are! I practice an ancient eastern breathing regimen.

EXT.   FIREHOUSE LANE. NIGHT

The team of horses gallops out of the firehouse. The FIREMEN *swinging aboard are met by the booming guns of the assassins. Two of the horses go down, the third is pulled over on its back, and the engine, pulled awry by the panicked horses, topples over on its side, crushing one of the* VOLUNTEERS. *The steam boiler makes a terrible clang in the street. The fire box under the boiler is scattered and flaming coals ignite the clapboard firehouse.*
 One of the VOLUNTEERS *has somehow escaped injury but his clothes are on fire, and as he begins to crawl in the road* COALHOUSE WALKER *runs over to him and beats out the flames. Then he kneels down gazing at the terrified fireman.*

COALHOUSE   *(calmly)* Where is Chief Conklin?

The VOLUNTEER *is too terrified to speak.*

See who I am?

The VOLUNTEER *manages to nod yes.*

You tell Chief Conklin who came looking for him.

EXT.   FIREHOUSE LANE. NIGHT

COALHOUSE *and his* MEN *calmly get into their car and drive off leaving carnage, dead horses and moaning men. The fire is now raging in the Emerald Isle Firehouse as flaming beams and timbers fall over the great capsized steam boiler.*

INT.   NEW ROCHELLE THEATER

HOUDINI *is trying to reclaim his audience.*

HOUDINI   Ladies and Gentlemen, please! These are just tricks! Illusions of the stage!

At this moment there is a thud of a dull, distant explosion of such force that the theater shakes on its foundations, and chunks of plaster fall from the proscenium arch. The audience, thinking this to be another of HOUDINI's *tricks, begins to leave en masse and runs up the aisles.*

INT.   BROADVIEW AVENUE HOUSE. MOTHER AND FATHER'S BEDROOM. NIGHT

FATHER *is hurriedly getting out of bed.*

FATHER   What was that!

He runs to the bedrooom window. There is a bright red glow on the horizon.

My God.

MOTHER   *(getting out of bed, pulling on her robe)* What is it?

FATHER   It's the factory. It must be the factory.

MOTHER   *(coming to window)* No. It's not in that direction. But it's something—something awful.

EXT.   FIREHOUSE LANE. DAY

Municipal FIREMEN *are poking around the smoking ruins of the Emerald Isle station. New Rochelle* POLICE *keep a crowd at bay behind ropes.* REPORTERS *we saw watching* HARRY HOUDINI *from the wings are on the scene. The* POLICE CHIEF *in pantomime reconstructing the crime for the reporters.*

A well-dressed man walking on the edges of the onlooking crowd is FATHER. *He strolls down the sloping field to the pond and looks in the water.* COALHOUSE WALKER's *Model T Ford is completely submerged and it looks more like a sunken cathedral, shimmering and undulating in the refraction of the water.*

INT.   BROADVIEW AVENUE HOUSE. DINING ROOM. EVENING

At the bare dining-room table, FATHER *holds an old army pistol from the Philippine campaign. He is cleaning and oiling it.* MOTHER *sits numbly holding the brown* BABY. YOUNGER BROTHER *is slumped in his chair. The local newspaper is spread in the middle of the table. The headline is* NEGROES KILL FIVE.

FATHER   *(to* MOTHER*)* We are suffering a tragedy that should not have been ours. What in God's name possessed you on that day? The county has facilities for indigents. You took her in without sufficient thought. You victimized us all with your foolish female sentimentality.

Tears spring from MOTHER's *eyes.*

YOUNGER BROTHER   Are you going out to find him and shoot him?

FATHER   I'm going to protect my home. This is his child here. If he makes the mistake of coming here to my door I will deal with him.

YOUNGER BROTHER   *(drily)* But why should he come here? We did not desecrate his car.

FATHER   In the morning I will go to the police and have to tell them this murdering madman was a guest in my home. I will have to tell them we are keeping his bastard child.

YOUNGER BROTHER   I think Coalhouse Walker Jr. would want you to tell the police everything you know. You can tell them he's the same Negro maniac whose car is lying at the bottom of Firehouse Pond. You can tell them he's the fellow who visited their own headquarters to make a complaint against Willie Conklin and his thugs. You can tell them he's the same crazed killer who sat by the bedside of someone who died in the hospital of her injuries.

FATHER   *(voice rising)* I hope I misunderstand you. Would you defend this savage? Does he have anyone but himself to blame for Sarah's death? Anything but his damnable nigger pride? Nothing under heaven can excuse the killing of men and the destruction of property in this manner!

YOUNGER BROTHER *stands abruptly knocking his chair over.*

YOUNGER BROTHER   *(trembling)* I did not hear such a eulogy at Sarah's funeral. I did not hear you say then that death and the destruction of property was inexcusable.

INT.   NEW ROCHELLE. OFFICE OF THE POLICE CHIEF. DAY

Sense of emergency as the POLICE CHIEF, *the* MAYOR, WILLIE CONKLIN, *and several* OFFICERS *group around* FATHER.

POLICE CHIEF   *(to* FATHER*)* But we know who he is. We received a letter from him this morning. So did the newspapers. His name is Coalhouse Walker Jr. Some grievance about a car.

FATHER   Yes. That's it.

MAYOR   *(a nervous individual)* And while we sit here he's still on the loose!

POLICE CHIEF   Please Mr. Mayor. *(to* FATHER*)* We're searching the Negro quarter. The police in Pelham and Mount Vernon are going through their Negro quarters. *(to* FATHER*)* But I don't think he's a local.

FATHER   Definitely not. He was a musician. A pianist. He lived in New York.

MAYOR   You say he worked for you?

FATHER   No. No. His fiancée was in our service.

POLICE CHIEF   He says if we don't restore his car and turn Willie Conklin over to him he's going to make another raid. Would he?

FATHER   The man is nothing if not persevering.

CONKLIN   I'm not leaving this station house. That coon is going to get us all!

POLICE CHIEF   (*to* CONKLIN) It would have been our great good fortune had he gotten you last night, you dumb son of a bitch.

CONKLIN   Oh, for Christ's sake! (*He turns from the* POLICE CHIEF *to a couple of the senior* OFFICERS *standing there.*) Pat! . . . Tommy! . . . For Godsake! I've got a wife and kids! You're not gonna desert me now!

POLICE CHIEF   (*to his* MEN) I don't care where you put him, but get him out of my hair.

CONKLIN *is escorted out.* POLICE CHIEF *goes to a wall map of New Rochelle.*

We'll put twenty-four-hour patrol on every street leading into town. We'll put two men on watch at every firehouse.

MAYOR   Is that enough?

POLICE CHIEF   For a start. (*to one of the* OFFICERS) I want to talk to the Chief of Detectives in New York City. Could you find out who that is and get them on the phone?

EXT.   MANHATTAN CASINO ON EIGHTH AVENUE. NIGHT

Showbills in glass cases advertise the Jim Europe Clef Club Orchestra. PEOPLE *arriving for the evening show. Sound of traffic.*

Separate from the crowd are THREE WHITE MEN *talking to* THEATER OFFI-CIALS, *who are black and who are shaking their heads and appear to disclaim any connection with what the* WHITE MEN *are asking. The* WHITE MEN *leave and get into cars at the curb and drive off.*

At this point the camera finds YOUNGER BROTHER *standing under the mar-quee observing all. Just before the* TWO BLACK MEN *go into the lobby he approaches them and the glass doors close on all three in the lobby. In pan-tomime we understand that* YOUNGER BROTHER *is having difficulty persuad-ing them of whatever it is he wants.*

We see him take a letter out of his breast pocket and hand it to one of the men.
At this moment the Eighth Avenue el is heard. It overwhelms the scene in a
great rushing sound.

EXT.   MANHATTAN CASINO. NIGHT (LATER)

The glass doors are open and we hear the syncopated music of the Clef Club
Orchestra merging with the street sounds of horns and so on. Two New York
City POLICEMEN *are standing near the entrance, leaning idly against one of the*
showbill cases.

A YOUNG NEGRO MAN *in a correct black suit and tie and bowler hat comes*
down the street, passes the two POLICEMEN. *He ignores them and shoots a*
glance at YOUNGER BROTHER, *who is standing nearby.* YOUNG MAN *keeps*
walking. YOUNGER BROTHER *makes no move for a moment, then idly, as if he*
had nothing better to do, he strolls slowly after the YOUNG BLACK MAN. *The two*
policemen are oblivious to this.

EXT.   ANOTHER HARLEM STREET. NIGHT

YOUNGER BROTHER *comes around the corner. The street is empty of pedestrians.*
YOUNGER BROTHER *hurries on, coming abreast of a large black touring car*
parked at the curb corner. The door opens and another YOUNG MAN *dressed*
identically to the first steps out and holds the front door open and gestures to him.
YOUNGER BROTHER *gets in. Doors close, gears are engaged. The car drives off.*

INT.   DINGY BASEMENT HALLWAY. NIGHT

YOUNGER BROTHER *and his* TWO ESCORTS *come down this hall to a door. One*
of the young men opens it and YOUNGER BROTHER *walks inside.*

INT.   BASEMENT ROOM. NIGHT

In a room otherwise bare of furniture COALHOUSE WALKER *sits at a bare table*
under an electric light bulb. The two YOUNG BLACK MEN *are standing behind*
him and a third takes his place just inside the front door. Like COALHOUSE *they*
are all well dressed, in dark suits, collars, and ties. COALHOUSE *sits with his*
arms folded and looks at YOUNGER BROTHER.

COALHOUSE   What is it you want?

YOUNGER BROTHER *is very nervous at this moment. Once or twice he starts to say something, some kind of general statement he might have prepared, but when he finally says something he blurts it out almost surprising himself.*

YOUNGER BROTHER   I know how to make bombs. I know how to blow things up.

INT.   NEW ROCHELLE POLICE STATION. NIGHT

In front of the raised SERGEANT's *desk* PEOPLE *are going back and forth busily. On a bench along the side of the room sits* WILLIE CONKLIN. *His florid face is now the color of veal, and when he thinks no one is looking he stands facing the wall and takes a swig of whiskey from a bottle in a paper bag. A couple of* POLICE OFFICERS *are standing nearby.*

CONKLIN   (*to* OFFICERS) What we ought to do is go down there to coon-town and clean out all the niggers once and for all.

FIRST OFFICER   Well, that's an idea. (*to* FELLOW OFFICER) Of course the simplest thing would be to turn Willie over to the boogie-man. A small enough price to pay to get some peace around here.

SECOND OFFICER   A good thought. Do you think we ought to take it to the Mayor?

CONKLIN   (*unable to bear the teasing*) God love you. You were cruel lads at St. Catherine's and yer cruel now. Are we not in this together? Do we not face this danger together?

FIRST OFFICER   Willie, we had to hear from the black man himself that one of your shenanigans was what started this, you dumb Mick . . . telling us now we're in this together.

At this moment FATHER *comes out of an inner office.* CONKLIN *spots him and goes over to him.*

CONKLIN   It's a tragic thing, Captain, a tragic thing indeed.

He puts his hand on FATHER's *shoulder.* FATHER *is shocked. He shakes* CONKLIN's *hand off, puts his derby firmly on his head, and walks out the door.*

Ragtime: A Screenplay

We're at the funeral of the five dead volunteer firemen. All the city officials are here: POLICEMEN *and* FIREMEN *in their uniforms and white gloves.* REPORTERS.

A PRIEST *incants over five open graves.* WIDOWS *and* CHILDREN *are crying bitterly. It is a scene of genuine grief and mourning. Off to the side the* POLICE CHIEF *is giving an interview to several reporters.*

REPORTER   Where's Conklin?

POLICE CHIEF   We have him under guard. We don't want him here. If that maniac were to come after him in a crowd—well, you can imagine.

SECOND REPORTER   What steps are being taken to resolve this crisis?

POLICE CHIEF   You must be from the *Times*.

REPORTER   You gonna try talking to this Coalhouse Walker?

POLICE CHIEF   Look at those widows and children over there. Five upstanding family men dead and you want me to talk to some maniac coon about his car? What would I tell those widows? What would I say to those children?

INT.   FLAG AND FIREWORKS FACTORY. DAY

FATHER *is seen entering with a troubled expression, waving away his* FOREMAN, *telling him he can't be bothered at the moment.* FATHER *goes into his office and slams the door.*

Down the aisle between the rows of sewing machines and workers stand two men, the ASSISTANT FOREMAN *and a* WAREHOUSE MAN.

WAREHOUSE MAN   He don't look too happy.

ASSISTANT FOREMAN   Look, what did you say is missing?

WAREHOUSE MAN   I ain't even sure. Two ten-pound sacks of sulphur, a keg of gun cotton, and a fifty-foot wheel of fuse line.

ASSISTANT FOREMAN   He's got too much on his mind as it is. Just flag it on the monthly inventory and it'll get to his desk.

EXT.   NEW ROCHELLE. COBBLESTONE STREET. DAWN

A large automobile is coming down the dark street. It is running without lights. The car comes abreast of Municipal Fire Station Number Two. The car comes to a stop across the street from the fire station.

EXT.   MUNICIPAL FIRE STATION NUMBER TWO. DAWN

TWO POLICEMEN *are standing sleepily before the doors. They look at the car and are astounded to see* SEVERAL BLACK MEN *disembark holding shotguns and rifles. One of the* POLICEMEN *has the presence of mind to drop to the ground. The other stands hypnotized as the black men stand formally, like a firing squad and upon signal, fire in unison. The blast kills standing* POLICE-MAN *and shatters the window panes of the firehouse doors.*

One of the raiders runs up to the door and tosses several small packages through the broken windows. COALHOUSE *calmly comes to the terrified* PO-LICEMAN *on the sidewalk and places a letter in his hand.*

COALHOUSE   This is to be published in the newspapers.

COALHOUSE *joins the others, who get back into the car. The car moves off down the street. By the time it reaches the corner and disappears three explosions, coming one on top of another, blow out the doors of the Municipal Firehouse and instantly turn it into an inferno.*

INT.   POLICE CHIEF'S OFFICE. DAY

The office is packed with NEWSPAPERMEN, POLICE OFFICERS, *etc. The* POLICE CHIEF *is standing behind his desk emptying the drawers and filling a small overnight bag with the personal accouterments of his office: paperweights, pen and ink stand, etc. The* CHIEF *has a cigar in his mouth.*

CHIEF   The man uses automobiles to get around. He strikes and disappears God knows where. For several years the Association of Police Chiefs of the State of New York has passed a resolution calling for the licensing of automobiles and automobilists. If that were the law today we could track the brute down.

His desk cleaned out, the POLICE CHIEF *snaps his valise shut, takes his derby off the hatrack, and walks out through the reporters.*

Ragtime: A Screenplay

INT.   CITY HALL LOBBY. DAY

MAYOR *surrounded by angry citizens including* UNIFORMED FIREMEN. *Lots of shouting, panic. To a group of angry mothers the* MAYOR *says go home and lock the doors. Schools are closed. Several uniformed firemen are demanding to be sworn in as police deputies and be given arms to defend themselves.*

REPORTERS *join this swirling crowd and call on the* MAYOR *for a statement. He announces that he has telegraphed the* GOVERNOR *and requested that units of the State Militia be sent to the city.*

EXT.   MODEST WOODEN HOUSE. DAY

A BLACK MOTHER *is pulling her* CHILDREN *off the porch and rushing them in the house. She slams the door and pulls the shade down. Down the street can be seen two or three* WHITE TOUGHS *looking for action.*

MONTAGE: NEWSPAPERS COMING OFF PRESSES

The headlines vary: RAGTIME KILLER GETS SEVEN, COMMUNITY IN TERROR, GOVERNOR SENDS TROOPS, *etc. Each newspaper comes off the press at a different angle. In the* St. Louis Post Dispatch *is an exclusive picture of the killer sitting at a piano in tails and white tie, smiling, obviously from earlier days.*

EXT.   NEW ROCHELLE STREET. DAY

State MILITIAMEN *armed, standing in the backs of open Reo trucks as they patrol the streets.*

EXT.   BROADVIEW AVENUE. DAY

Two MILITIAMEN *lounge in front of the house. A car pulls up in front and a* RE-PORTER *jumps out. A minute later another car pulls up with more* REPORTERS.

INT.   BROADVIEW AVENUE HOUSE. DAY

In the front hall MOTHER *holding the brown* BABY *refused to answer the knocking at the front door.* LITTLE BOY *looks at her expectantly and she puts her hand on his shoulder.*

EXT.   BROADVIEW AVENUE. DAY

Several REPORTERS *are now camped on the front porch. They peek through the windows, smoke cigarettes, and crush them under their heels.*

EXT.   REAR OF BROADVIEW AVENUE HOUSE. DAY

A REPORTER *and a* PHOTOGRAPHER *come around to the kitchen door, surreptitiously peek in, and see* MOTHER *and the brown* BABY.

INT.   BROADVIEW AVENUE HOUSE, KITCHEN. DAY

MOTHER *gasps as the door flies open and a* PHOTOGRAPHER *comes in and shoots her picture in a great flash of light.* REPORTER *yelling: "Get it! Get it quick!"*

EXT.   DOWNTOWN NEW ROCHELLE CORNER. DAY

NEWSBOY *shouting "Wuxtry! Wuxtry!"* PEOPLE *are buying the papers at a good clip. We look over one man's shoulder. Headline reads:* WHITE FAMILY HARBORS KILLER'S SON! *and underneath the headline is the picture of* MOTHER *holding the baby.*

EXT.   BROADVIEW AVENUE. EVENING

A steady stream of sight-seeing cars slowly driving past the house, perhaps just staring and pointing.

INT.   BROADVIEW AVENUE HOUSE. GRANDFATHER'S BEDROOM. DAY

Here everyone in the family is gathered except YOUNGER BROTHER. *The most agitated is* MOTHER, *who paces up and down. Uncharacteristically, she is not fully dressed but wears a robe. Her hair is undone and comes to her shoulders. She is clutching the brown* BABY. *She is gaunt and verging on hysteria.* FATHER *stands by the window dressed for work. His hands are behind his back.* GRANDFATHER *is propped up on his pillows looking weak and pale, with his alert eyes taking in everything. The* BOY *stands by* GRANDFATHER's *bed.*

Ragtime: A Screenplay

MOTHER   You know what's going to happen, don't you? They're going to revenge themselves on the infant. They're going to take him away from me and put him in an orphan home.

FATHER   Please calm yourself. I don't think . . .

MOTHER   You don't think, you don't think. You go off to the office or down to City Hall and you leave us here cowering in our bedrooms. How long before those horrible reporters break down the doors and the State Militia tears this child from my arms?

GRANDFATHER   We must go away.

FATHER   Go away? Yes. That is clear. But there are problems.

GRANDFATHER   Well, I'm not one of them. I'm about ready to get up anyway. You know where we should go?

BOY   Where, Grandfather?

GRANDFATHER   To Atlantic City. It should be beautiful there now. Yes, that is the answer to everything, Atlantic City.

EXT.   FIREHOUSE POND. DAY

A crowd standing behind police barriers, watching as a crane lifts COALHOUSE WALKER's *Model T Ford from Firehouse Pond. Photographers' flash pans and flash bulbs explode on the scene like lightning. The automobile is brought up out of the water, mud dripping from its tires, slime pouring out of its hood. It is swung over to the bank and deposited on the ground for everybody to see.*

MAYOR   *(voice over, reading)* One: That the white excrescense known as Willie Conklin be turned over to my justice. Two: That the Model T Ford with its custom pantasote top be returned in its original condition. Until these demands are satisfied let the rules of war prevail. Signed, Coalhouse Walker Jr., President, Provisional American Government.

INT.   MAYOR'S OFFICE. NIGHT

The MAYOR *is in his shirt-sleeves. Also present is the* COMMANDER *of the State Militia assigned to the town, a couple of* POLICE OFFICERS, FATHER, *a* BANKER, *and an* ALIENIST *(shrink). All are sitting around a conference table.*

MAYOR   That's how it's signed: 'Coalhouse Walker Jr., President Provisional American Government.' *(He removes his spectacles.)* Well, Gentlemen?

ALIENIST   This letter is much advanced in its signals of mental deterioration. To deal with someone in the throes of a progressive delusionary madness as if he were open to reason would be a tragic mistake.

COLONEL   I agree, Doctor. You negotiate with this nigger and you'll have every coon in the country flouting the law and spitting on the American flag. To say nothing of the Reds.

BANKER   We cannot let New Rochelle become a symbol for the beginning of the end of American Civilization.

MAYOR   I think we're all agreed. But what in hell are we gonna do?

FATHER   *(clearing his throat)* The first thing I should think would be to get Willie Conklin out of town . . . like you'd pick a burr out of your hair.

MAYOR   I can't do that.

POLICE LIEUTENANT   His wife and kids are in New York, Mr. Mayor. They're staying with some relatives in Hell's Kitchen. I'm for sending him down there.

FATHER   We can give a statement to the papers, Mr. Mayor, to this effect: That Willie Conklin is no longer residing in New Rochelle and that Coalhouse Walker may now burn down the entire metropolis of New York or accept the principle that any man who takes the law into his own hands places himself against a civilized and resolute people and defames the very justice he seeks to enforce.

COLONEL   *(admiringly to* FATHER*)* That's good. That's damn good.

MAYOR   We can't look like we're giving in. We already brought up the car— just so the damn papers could take pictures of it.

POLICE LIEUTENANT   *(clearing his throat)* Your Honor, Conklin's own neighbors are ready to do the coon's job for him. There ain't no white man less popular in New Rochelle right now than Willie Conklin.

BANKER   *(leaning forward)* Do it.

EXT. FIREHOUSE POND. DAY

A crowd is behind police cordon. POLICE LIEUTENANT *is talking to a few* REPORTERS.

POLICE LIEUTENANT   The explosives used in the bombing of Municipal Station Number Two was a combination of gun cotton and fulminating mercury. Whoever made those bombs knew his stuff. Now, we know that Coalhouse Walker was a piano player. Piano players don't know that sort of thing. We know he's got help. He's got a gang of colored men all armed. He's got cars. All that costs hard cash. Where does he get his money? Where does he hide out? I know a half dozen Reds I'd like to have in my lock-up. I betcha I'd get some answers then.

The camera inspects the car and the faces of the people looking at it.

INT.   HARLEM. COALHOUSE WALKER'S BASEMENT HIDEOUT. NIGHT

COALHOUSE *and his* MEN *are gathered here.* COALHOUSE *sits on a chair with a towel around his shoulders. His head and moustache are being shaved by one of the* YOUNG MEN. *His expression is impassive. Two of the other* YOUNG MEN *have copies of newspapers, on the front page of which are to be seen pictures of the Model T Ford being raised from the pond and a headline:* FIRE CHIEF FLEES TO NEW YORK.

FIRST YOUNG MAN   Coalhouse gone to Willie's house. Willie be a dead man now. We missed our chance.

·SECOND YOUNG MAN   Naw, Brother. He better to us alive. He keeping Coalhouse in the folk's minds.

The YOUNG MAN *shaving* COALHOUSE *chuckles.*

THIRD YOUNG MAN   He a plague.

SECOND YOUNG MAN   Now we gone do somethin' so terrible bad in this town no one ever mess with a colored man for fear he belong to Coalhouse.

They're all taken with a kind of solemn joy. The barber with a hot towel covers COALHOUSE's *face and head, wiping it clean of soap. When the towel is slowly* removed we see COALHOUSE, *his head shaved, his face hairless, impassive, like some ancient warrior preparing ritualistically for the final battle.*

INT.   ATLANTIC CITY. MOTHER'S HOTEL BEDROOM. DAY

A beautiful early morning light lays upon white-curtained glass doors. MOTHER *comes into the picture in her nightgown, her hair down, and throws open the doors and stands looking at the sun as it rises above the sea.*

INT.   HOTEL DINING ROOM. DAY

The FAMILY *is at breakfast at a table covered with a starched white cloth. The service is heavy hotel silver. Enormous amounts of food: shirred eggs, halves of grapefruit, hotbreads, broiled fish, ham slices, sausage, a variety of preserves, etc.*

Other guests are in the dining room. The camera lingers on a SMALL MAN *dressed dramatically in a white silk shirt open at the neck and riding breeches who sits at a table with a* LITTLE GIRL.

EXT. BOARDWALK. AFTERNOON

The FAMILY *strolling along the boardwalk. The sun is going down and the crowds are out in force.*

MOTHER *holds* FATHER'S *arm. Occasionally* FATHER *tips his straw hat to other strollers.*

Behind MOTHER *and* FATHER, GRANDFATHER *in a wheeled boardwalk chair made of wicker with a fringed canvas top is being pushed by the* BOY. *Occasionally, when* GRANDFATHER *is impatient with the rate of speed, he prods a pedestrian with his cane, calls to clear the way.*

In these shots we should get another glimpse of two of the other hotel guests—the SMALL MAN *in the white shirt with the open neck, jodhpurs, and flat white linen cap seen again with a beautiful dark-haired* LITTLE GIRL.

EXT.   BAND PAVILION. NIGHT

A NEGRO *brass band is playing a rag. The* MUSICIANS *are dressed in red and blue military uniforms with epaulets and braided caps.*

Ragtime: A Screenplay

MOTHER, FATHER, *the* BOY *are in the audience. The music should be one of the same rags played by* COALHOUSE WALKER *on the family piano. Close-ups of* MOTHER *and* FATHER, FATHER *looking troubled and tears streaking* MOTHER'S *cheeks.*

INT. MOTHER'S HOTEL BEDROOM. NIGHT

MOTHER *and* FATHER *are in their robes.* FATHER *is in an amorous mood. He is having trouble communicating this to her.*

FATHER   Are you not having a good time?

MOTHER   Yes. Moments when I think our lives are very fine in the sun and salt air, when it's hard to believe that anything is wrong. Poor Sarah. Poor Coalhouse.

FATHER   I spoke to the office this afternoon.

MOTHER   Has my brother appeared?

FATHER   Briefly.

MOTHER   I used to think that our life was a kind of preparation, that we would lift ourselves out of our existence someday.

FATHER   Preparation for what?

MOTHER   I don't know. Some kind of life of genius. I don't know, but I don't have that feeling anymore. *(She goes to her dressing table, begins to brush her hair.)* I wish my brother were here with us. I feel a passionate admiration for him. I think I've neglected him.

FATHER *loses all hope for the evening and his head bows as he listens to her.*

EXT. HOTEL PORCH. DAY

MOTHER *and the* BOY *are playing on the wicker settee with the brown child.*
    The BOY *is alert to something at the far end of the porch. It is the* SMALL MAN *who dresses always in open-neck shirt and riding pants. He is walking toward them. He holds up to his eyes a rectangular piece of glass framed in metal which is attached to a chain around his neck. He is peering at* MOTHER *through this glass.*

The BOY *sees the dark-haired* LITTLE GIRL *who stands behind her father, not advancing with him, but standing and returning the* BOY's *gaze from a distance.*

At this point MOTHER *notices the attention the man is giving her. Caught in the act he drops the rectangular glass, bows stiffly, and then comes over to her making profuse apologies. His hair is totally black and his little trim beard is black, but we should see at this moment, if we haven't guessed already, that this is* TATEH *in a rejuvenated state.*

TATEH   Forgive me, gracious Madame. I am the Baron Ashkenazy. I am in the moving-picture business and this *(holding up the glass rectangle)* is a tool of the trade which I cannot forbear using even when I am on vacation as I am now with my daughter. *(He turns and summons her from the far end of the porch.)* Come, come! *(to* MOTHER*)* I have looked forward to an introduction to you and your family.

The LITTLE GIRL *advances as* TATEH *chatters.* MOTHER *is clearly charmed by the man. The* LITTLE GIRL *and the* BOY *stare at each other as she comes up along the porch.*

INT.   BASEMENT HIDEOUT. DAY

COALHOUSE's *band is having a meal. The meal should be frugal. There are four* YOUNG MEN *and a fifth,* YOUNGER BROTHER. *All, including* YOUNGER BROTHER, *have shaved heads.* YOUNGER BROTHER *has also shaved his drooping blonde moustaches. He is one of them. As they talk they eat.*

FIRST YOUNG MAN   Finding Willie in Hell's Kitchen ain't gonna be easy.

SECOND YOUNG MAN   Yeah, man. Finding an Irishman in Hell's Kitchen 'bout as easy as findin' Coalhouse in Harlem.

They laugh.

YOUNGER BROTHER   Maybe we shouldn't even try.

COALHOUSE   *(nodding)* Let's hear your thought.

YOUNGER BROTHER   Well, it's one of our two demands, Willie and the car. But tactics that worked in New Rochelle don't necessarily work in New York. The situation has changed. We can't, for instance, start burning down firehouses in New York City.

THIRD YOUNG MAN   That's right. We tire ourselves doin' that.

Everyone laughs.

YOUNGER BROTHER   If Willie is our demand *they've* got to summon him up, not us. *They* . . . Just like they have to return the car as it was.

THIRD YOUNG MAN   We're to the heart of things now. Can't scare four million people by burning down a firehouse. This the big city. Who the big man in New York? Get to him and you'll have Willie Conklin. Then you'll have your car soon enough.

INT.   HOTEL DINING ROOM. EVENING

MOTHER, FATHER, *the* BOY, BARON ASHKENAZY (TATEH), *and his* DAUGHTER *are dining together. There is candlelight. A pianist and a fiddler play dinner music. Both* TATEH *and* FATHER *wear black tie.*

BARON ASHKENAZY   Such good wine. You really know a good wine. That's no small achievement, to know a wine.

FATHER   Thank you.

BARON ASHKENAZY   And see how the candlelight is reflected in the glass and the redness of the wine and how the room for dining glows!

He holds his rectangular glass aloft from MOTHER, FATHER, *and the two* CHILDREN, *framing the room.*

In the movie films we only look at what is there already. Life shines on the shadow screen as from the darkness of one's mind. It is a big business. People want to know what is happening to them. For a few pennies they sit and see their selves in movement, dining, racing in motor cars, fighting, and, forgive me, embracing one another. This is most important today in this country, where everybody is so new. There is such need to understand.

As the BARON *talks* MOTHER *and* FATHER *are spellbound by his incessant chatter, by his excitement for life, by his simple delight in everything.*

BARON ASHKENAZY   (*to* LITTLE GIRL) Eat, eat, my darling. (*to* MOTHER *and* FATHER) She is an orphan on her mother's side. Her mother died some years ago. I have never remarried. How terrible of me. How terrible of the BARON.

The LITTLE GIRL *and the* LITTLE BOY *are sitting next to each other at the table but don't say anything and don't look at one another.* MOTHER *gazes at them, and we can tell from her expression that she finds them incredibly appropriate side by side: her handsome son, his hair combed back, his little man's suit and flowing tie, and beside him this beautiful creature with the darkest eyes and thick black hair and olive complexion.*

INT. BASEMENT HIDEOUT. EVENING

The COALHOUSE BAND *in discussion.*

FIRST YOUNG MAN   How about the Mayor?

SECOND YOUNG MAN   Naw, he no account. No one likes him enough.

THIRD YOUNG MAN   The Governor of New York State.

SECOND YOUNG MAN   Naw, he too well-liked.

FOURTH YOUNG MAN   Gotta have the people interested in what you're doing. Gotta have them say "How about that Coalhouse . . . ain't he somethin'?"

YOUNGER BROTHER   That's exactly it! If we do this thing right there won't be five of us, there'll be five thousand.

COALHOUSE   *(with a smile)* The Provisional American Government seems to be getting larger.

YOUNGER BROTHER   And why not? With an enemy as vast as the white American race the restoration of your automobile is as good a place to start a revolution as any.

FIRST YOUNG MAN   The President?

SECOND YOUNG MAN   Naw, he in Washington.

INT. HOTEL DINING ROOM. EVENING

The dinner continuing.

BARON ASHKENAZY   . . . and so from the movie books I made for the Franklin Novelty Company I discover that others are doing animation drawings like mine own except for projection on celluloid film with a magic lantern. And so I become interested in the celluloid film and what do I find? The images do not even have to be drawn. Light may draw the images! God's light as it touches the film. *(He drinks some wine.)* You have seen of course *His First Mistake?* Not God's. *(He laughs.)* That is the name of my first picture play. No? *A Daughter's Innocence?* *(He laughs.)* Don't embarrass! They are one-reelers. I made them for under five hundred dollars and each has brought ten thousand dollars in receipts. Yes, it's true!

FATHER *is embarrassed by the mention of specific sums. He blushes and coughs.*

BARON ASHKENAZY   No, I tell the truth! It is a good profit but not unusual. Today in the film business, there is no limit. I have become myself a company in purchasing with the Pathe Exchange for a story fifteen reels long! And each reel will be shown one a week and the customer will come back every week to see what next happens.

INT.   BASEMENT HIDEOUT. EVENING

The BAND *are all leaning forward around the table suggesting the excited culmination of their debate.*

FIRST YOUNG MAN   He the richest they got?

YOUNGER BROTHER   My God. He runs a hundred banks. He runs a thousand companies. He owns the ships and the trains and the mines and the steel mills. I'll say he's the richest they got.

SECOND YOUNG MAN   Mighty fine. Then that what Coalhouse do. Take the richest they got with his big cee-gar and his top hat. *(He laughs and claps his hands.)* That worth a million Willie Conklins. That worth a Model T made of gold.

The YOUNG MEN *contemplate the strategy with excitement and laughter. They congratulate each other but then they quiet down and turn expectantly to* COALHOUSE, *who the party realizes has not said a thing. He is leaning back in his chair with his arms folded. He looks at them one by one and nods.*

COALHOUSE   Yes. That's what we'll do.

The YOUNG MEN *cheer and pound each other on the back.*

INT. HOTEL DINING ROOM. EVENING

The BARON *takes a shiny coin from his pocket and flips it into the air. It goes nearly as high as the ceiling. Everyone watches. The* BARON *catches the coin and flattens it under his hand on the table with a loud smack that makes the silver jump. He lifts his hand.*

INSERT: CLOSE-UP ON THE WHITE TABLECLOTH OF A SHINY BUFFALO NICKEL

BARON ASHKENAZY   You don't understand?

FATHER   I'm sorry. I . . .

BARON ASHKENAZY   How I named myself! I am the "Buffalo Nickel Photoplay Incorporated"!

EXT. OCEAN. DAWN

The sun spreads over the sea at dawn.

INT. HOTEL CORRIDOR. DAWN

The LITTLE BOY *comes out of his room and closes the door. He goes down the long corridor looking at the door numbers. At the end of the corridor another door opens and the* LITTLE GIRL *peeks out.*

EXT. GRAND STAIRCASE. DAWN

The TWO CHILDREN *are running together down the carpeted stairs.*

EXT. HOTEL PORCH. DAY

The CHILDREN *are running hand in hand down the wide painted porch steps into the sun.*

Ragtime: A Screenplay

EXT. BEACH. DAY

The BOY *and* GIRL *run in the sand, running for the joy of running and for being with each other. The audience should have some sense that at last they are together as they were meant to be.*

They run and suddenly she stops, drops to her knees, and becomes interested in a shell. After a few steps he turns, sees that she is not following, comes back, hunkers down beside her and looks at what she is looking at. He finds another shell and hands it to her.

INT. COVERED VAN. NIGHT

YOUNGER BROTHER *crouches in the back of a covered van loaded with explosives and supplies. He is in blackface.*

The sound of gunfire and a scream. The van comes to an abrupt halt. Suddenly the back flap is lifted and one of the other YOUNG MEN *sticks his head in.*

YOUNG MAN   Let's go!

YOUNGER BROTHER *begins to unload the supplies.*

EXT. MORGAN LIBRARY. NIGHT

The conspirators' van is up on the sidewalk with its back actually on the stairs leading to the great brass doors. There is a DEAD POLICEMAN *lying on the steps. A whistle blowing in the distance.* COALHOUSE *comes out of the library doors, a carbine in his hands.*

COALHOUSE   Quickly now.

EXT. THIRTY-SIXTH STREET

Lights are going on in houses all up and down the street.

EXT. MORGAN LIBRARY

The YOUNG MEN *carrying the supplies and explosives from the van into the library,* COALHOUSE *covering them.* YOUNGER BROTHER *jumps out of the van, stares at the library doors, reacts.*

YOUNGER BROTHER   *(screaming)* This is wrong! This is the library!

COALHOUSE   Never mind that. Get inside.

YOUNGER BROTHER   It's the wrong building!

He is pulled inside by one of the others.

COALHOUSE   *(shouting)* Get that truck out of here!

INT.   MORGAN LIBRARY. NIGHT

By electric torchlight: the great brass doors are closed and bolted. COALHOUSE
assigns positions to the YOUNG MEN *at various windows. They are all armed.
He sends one man to the roof, pointing to the skylight in the ceiling of the East
Room. He strides through the front hall, the East Room, the West Room.*

   YOUNGER BROTHER *is in the front hall unpacking packs of dynamite and
wheels of fuse.* COALHOUSE *comes back.*

YOUNGER BROTHER   This is his library. This is Morgan's library! *(pointing
   vaguely)* That brownstone is where he lives!

COALHOUSE   Never mind that now. We wanted the man, so we have him
   since we have his property.

EXT.   BEACH, ATLANTIC CITY. DAY

The BOY *has buried the* GIRL *in the sand and made a pillow for her head and he
is sculpting an enlarged feminine form over her contours, packing wet sand in
exaggerated projections of her breasts and belly and thighs and feet. Her dark
eyes never leave his face. There is a sound of distant thunder and he sees her
looking up at the sky. Large drops of water begin to pelt the sand. A loud crash of
thunder. He takes her hand, pulls her up, destroying the sand sarcophagus, and
they start back through the dunes.*

EXT.   BEACH. DAY

The rain is heavy now and the CHILDREN *are running. Water streaking the
encrustations of sand on their backs. Their hair quickly becomes wet. The sky
becoming very dark.*

EXT.   BEACH. DAY

There is a furious storm now: thunder and lightning and torrents of rain. We see them coming, the CHILDREN, *coming toward us running, totally soaked, and they duck in where the camera is, under the boardwalk.*

EXT.   BENEATH BOARDWALK. DAY

The CHILDREN *crouch in the cold sand and listen to the rain spatter the boardwalk over their heads.*

    From their point of view: Coming through the wind and rain are TWO ADULT FIGURES *with their heads down and their arms shielding their eyes.*

EXT.   BEACH ALONG SURF. DAY

Close up the two figures are MOTHER *and* TATEH. *They stumble down the wet sand looking for the* CHILDREN. *They turn with their backs to the wind. They cup their hands and call.*

    MOTHER's *dress sticking to her.* TATEH's *shirt soaked. They are distraught and run or walk or call.*

    Cut once or twice between this shot and the CHILDREN *watching silently from under the boardwalk. Then, standing on the beach,* MOTHER *and* TATEH *see the children coming out from under the boardwalk and running toward them.*

    The adults drop to their knees and hug the children, hugging, laughing, crying, admonishing.

MOTHER   Where were you? Where were you? Didn't you hear us call?

TATEH   (*hugging the* GIRL) *Gottzudanken. Gottzudanken.*

EXT.   BEACH. DAY

The storm has passed as quickly as it came. MOTHER *and* TATEH *and the two* CHILDREN *are walking along, all very familiar with each other, all happy.* MOTHER *negotiates a dip in the sand by placing her hand for a moment on* TATEH's *shoulder. He gazes at her with admiration.*

    Suddenly MOTHER *points to the horizon.*

EXT. SKY. DAY

Over the sea the black clouds have broken: an opening of blue widens and the sun appears.

TATEH *runs ahead of the others in a burst of exhilaration and does a somersault and then a cartwheel. He stands on his hands in the sand and walks upside down.* MOTHER *and the two* CHILDREN *laugh.*

EXT. BREAKERS HOTEL PORCH

The TWO COUPLES *are happily coming up the stairs.* FATHER *comes out of the front door with an anxious expression on his face. He holds a telegram in his hand.*

MOTHER   We found them, these naughty children.

FATHER   Never mind that. Come inside. Something quite awful has happened.

INT. HOTEL BEDROOM. DAY

FATHER *is packing a bag.* MOTHER *is sitting in a chair holding the brown* BABY.

MOTHER   I do hope you'll be careful.

FATHER   This proves justice is not the issue. He's insane. Who but an insane man would confuse that miserable Willie Conklin with Pierpont Morgan.

MOTHER   I wish you did not have to go.

FATHER   Your Mr. Walker has made me a celebrity. District Attorney Whitman finds himself unable to deal with the problem without my help.

MOTHER   How many times in our life I've had to say goodbye to you.

FATHER   This time I'll be back soon. The authorities are not going to put up with such nonsense for very long.

MOTHER *reacts to this by holding the* BABY *closer and then* FATHER *continuing says:*

I'll come back and get you. And then we'll all go back home and resume our lives.

He snaps shut the hasps of the valise and prepares to leave.

I wish as you dote on this child you would consider the possibility that he is the same blood as a madman.

EXT.   THIRTY-SIXTH STREET. MORGAN LIBRARY. NIGHT

All of 36th Street is cordoned off. At the end of the block (corner of Madison) crowds stand behind police lines. Floodlamps run by portable generators are trained on the white marble library. Police are stationed everywhere, on foot and on horseback.

Coming through the line are TWO POLICEMEN *escorting* FATHER, *who carries his valise. As he comes down the empty street on the sidewalk directly across from the Morgan Library he reacts to an enormous crater in front of the library gates: A broken water main bubbles up like a spa.*

EXT.   BROWNSTONE ACROSS FROM LIBRARY. NIGHT

The windows of this private residence have been blown out. POLICEMEN *lead* FATHER *up the stairs rapidly with anxious glances toward the library. The sound of the generators is the only sound that can be heard, the crowd being quite silent.*

INT.   BROWNSTONE. NIGHT

As FATHER *enters the downstairs hall he is immediately engulfed in a swirl of people—*POLICE OFFICERS, DETECTIVES, *and* REPORTERS, *all milling about. A* POLICEMAN *holds* FATHER's *arm and leads him to a door, which opens to admit him.*

INT.   BROWNSTONE PARLOR. NIGHT

FATHER *and the* POLICEMAN *enter a room that seems to be the nerve center of officialdom. The fine furniture of this residence has been pushed back against the wall.*

Standing in the bay window, a pair of binoculars in his hand, is DISTRICT ATTORNEY WHITMAN, *the man in charge. With him are* MORGAN's *museum curator,* MACLEAN, *whom we have seen previously (p. 202), a man in the uniform of the* COLONEL *of the New York State Militia, and a drably dressed bureaucrat who is a* CITY ENGINEER.

WHITMAN *peers out the window with binoculars and then allows the heavy velour drapes to fall in place. Then he turns toward the room.*

WHITMAN   *(to nobody in particular)* I had every reason to think I would be dining this evening in Newport. *(shouting)* What about that cable to Mr. Morgan?

DETECTIVE   Yes sir. It's on its way.

WHITMAN   *(to* CURATOR*)* That's cable number three. Why doesn't he answer? What's he doing in Egypt, anyway? Egypt! I can't even get to dinner.

They go to a table where plans of the Morgan Library are spread out.

CURATOR   *(to* WHITMAN*)* The library is built of fitted marble blocks. Stanford White designed it. You can't get a knife blade between the stones.

POLICE SERGEANT *comes in.*

SERGEANT   We got the volunteer, Sir.

WHITMAN   Bring him in.

A very YOUNG PATROLMAN *is brought in.*

WHITMAN   All right, Son, you know what you have to do. We want to know how many coons are in that place. We want to know their positions. Come over here *(pointing to the blueprints of the library)*. You see here two domed skylights, one in the center hall, one over the East Room? You've got to get up there, look down, and see what you can see.

YOUNG PATROLMAN   Right.

EXT.   THIRTY-SIXTH STREET. NIGHT

The YOUNG PATROLMAN *masked by two burly* POLICE OFFICERS *walks down the street to Madison Avenue and disappears into the crowd.*

INT. BROWNSTONE PARLOR. NIGHT

WHITMAN   *(on phone)* You tell the Mayor if he wants to come here and handle things he's welcome to do it. Until he does I'll handle things the way I think they ought to be handled. *(slams down receiver)*

At this moment there is a dull explosion across the street, followed by a single piercing scream. WHITMAN *runs to the window and grabs his binoculars. The doors to the hall open and from the noisy milling throng a* POLICE SERGEANT *runs in.*

SERGEANT   They've got the goddamn place mined.

EXT.   MORGAN LIBRARY. NIGHT

The white marble building stands impregnable, in silence.

INT.   BROWNSTONE PARLOR. NIGHT

WHITMAN *is now pacing with his tie loosened and his jacket off. The parlor is crowded.*

WHITMAN   Get these people out of here! What's everyone doing in here! Out! Out!

REPORTERS, POLICEMEN, ETC., *are pushed out the door leaving* WHITMAN *with his inner circle. Somehow* FATHER *has managed to stay in the room inconspicuously, as the doors close, an observer.*

MILITIA COLONEL   You got to think of this as a full-scale military action. I don't care how many coons are in there and I don't care how much dynamite they have. I can take them with one company of men in three and a half minutes or less.

MACLEAN, MORGAN's *curator, ignores the* COLONEL, *and walks directly up to* WHITMAN.

MACLEAN   *(trembling)* Let me remind you of the value of Mr. Morgan's acquisitions. We have in the library four Shakespeare folios. We have a Gutenberg Bible on vellum. We have seven hundred incunabula, and an important letter of George Washington numbering five pages.

COLONEL   (*waving his finger in the air—at* MACLEAN) If we don't take care of that son of a bitch, if we don't go in there and cut off his balls you'll have every nigger in the country at your throat. Then where will you be with your Gutenberg Bible?

WHITMAN *walks over to the drab little* CITY ENGINEER.

WHITMAN   And what have you got to say?

ENGINEER   If we could repair that broken water main in the street we might be able to tunnel in through the library foundation.

WHITMAN   And how long would that take?

ENGINEER   Not more than two, three days.

WHITMAN   Is that all.

ENGINEER   I have one other idea. Poison gas.

WHITMAN   (*mildly*) Yes, that might do it. Of course, everyone else in midtown Manhattan would die too. But I like your thinking.

WHITMAN *turns and faces the room and sees the old* SERGEANT *standing there eyeing him.*

SERGEANT   The crucial thing, Sir, is to get this Coalhouse Walker engaged in conversation. With an armed maniac, talking calms him down. You get him talking and keep him talking and then you have a wedge into the situation.

WHITMAN *looks at the old policeman with grudging admiration.*

EXT. THIRTY-SIXTH STREET. NIGHT

DISTRICT ATTORNEY WHITMAN *standing on the sidewalk in front of the brownstone is shouting through a megaphone and waving his straw hat.*

WHITMAN   Did you hear me in there? Why don't you answer? If there's a problem maybe we can solve it together. I'm District Attorney Charles S. Whitman. You know me. Everyone knows me.

EXT.   MORGAN LIBRARY. NIGHT

A small window adjacent to the great brass doors opens and a cylindrical object comes flying out.

EXT.   THIRTY-SIXTH STREET. NIGHT

The cylindrical object lands at WHITMAN's *feet with a clank. He flinches and then turns, and with the* POLICEMEN *on the steps of the brownstone shouting to him, he runs back and they all go inside the house. After a moment the brownstone door opens and* WHITMAN *and two or three officers peek out. To their astonishment there has been no explosion.*

WHITMAN   That's no bomb. That's some kind of metal cup. Someone go on out there and pick it up and bring it back.

Reluctance on the part of the officers.

Go on, go on! They didn't take a shot at me. Why should they bother killing you?

INT.   BROWNSTONE PARLOR. NIGHT

WHITMAN *and his* BRAIN TRUST *stand around looking at the object, which is being examined by the curator,* MACLEAN.

MACLEAN   Yes, this is a medieval drinking stein. A tankard. Solid silver with a hunting scene in relief. It is early seventeenth century and belonged to Frederick the Elector of Saxony.

WHITMAN   I'm gratified to hear that.

The CURATOR *raises the lid of the drinking stein and finds inside a piece of paper. He unrolls the paper.*

MACLEAN   My goodness!

WHITMAN   What is it?

MACLEAN   It's my office phone number.

INT. BROWNSTONE PARLOR. NIGHT

The DISTRICT ATTORNEY *is sitting on the edge of a table holding the speaker of the phone in his left hand and the receiver attached by a cord in his right.*

WHITMAN   *(heartily)* Hello, Mr. Coalhouse Walker? This is District Attorney Whitman speaking!

INT. MORGAN LIBRARY. NIGHT

COALHOUSE *is at the phone on* MORGAN's *desk in the West Room. All the drapes are pulled. At each window stands a young man on guard with a rifle.*

COALHOUSE   My demands are the same. I want my car returned in just the same condition it was when my way was blocked. You can't bring back my Sarah but I want for her life the life of Fire Chief Willie Conklin.

INT. BROWNSTONE PARLOR. NIGHT

WHITMAN   *(on phone)* Now you know that I as an officer of the court could never give to you for sentencing outside the law a man who has not had due process. That puts me in an untenable position. What I can promise is to investigate the case and see what statutes apply if any. But I can't do anything for you until you're out of there.

INT. MORGAN LIBRARY. NIGHT

COALHOUSE   I will give you twenty-four hours and then I'll blow up this place and everything in it.

INT. BROWNSTONE PARLOR. NIGHT

WHITMAN   Hello? Hello? Goddammit. *(He clicks the phone lever.)* Hello? *(He slams the phone down on the desk.)* Son of a bitch. *(He turns to the assembled company.)* Is there a bottle of whiskey anywhere in this house?

INT.   PIERPONT MORGAN'S CABIN ABOARD HIS NILE RIVER
PADDLE STEAMER. DAY

MORGAN's *stateroom aboard his paddle steamer is incredibly luxurious: ma-*
hogany paneling, rugs, "turkish" sofa, lamps with tasseled shades, art on the
walls, etc.

MORGAN *is conferring in his stateroom with an* ARCHITECT; *an* ENGINEER,
who appears to be Egyptian; and a ship's CAPTAIN, *who looks British. Blueprints*
are spread out on a table. Also a working model of a pyramid, which MORGAN
disassembles piece by piece to point out its features.

MORGAN   My pyramid, Gentlemen, was secretly designed for me by Stanford White's firm. As you can see, there is to be a false king's chamber as
well as a true king's chamber, an impregnable treasure room . . . a grand
gallery, and here . . . a descending corridor and . . . here an ascending
corridor. And a causeway to the banks of the Nile. I hope you are all
properly appreciative of the secret to which you are now privy.

CAPTAIN, ARCHITECT, *and* ENGINEER *are properly appreciative.*

I expect that with modern construction techniques—the use of precut
stones, steam shovels, cranes, and so forth—a servicable pyramid can be put
up in less than three years. (*to* ENGINEER) Do you agree with that?

The engineer scratches his head. Is about to say something.

Well, anyway, that's what I want. (*to* ARCHITECT) Your job is to help me
pick out the site.

ARCHITECT   (*clearing throat*) The Egyptian government . . .

MORGAN   Don't you worry about the Egyptian government. They will find
my negotiating position very strong. (*He chuckles.*)

There is a knock at the stateroom door and a voice calls out "Cable for Mr.
Morgan!" The CAPTAIN *goes to the door, takes the cable, and comes back into the*
room.

CAPTAIN   Another cable from New York, Sir.

MORGAN *accepts the paper from the* CAPTAIN *but doesn't look at it. Something*
has occurred to him.

MORGAN   (*to* CAPTAIN) We're not moving! Why has this boat stopped moving?

CAPTAIN   We're docked, Sir. We're at Giza.

MORGAN   What? *(He rushes to porthole stuffing cable in his pocket. Looks out.)* Ah! Yes, there it is.

EXT.   GIZA. NIGHT

In the blue-black starry night we see the great pyramid, even blacker, silhouetted against the night sky.

MORGAN'S VOICE   I will spend the night there. I want to feel the energies I'll exemplify when I die in order to be born again.

INT.   BROWNSTONE HEADQUARTERS. NIGHT

DISTRICT ATTORNEY WHITMAN, *looking a shade more ragged, sits at his command desk with a bottle of whiskey. The only other person in the room with* WHITMAN *is* FATHER.

WHITMAN   So the coon used to work for you, eh?

FATHER   Well no, that's not quite right.

WHITMAN   All the same . . . *(boozy and distracted)* I made a bad mistake by stepping into this one. Some crazy nigger. I thought it would take five minutes. And then I'd pick up my wife from here and go on to Newport for the weekend. Do you know Newport?

FATHER   Yes.

WHITMAN   We were to stay with Mrs. Stuyvesant Fish. I hope she reads the newspapers . . . I think I'm presidential material to tell you frankly. But I've got myself into a pickle here. A real pickle. I can't leave that coon in there too long. But I have to watch out for Morgan's furnishings. *(He suddenly slams the table with his open hand.)* What to do, what to do . . . *(He bellows.)* Lieutenant!

Door opens and a POLICE LIEUTENANT *comes in.*

We got any reds in town?

LIEUTENANT   Emma Goldman, Sir. Red Emma's in town.

WHITMAN   Well arrest her. Bring her in.

INT.   EMMA GOLDMAN'S BOARDINGHOUSE ROOM. NIGHT

GOLDMAN *is standing in the door, which is open, putting on her coat and talking to* TWO DETECTIVES *and a* POLICEMAN.

GOLDMAN   How are you boys feeling this evening? You see this little bag here? *(She points to a little valise by the door.)* I always have it packed and ready to go. I'm a resource for law enforcement. They bring me in anytime they don't know what else to do. *(She pins on her hat.)* You won't believe this, but I look forward to jail. It's the one place I get some rest. *(over her shoulder)* I'm going now, Ben.

REITMAN *comes into vestibule, gives her a peck on the cheek. He is holding a napkin and still chewing something.*

REITMAN   All right, my darling. I'll be down to see you tomorrow.

INT.   CENTER STREET. POLICE HEADQUARTERS. NIGHT

GOLDMAN *is being booked at the front desk, surrounded by* REPORTERS. *They clamor for a statement.*

GOLDMAN   *(holding up her hand)* I only know what I read in the newspapers. I'm sorry for the firemen in Westchester. I wish they had not been killed. But the Negro was tormented into action, so I understand, by the cruel death of his fiancée. As for the appropriation of the Morgan property? Mr. Morgan has done some appropriating of his own.

REPORTERS *shout questions: "Is he a follower of yours, Emma?" "Do you know him?" "Did you have anything to do with this?"*

The oppressor is wealth, my friends. Wealth is the oppressor. Coalhouse Walker did not need Emma Goldman to learn that.

INT.   PENN STATION. DAY

Eminent Negro educator BOOKER T. WASHINGTON *is greeted by* REPORTERS *as he steps off the train. He is a distinguished middle-aged man of great dignity.* REPORTERS *clamor for a statement.*

BOOKER T. WASHINGTON   I will say only this. I deplore Madame Goldman's remarks and condemn the actions of Coalhouse Walker. Negro America cannot support the acts of a desperado. I am in the city to do some fund-raising on behalf of Tuskegee Normal and Industrial Institute, which is dedicated, as you know, to the training of responsible and clean-living Negro young men and women. But if the authorities think I can be of some help in this unfortunate matter, I of course will offer my services.

EXT.   THIRTY-SIXTH STREET. BROWNSTONE. DAY

WHITMAN *stands peeking through the curtains of the bay window. He is anxious and strung out, but a light of shrewd cunning is in his eyes.*

EXT.   MORGAN LIBRARY. DAY

BOOKER T. WASHINGTON *is standing in the middle of the street dressed in his black suit and homburg. Disdaining the use of a megaphone he calls out to* COALHOUSE. *There is nothing in his manner that indicates that he expects to be rebuffed.*

BOOKER T. WASHINGTON   All right, Mr. Walker, I'm coming in now. You will please open the door.

WASHINGTON *steps around the crater in the street, walks up to the sidewalk and up the steps. He waits confidently for the door to open. After some moments the door opens quickly and* WASHINGTON *disappears inside.*

INT.   BROWNSTONE. DAY

WHITMAN *turns, sinks into a chair, and wipes his brow with a handkerchief.*

INT. MORGAN LIBRARY. ENTRANCE HALL. DAY

In the entrance hall fascia of dynamite strapped to the marble pilasters. Wires leading out of the doorways of the East and West Rooms. The library is wired and ready to blow.

BOOKER T. WASHINGTON *takes this in, a terrible frown on his face. He strides to the entrance of the West Room and looks in here.*

INT. WEST ROOM. DAY

The paintings, statuary, priceless Florentine furniture are all wired for demolition. A YOUNG MAN *standing by the draped window with a rifle. Washington's brow becomes more furrowed.*

INT. ENTRANCE HALL. DAY

He walks back through the entrance hall and looks in the East Room.

INT. EAST ROOM. DAY

Here too the tiers of rare books, the furnishings, etc., are wired. At each window stands a single YOUNG BLACK MAN, *armed.*

INT. ENTRANCE HALL. DAY

In the hall behind him he finds COALHOUSE WALKER *himself, impeccably dressed in a well-pressed hound's-tooth suit and tie and collar.* WASHINGTON *looks over* COALHOUSE. *His eyes flash.*

WASHINGTON   For my entire life I have worked in patience and hope for a Christian brotherhood. I have had to persuade the white man that he need not fear us or murder us, because we wanted only to improve ourselves and peaceably join him in enjoyment of the fruits of American Democracy. What will your misguided criminal recklessness cost me? What will it cost my students laboring to learn a trade by which they can earn their livelihood and still white criticism! A thousand honest industrious black men cannot undo the harm of one like you. Monstrous man! Had you been ignorant of the tragic struggle of our people, I could have pitied you this adventure. But you are a trained musician! I look about me and smell the sweat of rage, the rebellion of wild unthinking youth. What have you taught them! What injustice done to you, what loss you've suffered, can justify the doom you have led them into, these reckless youths?

At this moment a man sitting hunched over a box with a T*-shaped plunger turns to face the scene and it is* YOUNGER BROTHER *in blackface.* WASHINGTON *sees this and is stunned.*

And, may you be damned, you add to this unholy company a white who smears himself with color and adds mockery to your arsenal.

COALHOUSE   *(softly)* It is a great honor for me to meet you, Mr. Washington. I have always stood in admiration of you. It is true I am a musician and a man of years. But I would hope this might suggest to you the solemn calculation of my mind. And that therefore, possibly, we might both be servants of our color who insist on the truth of our manhood and the respect it demands.

WASHINGTON *is so shocked by this suggestion that he feels faint. His hand goes to his brow and he totters.* COALHOUSE *leads him to the West Room.*

INT.   WEST ROOM. DAY

COALHOUSE *brings* WASHINGTON *to one of the red plush chairs.* WASHINGTON *mops his brow with a handkerchief. He gazes around at the red damask walls. He glances at a portrait of* MORGAN. *He closes his eyes and locks his hands in his lap.*

WASHINGTON   Oh Lord, lead my people to the promised land. Take them from under the Pharaoh's whip. Free the shackles from their minds and loosen the bonds of sin that tie them to hell.

COALHOUSE WALKER *sits down in an adjoining chair. The two well-dressed black men are the picture of probity positioned now exactly as* FORD *and* MORGAN *were on p. 225.*

WASHINGTON   Come out with me now and I will intercede for the sake of mercy that your trial shall be swift and your execution painless. Dismantle these engines of the devil. *(waving his hands at the packs of dynamite attached to the ceiling and walls)* Take my hand and come with me. For the sake of your young son and all those children of our race whose way is hard and whose journey is long.

COALHOUSE *sits lost in thought.*

COALHOUSE   Mr. Washington, there is nothing I would like more than to conclude this business. *(Tears of emotion spring to his eyes.)* Let the Fire Chief restore my automobile and bring it to the front of this building. You will see me come out with my hands raised and no further harm will come to this place or any man from Coalhouse Walker.

Taking this for a refusal WASHINGTON *rises and leaves the room walking through the front hall and out the front door. One of the* YOUNG MEN *lets him out and the great brass doors slam behind him.*

INT.   GREAT PYRAMID. NIGHT

A portable lantern throws bounding shadows against the great stone-block walls and ceiling of the king's chamber of the Great Pyramid. Here sits PIERPONT MORGAN *waiting for the visions that will confirm his expectations of immortality.*

He decides to get some rest and with difficulty lies down on a blanket spread out on the earthen floor, but this too is unsatisfactory. He has the unmistakable feeling of being crawled upon. An examination shows bed bugs all over the ground. He jumps up and begins to slap himself free of the nasty little creatures. He paces the room and then quite accidentally feels the several telegrams in his pocket and takes them out to read by torchlight for want of something better to do. We watch him react to the message in these telegrams. Jumps up. Rushes to the stone door but it is sealed shut for the night and he is furious that he can't get out.

INT.   THIRTY-SIXTH STREET. BROWNSTONE VESTIBULE. NIGHT

BOOKER T. WASHINGTON *is giving an impromptu press conference in the vestibule.* REPORTERS *with their pads take down every word.*

WASHINGTON   Mr. Morgan's library is a dynamite bomb ready to go off at any moment. We are faced with a desperately mind-sick man. I can only pray that the Lord in his wisdom will bring us safely out of this affair. In fact I feel the need at this moment to offer a prayer.

He bows his head and clasps his hands in front of his chest. REPORTERS *look at each other incredulous, unbelieving. Muttering to themselves they remove their hats and take their cigars out of their mouths.*

INT. BROWNSTONE PARLOR. NIGHT

WHITMAN's *Brain Trust: the* CURATOR, *the* SERGEANT, *and* FATHER *are deep in conference.*

FATHER If Mr. Washington heard him correctly Coalhouse Walker has modified his demands.

WHITMAN Tell me again.

FATHER He said nothing about the life of Willie Conklin. He said only that he wanted the Fire Chief to restore his automobile and that if that happened he would come out with his hands raised. I think Mr. Washington got a concession out of him and didn't even realize it.

EXT. GREAT PYRAMID. DAY

Two or three burnoosed ARABS *are leading* MORGAN *into the daylight. He is blinking and is stiff and tired. He holds his hand in the small of his back.*

MORGAN Which of you understands English?

One ARAB *steps forward nodding and smiling amiably.* MORGAN *writes something quickly with a pencil on a piece of paper, folds the paper.*

(*to the* ARAB) Run this down to my ship. Fast. Chop chop. Understand? (*He points.*)

ARAB (*bowing*) Yes, your Excellence.

INT. BROWNSTONE HEADQUARTERS. NIGHT

DISTRICT ATTORNEY WHITMAN *and his* BRAIN TRUST *are all in shirt-sleeves and their ties are askew. He is reading a cable shaking his head in disbelief.*

Ragtime: A Screenplay

WHITMAN   "Give him his automobile and hang him."

He shakes his head and reads it again as if to make sure he hasn't made a mistake.

"Give him his automobile?" That's insane. That is the one thing I would never consider. I can't give in to the coon. Even to hang him. It would finish me. The District Attorney giving in to a nigger.

WHITMAN *hands the cable to* FATHER *and begins to pace the room in agitation.* FATHER *reads the cable thoughtfully.*

FATHER   The whole matter can be resolved quickly. Coalhouse Walker has softened his demand. The car has no real value. Besides, it's Mr. Morgan's idea.

WHITMAN   I'll say. Only J. P. Morgan would think of it. Who else would have the nerve?

FATHER   No, I mean it's Mr. Morgan's idea. Of course I don't know anything about politics but doesn't that absolve you of the responsibility?

WHITMAN *stops in his tracks and gazes at* FATHER.

EXT.   NEW ROCHELLE. FIREHOUSE POND. NIGHT

A group of POLICE OFFICIALS *and* TEAMSTERS *attaching a team of dray horses to* COALHOUSE WALKER's *ruined Model T. The horses are hitched to the bumper of the car as they pull it up to the road. A man standing in the driver's seat grasping the reins in one hand, the steering wheel with the other. He hollahs the horses and they start down the road.*

INT.   BROWNSTONE. MORNING

The parlor door flies open and two POLICEMEN *come in holding* WILLIE CONKLIN *by the collar.*

POLICEMAN   Here he is.

WHITMAN   Well, well. So that's the fellow.

CONKLIN *is disheveled and frightened. He is shoved into a chair. His teeth are chattering and his hands shake. He reaches in his back pocket for his pint and one of the* POLICEMEN *slaps his hand away and cuffs him in the head.*

POLICEMAN   Sit up straight when you're talking to Mr. Whitman.

WHITMAN   (*to* FATHER) All right. We've got Conklin and we've got the car. It's time to settle this thing. (*He picks up the phone.*) I'm going to call the coon now but I don't want to negotiate over the phone. I'm going to tell him I'm sending my ambassador.

FATHER *looks startled.*

WHITMAN   Please. I need a pair of eyes in there. He'll trust you.

EXT.   THIRTY-SIXTH STREET. DAY

FATHER *coming out of the brownstone. The street is empty and quiet. The generators are still and on the corner of Madison Avenue the ever-present crowd of witnesses is quiet.*

Parked at the curb in front of the brownstone is COALHOUSE WALKER'S *ruined Model T, rusted and gutted, mud-caked, tires flat, a total wreck.*

FATHER *takes a deep breath and walks resolutely across the street and up the steps of the Morgan Library.*

INT.   MORGAN LIBRARY. ENTRANCE HALL. DAY

The brass door opening and admitting FATHER. *The door slams shut behind him and he blinks in the dim light.*

From FATHER'S *point of view we see the figure at the rear of the entrance hall sitting hunched over the demolition box. The figure rises and approaches—* YOUNGER BROTHER *undressed to the waist with face blackened and a holster pistol under his arm. He is smiling.*

FATHER   You!

YOUNGER BROTHER *pulls out the pistol and taps the barrel against his own temple in a kind of salute.* FATHER'S *knees buckle.* COALHOUSE *and* YOUNGER BROTHER *help him to a chair and someone brings a canteen with water.*

EXT. MORGAN LIBRARY. DAY

FATHER *comes out of the library and walks quickly across to the brownstone.*

INT. BROWNSTONE. DAY

FATHER *is in a chair. He sips whiskey.* WHITMAN *hangs on his every word.*

FATHER   He agreed to extend the deadline for twelve hours. He wants wooden planks laid over the hole on the street.

WHITMAN   He blew that hole in the street himself with his goddamned grenade bomb.

FATHER   He wants to see Willie Conklin. He wants us to show him.

INT. BROWNSTONE VESTIBULE. DAY

WILLIE CONKLIN *struggling and protesting as* TWO POLICEMEN *hold him under the shoulders, open the front door, and drag him outside.*

CONKLIN   What are you doing? He'll kill me! You're going to get me shot! Help!

EXT. BROWNSTONE. DAY

WILLIE CONKLIN *in abject terror hangs limply from the arms of the* TWO BURLY POLICEMEN *on either side of him at the top of the brownstone stairs. They drag him back inside.*

INT. MORGAN LIBRARY. DAY

In the West Room COALHOUSE *sits behind* MORGAN's *great Florentine desk like a head of state as* FATHER *stands in front of the desk and delivers terms. As* FATHER *talks the* TWO YOUNG MEN *stationed in the West Room drift closer to* COALHOUSE *in their desire to hear what is being said.*

FATHER   The District Attorney has brought your car here as you have seen. It is parked across the street. He has shown you Willie Conklin. And now his terms: He will urge the authorities of Westchester to bring charges against Willie Conklin for malicious mischief, vandalism, and illegal detainment of a citizen. In addition he proposes that Conklin will, right here in full sight of everyone, restore your automobile. This is a humiliation he will live with for the rest of his life, and of course the car will be made over new. Mr. Morgan will pay for the work that has to be done and the Ford motorcar people are ready to deliver all the necessary parts.

COALHOUSE   And in return for this beneficence?

FATHER   (clearing his throat) In return the District Attorney demands your surrender and guarantees that you and your men will have full rights and privileges under the law.

The two YOUNG MEN *begin to laugh and hoot.*

FIRST YOUNG MAN   We got him! He givin' in!

SECOND YOUNG MAN   Oo wee! We goin' to get the whole pie!

COALHOUSE   Please go back to your posts.

Taken aback they return to the far ends of the room. COALHOUSE *sits back in his chair. He folds his hands under his chin and becomes very thoughtful.*
    Shot of faces of his followers looking at him anxiously. Shot of FATHER *grim-lipped and tense awaiting* COALHOUSE's *response.*

INT.   BROWNSTONE. DAY

WHITMAN *sits at his table twisting a handkerchief with his hand and chewing on a corner of the handkerchief.*

INT.   MORGAN LIBRARY. WEST ROOM. DAY

COALHOUSE *with his hands behind his back paces the room. He comes to a decision. He comes up to* FATHER.

COALHOUSE   In return for the restoration of my car under the conditions which you have described I will surrender myself. I will not surrender my boys. For them I want safe passage away from here and full and total amnesty. But stay here please, until I have a chance to tell them.

COALHOUSE *motions to the* TWO YOUNG MEN *by the windows of the West Room and they follow him out the door, which he closes.*

INT.   ENTRANCE HALL. DAY

COALHOUSE *is gathered with the band and* YOUNGER BROTHER *over the detonation box. The* YOUNG MEN *are stunned and angered.*

FIRST YOUNG MAN   You don't have to give him nothin'.

SECOND YOUNG MAN   We got Morgan by the balls. You don't have to negotiate nothin'.

THIRD YOUNG MAN   Give us Conklin and that car and let us out of here and you get back your library. That's the negotiation, man. That's the kind of negotiation!

COALHOUSE   *(calmly)* None of you is known to the authorities by name. You can disappear into the city and reclaim your life.

FOURTH YOUNG MAN   So can you.

COALHOUSE   No. They would never let me out of here. You know that. And if they did they would spare no effort to hunt me down and everyone with me would be hunted down and you would all die. To what purpose? For what end?

FIRST YOUNG MAN   We always talked before. Now you're doing this. You can't, man. We all Coalhouse!

SECOND YOUNG MAN   We can't get out. We'll blow it up.

YOUNGER BROTHER   Either we all ought to go free or we all ought to die. You have an obligation to us. Each and every man here joined you in your cause. We found you and joined you.

COALHOUSE   That is true.

YOUNGER BROTHER   You can't betray us for a car. You can't reduce the meaning of your demands.

COALHOUSE   I have not.

YOUNGER BROTHER   Is the goddamned Ford your justice? Is your execution your justice?

COALHOUSE   As for my execution my death was determined the moment Sarah died. As for my godforsaken Ford it is to be made over as it was the day I drove past the firehouse. It is not I who reduced my demands but they who magnified them as long as they resisted them. I will trade your precious lives for Willie Conklin's and thank God for him.

INT.   BROWNSTONE. DAY

FATHER *is closeted with* WHITMAN *and here is able to express his emotion as he was not in the library.*

FATHER   They're not human. They're monstrous! If not for Coalhouse himself they would happily destroy the library and themselves with it. They're nothing more than filthy revolutionaries.

WHITMAN *pours himself a shot and throws it back. Stubble covers his face. His eyes are red and his collar wilted. He paces. He stands at the window, makes a fist of his right hand and smacks the palm of his left. He looks again at the wire from* MORGAN.

FATHER   *(clearing his throat)* It does not say you have to hang the confederates.

WHITMAN   What?

He finds a chair and sits down.

How many of them are there, did you say?

FATHER   Five or six.

WHITMAN *shakes his head and sighs.*

FATHER   I think this is the best you can do.

WHITMAN   Sure. And what do I tell the newspapers?

FATHER   You can tell them, one, Coalhouse Walker is captured, and two, Morgan's treasures are safe, and three, the city is safe, and four, the entire might of the Police Department will be used to track down the underlings until every last one of them is behind bars, where he belongs.

WHITMAN   *(thoughtfully)* We'll tail them right back to the woodpile.

FATHER   *(delicately)* Well that may not be possible. They're taking a hostage and won't let him go until they know they're safe.

WHITMAN   *(looking up)* Who is the hostage?

FATHER   *(taking a deep breath)* I am.

WHITMAN   I see. And what makes the coon think he can hold the building alone?

FATHER   Well, he will be out of the sightlines of skylight or windows with his hands on the dynamite box. That would do it I should think.

WHITMAN *rises from his chair with a strangled cry of frustration. Walks across the room raising his arms and letting them fall against his sides.*

WHITMAN   All right. All right. You tell that son of a bitch it's a deal. Maybe if we wait till dark nobody will see what we're doing. For Mr. Morgan's sake. *(looking at* CURATOR*)* And his goddamned Gutenburg Bible. And his five-page goddamn letter from George Washington.

MONTAGE: EXT.   THIRTY-SIXTH STREET. DAY AND NIGHT

In the street, with the help of TWO MEN *and with a* MECHANIC *to direct him, Fire Chief* WILLIE CONKLIN *piece by piece dismantles the Ford and makes a new Ford from the chassis. Fenders are replaced. Seats. A new canvas top is attached. Etc. Block and tackle to drop in a new engine. Sweating, grunting, complaining, and at times actually crying,* WILLIE CONKLIN *restores the Ford. There should be a special music for this event.*

INT.   MORGAN LIBRARY. WEST ROOM. DAY

The YOUNG MEN *peer through the drapes at the scene in the street. It should be a happy time, a cause for rejoicing, but it is not. They're very grim.*

At MORGAN's *desk* COALHOUSE *sits, not even bothering to look at the car for whose restoration he has fought.* YOUNGER BROTHER *is still with him petitioning.*

YOUNGER BROTHER You signed your letter "President of the Provisional American Government."

COALHOUSE It seemed to be the rhetoric we needed for our morale.

YOUNGER BROTHER But we meant it! We meant it! There are enough people in the streets to found an army!

FATHER *peering through the drapes of the West Room window.*

FATHER It's done. (*to* COALHOUSE) There's your car as it was the day you were stopped.

COALHOUSE *rises from the desk and as* YOUNGER BROTHER *and the others watch he walks to the window and looks out.*

INT. MORGAN LIBRARY. DAY

A close-up of COALHOUSE's *face as he looks at his car.*

EXT. STREET. DAY

A brand-new shining black Ford stands at the curb.

INT. MORGAN LIBRARY. NIGHT

The lights are on and the YOUNG MEN, *silent and subdued, are reluctantly preparing to leave. One of them takes* YOUNGER BROTHER's *place at the dynamite box and he retires to a lavatory behind the entrance hall.*

INT. LAVATORY. NIGHT

At a luxurious marbled basin YOUNGER BROTHER *washes the burnt cork from his face. He glances up at the mirror over the washbasin and sees* FATHER *standing in the door.*

FATHER I myself require nothing from you but don't you feel your sister deserves an explanation?

YOUNGER BROTHER   If she thinks about me she will have her explanation. I could not transmit it through you. You're a complacent man with no thought of history. You pay your employees badly and are insensitive to their needs.

FATHER   I see.

YOUNGER BROTHER   The fact that you think of yourself as a gentleman in all your dealings is the simple self-delusion of all those who oppress humanity.

FATHER   You have lived under my roof and worked in my business. I put my trust in you.

YOUNGER BROTHER   Your generosity was what you felt you could afford. Besides, I have repaid that debt, as you will discover.

Having washed his face with soap and hot water YOUNGER BROTHER *now dries himself with a hand towel embroidered with the initials "JPM."*

You'll find in my office at the plant numerous mechanical drawings for armaments I've invented. Also a sealed letter in which I deed to you all rights to those inventions. You may patent any of those you deem worthy. Various explosive devices and weapons the world will find it needs.

He throws the towel on the floor, puts on his shirt, places his collar over the shirt, ties his tie, raises his suspenders.

You have traveled everywhere and learned nothing. You think it's a crime to come into this building belonging to another man and to threaten his property. In fact, this is the nest of a vulture. The den of a jackal.

He puts on his coat and runs his palm over his shaved head. Places his derby on his head and glances at himself in the mirror.

You may tell my sister that she will always be in my thoughts. *(gazing at the floor and clearing his throat)* You may tell her I've always loved her and admired her.

INT. MORGAN LIBRARY. ENTRANCE HALL. NIGHT

All of the BAND *is dressed now in their uniform of suit and tie and derby.* COALHOUSE *has them pull their hat brims down. He explains to one of the* YOUNG MEN *how to set the spark and throttle and how to turn the crank.*

COALHOUSE   You will ring the telephone when you're free.

FATHER   Am I not coming?

COALHOUSE   (*pointing to* YOUNGER BROTHER) Here's the hostage. One white face looks just like another.

They all laugh.
     COALHOUSE *embraces each* YOUNG MAN *before the brass doors. He embraces* YOUNGER BROTHER. *He looks at his pocket watch.*

EXT. THIRTY-SIXTH STREET. NIGHT

Floodlights in the street go out.

INT. MORGAN LIBRARY. NIGHT

COALHOUSE *takes his place in the alcove at the back of the hall straddling the bench with his hands on the dynamite box.*

YOUNGER BROTHER   There is slack in the plunger to a point halfway down.

COALHOUSE   All right. Go on now.

The YOUNG MEN *look at their leader. The light is turned out in the hall and in the darkness we hear the sounds of the doors unbolting and we watch the silhouettes of the* YOUNG MEN *filing out. Then the doors are closed.*

COALHOUSE   Bolt them, please.

FATHER *moves in the darkness to the doors and bolts them. He puts his ear to the doors.*

Ragtime: A Screenplay

EXT. THIRTY-SIXTH STREET. NIGHT

The shadows of the FIVE FIGURES *climb into the Model T Ford.*

INT. MORGAN LIBRARY. NIGHT

After what seems a torturously long interval FATHER *hears the sound of the Model T engine sputtering into life and then the sound of the car driving off.*

COALHOUSE'S VOICE   Now I suppose we can turn on the light.

FATHER *turns on the lights in the hall. He goes to sit on the floor with his back to the marble wall not far from* COALHOUSE WALKER. *Father raises his knees and rests his head. These two men from the same generation sit quietly.* COALHOUSE *sits contemplatively with his hands on the plunger.*

COALHOUSE   I would like to have seen my son. I would like to have seen him grow. Tell me, has he said any words? Is he walking?

FATHER *raises his head and looks at* COALHOUSE.

EXT. A HARLEM STREET. NIGHT

The Model T Ford comes down the street, slows up. TWO FIGURES *leap out and run off in different directions into the shadows. The car picks up speed.*

EXT. THIRTY-SIXTH STREET. NIGHT

The generator lights are back on and POLICE *on horseback are coming into the street and seem to be arranging themselves in some sort of formation.*

EXT. ANOTHER HARLEM STREET. NIGHT

Again the Model T passing the camera and ONE *of the silhouetted figures jumps off and disappears into the night. The car speeds up.*

EXT. WATERFRONT STREET. NIGHT

The car pulls into the scene and comes to a stop. We hear the gentle lap of the river against the pilings. Sound of a foghorn. While the car idles YOUNGER

BROTHER *and the* FIRST *and* SECOND YOUNG MEN *have a hasty whispered conversation.*

FIRST YOUNG MAN   We don't know. The car might have some marking.

YOUNGER BROTHER   It doesn't matter. I'm leaving town. I'm taking the ferry. You give me a half hour or so to be across the river in New Jersey and then you can call.

SECOND YOUNG MAN   Be careful, Brother.

FIRST YOUNG MAN   Never forget.

YOUNGER BROTHER   Never.

The TWO YOUNG BLACKS *leave the car and run off and now we see* YOUNGER BROTHER *getting behind the wheel of* COALHOUSE WALKER's *Model T. He leans over and releases the handbrake and holds the wheel tightly with both hands.*

EXT.   THIRTY-SIXTH STREET.   NIGHT

In the glare of the floodlights: lined up from one sidewalk to the other, from the steps of the library to the brownstone, two troops of MOUNTED POLICE *facing each other at a distance of thirty yards, the horses shoulder to shoulder, so that a kind of corridor is formed. At the end of the corridor in front of the brownstone steps, a squad of* NEW YORK'S FINEST *armed with carbines.*

It should be clear to us that there is no way bystanders on the corner behind the police corridors could see anything taking place.

The great brass door of the Morgan Library opens and COALHOUSE WALKER *in his shirt-sleeves steps boldly out and slowly walks down the steps between the two stone lionesses and the lines of mounted troopers.*

He has a bitter smile on his face. He regards the entire scene before him with total understanding; and, a beatific expression beginning to come over him, he slowly raises his hand as if to bless the armed might arrayed against him.

INT.   MORGAN LIBRARY.   NIGHT

FATHER *starts as he hears the volley of a firing squad. He screams and runs to the window.*

Ragtime: A Screenplay

EXT.   THIRTY-SIXTH STREET. NIGHT

On the white marbled sidewalk COALHOUSE WALKER's *body jerks in a sequence of attitudes as the bullets hit him.*

The POLICE *fire at will. The horses forming the wall on either side whinnying and bowing their heads and pawing with their front hooves.*

MUSIC: A RAG

The final musical statement of the film begins here—a rag, which runs to the end. It should begin as an ironic, painfully sad counterpoint to COALHOUSE's *death, but later it should be heard as something bright and relentless as the events of the picture spin out with increasing speed.*

INT.   STAGE

On a small stage decorated with a listless palm, EVELYN NESBIT *and a greasy-looking* PARTNER *in black tie are dancing ritualistically to the rag that we hear.*

MONTAGE: DAY AND NIGHT

YOUNGER BROTHER *driving to Mexico.*

A sequence of day and night scenes in which YOUNGER BROTHER *is shown riding* COALHOUSE's *Ford across various landscapes. As he goes the car gets dustier and more beat-up looking.*

YOUNGER BROTHER *himself begins to change. His hair growing out, a blonde beard appearing.*

The culmination of the sequence comes with YOUNGER BROTHER *pulling up to the edge of a river, cutting the engine, and standing up in the seat. The river is the Rio Grande and on the other side is a Mexican village with* MEN *and horses visible. The men carry rifles.* YOUNGER BROTHER *reaches behind him and brings out a sombrero, which he puts on his head.*

He jumps down from the car taking with him only the desert water bag slumped from the radiator cap and begins to wade across the river.

INT.   STAGE

EVELYN *dances the rag.*

EXT.   TOWN HALL SQUARE.   DAY

The ARCHDUKE FRANZ FERDINAND *and his wife, the* COUNTESS SOPHIE, *stand on the steps of town hall with several dignitaries.*

Suddenly there is an explosion and smoke covers the screen, and when it blows away the DUKE *and the* COUNTESS *are standing there stunned and covered with chalk dust. Someone has thrown a bomb. Much confusion.*

In the midst of the shouting and the running this way and that of the dignitaries, the ARCHDUKE *helps his Lady into the back of their car. Furious, he commands his* CHAUFFEUR *to leave the city.*

EXT.   SARAJEVO STREET.   DAY

The CHAUFFEUR *turns into this narrow cobblestone street and appears to lose his way. The* ARCHDUKE *commands him to back up and go in the other direction.*

The CHAUFFEUR *is engaging the gears and turning in his seat preparatory to backing the car. A* YOUNG SERBIAN *jumps on the running board of the touring car. He pulls a pistol out of his belt and shoots the* ARCHDUKE *and the* COUNTESS SOPHIE.

The COUNTESS *falls over between the* ARCHDUKE's *knees. Blood spurts from the* ARCHDUKE's *throat.*

EXT.   NEW YORK CITY.   TIMES SQUARE.   DAY

HOUDINI *is standing looking at the front page of a newspaper in which a big black headline announces the death of the* ARCHDUKE FRANZ FERDINAND *over his picture.*

HOUDINI   Imagine that. Imagine that.

We pull back now and see that a CROWD *has gathered to watch* HOUDINI *perform one of his feats. He is still preoccupied by the news as he puts the paper down and allows an* ASSISTANT *to help him off with his hat and coat. There is great applause as* HOUDINI *is wrapped in a straitjacket and chained at the ankles.*

This event is taking place at the foot of the Times Tower building, from the roof of which there hangs a cable.

HOUDINI *is soon swinging upside down above the street, rising higher and higher with each crank from the winch above. The crowd cheers.*

EXT.   TIMES TOWER. DAY

HOUDINI *is several stories above the street hanging upside down twirling gently in the wind, which we hear now.*

He rises past the baseball scoreboard attached to the building. We see from his point of view everything upside down: the automobiles, people, the sidewalks, police on horseback, the buildings. The sky is at his feet.

HOUDINI   Imagine that. Imagine that.

When he is at his assigned height he begins his feat twisting and struggling and swinging back and forth above the street. His head disappears inside the strait-jacket. We hear the oohs and aahs of the crowd.

INT.   STRAITJACKET. DAY

We hear HOUDINI *breathing and see imposed on the inside of the sunlit canvas of the straitjacket as on the screen, the image of the* LITTLE BOY. *We hear the magician gasp.*

LITTLE BOY   *(whispered)* Warn the Duke.

INT.   STAGE

EVELYN *dancing.*

SOUND: THE BASSO HORN OF AN OCEAN LINER

EXT.   NEW YORK CITY DOCK. DAY

At the foot of the gangplank leading to the Lusitania *passenger liner stand* MOTHER *and* FATHER. *Amid the hustle and bustle they stand terribly still, very constrained, and with a curious formality about them as if they were no longer husband and wife.*

FATHER   Under the circumstances I appreciate your coming to bid me goodbye.

MOTHER   Why would I not? I don't hate you.

FATHER   America is going to be in a war and my sympathies are with the Allies.

MOTHER   I cannot say we were not at one time made for each other. But I do not wish to be affiliated with a munitions maker.

EXT.   U-BOAT DECK. NIGHT

A Secret Service Man runs along the deck, meets a German sailor and socks him in the jaw. (black and white)

The camera pulls back. We are in a screening room and TATEH *and* MOTHER *and the two* CHILDREN *are watching* TATEH's *new film,* Shadows of the U-Boat.

TATEH   That is my new hero. Slade of the Secret Service. He will now capture entire German U-Boat with crew single-handed.

EXT.   UNDERWATER

The sound of a monstrous explosion. In the richness of a marine environment, creatures of the deep in great numbers gliding past our camera. We see the feet, legs, and torso of a human creature descending. Then the face with the hair risen in astonishment. It is FATHER.

INT.   STAGE

EVELYN *dancing.*

INT.   CONGRESS OF THE UNITED STATES (NEWSREEL)

President Woodrow Wilson is addressing both houses of Congress. (silent.)

WAR MONTAGE

Sequence of stock scenes of the war in Europe. Americans going over on troop ships, waving and smiling, trenches, Argonne Forest, Big Berthas, doughboys going over the top, the mud, the death, etc.

These scenes should pass over the screen at such speed as to suggest a gigantic fireworks display, with appropriate sound effects, and with the ever-present Ragtime music underneath.

We see American troops marching down Broadway for the first Armistice Day Parade. A crazy civilian figure following alongside troops is HARRY K. THAW. *He is ecstatically happy.*

The music should be lively and at this point the audience should realize that the color of the film has gradually been leaching out—something that has been going on since the death of COALHOUSE WALKER. *By this point everything is in black and white and continues so to the end—the picture becoming flickier and more rudimentary as in early silent film.*

EXT.   NEW ROCHELLE. BROADVIEW AVENUE. DAY

We see HOUDINI, *now a black-and-white newsreel character, driving up jerkily to the house on Broadview Avenue, running quickly up the steps and finding the door locked, the shades pulled, and a* TO LET *sign in the window. There is no sound accompanying this except music.*

EXT.   LARGE WHITE STUCCO CALIFORNIA HOUSE WITH ARCHED WINDOWS. DAY

Palm trees along the sidewalk in front of the house. TATEH *and* MOTHER *come out of the door arm in arm looking like absurd silent film home movies jerkily bowing and smiling and pointing.*

EXT.   LITTLE BOY, LITTLE GIRL, AND BROWN BABY SIT ON FRONT LAWN. DAY

Near a tricycle, they smile and wave back at the TWO GROWN-UPS.

TATEH *is suddenly excited. What he says is delivered to us on a title card. The card reads:*

"I have inspiration for a film! A gang of kids who are pals. White, black, fat, thin, rich, poor."

MOTHER *nods with a broad smile.* TATEH *lifts an arm expansively.*

"Together they have adventure. A gang of ragamuffins, like all of us, getting into trouble and getting out again."

The THREE CHILDREN *on the sidewalk get up jerkily and waddle quickly down the street doing an Armistice Day march, waving a toy flag. We watch them get smaller and smaller.*

The light flickers and fades and goes black, and on the black screen we hear the theme music in the rinky-tink Ragtime of a player piano.

E N D

The Metamorphosis
of *Loon Lake*

IN THE 1980s E. L. Doctorow published three quite different novels, which all take place during the 1930s. *World's Fair* is a seemingly autobiographical novel in the form of a memoir about a young Jewish boy named Edgar growing up in the Bronx during the Depression. *Billy Bathgate* also concerns a Bronx boy's coming-of-age, only this time the slightly older protagonist rises from the slums to a high life of crime in the company of gangster Dutch Schultz. The third novel, written first, is *Loon Lake*, another account of a proletarian youth who makes his way to the top of the social ladder as the adopted son of a business tycoon.

All three novels have several things in common. They are first-person accounts of youthful initiation into modern society told retrospectively; they all explore different aspects of the same American dream; and they interpret the thirties through the lens of its multifaceted culture. Since this was the decade in which the author himself grew up, the strong influence of popular culture, from radio shows to moving pictures, should not be surprising.

Loon Lake, the most complex narrative of the three Depression novels, portrays the odyssey of three children of the working class who wish to rise in the world and claim a part of the American dream. Penfield, Clara, and Joe are in flight from their proletarian origins. In renouncing their respective familial legacies, they all reject the idea of class solidarity for the ideal of individual self-fulfillment. In each case, their journey takes them to Loon

Lake, the idyllic domain of a wealthy capitalist named Bennett, whose private empire is carved out of the American landscape.

Thoughout, *Loon Lake* explores different resonant images of American culture. The descriptions of the lake recall not only the setting of Thoreau's retreat in *Walden* but also the scene of the crime in Dreiser's *An American Tragedy*. The representation of Bennett's fabulous estate suggests Fitzgerald's fantasy, "The Diamond as Big as the Ritz," and the portrayal of the poor young hero doggedly pursuing his dream girl echoes, of course, *The Great Gatsby*. But the other side of the novel, the description of Depression-ridden America wracked by class conflict and labor strife, also draws on the rich vein of popular and proletarian culture produced in the thirties. *Loon Lake* is very much a book about the 1930s but, as Doctorow has suggested, it is "about our idea of the Thirties."[1]

IN ITS rich imagery and range of cultural reference, *Loon Lake* is perhaps the most cinematic of Doctorow's novels. First of all, the novel originated in images. In the *Paris Review* interview, Doctorow says that the novel came to him in a vision. "I had these opening images of a private railroad train on a single track at night going up through the Adirondacks with a bunch of gangsters on board, and a beautiful girl standing, naked, holding a white dress up in front of a mirror to see if she should put it on."[2] The narrative is ignited by this momentary glimpse of Clara. In the novel, Joe sees Clara bathed in light and drops to his knees as if he has had a religious experience. In the screenplay we see what Joe sees and perhaps we, too, genuflect as the camera zooms in on gorgeous Clara. "Suddenly this golden vision is gone," Doctorow writes in the scenario. The camera shifts to the protagonist. "Joe stands as if struck dumb. He stares after the train. Music begins."

But movies resonate throughout the novel, from Joe's emulation of Charlie Chaplin at Loon Lake to Doctorow's sly reference to young Frances Farmer in Seattle. Douglas Fowler suggests that *Loon Lake* was inspired by the American movies of Doctorow's childhood.[3] Certainly, in describing Joe's progress, Doctorow draws on his intimate knowledge of thirties films, from *Modern Times* to *It Happened One Night*. But if *Loon Lake* is a novel whose vision is shaped by Hollywood movies, how then was the novel transformed into a film scenario?

In *The Screenwriter's Workbook*, Syd Field argues that the process of writing a screenplay follows the same linear logic as the screenplay itself. "A

The Metamorphosis of *Loon Lake*

screenplay follows a certain, lean, tight, narrative line of action, a line of development," he says. "A screenplay always moves forward, with direction, toward the resolution. You've got to be on track every step of the way; every scene, every fragment, must be taking you somewhere, moving you forward in terms of story development."[4] But, as we have already seen, fiction writing is a very different, often elliptical experience in which the writer discovers his tale in the process of writing it.

But fiction writing is not only an heuristic experience; it is also a polyphonic process. In his celebrated essay "False Documents," Doctorow suggests that the different realms of fact and fiction represent the conflicting powers of what he calls *"the regime"* and *"freedom."* By *"the power of the regime"* Doctorow means our acquiescence to the authority of brute facts which goes by the name of realism; by *"the power of freedom"* he means the ability of the imagination to subvert that authority. "There is a regime of language that derives its strength from what we are supposed to be and a language of freedom whose power consists in what we threaten to become," says Doctorow. "And I'm justified in giving a political character to the nonfictive and fictive uses of language because there is a conflict between them."[5]

John G. Parks claims that all of Doctorow's writing is concerned with opposing this regime of received facts. He says that "the ultimate political enterprise of the novelist is to prevent the power of the regime from monopolizing the compositions of truth, from establishing a monological control over culture."[6] Parks employs Mikhail Bakhtin's notion of a "dialogic" culture and the "polyphonic" novel to describe Doctorow's method of challenging the authority of the dominant culture and recovering the lost voices of silenced subcultures. Bakhtin described the polyphonic novel as "a plurality of independent and unmerged voices and consciousness, a genuine polyphony of fully valid voices."[7] This is, as we shall see, a fairly accurate description of the method of *Loon Lake.*

Already in *The Book of Daniel* Doctorow had begun to break up his narrative by fracturing chronology and splitting point of view. But in *Loon Lake* the principle of discontinuity is taken a step further. Here we encounter a number of narrative voices with characters speaking in both first and third person, shifting suddenly in time and space. The novel moves swiftly, changing voice or scene often, and filling in the necessary exposition with computer printouts, a device that resembles the movie montage in its ability to provide information in shorthand. Thus the narrative is both compressed and polyphonic: "It is the account in helpless linear translation of the unending love of our simultaneous but disynchronous lives."[8]

The narrative of *Loon Lake* evolves through a polyphony of voices in which Joe discovers his own identity by modulating and absorbing the contrapuntal viewpoints of Bennett, Penfield, and Clara. In his screenplay, Doctorow has sought to retain some of the complexity of his narrative strategy by the use of "flash forward": the insertion and repetition of short scenes out of chronological order which disrupt the linear narrative and represent the synchronicity of events. But he has simplified the polyphony of narrative voices by significantly reducing the role of the poet Warren Penfield. In the novel, Joe and Warren are depicted as spiritual brothers, sons of the working class torn between their desire for personal freedom and their allegiance to their proletarian origins. But Penfield is also Joe's surrogate father, who leaves the legacy of his writing—"all that is left of me"—with the message: "You are what I would want my son to be."[9] Thus, the ultimate conflict in the book is the struggle between two putative fathers, Penfield and Bennett, for possession of Joe's soul. In the end, having become Bennett's adopted son, Joe writes the book in an agonizing attempt to be true to both his fathers.

There are good practical reasons for reducing Penfield's role in the scenario. In the first place, giving Warren his due would unduly lengthen an already long screenplay. Second, the Penfield scenes would be the most difficult and expensive to film: labor unrest in Colorado, the General Strike in Seattle, the earthquake in Tokyo. But lessening Penfield's long shadow subtly changes the emphasis in *Loon Lake*. Now Joe's fate is directed almost exclusively toward his attempts to resist or emulate his other father figure, Bennett. Thus, the key dramatic scene in the first half of the screenplay is Joe's interview with Bennett. Standing before his employer, Joe rejects Bennett's job offer in a curt declaration of independence, but then he sits and listens to the tycoon's eloquent account of his Darwinian philosophy. Joe's alertness to Bennett's speech indicates that he will be leaving Loon Lake with more ideological baggage than he came with.

It is, of course, Joe's initial assertion of self-reliance that identifies him as Bennett's true son among the proletariat. This identification is sealed in the dramatic climax, when Joe first declares himself to be Bennett's son in his police interrogation and then echoes Bennett's philosophy in explaining to Sandy the difference between making "a new start" and making "a new *life*." Joe's inevitable decision to return to *Loon Lake* is triggered when he learns

The Metamorphosis of *Loon Lake*

that Lucinda and Warren have vanished. In a nice cinematic touch, Doctorow alters this climactic scene slightly. In the novel, Joe reads about their disappearance in the newspapers. In the screenplay, he sees it at the movies.

Penfield's diminished role has other consequences for the screenplay, as well. In the novel, the symbolic value of Loon Lake is adumbrated through Penfield's poem, which is annotated by Joe. In a computer printout Doctorow briskly traces the corruption of Loon Lake from its simple exploitation by trappers and hunters through its symbolic appropriation by painters and poets to its physical appropriation by capitalists like Bennett. In Doctorow's version of capitalist development, artists play a significant role in the cultural transformation of nature from landscape to commodity.

In the novel, Loon Lake is described as cold and remote, like its owner. Traditionally, the lake in classic American literature has symbolized the inviolable purity of nature, as in Cooper's Lake Glimmerglass or Thoreau's Walden Pond. But here Doctorow describes Loon Lake as icy and insular: the perfect objective correlative of capitalism, in which the pursuit of wealth is motivated by the desire for complete isolation. Joe says, "I looked back up the hill to the house and felt the imposition of an enormous will on the natural planet. Stillness and peace, not the sound of a car or a horn or even a human voice, and I felt Loon Lake in its isolation, the bought wilderness, and speculated what I would do if I had the money."[10]

In the screenplay, the icy resonance of the lake is not depicted in watery images alone. Instead, Doctorow shifts his focus from the lake to the loons. In the novel, Joe witnesses the bird's predatory behavior:

The wind rose in a sudden gust about my ears, and as I looked back to the lake, a loon was coming in like a roller coaster. He hit the water and skidded for thirty yards, sending up a great spray, and when the water settled he was gone. I couldn't see him, I thought the fucker had drowned. But up he popped, shaking and mauling a fat fish. And when the fish was polished off, I heard a weird maniac cry coming off the water, and echoing off the hills.[11]

In the screenplay, this scene is neatly reproduced in the beginning and then briefly reprised at the end. But Doctorow has made one significant change: now there are *two* loons. This doubling symbolizes the twinning of those other two predators, Bennett and Joe. In the final scene, when Joe has returned to

Loon Lake to be adopted, he and Bennett spot two loons. "I like those damn birds," Bennett remarks. "I like the way they move out of one element into another. (*looking at* Joe) Pretty as you please." Their identity is confirmed in the last scene when Joe dives naked into the lake to the accompanying cry of a loon. Doctorow describes the scene: "Joe, water falling from him, arms aloft, like wings about to lift him into the air. He falls back, surface dives, and disappears under the water."

Thus Doctorow's screenplay subtly transforms the theme of Joe's pursuit of a father figure. Details that appear in the complex novel emerge more clearly in the stripped-down screenplay. For instance, Joe is first drawn to the lake lodge by the strains of a popular song, "Exactly Like You." Here we identify it with his pursuit of the elusive Clara. In the later scene, when he returns to Loon Lake, we hear the same song. But now "Exactly Like You" refers to his similarity to Bennett. In the closing montage, their faces gradually impose on each other. The extraordinary final shot is of Joe, who has supplanted Bennett as proprietor of Loon Lake. The impersonation is complete. Doctorow's final directions read: "A shift in the light. No sound. Bennett from the rear, hands on the parapet. He turns around to us. It is not Bennett. It's a man the same age, with the same white hair. It's JOE. He glances at us, anguished."

I HAVE already indicated the symbiosis that exists today between the novel and film, but perhaps there is another way to read a scenario, especially when a writer adapts his own fiction. Could the screenplay offer a chance for a writer to work out his second thoughts about his novel? We have seen how Doctorow's slight change from one to two loons in the scene by the lake subtly links the two human predators. In our interview, he suggests that there might actually be an improvement on the novel, clarifying the connection between Joe and Bennett, in the old man's speech about the adaptability of loons.

Certainly it underlines a major theme the novel shares with *Ragtime:* the corruption of working-class solidarity in the United States. Like Tateh, Joe betrays his class origins and "point[s] his life along the lines of flow of American energy."[12] Richard King suggested that *Loon Lake* might be sub-titled "Why There Is No Socialism in America" because it vividly describes "the immensely seductive power of the bourgeoisie and its ability to 'buy' everyone off." According to King, the novel "charts the triumph of energy over ideology, status over solidarity."[13] The seductive power of fabulous wealth unfolds in the screenplay as the camera lingers lovingly over the luxury of Bennett's estate at Loon Lake.

But there are other ways in which a screenplay might clarify or "improve" on a novel. A simple example of clarification occurs in *Ragtime*, where an image crystallizes a concept. In the novel, the escape artist Houdini is described as an unwitting symbol of revolutionary possibility. He "never developed what we think of as a political consciousness. He could never reason from his own hurt feelings. To the end he would be almost totally unaware of the design of his career, the great map of revolution laid out by his life."[14] In Doctorow's scenario, the ironic connection between Houdini's performance and political action is made explicit as we watch this son of the working class escape from his manacles and we recall the revolutionary slogan: "Workers of the world, unite! You have nothing to lose but your chains."

Similarly, some might point to an example of "improvement" in *Loon Lake*. Several critics have complained about the abrupt ending of the novel, in which, after Joe's return to Loon Lake, Doctorow appends a computer printout of his future career, culminating with the chilling words "Master of Loon Lake."[15] I have never understood this criticism; Doctorow's surprise ending is sufficient in its exposition and powerful in its economy. Jean-Paul Sartre once remarked of the characters in John Dos Passos's *USA* that they did not have lives but destinies.[16] We might say of the mature Joseph Bennett that he has no life but only a career. Having charted Joe's spiritual fall, Doctorow does not have to recount the inevitable steps of his decline. Instead, the computer printout symbolizes the depersonalized character of his future life: his barren marriages, covert government work, and myriad business connections. In Doctorow's description, "the image I use for Joe is emptiness."[17] The final scene, in which Joe supplants Bennett, suggests the nature of his destiny without spelling it out. But to those who are troubled by the abrupt ending of the novel, Doctorow's use of montage in the screenplay may provide a more satisfactory resolution of Joe's odyssey from rebellion to acquiescence.

NOTES

1. Unpublished interview.
2. *The Writer's Chapbook*, ed. George Plimpton (New York: Viking, 1989), 69.

3. Douglas Fowler, *Understanding E. L. Doctorow* (Columbia: Univ. of South Carolina Press, 1992), 86.

4. Syd Field, *The Screenwriter's Workbook* (New York: Dell, 1984), 12.

5. E. L. Doctorow, "False Documents," *Jack London, Hemingway, and the Constitution: Selected Essays, 1977–1992* (New York: Random House, 1993), 153.

6. John G. Parks, *E. L. Doctorow* (New York: Continuum, 1991), 18.

7. Quoted ibid., 19.

8. E. L. Doctorow, *Loon Lake* (New York: Random House, 1980), 254.

9. Ibid., 177.

10. Ibid., 75–76.

11. Ibid., 76.

12. E. L. Doctorow, *Ragtime* (New York: Random House, 1975), 111.

13. Richard King, "Two Lights That Failed," *Virginia Quarterly Review*, Spring 1981, 344.

14. Doctorow, *Ragtime*, 29.

15. Doctorow, *Loon Lake*, 258.

16. Jean-Paul Sartre, "John Dos Passos and 1919," *Literary and Philosophical Essays* (New York: Collier Books, 1962).

17. Unpublished interview.

The Metamorphosis of *Loon Lake*

LOON LAKE

A Screenplay

EXT.   PINE WOODS. DAY

*Someone is running through the woods. A young man (*JOE*). He runs with his cap in his hand. We hear his breathing. He passes through patches of sunlight. Branches and twigs break under his feet. He makes a lot of noise. Even after he passes out of sight we hear the noisy passage he makes. He's no woodsman.*

EXT.   ROADSIDE BLUFF. DAY

JOE *stands at the treeline, looking down at a two-lane country road. Satisfied it is clear, he makes a brief attempt to spruce up—using his cap to beat the dust from his lumber jacket and trousers. He scrambles down the bluff.*

EXT.   COUNTRY STORE. DAY

A small general store with a crank-handle gas pump in front. Siding of hammered tin advertising signs—Moxie, Bull Durham, Silvercup Bread, etc. JOE *comes in off the road, sits on the sprung-upholstered divan outside the door, takes off one shoe and removes a folded dollar bill. Slips the shoe back on, looks up and down the road, and enters the store.*

A dingy, poorly stocked emporium. A sack of dried beans near the counter. A few cans and packaged goods on the shelves. The STOREKEEPER, *a stolid, middle-aged woman with thick eyeglasses, cuts slices of bologna onto a sheet of wax paper. After each slice she looks at* JOE *before slicing another.*

JOE   OK.

She weighs the slices, wraps them, puts them next to his other purchases on the counter. She takes a pencil from behind her ear, licks the point.

STOREKEEPER   Let's see; bottle of Grade A, sixteen cents. Twelve for the bread, thirty cents for the meat, fifteen for the cigs.

She adds the figures laboriously.

JOE   *(impatiently)* Seventy-three cents.

STOREKEEPER   *(continuing)* Carry the one. Five, six, seventy-three it is. You're the smart one.

She makes change from the dollar.

You ain't from around here.

JOE   No.

STOREKEEPER   I didn't figure. Say, you couldn't be with the Hearn Brothers?

JOE   *(a moment of panic)* What?

STOREKEEPER   The carnival stopping over to Chester. That freak show?

JOE *grabs the bottle of milk, the packaged bread, the meat, shoves the cigarettes in his pocket.*

JOE   I may be on the bum, lady, but that don't make me a freak.

He gets out of there fast.

EXT. TWO-LANE ROAD. DAY

JOE *half running, half walking along the road. He stops, listens, scrambles up the bluff and dives for cover in the woods. We hear the sound of an approaching engine. From* JOE's *point of view we see a state police car roaring by.*

EXT. PINE WOODS. DAY

JOE *sits cross-legged in a small clearing and makes his lunch. Slaps the meat between slices of the white bread. Tears into the sandwich ravenously. Shakes the milk bottle, lifts off the cap, eats and drinks, stares straight ahead, unseeing.*

INT. SIDESHOW TENT. DAY (SILENT)

FANNY THE FAT LADY *sitting on a scale as big as a porch swing. She's dressed like Shirley Temple—short jumper, bow collar, ribbon in her hair. Heavily made up. Dyed hair set in waves. She is sucking an enormous lollypop. She smiles.*

EXT. PINE WOODS. DAY

Reprise of JOE *running.*

EXT. BESIDE A RAILROAD EMBANKMENT. FADING DAYLIGHT

JOE *shares a fire with an* OLD HOBO. *Scruffy weeds all around. Behind the curving embankment an outcropping of rock. The* OLD HOBO *holds out a pint of rotgut.* JOE *drinks.*

OLD HOBO   Most stiffs know to get out of the mountains by the end of summer.

JOE   Yeah, well, I'm hoppin' a Red Ball. *(gestures toward the track)*

OLD HOBO   *(grinning)* Shit. You and Hell both can freeze over. *(reclaims bottle)* That there's just some spur line.

JOE   Well, the joke's on us.

OLD HOBO   Nosir. Wrong again. I ain't planning to go nowhere. This is it far's I'm concerned. *(He clutches his bundle.)* The last stop.

JOE *looks at the man with interest as the significance of this statement dawns on him.*

OLD HOBO   *(suddenly enraged)* I suppose you're gonna tell me I got something to live for!

JOE   I didn't say nothin'.

EXT.   BESIDE RAILROAD EMBANKMENT. NIGHT

The OLD HOBO *sleeping, back to the fire. He snores.* JOE *hunkers by the fire. He smokes a cigarette, stares into the flames. He hears something, lifts his head. We hear it now—the distant sound of a train whistle.* JOE *stands, turns toward the track. We watch his face as we hear the whistle again, closer, and hear the chuffing of the engine.*

EXT.   RAILROAD TRACK (JOE'S POINT OF VIEW). NIGHT

A paling of the night along the curved embankment and the outcropping. Suddenly a powerful white light swings into view and fills the screen.

EXT.   BESIDE EMBANKMENT. NIGHT

Illuminated in the engine's headlamp, JOE *throws his arm across his eyes, sinks to his knees.*

EXT.   RAILROAD TRACK (JOE'S POINT OF VIEW). NIGHT

*The train passing from left to right. Slowly, screechingly, magisterially. The looming black shapes of the steam locomotive and a coal tender. Followed by a brightly lit private passenger car: we see a porter in a white jacket serving drinks to three men at a table. Wood paneling, shelved books in leather bindings, tasseled lampshades. Two older women in wing chairs. And then a white bedroom with a canopied bed, and a blonde girl (*CLARA*) standing naked in front of a mirror. We zoom in on her: she holds up for inspection a white dress on a hanger.*

Suddenly this golden vision is gone. The train has passed through the clearing, around the curve, a red lantern swinging at the rear as, the noise receding, it disappears into the night.

EXT.   BESIDE EMBANKMENT. NIGHT

JOE *stands as if struck dumb. He stares after the train. Music begins. Dissolve to:*

MONTAGE UNDER CREDITS: JOE'S JOURNEY ALONG THE TRACK TO LOON LAKE

Sequence of scenes of JOE *walking the track.*

At first, in the early morning, his collar is up, he walks with his hands in his pockets, hunched against the chill, his cap pulled down low.

Later, the sun high, he carries his jacket slung from his shoulders.

The terrain changes, the track traverses open fields, goes over narrow bridges spanning deep gorges, winds its way around forested mountains.

The grade of the track changes: it climbs now, we see sky.

The track curls around the side of a mountain and a silvery lake comes into view.

It is dusk. JOE *is only a shape, a silhouette, and we hear his feet on the cinders and hear the distant cry of a loon over the darkening silver lake.*

Credits end. Music ends.

EXT.   RAILROAD SIDING AND PLATFORM. NIGHT

The immense locomotive stands dark and still. Something is moving along the platform, alongside the drive wheels, alongside the tender, back to the private car. It is JOE. *He steps out of the shadow of the train, stands looking up at it.*

He goes to the rear of the private car, hauls himself up on the observation deck. Stands listening. Tries the rear door, finds it open, slips inside.

INT.   PRIVATE RAILROAD CAR. NIGHT

By the light of a match JOE *explores the luxurious appointments of the car. A think Persian rug under his feet. Club chairs. Etc. On a side table lies a leather-bound book. He opens it and we see the bookplate:* EX LIBRIS F. W. BENNETT.

Loon Lake: A Screenplay | 319

The match goes out. He strikes another, drops the dead match carefully in a brass spittoon.

He follows the narrow corridor to the next door, a shining, immaculately clean stainless-steel kitchen. And finds beyond that the room he's been looking for: the bedroom with the canopied bed.

He lights another match, feels the plump lace pillows and down coverlets of the bed. He runs his hands over the bed as if over a girl. We hear his breathing.

He bends over the vanity table looking for something, a trace, a sign of the blonde girl. He finds nothing, but catches sight of himself by matchlight in the mirror: he's appalled by his dirty derelict appearance, so out of place here. The match goes out.

EXT.   THE F. W. BENNETT LODGE ("LOON LAKE"). NIGHT

A spectacular rustic mansion seen from the land side across a rolling meadow. All the lights are lit. But the wind is blowing and there is a feeling of menacing isolation.

JOE advances toward the great house slowly—drawn to it but cowed by its grandeur. As he gets closer the music of a dance band comes off the wind. The song is "Exactly Like You."

He does not approach the house head on, but moves to the side, to the cover of some trees, and here he sees that the house is situated on a bluff, and behind it, in moonlight, is the lake.

INT.   BENNETT LODGE. LIVING ROOM. NIGHT

Three or four COUPLES in evening dress are dancing to the music. They verge on middle age. But one of the women is the young blonde (CLARA), and she seems the most far gone. She dances indolently, her back arched over her partner's arm. A champagne glass is held lightly in her fingers. Her eyes are closed. The music ends and though her partner (TOMMY CRAPO) tries to stop, she goes on dancing.

A SERVANT moves forward and winds up the console Victrola and puts the record on again. He moves on, passing a window: JOE looking in, ducks out of sight.

       Loon Lake: A Screenplay

EXT. TENNIS COURT AND SHACK. NIGHT

JOE *sits on his haunches in the shadow of the Loon Lake tennis court shack. Behind him the court is in moonlight. He cups his hand around his Lucky to hide the glow as he takes a drag. Now that he's found her, he doesn't know what to do about it. His eyes are fixed on the great house. He's angry with himself.*

He hears something and reacts.

EXT. MEADOW BEHIND TENNIS COURT AND SHACK. NIGHT

A pack of dogs bearing down on JOE. *They are not hunting dogs but a mongrel lot of starved, cadaverous curs yelping with murderous excitement.*

The lead dog flying through the moonlight, eyes red, fangs extended.

The dogs are all over JOE, *leaping for his throat, getting in each others' way, snarling, turning on each other.* JOE *screaming, fighting them off, kicking out, howling like a dog himself.*

He is slammed against the side of the tennis shack and tumbles back through its unframed window, taking one of the dogs, jaws locked on his arm, inside with him.

INT. TENNIS SHACK. NIGHT

The dog has been stunned loose by the fall. JOE *grabs a tennis racquet hanging on the wall in its wooden press and brings it down side edge on the dog's back before it can get to him.*

A fountain of dog faces leaping and falling back in the window frame. One dog catches the window sill and begins to haul itself in. JOE *slams the racquet down on its paws. It falls back.*

He heaves the dog who came in with him through the window. Suddenly the yowling stops and the dogs are no longer trying to get in. JOE *slumps to the floor and listens now as the dogs grunt in appeasement as they begin feeding on the dog he has thrown to them.*

JOE *is pretty well torn up. Blood streaming down his face, neck, through his jacket. He looks up through the tennis shack window.*

EXT. A STARLIT SKY. NIGHT

The stars begin to blur as we hear the dogs feeding. The screen goes black.

INT. CARNIVAL SIDESHOW TENT. DAY

FANNY THE FAT LADY *sitting on her scale in her Shirley Temple outfit. She sucks on her giant lollypop and smiles.*

The camera pulls back to find a crowd of country RUBES *observing her. They are in summer clothes—overalls, thin frocks, the children barefoot, etc. But in the crowd is* JOE. FANNY *seems to be smiling at him. He carries his belongings in a bundle slung from one shoulder. He's smiling back.*

The scale over FANNY's *head points to the number 600.*

RUBE   *(man)* Hell, ain't no one weighs that much and lives.

For an answer, FANNY *responds with an emphatic sigh, bouncing the red arrow on the scale all the way up to 900. Crowd laughs.*

INT.   SIDESHOW TENT. STALLS OF OTHER FREAKS. DAY

JOE *wandering past the various acts, enjoying them all: the* FINGERLINGS, *a midget family,* WOLF WOMAN, LIZARD MAN, *etc. They are all bored, monotonously reciting their life stories to the onlookers or trying to sell pictures of themselves. But one of the* FINGERLINGS *for amusement darts into* WOLF WOMAN's *stall and, sneaking up behind her, pulls out a tuft of hair on the back of her leg. She yowls and turns and swings at him, but too high. He scurries out of the way, taunting her, and the crowd enjoys this mightily.*

EXT.   CARNIVAL MIDWAY. DAY

This the Hearn Brothers Show, a fifth-rate country carnival with tattered tents, paint-peeling trucks, broken-down attractions. It is situated on a hard dirt lot between two stands of trees. A hot day, the sun shining.

The crowd is sparse and generally indifferent, but JOE, *strolling past the game booths, shooting gallery, etc., is obviously drinking in the whole sleazy scene. Scratchy circus music is coming out of the loudspeakers. A couple of* ROUSTS *are struggling to lay the tracks of a kiddy-car ride.* JOE *drops his bag and ostentatiously helps them. They are not in good shape—rummies from the looks of them, and not young.*

FIRST ROUST   Fuck'n' kid.

SECOND ROUST   Hey, get outta here. Scram!

JOE *laughs. The carny owner's wife* (MAGDA HEARN) *observes the scene.*

EXT.   CARNIVAL MIDWAY. NIGHT

It's late, the wind is blowing, the string lights swinging in the wind. The RUBES
*are leaving. They carry their sleepy children. They hold Kewpie dolls, pin-
wheels.*

   FANNY THE FAT LADY *emerges from the sideshow tent, her enormous flesh-
slathered self quivering with each step. For support she holds onto the shoulder
of a woman attendant* (AUNT). *And with her other hand touches* JOE's *shoulder.
They make a stately procession. A* LITTLE KID *stops to watch. His* MOTHER
pulls him away.

   JOE *is self-consciously pleased to be associated with the act. But not so
occupied as to miss the passing scene: the* GIRL *who sells the tickets has locked
the door of her booth and stands outside, looking in a hand mirror and primping
her hair. A* RUBE *comes up, says something to her, she puts her hand on her hip.
He gives her a dollar. She tucks it in her blouse, gestures with her head, walks
off, and the rube follows her.* JOE *twists around to see where they go, but the
figure of* FANNY *blocks his view.* FANNY *smiles at him.*

EXT.   FANNY'S TRAILER. NIGHT

JOE, FANNY, *and the* AUNT *come to the foot of the steps leading to* FANNY's
trailer.

AUNT   Gracias.

JOE   Can she get up the steps?

AUNT   *(nervously)* Si. Gracias. Goodnight.

JOE   Glad to help. Well. Goodnight.

FANNY's *beaming at him. She utters something unintelligible. If we didn't know
before, we know now that she is retarded.*

The lights are going off now. The canned music abruptly shuts off. The wind blows litter across the lot. The FREAKS *are going off to their trailers.* JOE *finds himself confronted by* MAGDA HEARN, *a middle-aged foreign woman with platinum hair and a sort of beat-up glamour about her.*

MAGDA HEARN   I am Mrs. Hearn. *(pause)* Of the Hearn Brothers Attractions? Where all day you are hanging around.

JOE   Oh—

MAGDA HEARN   A young man who needs job.

JOE   I guess it shows.

MAGDA   You did not intend it to show?

She has him.

    What can you do?

JOE   *(eyeing her)* Just about anything.

MAGDA   You are not a local.

JOE   Does that show too?

MAGDA   All peasants are given weak eyes, weak hair, weak bones. In Hungary, in America. For this you don't qualify. Where you are from?

JOE   Paterson.

MAGDA   Where?

JOE   Paterson. That's in New Jersey.

MAGDA   So. You have jail record.

She begins walking, JOE *by her side. She walks with a limp.*

JOE   No I don't, lady.

MAGDA   So far off the track—up here?

JOE   That's right. I just don't like sharing boxcars with a hundred other stiffs.

Loon Lake: A Screenplay

MAGDA   A private boxcar or nothing.

JOE   That's right.

MAGDA   Why not?

She stops, faces him.

  Come tomorrow. To my husband I will speak. The work is hard. But you
  learn something. How to make money from the poor.

*She walks off. JOE watches her. Her limp is not unpleasant. Her figure is good
and the rolling gait is provocative.*

EXT.   FANNY'S TRAILER. NIGHT

*It is later. Quite dark. Standing queued up in front of the trailer are several men.
At the foot of the steps sits FANNY'S AUNT. She holds a cigar box on her lap.*
  Strange sounds come from the trailer: moans, shrieks, hoarse cries.
  SIM HEARN, *the carny owner, arrives: a tall thin man in a shabby black suit,
black string tie and fedora. He exchanges cigar boxes with the AUNT. He leaves.*
  *The weird sounds cease and from the trailer a MAN comes down the steps,
fixing the belt on his pants. The FIRST MAN ON LINE gives the AUNT a couple of
dollars, which she puts in the cigar box. She nods and the first man on line goes
into the trailer.*
  A couple of MEN ON LINE share a flask of whiskey.
  *The camera finds JOE sitting with his back to a tree. His bundle is beside him.
He smokes and looks at the stars as the shrieks and moans issue once more from
the trailer.*

EXT.   TWO-LANE ROAD. DAY

*The beat-up trucks and trailers of the Hearn Brothers carny, in convoy, coming
down the road.*

INT.   TRUCK CAB. DAY

JOE *at the wheel.* MAGDA HEARN *sitting beside him.*

MAGDA   You are what—nineteen? Twenty?

JOE   Close enough.

MAGDA   You have family? A mother, a father?

JOE   Yeah.

MAGDA   What do they do?

JOE   Well, he works in the factory there when they let him.

MAGDA   And your mother?

JOE   She's just there. The two of them together, all the fight's gone out of them.

MAGDA   But not you.

JOE   That's right.

MADGA   You have dreams.

JOE   That's right.

MAGDA   I knew it. You have dreams, you want more.

She removes a snapshot from her wallet. It shows a young blonde in spangled tights, sitting sexily on a trapeze.

JOE   That you?

MAGDA   Yes. In the Hagenbeck-Wallace Circus. Me and my husband and his brother, we were big star. My husband was catcher. One day I missed his hand and fell badly in the net.

She puts the photograph back in her wallet.

It did not heal right. I fell also from his love down through all the years further and further until I struck bottom *(she smacks the seat of the truck with the flat of her hand)* in the Hearn Brother Carnival.

JOE   From where I'm looking it's not the bottom. You ain't exactly one of the hands.

MAGDA   *(with a bitter laugh)* Shall I tell you how I Mrs. Hearn become? I have always been with numbers clever, even as child. I say to Hearn I will keep your books. And then, as I know by looking at this man, he afterwards has to marry me. He will not for long trust to keep his books who is not related.

Joe reacts.

Is true. In the American law a wife cannot be made to testify against husband.

JOE *looking ahead, again down the truck. The convoy is slowing, bunching up to a stop.*

Speak of devil.

EXT.   TWO-LANE ROAD INTERSECTION, EDGE OF TOWN. DAY

SIM HEARN, *the carny owner, standing beside a Model A; intersection at right angles to the convoy. He gestures to the lead truck to follow him, gets in behind the wheel, and turns into the road to head the caravan.*

EXT.   CARNIVAL MIDWAY. DAY

The Hearn Brothers Show once again set up in a hard dirt lot. The crowd of country RUBES, *barefooted* CHILDREN. *The rides going around. Canned music. The* BARKER *in front of the Freak Show tent:* FANNY *up on the platform beside him.*

EXT.   PINE WOODS. DAY

Reprise of JOE *running through the woods (opening scene). But there is no sound for this. What we hear instead is the canned carny music continued from the last scene.*

INT.   LOON LAKE STAFF HOUSE. BEDROOM. DAY

A simply furnished bedroom, a small window high in the wall. JOE *lies in bed, arms and legs and chest in bandages. Three people—two* MAIDS *and a* GROUNDSKEEPER—*standing in the doorway looking at him. They are all dressed in green livery.*

A commotion behind them and they make way for an older woman—the HEAD MAID (MRS. GROVE), *also in green—and the* DOCTOR.

MRS. GROVE   What is this! You know you have no business here! Libby (*to younger* MAID), I thought you had work to do.

LIBBY   Yes, ma'am.

LIBBY *leaves reluctantly, after the others, and with a glance back at Joe.*

MRS. GROVE   (*to* DOCTOR) You'd think it was the King of Siam.

The DOCTOR *has opened his black bag, popped a thermometer in* JOE's *mouth, and now he holds* JOE's *wrist, at the same time looking at his pocket watch.*

DOCTOR   Well, after all, the lad's a medical attraction. He's got more stitches in him than a three-piece suit.

MRS. GROVE   Anyone who's fool enough to prowl these mountains at night deserves what he got.

JOE *reacts with his eyes.*

DOCTOR   Compassion, Mrs. Grove. A youth. A mere stripling.

MRS. GROVE   (*fussing about the room)* I don't care. We've got enough to do without waiting on tramps.

The DOCTOR *removes the thermometer.*

DOCTOR   (*to* JOE) Well, your fever's down.

JOE   I didn't ask for this, lady. Those were your damn dogs, not mine.

MRS. GROVE   How dare you speak in that tone of voice!

DOCTOR   Now, now; tempers, everyone. Mrs. Grove, if you please, I've an examination to conduct.

MRS. GROVE *leaves.*

How do you feel?

JOE   Everyone's doing me favors.

DOCTOR   Actually, no favors are intended. Not when Mr. Bennett calls the shots. *(He prepares to change dressing.)* And as for me, I haven't had this much fun since the flu epidemic of 1918. You're strong as the devil. But I'm still hoping you'll develop something or other to try the limits of my medicine.

INT.   STAFF HOUSE. JOE'S BEDROOM. DAY

It is later in the day. A square of sun shines from the small window high in the wall into JOE's *eyes.*

LIBBY, *the young maid, appears at the door, sees the problem, and pulls the shade.*

JOE   Thanks.

LIBBY *stands looking at him, and he perceives that without even trying he's made a friend.*

What'd you say your name was?

LIBBY   Libby.

JOE   Well, you can sit down if you want.

LIBBY   I'm supposed to be working.

JOE   Maybe *you* can tell me where I am, Libby.

LIBBY   You don't know?

JOE   I must have got on the wrong track. I thought I was headin' for California.

LIBBY   This is Loon Lake.

Pause.

JOE   You don't say. And who's bed am I in?

LIBBY   It's an extra. In the staff house?

JOE   The staff house.

LIBBY   It's where we stay.

JOE   Who's we?

LIBBY   Mr. Bennett's people. We work for F. W. Bennett. *(sees it doesn't register)* You mean you don't know who he is? The Bennett Auto Works!

JOE   I may have heard of him . . . So. This is his layout.

LIBBY   All fifty-thousand acres! *(She giggles.)* Every tree, every leaf. He owns the forests, he owns the lake, he owns the water in the lake, the land under the water, and the fish that swim in it.

JOE   Don't forget the dogs.

LIBBY   Oh no—not the dogs. They're wild.

JOE   Sure.

LIBBY   It's the fault of the people who raise them. And then they can't afford to feed them anymore? And then they run off and forage and breed wild and hunt in packs.

JOE   The people?

LIBBY   The dogs! All through the mountains it's like that, not just here. *(pause)* Does it hurt?

JOE   It don't tickle.

LIBBY *shivers and holds her arms as if it's cold.*

JOE   *(patting the bed)* You can sit down, you know. I'm not Frankenstein, even if I look like it.

LIBBY *sits shyly on the edge of the bed, at the foot.*

JOE   They work you pretty hard?

LIBBY   Oh no. I wish they did. There's nothing to do.

JOE   Then why stick around?

LIBBY   I send money to my father in Albany. He's too sick to work anymore. *(She decides to put the best face on things.)* Besides, it's not that bad. I bet you don't know who comes here. Famous people.

JOE   What?

LIBBY   Famous people come here to visit with the Bennetts. They entertain a lot.

JOE   Who?

LIBBY   Why, big politicians and prime ministers from England, and Jeanette MacDonald was here in the spring! She's so beautiful! I unpacked her clothes.

JOE   Who else?

LIBBY   Oh well, it was before I ever came. But Charlie Chaplin.

JOE   Sure. On roller skates.

LIBBY   I can prove it!

Pause.

JOE   You say there's a Mrs. Bennett?

LIBBY   Of course! You know her.

JOE   I do?

LIBBY   She wins all the air races and her picture's always in the paper. Lucinda Bennett?

JOE   Oh, her. The one with the blonde hair?

LIBBY   *(smoothing her hair)* No! She's a brunette. Like me.

Pause.

JOE   Brunettes are my favorite.

EXT.   SEQUENCE OF LOON SHOTS. DAY

A pair of loons beating through the sky. We see them through several dissolves, at different speeds and angles; they are big, strange, beautiful, primeval birds, black and white with luminescent red eyes.

One of them peels off and dives.

Now we see not sky in the background, but mountain and forest. The dive seems heedless, destructive, and suddenly there is water behind the bird and it hits like a roller coaster, sending up a spray and skidding for several yards along the surface. The other comes in a moment later and we understand that this is the way they do it.

As we watch, both birds disappear; they are here one moment and gone the next. We look for them along the water.

And then, in a roll of agitation, one of them emerges from below, water falling from her, a wriggling fish in her beak. She tosses her head back.

We hear the uncanny, manic cry of the loons coming over the lake. We see other loons beating over the sky above the lake.

INT.   JOE'S BEDROOM. DAY

LIBBY *stands in the doorway with a large, flat leather-bound book clutched to her bosom. She is breathing fast from her run, or from excitement, or both.*

LIBBY   I better not get caught.

She fixes JOE's *pillows so that he can sit up better, and sits down beside him and opens the book.*

This is the Loon Lake guest book. Mr. Bennett asks them to sign their names and say something.

She turns the big, flat pages and stops and runs her finger down the page

There!

She looks at JOE *with an expression of triumph and pleasure.*

INSERT: THE GUEST BOOK

The top of the page is marked 1931, and halfway down the page LIBBY's *finger points to the signature "Charles Chaplin." Next to it is scrawled the comment: "Splendid Weekend. Gay Company!"*

LIBBY   *(voice over)* Splendid weekend! Gay company!

INT. JOE'S BEDROOM. DAY

LIBBY *has stood up and does a playful twirl around the floor.*

LIBBY   Charles Chaplin! Splendid weekend! Gay company!

JOE *is examining the book very carefully. He turns the pages, studies the names. He reads them aloud.*

JOE   Sir Thomas Beecham. Cornelius Vanderbilt Whitney.

LIBBY   He's so rich he's got three names!

JOE   That's class, all right. But look at this. This guy is such a big shot he needs only one name. Leopold. Of Belgium.

LIBBY *has come to see. She puts her head close to* JOE's. *Glancing up, he finds her eyes on the pages but her attention all on him. Her bosom rises and falls. She feels him looking at her and withdraws, sitting at the foot of the bed to regain her composure.*

JOE *turns to the last page with writing on it.*

JOE   Hey, Libby, how long have I been here, anyway?

LIBBY   We were taking the summer covers off the furniture. It was that night. *(looking at him)* I never hope to hear what I heard that night.

JOE   Well, how long ago was that?

LIBBY   Three weeks.

JOE   Wasn't someone here then? Weren't there guests? *(no response)* Libby, I saw them dancing. How come I don't find anything that recent in the guest book?

Pause.

LIBBY   *(not looking at him)* Not just anyone gets to sign.

JOE   Is that right! *(suddenly incensed)* Hey, I think someone's calling you—

She runs to the door and listens. JOE *reaches over to the bedside stand, yanks the drawer open, grabs a fountain pen there, unscrews the cap, shakes a blot on the floor. He spreads open the guest book and writes in it. Too late,* LIBBY *sees this. She lunges at him over the foot of the bed.*

LIBBY   What are you doing!

JOE   Joe . . . of Paterson. Splendid dogs. Swell company.

INT. JOE'S BEDROOM. EVENING

JOE *has just finished his dinner.*

A knock on the door. WARREN PENFIELD *enters: a stout, middle-aged man, bearded, overgrown hair, the ravaged, big-nosed face of a drinker. He wears baggy trousers, the belt below his belly, an ancient tweed jacket, a dirty tennis shirt, tennis sneakers.*

He closes the door, puts his back to it, peers at JOE *for a moment, begins to pace the room with his hands behind his back.*

PENFIELD   I can understand your feelings better than you can, Mr. Joe of
    Paterson. I spend my life understanding feelings—my own and, therefore,
    others. That's what poets do.

JOE   What?

PENFIELD   But by the same token, I understand poor Libby's feelings. Good
    God—she's one of the few decent people around here, and now she's in fear
    for her job. Do you realize what a disaster it would be for her to lose her job?
    (pause) Of course, I'll do what I can, the Bennetts aren't here right now,
    fortunately; there's time. I'll think of something—yes, I'll speak to Lucinda,
    that's what I'll do. But the point is, as a man of honor you should have
    realized she'd be held responsible for anything you did. She was nice to you,
    she made you her friend, and this is how you repaid. What?

JOE   Nobody's ever called me a man of honor.

PENFIELD   Oh. Well, what you did had quality, you see. "Joe of Paterson." A
    good, wicked joke. God knows I can enjoy a joke at his expense. I wish there
    were more of them. Incidentally, he himself is not devoid of humor, you
    know.

JOE   Who?

PENFIELD   Frank Bennett! A complicated human being. He's quite charm-
    ing at times. The mistake people make is to jump to conclusions before they
    even meet him.

Loon Lake: A Screenplay

JOE   Well I'll try not to.

They enjoy the laugh together. A female STAFF MEMBER *of the household* (ROSE) *comes in to take* JOE's *empty dinner tray.*

ROSE   If you're feeling so good, maybe it's time to get up out of that bed and start earning your keep.

She grabs the tray, giving PENFIELD *a withering glance, and marches out, snorting her disapproval.*

PENFIELD   Dreadful woman. They all are, except for Libby. They're all related, you know, like wood trolls. They despise me. I'm more than they are, but I have no place as they have. They never miss an opportunity to make my life miserable. I have to beg to get something to eat. But when the Bennetts are in residence and they ask me to dine with them, I'm served like the King of England.

JOE   Did I see your name in the guest book?

PENFIELD   What? No, hardly. I'm a friend of the family, you see, and I live on the grounds. Warren Penfield's my name. Actually, I'm Mrs. Bennett's friend, mostly, Lucinda, she's very generous, a patron of my work, you see. Actually, I suppose you might call me poet-in-residence. *(He clears his throat, pulls his shoulders back, tries without succeeding to tuck his shirt in.)* Yes, I'm Poet in Residence at Loon Lake.

JOE   I never met a real live poet.

PENFIELD   Yes, well, most of us are dead, that's true . . . I hadn't thought to ask you how you feel.

JOE   Lousy, thanks.

PENFIELD *pulls up his jacket sleeve and shows his bare left arm: a thick scar runs from the wrist to the elbow.*

PENFIELD   You're not the only one, I want you to know. Seven years ago the dogs treed me when I followed the track in one night—just like you.

A big shed with mowers, tools, bins, etc. MRS. GROVE *in light green talks to* MR. STONE, *an older man in dark green, while* JOE *leans against the door jamb. He too has on the dark green shirt and slacks. He looks pale, thin, with overlong hair. He's still not very strong.*

MRS. GROVE   Mr. Stone, this boy is good for some work.

JOE   I wouldn't count on that. I ain't been told what the wages are.

MRS. GROVE   As you might suspect, we'd just as leave see him on his way. But that's Mr. Bennett's decision for when he returns. It won't be soon enough, as far as I'm concerned.

She leaves.

MR. STONE   Relax, son. She's just an old iron-ass.

JOE   I've paid to stay here. You know? I'm a paying guest. *(He pulls his shirt collar down, shows the scars down his neck, on his chest.)* See?

MR. STONE   I see.

He hands JOE *a leaf rake.*

JOE   I mean, if I don't work, what'll they do, fire me?

MR. STONE   Kid, you don't know how lucky you are. If you was smart you'd do anything to make it permanent.

JOE   Yeah, and listen to the loons.

MR. STONE   Well, I suppose so. But you get three squares, a bed with clean sheets, a few dollars, and a day off to go to town every coupla weeks and spend 'em. Could be a better way to wait out the hard times, but I sure as shit don't know what it is.

JOE *looks out the open door.*

MR. STONE   You don't look too good anyways. Why don't you take it easy on yourself.

EXT.   LOON LAKE GROUNDS, LAKESIDE. DAY

The sun shines, a brilliant morning, the landscape in the colors of early autumn. We're seeing for the first time in daylight the Loon Lake lodge of F. W. BEN-NETT *in all its magnificence: a brown log motif, three sprawling storeys on a hill overlooking the lake—dormers, casement windows, screen porches, terraces, rock gardens.*

JOE *with other* WORKMEN *rakes leaves on the downhill slope. He works slowly, stops to look around. He's glad to be up and around; the sun feels good. He gazes at the lake.*

On the shore is a large boathouse of the same style as the lodge up above.

The deep blue lake seems cupped in the mountains like water cupped in hands.

Loons fly by.

EXT.   LOON LAKE GROUNDS, LAND SIDE. DAY

JOE *is among three or four* WORKMEN *with leaf rakes tossing leaves over the slat side of a small three-wheeled truck that moves slowly along. Stables, greenhouses, other outbuildings in the distance.*

Out of the far end of a meadow can be seen the top of the wire-mesh fence of the tennis court. JOE's *attention is caught by a white tennis ball flying high over the fence.*

EXT.   TENNIS COURT MEADOW. DAY

JOE *dragging his rake, leaving his post, going toward the tennis court. The other* WORKMEN *looking after him critically.*

EXT.   TENNIS COURT. DAY

PENFIELD *in white ducks and shirt too tight for his belly is on one side of the court with a pail of balls. He demonstrates the proper forehand stroke to a* YOUNG WOMAN (CLARA) *standing on the other side of the net. She wears a white tennis skirt, a halter, and a visor over her blonde hair. Perhaps we zoom in on her standing there in all her angry beauty and holding the racquet on her shoulder like a baseball bat.*

EXT. TENNIS COURT (JOE'S POINT OF VIEW). DAY

PENFIELD *takes a ball and gently hits it to* CLARA's *forehand. She swings with a wild lunge and poles the ball over the end-court fence into the meadow. We see several other balls in the grass, as if it is sprouting white flowers.*

PENFIELD *says something and hits her another. Again she knocks it a mile. A third time, and the ball rockets off the court at an angle, coming over the side fence toward us and rolling to a stop in the grass at* JOE's *feet. He picks it up.*

EXT. TENNIS COURT (ANOTHER ANGLE). DAY

CLARA *has followed the progress of this ball.* PENFIELD *comes to the net.*

PENFIELD   Take a level stroke, my dear. Keep your eye on the ball and don't worry about hitting hard.

CLARA *glares at him, drops the racquet, and strides swiftly off the court toward the woods on the far side of the distant lodge.*

PENFIELD   Clara? Is something wrong? Clara? Did I say something to offend you?

She ignores him, tosses her visor behind her, fluffs her hair. PENFIELD *watches her going as if in a trance. He comes to, finally, and rushes about the clay court picking up tennis balls.*

EXT. MEADOW BEYOND TENNIS COURT. DAY

JOE *too, after watching her, transfixed, runs around picking up the white balls from the grass, then hurries toward the court. It's her—the girl he followed to Loon Lake.*

EXT. TENNIS COURT. DAY

JOE *meets* PENFIELD *just inside the fence gate.*

PENFIELD   She can't bear to be taught. (*looking after* CLARA *almost proudly*) I told her not to hit so hard—but what game can it be, after all, in which one doesn't hit one's hardest!

The two men watch her going over a rise in the meadow and disappearing by degrees in the general direction of the lodge.

PENFIELD dumps his tennis balls into JOE's already laden arms and rushes after her.

EXT.   LOON LAKE LODGE. DAY

A car and a station wagon, LOON LAKE STAFFERS in civilian clothes piling in, including MRS. GROVE. Doors slam.

INT.   LOON LAKE STAFF HOUSE. JOE'S BEDROOM. DAY

JOE and LIBBY listen to the sounds of car doors slamming, cars driving off.

JOE   Let's go.

LIBBY   I'm afraid.

JOE   C'mon. They're gone for the weekend. All the wood trolls.

LIBBY   Not all. Cook stayed. Rose and Mary.

JOE   Aw hell, I'll do it without you.

He leaves.

LIBBY   Wait!

She runs after him.

INT.   LOON LAKE MAIN HOUSE. KITCHEN. DAY

It is grand, 1930s modern, spotlessly clean and empty. A door opens and the heads of LIBBY and JOE peeking in.

INT.   BUTLER'S PANTRY. DAY

Glass cabinets of china, silver service, etc. LIBBY pulls open a drawer to show JOE all the silver flatware.

LIBBY   Have you ever seen anything! They can serve thirty people at dinner.

Loon Lake: A Screenplay | 339

INT. LIVING ROOM. DAY

The grandest room of all—built-in furniture, huge fireplace, two levels, game table, trophies on walls, large double-bay windows looking out on terrace overlooking the lake. LIBBY, *proprietary, watching* JOE*'s reactions.*

LIBBY Of course, this is just one of their places! Can you imagine?

JOE *heads for upper level.*

JOE What's up here?

INT. FRONT HALL. DAY

A grand curving staircase of halved logs polished to a high shine. A chandelier made of antlers. JOE *gazes up the stairs.*

JOE I love roughing it! Don't you old girl?

He grabs LIBBY*'s hand and runs up the stairs.*

INT. UPSTAIRS CORRIDOR. DAY

JOE *is going down the corridor,* LIBBY *in hand.*

JOE What's this?

LIBBY The west wing bedrooms.

JOE Fancy that. Is anyone home? Any Bennetts? Any guests?

LIBBY No.

JOE No? You sure? What's in here?

He opens one of the doors.

INT. HABERDASHERY ROOM. DAY

JOE *enters, followed by an apprehensive* LIBBY. *Here are racks of sports clothes, shelves of sweaters, boxes of riding boots.*

LIBBY He gives people gifts when they visit.

JOE *takes an argyle sweater from the shelf, checks the label, pulls it over his head.*

You shouldn't.

JOE *looks at himself in the mirror, likes what he sees.*

JOE   Hey Libby, I could be a Bennett, couldn't I? What d'ya think?

He smoothes his hair.

You're pretty wowed by all this. But did you ever think what's underneath?

He's searching for trousers, finds some, takes his off.

LIBBY   Oh! *(hiding her eyes)*

JOE   Someone just like me, kid. Just like me.

He has knickers on now, finds saddle shoes in a box.

Look, I make a passing big shot don't you think? A goddam aristocrat!

LIBBY   You shouldn't. Take those thing off.

JOE   Look!

He finds a woman's riding helmet, puts it on her head; finds a velvet riding jacket, puts it on her.

Look. Mr. and Mrs. Mighty Muck-a-Muck themselves.

Despite herself LIBBY *gazes into the mirror.* JOE *grabs her around the waist, dances her about.* LIBBY *laughs and protests at the same time, giggling, telling him to stop. To her surprise he does—he's seen something out the window.*

LONG SHOT: GUEST COTTAGE ON HILLSIDE IN TREES
(JOE'S POINT OF VIEW). DAY

CLARA *and* PENFIELD *sitting on the porch steps.*

INT.   MAIN HOUSE. HABERDASHERY ROOM. DAY

LIBBY *comes to the window to see.*

LIBBY   What?

JOE *blocks her view, takes her in his arms again, resumes the dance. He's really manic now, dances her out the door and sings.*

INT.   UPSTAIRS CORRIDOR. DAY

JOE *is dancing* LIBBY *down the corridor, stopping at each passing bedroom door to throw it open. Squares of sunlight fill the corridor behind them.*

JOE   *(singing)*
  "I know why I've waited,
  Know why I've been blue,
  Prayed each night for someone
  Exactly like you."

INT.   STAFF HOUSE. DINING ROOM. NIGHT

JOE *in his green livery at a long table with the* PEOPLE *of the green, his dinner on a tray before him.* ROSE *taps him on the shoulder.*

ROSE   That Penfield called. You're to go over to the cottage.

JOE   Who, me? What for?

ROSE   *(walking away)* How should I know. I'll be glad when you're gone and them with you.

JOE *sees* LIBBY *and others looking at him. Affects cool. Shrugs. Resumes eating.*

INT.   JOE'S BEDROOM. NIGHT

JOE *enters casually, cigarette in mouth. Once door is closed, leaps into feverish action: tears off his uniform clothes, dresses in soft white shirt, argyle sweater, knickers, ribbed socks, saddle shoes.*

EXT.   LOON LAKE WOODS AND COTTAGE. NIGHT

JOE *coming through the trees to the front door of the cottage. He stops at the steps, takes deep breath, mounts porch steps, knocks on the door. He hears dogs howling, and looks up at the stars. The door opens, and firelight shines on his face.*

INT.   CLARA'S COTTAGE. NIGHT

Low beams, stone fireplace in firelight. CLARA *sits, holding a wineglass, on the sofa, crosslegged, in a robe of white satin fallen open across her thighs.* PEN-FIELD *is on the floor at her feet, reading from a thin sheaf of papers.*

PENFIELD   " . . . and after the old man retired
    and all the gangsters and their women stood around
    in their black ties and tuxes and long gowns
    the best gangster's girl saw a large Victrola in the corner
    of the big living room with its leather couches and
    grand fireplace
    the servants spirited away the coffee service
    and the best gangster's girl put on a record and commanded
    everyone to dance.
    And they danced to the Victrola music
    they felt better they did the fox-trot
    and the gangsters nuzzled their shoulders
    and their new shoes made slow sibilant rhythms
    on the polished floors
    as they danced in their tuxes and gowns of satin
    at Loon Lake
    in the rich man's camp
    in the mountains of the Adirondacks."

A moment of silence. He clears his throat.

    Well, what do you think?

CLARA *has tears in her eyes. She leans over, lifts his face, kisses him. His hand, holding a bottle, rises.*

JOE   *(leaving)* I can come back another time.

PENFIELD   *(struggling to his feet)* No no, not at all. Come in, come in. Here
    he is, Clara, Joe of Paterson, the fellow I wanted you to meet.

He runs, gets a glass for JOE, *pours wine from the bottle.*

   Miss Clara Lukacs.

JOE   How do you do.

CLARA *barely glances at him. She's still thinking about the poetry.*

PENFIELD   Sit down, sit down.

JOE *sits opposite* CLARA, PENFIELD *on the floor between them.*

PENFIELD   *(raising his glass)* To good verse. To freedom.

CLARA *raises her glass solemnly.* JOE *realizes that they are both sloshed. He raises his glass. Dissolve to:*

INT.   CLARA'S COTTAGE. NIGHT

The fire has died down. PENFIELD *is discoursing, pausing every now and then for a swallow of wine.*

PENFIELD   It was the battle of the Somme, you see, though I didn't know it. Signal Corporal Penfield is called to the battalion bunker. The field telephone is out, not even a damn pigeon left, just some feathers floating in the smoke. "Corporal, we need that artillery barrage." So I take the old semaphores and make my way to the front, to the top of a hill—a mound, really, a hummock—but the highest position in all this no-man's land. So I can be seen. And all hell breaks loose, all the deadly fireworks, star shells. Vary flares like daylight. And I hold up my flags *(he holds out bottle)* and send the urgent message. And a while later in comes the artillery, right on target. And that's what I got the medal for.

He digs in his pocket, hands silver star with faded ribbon to JOE. JOE *looks at it and leans over, hands it to* CLARA, *whose robe has now opened to reveal her wearing nothing underneath. His hand brushes hers.*

CLARA   Warren, you're a hero!

PENFIELD   But no, love, you haven't heard the whole story. I was so scared I never sent the message I was supposed to. What I semaphored was a poem.

JOE   What?

PENFIELD   Wordsworth's "Ode, Intimations of Immortality from Recollections of Early Childhood."

CLARA   What?

PENFIELD   *(pantomiming semaphore)* It was all I could think of.
    "There was a time when meadow, grove, and stream,
    The earth and every common sight,
    To me did seem
    Apparelled in celestial light,
    The glory and the freshness of a dream,"
    and so on. And a while later the shells came in on target. Very strange.

CLARA   *(beginning to laugh)* In the war—the battle? You did that?

PENFIELD   Surely you know it. The Wordsworth Ode. *(looks at each of them)* Don't they teach it in school? Anyway, that's what I got the medal for. They pinned it on my bathrobe in Nutley, New Jersey, where they sent me for observation after the war.

CLARA   Where? *(laughing)* Oh Warren, you old fuck, where!

JOE *can see her breasts through the open robe. He sees* PENFIELD *glance at him sadly, tears in his eyes. Dissolve to:*

INT.   CLARA'S COTTAGE. NIGHT

JOE *is fixing the fire. Smoke drifts into the room.* PENFIELD *is opening another bottle at the kitchen counter.*

CLARA   *(to* JOE*)* You live here? How do you stand it.

PENFIELD   Clara—I said he's my surprise for you.

CLARA   What's 'at mean?

They are all three standing drunkenly before the fireplace, PENFIELD *filling glasses.*

PENFIELD   You remember the night you heard the dogs? Joe here is taking each day as it comes, just like you.

She leans forward, traces the scar on JOE's *neck with her finger. She unbuttons his shirt, pulls it off his chest, down his arms. Traces the scar on his chest.*

CLARA   He told me they brought down a deer. That was a lie.

PENFIELD   Yes.

CLARA   What class.

She begins to cry.

PENFIELD   I could help you leave, Clara. I can get you out of here. We can leave together. There's still time.

CLARA   That son of a bitch Crapo. I wouldn't give him the satisfaction.

Fade out.

INT.   STAFF HOUSE. JOE'S BEDROOM. MORNING

JOE *is sleeping. Rapping on the door—it flies open.* LIBBY *comes in, shakes him.*

LIBBY   You better get up. Mr. Bennett's expected.

JOE   *(one eye open)* What?

He sits up in bed, winces, holds his head.

He's here?

LIBBY   He's due in. Mrs. Grove is driving everyone carzy.

She sees the argyle sweater, knickers, etc., strewn about.

You took those things from the house!

JOE   Yeah.

LIBBY   You stole!

JOE   Don't shout. My head . . .

LIBBY   Omigod.

JOE   *(putting his feet on the floor)* Nobody has to know a thing Libby. Unless you tell them. And you can't, can you.

Loon Lake: A Screenplay

LIBBY   You were with her!

She rushes out.

JOE   Close the door, dammit!

INT.   STABLES. DAY

In the dim light, JOE *is mucking out a stall. Down at the other end of the building a* MAN *in green is tightening the saddle cinches of two horses. Suddenly the stable doors swing open. A great flood of light. An authoritative male voice. The* STABLEMAN *leads the horses into the light.* JOE *climbs over the stall gate and goes toward the light.*

EXT.   OUTSIDE STABLES. DAY

Framed by the open stable doors, we see from JOE*'s point of view* F. W. BEN-NETT *mounting a magnificent bay mare. He is a broad-shouldered, white-haired man, obviously a skilled rider. The horse is skittish. He controls her. His face is tanned, his eyes blue.*

In the flurry the horses separate and we see CLARA *getting a hand up from the* STABLEMAN. *She sits astride a grey horse, somewhat smaller than* BENNETT*'s. Her helmet is askew. She is obviously an inexperienced rider.*

BENNETT, *speaking softly to her, leads them off into the woods,* CLARA *bouncing inelegantly on the wide-assed horse.*

EXT.   MAIN HOUSE. NIGHT

Lights ablaze. Dance music.

INT.   PENFIELD'S STUDIO APARTMENT. NIGHT

JOE *stands at the window. We hear, much diminished, the music of the previous scene.*

PENFIELD *drinks. The apartment is filled with books, dirty ashtrays, clumps of dust, empty wine bottles.*

JOE   I suppose I'll be out of here tomorrow.

PENFIELD   *(staring into his glass)* What?

JOE   When it comes to his attention.

PENFIELD   You can't be sure, Joe of Paterson. I have made a study of the very rich. The one way they're accessible is through their whim. *(drinks wine)* I haven't told you this, but six or seven years ago when I came up here at night along the track—like you—I knew where I was going. I had traced Bennett to Loon Lake. In my pocket was a switchblade. I intended to kill him.

JOE   *(turning from window)* I have the idea myself.

PENFIELD   Mr. Bennett was not impressed. Indeed, he was amused. He invited me to remain on the grounds and write my poetry. Yes. And now you see me.

JOE   I do. I see you.

PENFIELD   I know what you're thinking. You think living this way, year after year, and not going anywhere, not doing anything, I've lost my sense of proportion. It's true! So that every small thing that happens is monumentally significant. I know. I lie in wait like a bullfrog lying in wait, for whatever comes along for its tongue to stick to. Yes. That's the only part of me that moves, my tongue. You want to hear me croak?

JOE   What?

PENFIELD *imitates a frog, loudly and insistently.*

Jesus.

PENFIELD   I think I do that well.

JOE   Why were you going to kill him?

PENFIELD   Who?

JOE   Bennett.

Pause.

PENFIELD   People I loved died because of the policies of one of his companies. He owns lots of companies.

JOE   You know what he's worth?

PENFIELD   Worth? What can it matter? I haven't a dime myself. Millions, billions. The power over people. This one company mined coal in Colorado. Ludlow, Colorado. You never heard of it? Why should you. It was more than twenty years ago.

He gets to his feet, stumbles around looking among his books. Opens a closet door, rummages inside. Sound of things falling. He emerges, holding a thin book in his hands. Spanks the dust from it.

This is my first book of verses. *Flowers of the Black Hills.* That's where the coalfields are out there. I want you to have it.

JOE   Thank you.

PENFIELD   I published it myself.

JOE   Thank you.

PENFIELD   Just don't read it in front of me.

JOE   Who was killed there, Mr. Penfield?

PENFIELD   My father. He was a miner. The miners went on strike. The company had an armed militia . . . Also my mother. The company set fire to the workers tents, where women and children were hiding. And Clara too, when she was a little girl.

JOE   Clara?

PENFIELD   Clara was killed in Ludlow. She keeps coming back, you see, over and over. The same girl, the same true love. I get fatter and older but Clara stays beautiful.

JOE   Are you all right, Mr. Penfield?

.PENFIELD   *(enraged)* You don't believe me! Who are you to doubt me—a follower of trains in the night.

EXT.   LOON LAKE. DAY

A beautiful mahogany Chris-Craft backs out of the boathouse. Aboard are BENNETT *(in yachting cap and blazer) and* CLARA.

The boat rises in the water and zooms away, the two of them laughing. Loons start up into the sky.

Camera pans back. JOE *with a rake watches from hillside.*

EXT.   PATH TO CLARA'S COTTAGE. EVENING

JOE *helping* PENFIELD, *who is drunk, along the path to the cottage.*

JOE   Who is Clara, Mr. Penfield?

PENFIELD   A maiden in distress, my boy.

JOE   Is that what they call it?

PENFIELD   What?

JOE   Maybe I better take you back.

PENFIELD   I must get her away. I've got to save her.

He stumbles up the porch steps, pounds on the door.

Clara? Clara? Clara?

JOE *tries the door, which is open.* PENFIELD *pushes past him.*

INT.   CLARA'S COTTAGE. BEDROOM. NIGHT

CLARA *in camisole and step-ins is applying makeup before a mirror.* PENFIELD *comes in;* JOE *stops behind him in the doorway.*

PENFIELD   Clara, why don't you answer?

CLARA   Christ.

PENFIELD   I'm here now, Clara.

CLARA   Yeah.

PENFIELD   (*to* JOE) It's always the same. He destroys love. He kills her and he lets me live to grow older and more ridiculous. And then she comes back. I recognize her and she is as drawn to me as I am to her—despite the change in our circumstances.

Loon Lake: A Screenplay

CLARA *goes to the closet, removes an evening gown.*

PENFIELD   (*to* CLARA) But this time—this time I won't fail you, Clara. I swear it.

CLARA   Stop pawing me!

PENFIELD   Why have you no memory, Clara?

CLARA   War-rin! Do I have to spell it out?

She slips the gown over her head.

PENFIELD   (*to* JOE) We are drawn to each other in recognition as you see now, again, even though I'm indisputably fatter and more ridiculous as a figure of love. And even though (*looking at* CLARA) she is faithful to nothing but her own life.

CLARA   (*to* Joe) Zip this up, will you?

PENFIELD   (*sinking to his knees*) Oh God! (*he lifts his eyes*). Oh God, who made this girl, give her to me this time to hold. Let me sink into the complacencies of fulfilled love, let us lose our memories together, and let me die from the ordinary meaningless results of having lived.

CLARA   Goddammit what d'ya want from me! (*to* JOE) Jesus, what'd you bring him for? Take him home. Get this fucking drunk out of here!

EXT.   BRIDLE PATH. DAY

JOE *and* THREE WORKERS *in dark green, including* STONE *and* HEAD GROUNDSWEEPER (FOREMAN), *walking hurriedly, picks and shovels over their shoulders.*

STONE   What's this all about?

FOREMAN   Just hurry. The old man's on one of his tours.

Around a bend, two horses are tethered together along the trail. Beyond, standing on a boulder in the woods, is BENNETT.

BENNETT   (*calling*) Come up here!

EXT. BOULDER SITE, WOODS. DAY

Climbing to position, JOE *sees* CLARA *sitting against a tree to one side. She chews a stalk and looks at him idly. He pauses, goes on.*

BENNETT   That's it. Now here, look at the size of this thing.

The WORKMEN *look down dutifully at the boulder they stand on.*

I've always wondered about this. I want it exposed.

Pause.

FOREMAN   *(scratching his head)* You want us to dig this rock up?

BENNETT   Dig around it. You see here? This is the top of it, we're standing on top of it. That's what this rise is. I want the whole thing uncovered.

At their dumbfounded silence, he grabs a pick from one of them.

I don't know why it's here! You see? Work away at it like this. You see how it extends—goes all the way over here.

FOREMAN   Here Mr. Bennett. Don't you be doing that. (*pointing to* JOE *and* STONE) You, you—get to work.

JOE *and* STONE *begin to swing their picks at the earthen packing around the boulder.*

BENNETT   That's the way! That's what I want.

He goes back to the horses, CLARA *joining him; he helps her mount and mounts himself.*

Damndest thing, isn't it? It's the only one—nothing like it anywhere in these woods.

He trots off, CLARA *behind.* JOE *watches, leaning on his pick.* FOREMAN *takes off his cap, wipes his forehead.*

FOREMAN   Jesus, Mary, and Joseph!

Loon Lake: A Screenplay

INT. CLARA'S COTTAGE. NIGHT

It's dark. The door opens slowly. Pause. A hand turns on the light switch. It's
JOE. *He's still in his work clothes.*

The cottage is messy. Unwashed wine glasses, filled ashtrays. JOE *goes to the*
doorway of the bedroom, switches on the light.

INT. CLARA'S BEDROOM (JOE'S POINT OF VIEW). NIGHT

The room is empty. It looks well lived-in: clothes strewn everywhere, stockings
twirled and curled up like strips of bacon. Step-ins lying in perfect circle on the
floor where they'd dropped.

INT. CLARA'S LIVING ROOM. NIGHT

JOE *builds a fire in the fireplace. Takes a cigarette from the monogrammed*
("FWB") box on the table, packs it, lights it, sits back on an armchair facing the
fire. He stretches his legs luxuriously, as if it all belongs to him. He settles back
to wait. He smokes, gazes at ceiling.

INT. CLARA'S LIVING ROOM. DAWN

JOE *lies asleep, curled up on the sofa. What wakes him is the sound of an*
airplane. He listens as it grows louder, rises in pitch, grows faint.

Sunlight is on the windows and, coming in at a slant, lights the smoke
hanging under the ceiling.

The engine grows louder again, closer, so that the dirty wine glasses rattle
against each other on the table. JOE *jumps up and goes to the window.*

EXT. LOON LAKE. DAWN

A single-engine plane with pontoons is banking over the mountain on the other
side of the lake. It comes back, a green and white seaplane zooming toward us,
then flaring in the sun as it banks off again.

EXT. CLARA'S COTTAGE. DAWN

JOE *runs outdoors, peers up to watch the sight.*

Each run of the plane is different in speed and angle of descent. A sassy pilot, having a good time.

JOE's *wonderment, seeing an airplane this close.*

EXT. LOON LAKE. DAWN

The pilot has cut the engine. The plane comes in very low, overhead, drifts down over the lake and passes below the tree line.

EXT. LAKESIDE. DAWN

JOE, *pushing his way through brush, trees, comes to the water, sees plane taxiing toward a hangar at water's edge, perhaps fifty yards to his right.*

CLOSE-UP: PLANE

LUCINDA BENNETT *pushes back hatch cover of cockpit, removes her leather helmet, runs fingers through her hair.*

EXT. PATH TO CLARA'S COTTAGE. DAWN

CLARA, *in rumpled evening gown, is coming through the woods from the Main House. She carries her shoes. Her hair is not combed.*

EXT. CLARA'S COTTAGE. DAWN

CLARA *comes into the clearing in front of the cottage just as* JOE *emerges from the woods.*

CLARA   Are *you* here?

She strides past him into the cottage. He turns, follows.

INT. CLARA'S LIVING ROOM. DAWN

CLARA *stands, back to the open door* (JOE's *point of view), her hands on her hips. She realizes she's holding her shoes, and flings them across the room. The bedroom phone rings. She runs in there as if she's going to attack it.* JOE *moves into the middle of the living room and we listen with him as* CLARA *answers the phone.*

CLARA   *(off)* What! *(pause)* Yeah, well I wouldn't count on it!

We hear the phone slam down. Pause. Silence. JOE *moves to the door of the bedroom.*

INT. CLARA'S BEDROOM. DAWN

CLARA *sits on the edge of her bed. Slips off her shoulder straps, shrugs her gown to her waist. She sits hunched over, hair matted, tears streaming down her face and falling on her breasts.*

JOE   *(not moving)* Hey. Come on now. Come on.

After a moment, she stands, steps out of her gown and, nude, goes into the bathroom. A moment later the sound of the shower running.

INT. CLARA'S LIVING ROOM. MORNING

In the kitchen alcove, JOE *has put up coffee in the percolator.*

CLARA *comes into the room wearing a white bath towel with the FWB monogram in red. She accepts a mug of coffee from* JOE, *sits on the sofa with her legs folded, and holds the mug with both hands, as if for warmth. She's washed her hair; it lays about her head in wet curls. Her eyes are glistening.* JOE *has never seen anyone so beautiful.*

JOE   You don't belong here any more than I do.

CLARA   No.

JOE   When I first saw you I thought you were one of them.

CLARA   That's a laugh.

JOE   Then it began to dawn on me. You would know the game of tennis. You would know how to ride horseback.

He smiles, but she's having none of it.

CLARA   This place is getting on my nerves. How do I get out of here?

Pause.

JOE   I'll take care of it. Leave it to me.

She looks at him. He doesn't know if she's going to laugh in his face, throw the coffee, or what. But she seems satisfied with his answer. She puts her mug on the floor, curls up on the sofa with her back to him. JOE *realizes that she is going to sleep. He leaves, closing the door gently.*

EXT.   COTTAGE CLEARING AND WOOD PATH. DAY

JOE *ecstatic, exultant, running, turning around to look back, running again, leaping in the air. He can't believe his good fortune.*

EXT.   BOULDER SITE, WOODS. AFTERNOON

The WORKMEN *have unearthed the enormous boulder to its southern polar top: it sits now in an enormous trench on top of several smaller stones.* JOE *stands with* FOREMAN, *gazing at their handiwork. Unlike the others, who are exhausted and skeptical,* JOE *is gleaming with sweat, nervy, energetic.*

JOE   Is that enough you think? Maybe we should dig some more.

FOREMAN   (*to* OTHERS) What's gotten into him? Is he touched in the head?

JOE   Not, me, boss. I'm not the one touched in the head. *(He laughs.)*

EXT.   IN FRONT OF MAIN HOUSE. AFTERNOON

The WORKMEN, *dirty and tired, back from the boulder site, picks and shovels on their shoulders.* BENNETT *stands on his front porch, addressing them.*

BENNETT   Good work, boys. *(checks the sky)* The light's no good now. To-morrow when the sun is high, we'll check for markings. We may have to wash it down. I want to see if it has markings.

They take this news impassively. JOE, *in the middle of the* WORKMEN, *glances around at their lack of enthusiasm and he grins.*

You, Joe, you think it's just a rock, don't you.

JOE *is stunned that* BENNETT *knows his name.*

Come inside, I want to show you something.

BENNETT *goes into the house. Someone reaches over and takes the pick from* JOE's *shoulder.*

FOREMAN   There's a good lad.

Snickers as the rest of them leave. JOE *looks after them.*

INT.   MAIN HOUSE. LIVING ROOM. AFTERNOON

BENNETT *and* JOE *are examining a large folio spread flat on a long table.*

BENNETT   See this? And this? I'm not as crazy as you think. Megaliths. Dolmens.

Insert: Line drawings in color of primitive stone monuments—in all cases on large boulders resting on three or four smaller ones, much like the dig in the woods.

BENNETT   The Indian tribes of New England built them to honor their fallen chiefs. I know a little something about the ancient burial practices of the Adirondack tribe.

A MAID *enters, holding a phone with a long cord.*

MAID   Your call, sir.

BENNETT *takes just the headset, and begins to move all around the room as he talks. The* MAID *follows with the receiver, keeping the cord clear of furniture.* JOE, *uncomfortable and ill at ease, glances through the glass door. On the terrace a thin, elegant* WOMAN *arranges cut flowers in a vase—brown hair cut short, no make-up, longish skirt, loose sweater, low-heeled shoes. It is* LUCINDA BENNETT. JOE *reacts with recognition. She looks up and smiles at him, lifts the vase, closes the door.* JOE *slides open the door for her.*

LUCINDA   Thank you.

She puts the flowers down on the table beside the open folio, steps back to look at them.

There, that'll do. (*turns to* JOE) I'm Lucinda Bennett.

JOE   I know. You're famous.

LUCINDA   And you are—

JOE   Joe—

LUCINDA   (*overlapping*) Joe of Paterson. (*She laughs.*) You see? You're famous too. (*pause*) Don't be embarrassed. It's nice to see someone with a little spunk around here.

BENNETT *has finished his call.*

BENNETT   You don't know how to work cameras, by any chance.

JOE *realizes he's being spoken to.*

I've got all this equipment here, but it has to be set up just so. Can't get the hang of it myself. I want pictures of the dolmen, see if I'm right.

JOE   No—I don't know anything about cameras.

BENNETT   I thought you were smart. Come in here a minute.

He marches out of the room toward a short hall. JOE *glances for a moment at* LUCINDA BENNETT, *wipes his hands on his trousers, and follows* BENNETT.

INT.   FRONT HALLWAY AND CORRIDOR. DAY

BENNETT *leading* JOE *down the corridor.*

BENNETT   I wanted to take a look at you anyway; see if you belonged with me on a permanent basis. What's your opinion?

BENNETT *opens a door, steps in.*

INT.   BENNETT'S STUDY. DAY

A large room filled with books, trophies, photographs of BENNETT *with presidents, kings, etc., a globe on a stand, a ticker-tape machine, etc.* BENNETT *goes behind desk, takes a folder out of a drawer.* JOE *stands in front of the desk.*

BENNETT   Well?

JOE   You mean a job?

BENNETT   That's what I mean. Should I hire you?

JOE   No.

BENNETT   No?

JOE   I couldn't live here. It's not for me.

BENNETT   *(Studying contents of folder, he looks up, smiles slightly.)* You seem to have adapted well enough. From what I understand you've made the place your own. *(pause)* Are your injuries healed?

JOE   I suppose.

BENNETT   And what are your parents telling you to do?

JOE   My parents?

BENNETT   You have parents, don't you? They haven't called or written to see how you're getting along?

JOE   How would they know? I haven't seen them in years.

BENNETT   *(holding up a paper)* They signed a waiver. I'm not at fault for the injuries you incurred on my property. They receive two hundred and fifty dollars.

Pause.

JOE   I don't understand.

BENNETT   I'm not lying to you. This is your father's signature, isn't it? *(pause)* We looked through your billfold. You might have been on the way out.

JOE *has to sit down.*

You don't want to work for me. Fine. You can go home, and if you're smart you can use that money to make money. Buy something and sell it for a profit. Anything, it doesn't matter. Some of the great fortunes were built from less.

JOE   No. They can have it. It's theirs.

BENNETT *paces the room.*

BENNETT   I'll tell you, I always respect a man's decision. Never try to argue him out of it. You're not staying here and you're not going home. That leaves you back on the road, doesn't it? Back on the bum. Well, I say why not, if that's what you want. But be sure you can handle it. Just be sure you've got the guts. So that if you have to steal or take a sap to someone's head for a meal, you'll be able to. Every kind of life has its demands, its tests. Can I do this? Can I live with the consequences of what I'm doing? If you can't answer yes, you're in a life that's too much for you. Then you drop down a notch. If you can't steal and you can't sap someone on the head when you have to, you join the line at the flophouse. You get on the bread line. If you can't muscle your way into the bread line, you sit at the curb and hold out your hand. You're a beggar. If you can't whine and wheedle and beg your cup of coffee, if you can't take the billy on the bottoms of your feet—why, I say be a poet. Yes *(he laughs)*, like old Penfield, find your level. Get in, get into the place that's your nature, whether it's running a corporation or picking daisies in a field, get in there and live to it, live to the fullness of it, become what you are, and I'll say to you, you've done more than most men. Most men—and let me tell you, I know men— most of them don't ever do that. They'll work at a job and not know why. They'll marry a woman and not know why. They'll go to their graves and not know why.

BENNETT *now stands at window, his back to* JOE.

I've never understood it, but there it is. I've never understood how a man could give up his life, give it up, moment by moment, even as he lives it, gives it up from the second he's born. But there it is. Bow your head. Agree. Go along. Do what everyone's doing. Let it leach away. Sign it away. Drink it away. Sleep it away. *(coming back to desk)* Well, you're brash enough. Where are you going?

JOE   I don't know. As far as I can get.

BENNETT   *(a thoughtful pause—and then coming to a decision)* You may happen to need something—this is a private number. Not to be given out, you understand? *(He writes it down, folds the paper, hands it to* JOE.*)* But don't leave until I've got my dolmen. The stone of my Indian chief.

PENFIELD *is in bed, the covers drawn up to his chin.* LIBBY *stands, hands on hips, in the middle of the room.*

PENFIELD   *(tragic face)* Go away, Libby, you don't know anything.

LIBBY   I know what a hollow leg is. Look at this place; it's enough to make anyone sick!

She goes into a flurry of action—picking up dirty socks, papers, books.

PENFIELD   Go away! Get out! Let me die in peace!

JOE *arrives at open door.*

Joe, my boy, get her to stop! Must I die with the slanders of servants in my ears? *(to* LIBBY*)* Get out! Don't touch a thing, dammit! *(He rises in his bed.)* You're disrupting everything! *(He sinks back on his pillows.)*

LIBBY   *(snappishly straightening covers)* What do you care if you're dying!

She picks up a basket of trash, a pile of newspapers, and storms out, ignoring JOE, *her chin in the air.*
Silence.

PENFIELD   Joe, there's a bottle of wine under the window seat.

JOE *brings over the bottle and a glass and pulls a chair up to* PENFIELD's *bedside.* PENFIELD *sits up.*

JOE   Mr. Penfield, I've got something to tell you. But first I need to know who Clara is.

PENFIELD   Clara? An eastern industrial child. Born of the infinite class of nameless workers. Our very own exclusive class. *(He drinks.)*

JOE   What do you mean, Mr. Penfield?

PENFIELD   She's like you, Joe. She comes off the streets.

INT.   BENNETT LODGE. LIVING ROOM. NIGHT (SILENT)

Reprise scene of dancing COUPLES *in evening dress (p. 320).*
CLARA, *the most far gone, dances indolently, her eyes closed, her back arched*

over her PARTNER's (TOMMY CRAPO) *arm, a champagne glass held lightly in her fingers.*

JOE   *(voice over)* Who brought her here, Mr. Penfield?

PENFIELD   *(voice over)* Tommy Crapo.

CLARA's *partner,* TOMMY CRAPO, *holds her with an amused, slightly contemptuous look on his face.*

JOE   *(voice over)* Who?

PENFIELD   *(voice over)* Tommy Crapo. The labor consultant. Don't you read the newspapers? Don't you look at the tabloids?

CRAPO, *dancing, is a smoothie—he's short, trim, has shiny black hair, dark, enormous, almost feminine, eyes.*

PENFIELD   *(voice over)* Tommy Crapo, who likes to have his picture taken with a beautiful woman at his side.

The dancers turn past a window where JOE's *face is seen peering in.*

INT.   PENFIELD'S STUDIO APARTMENT. NIGHT

JOE *sitting beside* PENFIELD's *bed.*

JOE   Is he in the rackets?

PENFIELD   Mr. Crapo is a specialist in labor relations. *(drains the glass)* Yes, I think that's a fair description.

JOE   You mean he knocks heads for Bennett.

PENFIELD *looks at* JOE.

PENFIELD   Why these questions? Is Tommy Crapo back?

Pause.

JOE   He's on his way. That's what I came to tell you, Mr. Penfield. Clara Lukacs has to get out of here.

PENFIELD   What?

JOE   Miss Clara Lukacs is ready to make her escape.

PENFIELD *struggles out of bed and in a flurry of agitation pulls on his ratty bathrobe and gets on his knees to retrieve his slippers from under the bed.*

PENFIELD   She's ready? Did she say that? When? What shall we do? How?

Lurching to his feet he gets his slippers on, rushes about the room aimlessly, clasping his hands.

Oh Clara! Oh my darling—But how! I need a plan. Yes. I've got to make a plan, I've got to think.

JOE   Why don't you sit down, Mr. Penfield. Calm yourself. I *have* a plan.

PENFIELD *sinks into a chair, gazes at* JOE.

Miss Lukacs wants me to get her out of here.

PENFIELD   You?

JOE   She thinks if you leave together you'll be too easy to follow. Like a hot car.

PENFIELD   A what?

JOE   See, Crapo doesn't know me from Adam.

PENFIELD *takes this in. He becomes poised and calm.*

PENFIELD   *(softly)* I see. So that's the way it happens.

JOE   Clara—Miss Lukacs—says once she's safe she can get in touch with you.

PENFIELD   She said that?

JOE *nods, looks away.* PENFIELD *smiles sadly.*

JOE   I'll need money. And I'll need a car.

Long pause.

PENFIELD   All right. I'll help you *(nods to himself)*. Yes, the two young people. Of course. *(He begins to recover.)* Yes *(struggles to his feet)*. You can count on me. Yes. I have resources. I have allies.

He resumes his pacing. He's determined not to reveal his anguish.

I am not without resources. I am not without allies. Yes, Clara can count on me. You can both count on me. You'll find Warren Penfield comes through!

JOE *gets up, prepared to leave.* PENFIELD *rushes over to him. He rolls up his bathrobe sleeve, holds his arm out. After a moment* JOE *understands, rolls up his own sleeve showing his scars.*

PENFIELD   *(laughing, on verge of hysteria)* That's right. Brothers under the sign of the wild dog. You know how brothers do who share this secret sign? *(He crosses forearms with* JOE.) That's it. *(looking into* JOE's *eyes)* My pain is your pain. My life is your life.

EXT.   RAMP AND HANGAR, SHORE OF LOON LAKE. DAY

The green and white monoplane we saw in the air now sits moored a few yards from the shore. PENFIELD *stands just out of reach of the water lapping the concrete ramp.* LUCINDA BENNETT, *in overalls, comes out of the hangar, wiping her hands on a big trainman's handkerchief.*

PENFIELD   What do you do, Lucinda—paint the innards like a new toy?

LUCINDA   No, old bear. When I'm through its innards will be dark and oiled and refitted to tolerances that will take me to the top of the sky. *(pause)* Why are you sulking? I thought you loved me.

PENFIELD   Since I gave up my manhood to live here, I make no claims of that sort on anyone.

LUCINDA   *(smiling)* That's not the report I have.

PENFIELD   *(mournfully)* Oh, Lucinda!

LUCINDA   *(touching his face)* So much suffering—poor Warren.

PENFIELD   I need your help. Not for me. Your poor Warren is finished. Oh God—how much better if when I came here the dogs had torn out my throat!

LUCINDA   *(sighs)* Yes. I suppose you're right.

She heads back to the hangar, and after a moment he lumbers after her.

PENFIELD   Forgive me!

LUCINDA   Oh Warren, it's such a bore when you whine.

PENFIELD   Indeed! *(bitterly)* My agony does not divert.

They both pass into the hangar. Camera pulls back to discover JOE *eavesdropping in the nearby brush. He waits a moment and goes up to the hangar, standing just to the side of the open door. We hear* PENFIELD's *voice—intense, dramatic, but we can't hear the words.*

INT.   HANGAR. DAY

Here the light is dim. LUCINDA *is at a worktable beside another plane, the cowling removed from one of its two engines.*

LUCINDA   Of course, Warren. If that's what you want. It will give me pleasure.

PENFIELD   Thank you.

LUCINDA   You have a good nature.

PENFIELD   *(kissing her hand)* Oh, my dear!

LUCINDA   Would you like to go on a flight with me? Probably not. But a really long flight. Just the two of us. Would you consider it?

PENFIELD   What? Where?

LUCINDA   I don't know. Anywhere. The Far East. Shall we do that? Fly across the Pacific.

PENFIELD   The Far East?

LUCINDA   Yes, pooh bear. A long flight—you and I. What a *good* idea! Who knows what might happen. *(looks at him, bursts out laughing)* Oh Warren, if you could see your face right now—the dismay!

PENFIELD   Lucinda—how is it possible? Am I misunderstood?

LUCINDA   Oh foolish thing—I don't mean *that.* Good God. It's a practice made too thoroughly disreputable by its devotees, don't you think?

INT.   MAIN HOUSE. LIVING ROOM
(FROM TERRACE, JOE'S POINT OF VIEW). NIGHT

BENNETT, LUCINDA, PENFIELD, *and* CLARA *having drinks before dinner. Formal clothes: black tie, long gowns are the dress. The fire roars in the big fireplace. Despite his black tie,* PENFIELD *looks rumpled.* CLARA, *in something sequined, looks tawdry beside the understated elegance of* LUCINDA. *Her eyes are on the floor.* PENFIELD *gazes at her in torment, with mute glances of appeal at* LUCINDA.

BENNETT *seems oblivious to all of this. He merrily opens the guest book and laughingly reads something aloud.*

The whole scene is pantomimed—we are seeing it through a terrace window.

Outside on the terrace, JOE *in his stolen sweater and knickers catches* LUCINDA's *eye. She waits a moment, excuses herself, and walks out of the room.*

EXT.   FRONT DOOR, MAIN HOUSE. NIGHT

LUCINDA BENNETT *is handing* JOE *a set of keys.*

LUCINDA   It's grey. With a canvas top. You're leaving somewhat better off than when you came in.

JOE   Yeah. I'll take good care of it, if that's what's worrying you.

LUCINDA   It's not. That's not the sort of thing I care about.

JOE   You've got your own reasons for doing this—don't think I don't know.

LUCINDA   What a crude young man. Maybe I shouldn't worry about you.

JOE   Maybe you shouldn't.

LUCINDA   I have nothing more to fear from my husband. But I'd watch out if I were you.

JOE   Thanks. *(She turns to go in.)* I mean that. *(She looks back from the door, a face of misery.)* Happy flying.

EXT.   CLARA'S COTTAGE. NIGHT

JOE *coming off the porch, struggling with* CLARA's *luggage under his arms—valises, hatbox, etc. Hurries into the woods, after halting for a moment to listen to the distant cries of the loons.*

INT. LOON LAKE GARAGE. NIGHT

JOE, *in shadows, going down a line of four or five cars. The last one in the row is a small grey 1933 Mercedes convertible with spare tires in the front fender wells. He swings open the doors directly behind the car and, after releasing the hand brakes, pushes the car into the open.*

EXT. GARAGE AND PUMP. NIGHT

JOE *packing* CLARA's *bags in the trunk and the back seat. He looks around, quietly unhooks the gas hose, gasses up the car. Looks around again, takes the set of keys out his pocket, gets behind the wheel.*

INT. MERCEDES. NIGHT

JOE *familiarizes himself with the switches, the gearshift. Finds a chamois cloth in the glove compartment, dusts off the dashboard and passenger seat. The car hasn't seen much use.*

He reads a road map, using the map light on the dashboard. Then he settles back and waits. He hears the sound of the wind in the trees. The canvas roof snaps under the wind.

INT. MERCEDES. NIGHT

Some time has elapsed. JOE, *dozing, sits up suddenly. Someone is coming.* JOE *flicks on the parking lights.*

EXT. ROAD LEADING TO GARAGE. NIGHT

Hurrying along, WARREN PENFIELD, *holding* CLARA's *elbow. She wears a fur jacket over her gown. She holds the skirt, raising it to keep from tripping. They come around to the passenger side of the car.*

INT. MERCEDES. NIGHT

JOE *leans across the seat, pushes the far door open. Before* CLARA *can get in,* PENFIELD *is hugging her.* JOE *sees this without being able to see their heads.*

PENFIELD *is kissing her loudly, hugging her, moaning, carrying on.* JOE *sees* CLARA *pushing* PENFIELD *away.*

CLARA   War-rin—please!

And now she's bending down, getting in the car. She slams the door behind her. PENFIELD *is seen running around the front of the car, and then he's at* JOE's *window.* JOE *starts the engine, throws the toggle switch for the headlights, adjusts the throttle.* PENFIELD *has been tapping on the window.* JOE *rolls it down.*

PENFIELD   Remember, you turn left, not right, past the tennis court. That's the back road out of here.

JOE   Right.

PENFIELD   It's not paved, but it's generally downhill, and in three or four miles you'll hit the county road.

JOE   OK.

PENFIELD   Here (*he thrusts some folded bills into* JOE's *hand*)—I wish it were more.

JOE   Thanks.

PENFIELD   Clara, don't forget me! (*He throws a kiss.*) Clara, both of you, remember Penfield. Drive carefully. Sometimes the weather comes up fast in the mountains. Watch your step.

JOE   OK.

PENFIELD   You know how to reach me. My prayers go with you, Clara. I'll never forget you. Take care of her, Joe. I wish—

PENFIELD *is still talking as* JOE *puts the car in gear and lurches off, nearly taking* PENFIELD's *head with him.*

EXT.   MERCEDES. NIGHT

The car moves down the road. PENFIELD, *in his black tie, is standing behind, waving after it.*

INT. MERCEDES. NIGHT

JOE *adjusts the rear mirror, sees the figure* PENFIELD *waving, then veering out of sight as the road curves into the woods.*

EXT. UNPAVED ROAD THROUGH WOODS. NIGHT

The headlights light up the trees and animal night life as the car comes down the mountain road. Intercut exterior shots with:

INT. MERCEDES. NIGHT

CLARA *hangs onto the leather loop strap over the window.* JOE *is getting the hang of the car, its strange gearshift.*

Dogs appear, running in the woods beside the road, yelping, baying—first one or two, then the whole pack. JOE *curses, speeds up as the dogs hit the road and run alongside the car.*

The car outdistances the dogs and then nothing is heard but the hum of the engine.

CLARA *leans back in her seat, lights a cigarette.*

JOE   What do you think he'll do when he finds you gone?

CLARA   An interesting question.

In the dashboard light her eyes are clear, her face beautiful, as she watches the road. JOE *looks at her in her composure of total attention, going along with the ride.*

EXT. CARNIVAL MIDWAY. DAY

A grey afternoon. Just a few straggling customers. The rides go around empty. The wind rattles the tent flaps so that they sound like machine guns.

The GIRL *in the ticket booth is yawning.*

SIM HEARN *stands looking over his bleak domain, leaning against the platform beside the entrance to the main tent. A toothpick is in his mouth. We hear a* chirp chirp *sound as he sucks the air from the spaces between his teeth.*

EXT. FERRIS WHEEL. DAY

JOE *and* TWO ROUSTS *lounge at the controls of the ferris wheel, which is empty and not running.*

FIRST ROUST   Old Sim missed his town this time.

SECOND ROUST   No he ain't. You watch. See what happens. He's fixin' to take the wagons to Florida.

FIRST ROUST   I wouldn't mind Florida this winter.

SECOND ROUST   Shit, you get down there on yer own, he might take you on. But he might not. (*to* JOE) He tell you anything.

JOE   Who?

SECOND ROUST   Sim Hearn. Keepin' you on the job?

JOE   What job?

SECOND ROUST   (*to* FIRST ROUST) You hear that? (*He grasps the long lever of the ferris wheel motor and slides his hand up and down.*) What job!

The ROUSTS *laugh.* JOE *walks away.*

INT.   SIDESHOW TENT. DAY

JOE *walks among the stalls. A couple of* KIDS *are the only customers.* LIZARD MAN *reads a newspaper. The* FINGERLINGS *play cards.* WOLF WOMAN *nodding off.* JOE *finds* FANNY's *stall is empty.*

EXT.   FANNY'S TRAILER. DAY

The door opens and MAGDA HEARN *comes down the wooden stairs just as* JOE *walks up.*

JOE   What's the matter?

MAGDA   Fanny is not well. She wheezes like calliope.

JOE   Well, why doesn't someone get a doctor?

MAGDA *caresses* JOE's *face.*

370 | Loon Lake: A Screenplay

MAGDA   I worry to think someday if we are not together what will happen to you.

Appearing at the top of the steps is FANNY'S AUNT, *holding her rosary beads.*

EXT.   CARNIVAL LOT. EVENING

Tents, rides coming down. Shutters up on the trailer windows. Signs everywhere of the carny's wrap-up: no music, no carny lights.

At the edge of the lot, near the road, JOE *stands beside a flatbed truck, while the* FREAKS *in street clothes now throw their bags aboard and clamber up after them. Other* CARNY FOLK *intermingling with them—the* BARKER, *etc. But* FANNY THE FAT LADY *is not among them.*

At a distance, SIM HEARN *is instructing* MAGDA *about something. She nods, he leaves, and she comes over to* JOE.

MAGDA   There's a town, Chester, where is railroad station—fifteen miles from here. To Chester only you take them. Don't let them tell you otherwise. You do this only and come back.

JOE   Will somebody tell me what's going on?

MAGDA   Shh! I will be waiting.

INT.   CAB OF TRUCK. NIGHT

As JOE *climbs up behind the wheel, he is surprised to find* FANNY'S AUNT *sitting in the passenger seat, her bundles and bags beside her.*

EXT.   TWO-LANE ROAD. NIGHT

The truck comes down the road. We see in the back, cold and huddled, the assembled FREAKS, *even stranger looking in their coats and hats, sitting among their trunks and bags—eyes of real intelligence in their faces, thought flashing there, a true perception of their condition and the journeys they must make.*

INT. CAB OF TRUCK. NIGHT

JOE, *behind the wheel, lights a cigarette, sees from the corner of his eye* FANNY'S AUNT *lift her skirt, check the metal clip of her garter, and touch a wad of bills tucked in the top of her stocking. She glances at him nervously and pulls her skirt down.*

EXT. CARNIVAL LOT. NIGHT

The empty truck returning to the lot. JOE *switches off the engine, steps out on the running board.*

In the darkness he sees many parked cars, trucks, wagon teams, that weren't there when he left.

The wind is blowing, but he hears another sound under this—a muffled scream and then what might be a rug being beaten. These sounds seem to be coming from the main tent—the one tent still standing.

JOE *walks toward it. A flashlight is suddenly shining in his eyes. Someone grabs his arm.*

MALE VOICE   Who's this?

MAGDA HEARN'S VOICE   It's all right. He's with show.

The light goes out. JOE *makes out the figure of a* STATE TROOPER—*blocked hat, gun, Sam Browne belt. The* TROOPER *releases his arm.*

Then MAGDA *is walking* JOE *toward the main tent.*

MAGDA   *(whispering, urgent)* Joe, I want you to see, to understand. And I wait for you in car. Please hurry.

JOE   What's going on? What are the police doing here?

MAGDA   Go. Hurry.

She propels him toward the entrance.

INT. MAIN TENT. NIGHT

A few rows of wooden bleachers, but these are empty. A large CROWD OF MEN *stands in the dirt ring surrounding something that* JOE, *in the entrance chute,*

Loon Lake: A Screenplay

cannot see. Their backs are to him. One bulb strung high on the tent pole is the only lighting.

We hear that peculiar rug-beating sound—as if the earth itself is being drummed. We hear the night music of FANNY THE FAT LADY—*the screams and grunts. The* MEN *shout their encouragement as the drumming accelerates. At the peak—silence—and then the hoarse male roar of expiration. The* CROWD *cheers.*

A moment later a MALE *staggers outside the circle of* MEN. *He is buttoning his pants. He sinks down on his knees, removes a flask from his back pocket, and takes a long swig.*

Then JOE, *in hysterical rage, is pushing through the* CROWD, *screaming unintelligibly. The drunken roistering* MEN *don't take well to this.*

VOICES   Hey . . . Who're you pushing? . . . Look at this . . . Wait your turn, punk . . . (etc.)

JOE *sees* FANNY, *nude, on her back in the dirt, another lover on top of her now. The music begins again.* JOE *is shoved back, punched around, and left deposited back behind the crowd again.*

Blood streams from a cut over JOE's *eye. The earth drums,* FANNY *moans, the* CROWD *cheers.* JOE *sees the shadow of a man leaning against the bleacher support. We hear over the pandemonium the thoughtful, preoccupied sucking of* SIM HEARN's *tongue on his own teeth.*

EXT.   HILLY TWO-LANE ROAD. NIGHT

A Model A (identified as SIM HEARN's, *p. 327) going fast down the road. It skids on a curve, comes up over the top of a hill with a bump, headlights stabbing the night sky.*

INT.   MODEL A FORD. NIGHT

MAGDA HEARN *is driving,* JOE *is sitting beside her.*

MAGDA   Hearn watches till he sees the signs. She doesn't take breath easily. From the bed she cannot lift herself . . . The people know Hearn. He gives something always at end of summer. A grand finale. The word goes through the mountains. Look where we are—we make better time than I hoped.

EXT. PINE GROVE MOTOR COURT. NIGHT

The Model A is parked in front of one of the run-down little cabins of this 1930s motel at the edge of a pine woods.

INT. MOTOR COURT CABIN. NIGHT

The bed has a khaki blanket, two lumpy pillows. No sheets. JOE *sits on the edge of the bed and stares at the floor.*
    MAGDA *stands at the bureau counting bills.*
    A bare bulb hangs from the ceiling.

MAGDA   Sim knows to get the money out before the fun starts. To Albany to the bank he thinks I am going. *(She wets her thumb on her lower lip.)* Sixty. Eighty . . . Three. Four. Fifteen hundred and eighty-four dollars!

She is feverishly excited. She digs in her purse and comes up with another wad of bills.

And plus salary which he never paid! *(She counts.)* Two hundred I squeeze from you, you bastard!

She runs over to JOE, *bends down, kisses him on the mouth. She pulls the string tie of a canvas coin sack and pours a stream of coins on the bed. She laughs. Dissolve to:*

INT. MOTOR COURT CABIN. NIGHT

JOE *drinks from a pint flask.* MAGDA *has arranged the coins in stacks on the bed. But her glee causes her to shake the bed and the coins collapse into a pile. She rolls on her back in the coins.*

MAGDA   Come to me. Come to Magda. You know what? Tomorrow we trade his car and buy new. We drive to California, you and me, before Sim Hearn even thinks is something wrong.

She pulls JOE *back on the bed, takes the flask away from him, swigs, puts it on the bedside table. She begins to unbutton the buttons on his fly, loosens his belt buckle, unbutton his shirt.*

You know what? To Hollywood we are going. I have read the magazines, I understand the movie business. I sell my life story. A film of my life! Everyone will know who Magda is.

She kisses his chest, pulls the shirt off his shoulders.

And who knows—with your looks, my Joseph, with your body, why you cannot a movie star be. And we shall love and be famous and have great sooccess. Shall we? Shall we?

She goes down on him.

INT.   MOTOR COURT CABIN. NIGHT

The light is out now. In the darkness we hear something that might be lovemaking, but with a degree of intense passion to suggest violence, pain.

MAGDA'S VOICE   No more. Please. Don't—

The sound of covers spilling to the floor. Slapping. Hitting. It is a definite struggle now, with curses, moans. And then a figure seems to rise from the bed as if propelled—and then the sickening sound of someone hitting the floor. A whimper. A moan. Dissolve to:

INT.   MOTOR COURT CABIN. DAWN

JOE, *alone in the bed, is awake, watching the light coming up on the window shade. He gets out of bed, steps over* MAGDA, *asleep naked and snoring on the floor, rolls up his clothes and shoes into a bundle. He grabs the stack of bills from the bureau, unlatches the door quietly, and steps outside. The door closes.*

EXT.   PINE GROVE MOTOR COURT. DAWN

A thin frost on the windshield of the Model A. No other cars in sight. The first birds waking.

   JOE *goes behind the cabin, sees a privy and an outdoor shower up on the slope behind the Motor Court. He moves toward it and, halfway up the slope, turns and rears back and throws the bills into the wind.*

EXT.   OUTDOOR SHOWER. DAY

EXT.   OUTDOOR SHOWER. DAY

JOE *stands under the stream of cold water. Above him the tops of the pine trees sway in the wind. He's shivering, but makes no effort to hurry, wanting the water to wash everything away.*

EXT.   PINE WOODS. DAY

Reprise of JOE *running through the woods (opening scene).*

EXT.   RAILROAD TRACK EMBANKMENT. NIGHT

Reprise: JOE *crouching in the weeds, the private railroad train passing left to right, slowly, screechingly; the private car, the white-jacketed porter serving drinks, the white bedroom with* CLARA *standing naked in front of a mirror and holding up a white dress on a hanger.*

MONTAGE: JOE AND CLARA'S DRIVE OUT OF THE MOUNTAINS. (MUSIC)

The little grey Mercedes with the canvas roof coming down a long winding hill in the early morning, its headlights flickering over the bumps.

The Mercedes coming down a straight, slightly downhill stretch in the dawn, headlights still on.

The Mercedes bumping over railroad tracks at the outskirts of a city, going past freight cars, warehouses.

The Mercedes racing along a flat plain in the bright early morning in a stream of traffic—milk trucks, delivery vans, produce wagons, cars. Dissolve to:

EXT.   SIDEWALK IN FRONT OF A DINER. DAY (MUSIC ENDS)

The Mercedes pulls in front of a streetcar diner. The engine is cut. JOE *steps out, goes around the car, opens* CLARA'*s door. She steps out sleepily.*

JOE   You awake?

CLARA   Where are we?

JOE   The United States of America.

INT. DINER. DAY

A crowded, noisy, working-class diner during the breakfast hour.

When CLARA *and* JOE *enter—she in her long gown and fur jacket, he in fancy sweater and knickers—a silence descends.* WAITRESS, CUSTOMERS, SHORT ORDER COOK *stare at them.*

JOE *takes* CLARA'S *arm and hustles her back out the door.*

CLARA   What's the matter?

JOE   Jesus! What d'ya think?

EXT. ARMY-NAVY SURPLUS STORE. DAY

The Mercedes pulls up to a sharp stop in front of the store. JOE *jumps out, hurriedly opens* CLARA'S *door, takes her arm, helps her out, grabs one of her valises from the back seat. He rushes* CLARA *into the store.*

INT. ARMY-NAVY SURPLUS STORE. DAY

A dingy surplus store stuffed with racks of military surplus, the counter piled with khaki trousers, shelves bending under the weight of boxes, etc.

JOE *is counting out bills into the hand of the* PROPRIETOR. JOE *is wearing dark trousers, a work shirt, a khaki greatcoat. His knickers and argyle sweater, and* CLARA'S *fur jacket are under his arm.*

Behind him, CLARA *is checking herself in a floor-length mirror: she wears a normal skirt, turtleneck sweater, sailor's pea jacket. The* PROPRIETOR *can't help looking at her—even as the cash is being counted into his hand.*

EXT. STREET LEAVING TOWN. DAY

The Mercedes is moving fast.

INT. MERCEDES. DAY

JOE   What kind of money do you have?

CLARA   Money?

JOE   These duds came to almost thirty dollars. We've got eighty left.

CLARA   I don't have any money.

JOE   I have to know what our cash assets are.

CLARA   I never use the stuff.

Pause.

JOE   That's really swell.

CLARA   Look in my bag if you don't believe me.

JOE   Well how far did you think you could go without money?

CLARA   I don't know. You tell me.

EXT.   TWO-LANE ROAD. DAY

The Mercedes picks up speed.

INT.   MERCEDES. DUSK

JOE *is bleary-eyed.*

CLARA   I feel like I've been in this car all my life.

JOE   Every mile is a mile between us and Bennett.

CLARA   I want a bath.

JOE   A what?

CLARA   You've heard of them? Well, that's what I want.

INT.   RUTHERFORD B. HAYES HOTEL. LOBBY. NIGHT

Small-town, commercial hotel lobby—worn upholstered chairs, half-dead rubber plants, a counter with a few mail slots behind it, one elevator with polished brass folding doors.
    JOE *is checking in. It's clear that he's never done this before, though he makes*

a great show of being a man of the world. The CLERK *has to point to the register and hand him the pen.*

CLARA *waits at the elevator.*

CLERK   Front!

An old Negro BELLBOY *appears, buttoning his tunic.*

BELLBOY   Yes *suh!*

JOE *has started to pick up* CLARA's *valise. The* BELLBOY *takes it from him, as well as the key he has picked up from the counter.*

Thank you, young gen'man.

JOE *follows the* BELLBOY *to the elevator, digging in his pocket for a tip.*

INT.   HOTEL ROOM. NIGHT (BRIGHT LIGHT)

A large room, with big windows with dark green pull shades, fluffy white curtains. A double bed. A worn-out carpet.

    CLARA *removes things from her overnight bag.* JOE *comes out of the bathroom.*

JOE   They even got a tap for ice water. Too bad it's not summer no more.

CLARA *marches past him into the bathroom, closes the door smartly.* JOE *hears the sound of the tub running. He pulls all the shades down to the sills.*

    He sits on the double bed. Bounces it. He lights a cigarette. Looks at the bathroom door. Comes to a decision. Removes his shoes and socks, unbuckles his belt, begins to unbutton his shirt. Interrupts his undressing to turn on the bed-table lamp and switch off the ceiling light.

INT.   HOTEL ROOM. NIGHT (DIM LIGHT)

CLARA *comes out of the bathroom. She is nude. She matter-of-factly turns back the covers, slips into bed.*

    JOE, *already in bed, watches her. She turns her back to him, curling up on her side. When he moves toward her, touching her shoulder, she growls in a high pitch and pokes her elbow into his chest.*

He falls away on his back, making a soundless whistle. He turns off the bedside lamp, puts his hand behind his head, smiles. His eyes close.

INT.   HOTEL ROOM. DAY

JOE *awakens, realizes* CLARA *is not in bed. A window shade snaps up. She is in a robe and looking out the window.*

CLARA   What in hell am I doing here? (*turns, looks at* JOE) I must be out of my mind. Look at him—hunky king of the road there. Oh, this is great—this is really great!

She begins to dress—pulls skirts, blouses, out of her valise, looks at them, flings them aside.

God damn him! And his wives. And his boats and horses and fucking choo-choo trains.

She abruptly sits on her side of the bed, her arms full of clothes, and she stares at the floor.
   JOE *has sat up.*

JOE   Hey. I told you I'd get you out of there and I did. Didn't I? (*She doesn't answer.*) Hey, girlie—didn't I?

He puts his feet on the floor, grabs his pants.

You have a complaint? You think you're some hot-ass bargain?

CLARA   You bet I am, hunky. I can promise you.

JOE   Well then, go on. Go back to your fancy friends and see what they do for you. After all, look what they already done.

He is out of bed, buckling his pants, pulling on his socks, sticking his feet in his shoes.

CLARA   Where are you going?

He takes his wallet out of his back pocket.

JOE   Here.

Loon Lake: A Screenplay

He crumples a couple of single dollar bills and throws them on the floor.

That and a twitch of your ass will get you back to the loons.

CLARA   You're not leaving—you're not leaving me here!

He is in his shirt now. He stands in front of the bureau mirror, takes out his pocket comb.

JOE   You can go back to your career—fucking for old men. *(combing his hair)* It's probably as good as you can do anyhow.

The mirror shatters. JOE *goes for* CLARA, *now on her knees on the bed, about to throw something else.*
   He pins her to the bed, the robe falls away from her. She tries to bite him. He holds her wrists, puts his knees between her legs.

CLARA   You're hurting me!

He kisses her. She struggles. One way or another, twisting and contending, they are soon making love.

MONTAGE: EXT.   ROAD. DAY

The Mercedes going breezily along a road in flat, plains countryside. The top is down.
   The Mercedes going toward the setting sun.
   The Mercedes going down the main street of a deserted, boarded-up town.

CLARA   *(voice over)* I didn't know dead people were that unusual. I saw them all the time. I wandered around, holding my bottle, dragging my blanket behind me, and seeing dead hunkies on tables. My father would smile at me.

EXT.   MOTOR COURT CABIN. NIGHT

The Mercedes is pulled up in front of a cabin. Stars are out. Crickets are chirping.

CLARA   *(voice over)* When I got older, I began to understand more. I had thought, for instance, anyone who was dead had to have a hole in them.

INT. MOTOR CABIN. NIGHT

JOE and CLARA in bed—she sitting up, he lying against pillows, smoking a cigarette, listening.

CLARA   Then I saw some old guy being dressed who'd died of natural causes. He'd made it all the way. So I knew then about natural death.

JOE   Was your father in the rackets himself?

CLARA   Nah. He was just some dumb hunky, he didn't talk much, he just did his work. And he got this clientele over the years because he kept his mouth shut and didn't make judgments—he didn't care who he buried. Why should he, the kind of work he did, why get excited?

She lies down beside him, stares at the ceiling.

But if it was really a big affair it was worth watching. My father in his shiny black suit, people filling the parlor, paying their respects; crowds in the streets. And all the black cars in a line around the block—double-parked with their headlights on. And the cops checking on who showed up and the photographers with their big flash cameras, and the next morning in the *News* and the *Mirror* there was a picture of somebody and in the background the canopy said Lukacs' West 29th Street Funeral Parlor.

JOE   West 29th Street?

CLARA   Yeah. To this day I hate cut flowers. What a stink they made—came right up through the floor, the dumbwaiter.

JOE   We were practically neighbors.

CLARA   Anyway, when I was fifteen my father asked me to be his receptionist. Business was booming. I didn't mind. I hated school. And now I got to wear dresses and hose and high heels. I had an allowance for the beauty parlor. And I got to meet some real big shots. It was an entree—as they say.

JOE   Hey Clara, we lived right across the river from each other—you realize that? Two snot-nosed kids! Little did we know we were destined to meet!

CLARA   What?

JOE   *(laughing)* We saw the same Tom Mix movies. We ran along the sidewalks and pointed to the sky at the same airships.

He has put out his cigarette. He's on his side, smiling at her.

CLARA   What are you talking about?

JOE   Don't you remember the I-cash-clothes man? And the water wagon— going down the street—running alongside it for the spray? Listen—don't you remember how we went to the candy store for ice cream?

CLARA   Jesus.

JOE   No, really, Clara—one afternoon we bought Dixie cups and stood in the sun with our wooden spoons. You remember. Licking the ice cream off Joan Crawford's face?

EXT.   TWO-LANE COUNTRY ROAD. DAY

The Mercedes going down the road. Thunderheads in the sky. Cracks of lightning.

EXT.   TWO-LANE COUNTRY ROAD. DAY (RAIN)

Heavy sheets of rain whipping against the Mercedes. It's wheel planing the water.

INT.   MERCEDES. DAY

Heavy drumming of rain on the convertible roof. Rain leaking in. JOE *peers through the rain pouring off the windshield.*

JOE   Son of a bitch.

CLARA *is laughing. She leans over and switches off the windshield wipers.*

What're you doing!

CLARA   Drive, you bastard! Drive!

Her face is flushed, her eyes large with excitement.

JOE   It's a fucking flash flood!

EXT. TWO-LANE COUNTRY ROAD. DAY (RAIN)

The Mercedes wobbles down the road, spins around completely (360°), con-tinues; the rain coming down, thunder, the sound of JOE *and* CLARA *laughing and shrieking as if on a carnival ride.*

INT. TAVERN. EVENING

A Midwest working-class tavern, a CROWD *bunched up at the bar.* JOE *sits in a plywood booth with two glasses of whiskey on the table. General bar noise. Someone whistles.* CLARA *is coming back from the restroom. She is the only woman in the place. She slips in the booth across from* JOE. *They are both damp, their hair wet.* CLARA *plucks her blouse away from her chest.* JOE *pushes a shot glass toward her.*

JOE Have some of that. Warm you up.

CLARA'S *eyes aglitter. She looks up, friendly, as a* MAN *in a plaid shirt and overalls approaches.*

MAN Hey, little lady.

CLARA How you doin'?

MAN My friend and me have a little wager goin'.

Laughter from the bar.

He thinks you're just an ordinary sensational lookin' lady. I think you must be one a them movie stars.

CLARA *laughs. The* MAN *takes a pull from his beer can. He is large, with a heavy gut. He leans over the table, ignoring* JOE *as if he's not even there.*

JOE Hey, buddy.

MAN (*to* CLARA) So who wins? If I'm right, my friend buys us a drink and he gets lost. If he's right, I buy him a drink and you and me can get lost.

CLARA *enjoys this sophisticate of the boondocks.* JOE *tugs at the* MAN'S *shirt.*

JOE Hey, buddy.

The MAN *turns to find a switchblade in* JOE'S *hand, the point just inches from his gut.*

Loon Lake: A Screenplay

The lady's with someone.

The MAN *draws back, arms raised.*

MAN   OK, friend. I can see that. No need for that there. No need.

He backs off. JOE *folds up the knife, slips it into his pocket.*

CLARA   (*to* JOE) Are you out of your mind?

JOE *sees the* MAN *talking to his friends at the bar.*

Do you know what you're doing?

JOE   I do. And if you don't stand up right now and get your ass moving, I'll do the same to you.

EXT.   STREET OUTSIDE TAVERN. EVENING

The street shining with the recent rain. JOE *holds* CLARA's *arm as he hustles her to the car.*

CLARA   You know something? You're crazy, you know that?

But she seems pleased by the episode. JOE *hears the words as praise.*

INT.   MOTEL BEDROOM. NIGHT

Headlights loom and fade on the windowshade as the traffic goes past.
    JOE, *nude, lies on his back, his arms flung out, the covers all over the place. He's gasping for breath.*
    CLARA, *nude, the perspiration shining on her breasts, raises herself on one elbow, looks at him with concern.*

CLARA   (*softly*) Hey, mister. You still alive?

EXT.   COLUMBUS, OHIO. STREET INTERSECTION. DAY

A TRAFFIC COP *blows his whistle, waves on the traffic. Among the proletarian cars that come through, the sleek gray Mercedes stands out. The* COP *stares after it.*

Loon Lake: A Screenplay | 385

INT.   MERCEDES. DAY

JOE *notices the staring* COP *in the rearview mirror.*

JOE   I have not been smart. I suppose my mind has been on other things.

EXT.   STREET IN COLUMBUS. DAY

The Mercedes makes a sudden, sharp turn into a side street.

INT.   MERCEDES. DAY

CLARA   What's wrong?

JOE   A German-made convertible with New York plates.

Pause.

CLARA   This is a hot car.

JOE   As hot as they come.

EXT.   COLUMBUS, OHIO. USED CAR LOT. DAY

JOE *and* USED CAR SALESMAN *walk around the Mercedes. Behind them are rows of black Fords, Chevys, etc. A big sign reads* BUCKEYE BILL USED CAR LOT.

SALESMAN   How you expec' me to move a car where you can't get the parts if'n they break?

JOE   Nothing breaks on a baby like this.

SALESMAN   Hell. There ain't even a book on this here car.

JOE   Course not. Nobody who owns one ever trades it. It's too good to have a book.

Pause.

SALESMAN   Son, I may end up offerin' you a job, but I can't buy this vehicle. Buckeye Bill ain't been in business all these years in the same spot by takin' in cars without papers.

Loon Lake: A Screenplay

JOE   Jesus! Since when do you walk around with papers of your own family's car!

SALESMAN   This is your family car?

JOE   Yessir. It's one of my mom and dad's cars.

SALESMAN   Now why you want to go and sell their car out from under 'em?

JOE *puts his hand on the* SALESMAN'*s shoulder, walks him away from the car, out of the range of* CLARA'*s hearing—she is seen looking bored in the front seat. She is wearing her fur coat.*

JOE   *(confidentially)* Why? Why is that bit of heaven you see there. (*gesturing back at* CLARA) Miss Lukacs, my fiancée. Miss Lukacs, of whom my family don't approve. I am giving up everything—my inheritance, everything—for her. We are running away to get married.

SALESMAN   How you gonna run if you don't have no car?

JOE   I'm gonna take part of what you give me for it in what you have here on the lot. I'm gonna buy a modest, well-tuned vehicle from you, Bill. The famous Buckeye Bill—that's you, ain't it?

SALESMAN   Yessir!

INT.   USED CAR. DAY

JOE *and* CLARA *back on the road. Through the window, the outskirts of Columbus, Ohio. The engine noise is loud.*

CLARA   *(loudly, so as to be heard over the noise)* Someday, maybe you can buy it back—or one like it.

JOE   What?

CLARA   I said someday you could hope to get it back.

JOE   *(pounds the dashboard)* I've got my car! I've got papers for it! I've got a hundred and ten simoleons in my pocket! Is that bad? We can get to California if we're careful.

CLARA   California?

JOE   That's where we're going. Didn't you know?

The ride is bumpy. CLARA *holds the leather strap over the door. She peers ahead.*

CLARA   I wasn't informed.

EXT.   TWO-LANE ROAD. DAY (MUSIC)

The car with JOE *and* CLARA *rattling along. It is a 1932 Chevy station wagon with wood-panel sides, a dented fender, and windows that tremble in their frames with every bump. We watch it go, sputtering into the distance. (Music ends.)*

EXT.   ROOMING HOUSE. DAY

A very heavy snowstorm. Snow banks the cars parked along this modest residential street, blows up against the porch steps of the houses, fills the grey sky.

The front yard of one house has a ROOMS FOR RENT *sign that is almost obscured by the blown snow.*

INT.   ROOMING HOUSE. BEDROOM. DAY

JOE *stands at the window looking out at the storm.*

EXT.   ROOMING HOUSE ALLEY THROUGH WINDOW. DAY

From JOE's *point of view we see the Chevy station wagon parked behind the house, half buried in snow. The sense is of a car out of commission—a rear tire is flat, the whole machine looking somehow askew.*

INT.   ROOMING HOUSE. BEDROOM. DAY

JOE *turns from the window. He stands for a moment at the foot of the double bed, where* CLARA, *fully dressed, is asleep under a throw blanket.*

The room is clean, small, sparely furnished.

JOE *puts on his khaki greatcoat and leaves, closing the door quietly so as not to awaken her.*

Loon Lake: A Screenplay

EXT. ROOMING HOUSE. DAY

JOE *comes down the front steps, raising his collar, buttoning his coat.*

An OLD WOMAN *watches him from the porch window. He looks both ways, makes up his mind, and walks off down the street, huddled against the storm.*

MONTAGE: EXT. JACKSONTOWN, INDIANA. DOWNTOWN CITY STREETS. DAY

A sequence of shots of this small Midwestern industrial city on a snowy day.

Architecture of red brick—bank, city hall, armory with cannon on front lawn. Traffic in the snowy streets, headlights on in the afternoon.

Black cars parked aslant at the curbs.

EXT. JACKSONTOWN. RAILROAD STREET. DAY

At a downtown intersection, JOE *is engrossed by the sheer busyness of the scene. Lots of cars going in the same direction, many with out-of-state licenses: jalopies of every description, with valises and duffel bags strapped to their fenders. Cars filled with families—children, and grandparents high in the rear seats, scarves wrapped around their heads. Broken-down trucks with furniture covered with blankets and tied down with rope.*

A trolley car comes clanging along, going in the same direction. It comes to a stop, takes on passengers. Impulsively, JOE *jumps aboard, and the trolley moves off.*

INT. TROLLEY CAR. DAY

The car is crowded with MEN *in overalls, some carrying toolboxes. Some* MEN *with* FAMILIES *and their suitcases and bundles.*

JOE, *standing, peers through the window; the trolley is barreling between rows of semiattached bungalows, one block like another.*

EXT. TROLLEY CAR. END OF THE LINE. DAY

The trolley moving slowly now in a narrow street alongside the walls and chain link fence of some vast factory. MEN *are walking in the street, and the trolley car clangs its bell as it pushes through.*

The trolley comes to a stop and everyone pours out, including JOE.

EXT. MAIN GATE, FACTORY. DAY

JOE *finds himself in a huge, quiet, intense* CROWD *standing in the snow before locked gates. Behind the gates, uniformed* MEN *stand talking with unconcern— as if nothing unusual is going on.*

JOE *sees over shoulders, through the fence gate and the whirl of falling snow, an enormous sign extending over the roofs of two buildings. Each letter of the sign is individually mounted.*

EXT. FACTORY SIGN. DAY

Panning, we are able slowly to assemble the name of this manufacturing plant: BENNETT AUTOBODY NUMBER SIX.

INT. JACKSONTOWN INN. NIGHT

JOE *and* CLARA *having dinner. This is the best restaurant in town: candlelight, white linen tablecloths, black* WAITERS, *a certain hotel heaviness. Roast beef au jus.*

JOE   I did a little exploring while you were having your nap. We could be in worse places. There are jobs here, people shopping in the stores. They have three movie houses open.

CLARA *says nothing, cuts her roast beef.*

And you want to hear something funny? The big employer, and why everything is humming, is none other than your friend and mine—Mr. F. W. Bennett.

CLARA *puts down her knife and fork, dabs at her mouth with her napkin, and sits there.*

Loon Lake: A Screenplay

It's his Number Six plant. *(He stops and gazes at her in the candlelight.)* Oh, Clara—I'd be happy if I could just look at you across this table for the rest of my life!

CLARA   That would be a lot of roast beef.

JOE   Hey, you're not wearing the gold band I bought you.

CLARA   *(looking at her hand)* I forgot.

JOE   It's for your own protection, Clara . . . *(resuming his eating and drinking)* Anyway, as long as we're stuck here—I mean the papers say every state from Indiana to the Rockies is snowed under—so long as we're here a while, I thought I'd tap into Mr. Bennett—build up our cash reserve for the run to California.

CLARA   What does *that* mean?

JOE   Well *(he takes a swig of beer)*—see, they're hiring at the Number Six plant.

CLARA   So?

JOE   *(the moment of truth!)* I caught on there this afternoon. (CLARA *doesn't seem to react; he's encouraged to continue.*) Nothing to it. All these old-timers have union backgrounds. Hell—it's unskilled labor; they look for the innocent faces, the ones who don't know any better. I caught on right away.

CLARA *resumes dining, smiling sweetly across the table. They eat in silence. The silence gets bigger and bigger. She is oblivious to his exasperated glances.*

I don't see why you should get on your high horse. Is it any worse than sleeping in his bed?

CLARA   I think I've got to leave now.

JOE   Goddammit, Clara. The rooming house is twelve-fifty a week in advance. How long do you think I can afford that? The guy wants eighty-five dollars to regrind the valves. We need money!

She has risen from the table.

Do you mind if I pay the damn check? The roast beef au jus goes for two-fifty!

EXT. JACKSONTOWN STREET. NIGHT

JOE *is following* CLARA *down the street. When he grabs her elbow, she shrugs him off.*

JOE   Clara, for God's sake, what is it I've done, after all? I got a job! A job! Is it a fucking crime to get a job? We're here in the real world, now, don't you understand? There's no money!

INT.   ROOMING HOUSE. BEDROOM. NIGHT

CLARA *is packing.* JOE *remonstrates, his voice low but urgent.*

JOE   Please don't be like this. Please listen. All right, this is the worst shit-hole in the country, and it's so freezing fucking cold I can't believe how cold it is. And there's no reason to stay here—except that it's Bennett's. *(He detects a flicker of interest on her part.)* That's why, Clara. That is the true reason why. Because I'm gonna work his line without his knowing, and I'm gonna walk away from his machine with my wages in my pocket and he's going to get us to California. That's why!

She sits on the edge of the bed.

You hear me, Clara? Because it's living under his nose. That's why. Because it's the riskiest thing. It's the toughest and most dangerous and the classiest thing. That's why.

CLARA   And what am I supposed to do all day while you work his line and make your classy wages? Huh, big boy? What am I supposed to do!

He is by now sitting next to her.

JOE   *(softly)* You don't know what you've done to me. Me, the carny kid! You're making an honest man of him—it's horrible! I have all these godaw-ful longings to support you, to make a life with you. I want us to live together in one place. And I don't care where it is; I don't care if it's the North Pole. *(He kisses her neck.)* I'll do anything to keep you in bonbons and French novels, Clara, and it's all your fault.

CLARA   Oh Jesus, he's crazy. This boy is crazy.

JOE   What do you say? A few weeks. In a company house. Working it all out in the hard life. You got anything better to do?

Pause.

CLARA   That's the crying shame of it.

INT.   BENNETT AUTOBODY. ASSEMBLY LINE. DAY

Inside the vast automobile plant, there is a thunderous racket of running machines, conveyor belts, acetylene torches, riveting, the rattling of moving treads, the creak of pulleys carrying black autobody sections overhead.

INT.   ASSEMBLY LINE (ANOTHER ANGLE). DAY

One of the figures working on the trim line (bumpers, grills, headlights) turns out to be JOE, *in overalls, cap, dirty face, like all the rest. The line moves fast and he is conscientious and harried, trying to keep up. His work gloves are shredded. Over the noise a steam whistle blows and he lifts his head up with exuberance.*

EXT.   BENNETT AUTOBODY. MAIN GATE. DUSK

The WORKFORCE *streaming out of the plant, a sea of bobbing soft caps. A sort of agitation in the crowd—it's* JOE, *pushing through, more in a hurry than anyone else.*

When he reaches open ground, in the street, he starts running. He gets the last available space on the back step of the trolley car, as it takes off down Railroad Street, packed to the gills with WORKERS.

EXT.   RAILROAD STREET, SEMIATTACHED. NIGHT

JOE *coming along the street, the sound of a trolley car receding in the distance. He stops in front of one of the block of two-family semiattached bungalows, undistinguishable from all the rest, counts in from the corner, and, satisfied that he's got the right one, he bounds up the porch steps and opens the right of the two doors and goes in.*

INT. RAILROAD STREET HOUSE. KITCHEN. NIGHT

The residue of dinner on the battered table in this small, primitive kitchen. JOE *sits bathing the cuts on his hands in a basin of warm water.* CLARA *sits as near to the small coal stove as she can get. She's wearing her fur coat and reading a screen romance magazine. She is hardly the girl from Loon Lake at this point— her hair is longer, wilder, her skin coarsened by the winter, no makeup—and to* JOE's *eyes, as he watches her lovingly, she is more beautiful than ever. He laughs.*

CLARA   I'm glad *you're* laughing.

INT. BEDROOM. NIGHT

CLARA, *fully dressed, standing and watching* JOE *flailing about under the covers, rolling from one side of the camp-style bed, hoofing and whistling. Suddenly he stops, lifts the covers.*

JOE   OK, it's warm. Quick!

CLARA *drops her fur coat, jumps into the bed, still dressed, is covered up by* JOE. *He hugs her while she shivers.*

JOE   It's OK, it's warmer now—you see?

He starts undressing her under the covers. It's a not unpleasant task, and soon they are kissing. But suddenly she pushes him away.

CLARA   Shhh!

JOE   What?

CLARA   You hear that? *(pause)* Next door. They've got a radio.

JOE *listens: the faint strains of a swing band.*

EXT. RAILROAD STREET. MORNING

WORKERS *carrying lunch pails, walking hunched up in the cold morning. A bell clangs and the trolley goes through.*

EXT.   PORCH, RAILROAD STREET. MORNING

JOE *is just leaving for work. He closes the front door, turns, finds the next-door* NEIGHBOR (LYLE RED JAMES) *coming out at the same time.*

A gawky, red-haired cracker in overalls—very thin, buck teeth, a face of freckles. He grins at the coincidence.

NEIGHBOR (LYLE RED JAMES)   How-do!

Together they go down the steps, join the throng in the street.

EXT.   RAILROAD STREET. DAY

The big Bennett plant in the distance.

JOE *walks hunched against the cold like everyone else going to work. But his* NEIGHBOR *lopes along, lifting his arms, inhaling, treating the day as if it's spring.*

NEIGHBOR (LYLE RED JAMES)   *(singing in an adenoidal hillbilly tenor)*
"Hear the mighty engine,
Hear the lonesome hobo's squall . . . "
(to JOE*)* I started out in trim. Just like you. Now I hang doors. You get a few more cents a hour. Hands don't cut up so bad. Lemme see your hands. (JOE *does)* Yeah. That's it. *(singing again)*
"Hear the mighty en-gine,
Hear the lonesome hobo's squall
A-goin' through the jungle
On the Warbash Cannonball!"

A particularly fierce blast of wind and snow gusts. JAMES *holds out his arms.*

Whooee! Toughen me up, God! Usen me up to it!

EXT.   RAILROAD STREET. DAY

BENNETT AUTOBODY *sign looming ahead. The crowd of* MEN *going to work is thicker.*

JOE's *neighbor,* LYLE RED JAMES, *is still talking.*

LYLE RED JAMES A course, all this hirin' ain't just seasonal. You're lucky you came to Jacksontown not till now. You wouldn't know it, but they was a wildcat strike last summer. Quite a to-do! *(singing)*
"She's mighty tall and handsome;
She's known to one and all . . . " *(to* JOE*)*
Company brought in strikebreakers. A feller was killed. They closed down the whole damn shebang, fired ever'one. Ever'one! *(singing)*
"She's the hoboes' 'commodation,
She's the Warbash Cannonball."

The two men fade into the crowd, JOE's *neighbor,* LYLE RED JAMES, *still talking.*

INT. JAMES'S LIVING ROOM. NIGHT

LYLE RED JAMES *is pointing out to* JOE *and* CLARA *what things in his house ought to be appreciated for their taste or expensiveness.*

JAMES Genuwine horsehair chairs and matching sofa. Got us our own private-line phone right here. Reach anywheres in the country with it. This floodlight *(a floor lamp with a square deco shade)* is the modern style of the times. I seen one jest like it in Chicago.

JOE *is somewhat puzzled. This company house has curtains on the windows, pictures on the walls, a braided rug on the floor.*

JOE Very nice, Mr. James.

JAMES None of this mister stuff, Joe. Lyle James likes his friends to call him Red.

JOE Red. I mean, the room layout is just like our place—but that's as far as it goes.

JAMES First thang we did when we moved in? Put all that company junk to storage. No use fer it. Brought all our own on my flatbed truck. *(gazing around with satisfaction)* Don't look much like Railroad Street, do it?

SANDY JAMES, *his wife, enters from the kitchen carrying a home-baked choco-late cake, cups and saucers, on a tray.*

SANDY JAMES   Loll, yo' braggin' agin!

SANDY JAMES *is a child bride, a young teenager, not half the age of her husband. She wears an unbuttoned sweater over her dress, school shoes, ankle socks.* CLARA *is intrigued.*

Move those magazines, Loll, so I can set this down?

He does as he's told—takes a stack of pulp detective magazines and puts them aside.
The sound of a baby crying.

'Scuse me, I won't be a minute!

She rushes into the other room.

LYLE RED JAMES   (*to* CLARA) Ain't she somethin'? 'Course I can't brag about *her,* leastwise to her face—makes her color up like the evenin' sun.

INT.   JAMES'S LIVING ROOM. NIGHT

We take a long close-up look at a splendid radio—a Philco console of burled wood, with a circular dial, glowing green, and a cat's-eye tuning light.
Dance music is playing.
LYLE RED JAMES *sits on a sofa with his hands on his overalled knees. His fingers tap to the rhythm of the music.*
JOE *and* CLARA *sit in the horsehair sofa.*
SANDY JAMES *sits on the floor, her legs tucked under her like a child. The doll she is crooning to is a real* BABY. CLARA *can't take her eyes off this teen-age madonna.*

SANDY   You hongry? Is she hongry? Well all right, her momma's gonna feed her. Yes she is!

Naturally, with no self-consciousness, SANDY *unbuttons her dress, slips it off one shoulder, and gives the* BABY *her breast.*
Pause.

CLARA   How old is she?

SANDY   Six months.

CLARA   Did you give birth here? In Jacksontown?

SANDY   No, Ma'am. Down to Grantham.

LYLE RED JAMES   Don't s'pose you folks would know Grantham, Tennessee. But that's where her people live, coal miners down at the edge of the holler there. I watched Sandy growin' up. One day I am drivin' myself past there and I like to a gone into a ditch, for there was this chile liftin' her arms to tie washclothes on the line. And I seen those legs on them tiptoes and her behind-the-knees, and I said Mr. James, if 'n you don't ask for the hand of that Sandy *right now*—well, she'll be gone by tomorra.

SANDY   Hush, Loll!

JAMES   So I did, it's just what I did, waited on her pappy to get home from his shift and 'fore he even got his face washed I popped the question.

SANDY   Y'all want some more cake?

CLARA   *(shakes her head no)* It's good, though. I couldn't bake a cake in a million years.

SANDY   *(blushing)* It's easy. *(pause)* I ain't never talked to someone from New York before. *(She giggles.)*

CLARA *laughs. She is fascinated.* JOE *sees this.*

JAMES   *(taking out a pocket watch)* Ten minutes to the "Mr. First Nighter." That's a New York show on the Blue network. We listen to it every week— not just 'cause you folks is here.

EXT.   PORCH, RAILROAD STREET HOUSE. NIGHT

JOE *and* CLARA *say goodnight to* SANDY *and* LYLE JAMES *at their door, then they open their own adjoining door and go in.*

INT.   JOE AND CLARA'S LIVING ROOM. NIGHT (DARK)

In the darkness JOE *and* CLARA *begin to giggle, laugh, shush each other, laugh some more.* JOE *imitates* LYLE RED JAMES's *voice.*

JOE   Hey Miss Clara. Lemme see yo' behind-the-knees, honey . . .

They bang into each other, make their way into the bedroom, laughing.

INT.   BEDROOM. NIGHT (DARK)

JOE   Lordy me, that was an excitin' tale on the Mr. First Nighter show from New York. Lift yo' arms, honey-chile, so as I c'n take yo' frock off.

EXT.   MAIN GATE, BENNETT AUTOBODY. DAY (DUSK)

The WORKFORCE *pouring out at quitting time,* JOE *in the middle of it all.*
A hand taps him on the shoulder. He turns; no one is there. When he turns back, LYLE RED JAMES *stand grinning at him.*

JAMES   You comin' to the meetin'?

JOE   What meeting?

JAMES   Union meetin'.

Pause.

JOE   Well, I'm not a member.

JAMES   Don't matter none. Let's go. See what they up to. This a recruitin' meetin'—anyone's got the balls.

JOE   Well, I don't know—I never told Clara I wouldn't be home.

JAMES   Boy, the little woman sure has a holt a you. She's with Sandy anyways—you come on with me, they'll figger it out.

He takes JOE's *arm.* JOE *gives a fleeting glance behind him at the departing trolley car.*

INT.   UNION MEETING ROOM. NIGHT

Several dozen MEN *sitting on camp chairs in a dirty loft with a wooden floor, dirty windows. They face a table at which the* OFFICERS *of the local preside—*

hard-looking men with buttons or union cards prominently displayed in the bands of their hats. An American flag pinned on the wall behind them.

One officer, the local's PRESIDENT, *addressing the meeting.*

PRESIDENT   We have a good program tonight. A brother from national to tell us about the sit-down tactic that has worked pretty good for some of our brothers. I won't waste much time on preliminaries. I don't have to tell you men how it feels to work in a Bennett speed-up. I don't have to tell you the difference between a man and a slave—you know that, or you wouldn't be here . . . I call on the Secretary to read the minutes.

JOE *is sitting in the back row, not terribly interested in what's going on. Then the* SECRETARY *stands and he sees who it is and reacts.*

LYLE RED JAMES   Herewith the o-fishul minutes a the last meetin'. As taken by yo' Sec'tary Loll Red Jimes, Bennett Local Seventeen, union card number three-six-oh-six-eight.

Cheers and a burst of laughter and applause.

PRESIDENT   Just read the damn minutes, James.

We hear the nasal singsong as we study JOE's *face in reaction: he's learned something he didn't know.*

INT.   RAILROAD STREET HOUSE. KITCHEN. NIGHT

JOE *and* CLARA *talking over coffee.*

JOE   I can't explain it. I thought we was just two guys goin' to a meeting. And it turns out he's a union official.

CLARA   So what?

JOE   I don't know. It was creepy. He sprung it on me. There's more to this hayseed than meets the eye. He keeps secrets.

CLARA   *(smiling)* So do you.

She holds out her hand: on her finger is a wedding ring.

JOE   Hey!

Loon Lake: A Screenplay

CLARA   They think you're an auto worker named Joe Paterson. They think I'm your wife. They think we're their friends living the life next door on Railroad Street. We keep some pretty good secrets ourselves.

JOE *holds her hand with his two hands, assuaged.*

JOE   (*smiling*) I seen the way you looked at that baby, Clara. That's the easiest thing in the world.

Pause.

CLARA   What knocks me out—Sandy James is all of fifteen years old. Did you know that? She got married at thirteen. Can you beat that? And she does everything—she goes to the store, she knows what's good and what isn't, she takes care of that kid like royalty, feeds that stupid hick of a husband better than he deserves, washes the floor on her knees, scrubs clothes, cleans—Jesus! The only thing I haven't seen her do is sew the American flag!

INT.   JAMES'S LIVING ROOM. NIGHT

CLARA *and* SANDY *are decorating a Christmas tree so tall its tip bends along the ceiling. It fills the already heavily furnished room. The radio is playing.*

    LYLE RED JAMES *pours two whiskeys, gives one to* JOE. *He pulls his chair so as to sit knee to knee with* JOE. *He glances at the two women.*

JAMES   I don't want 'em to hear this. We got the strike planned. You gotta keep quiet 'bout this.

JOE   What?

JAMES   In the exec'tive board meetin' last night. I can't tell you who came to visit from Detroit, but you would recognize his name from the papers, you can believe me.

JOE   I believe you.

JAMES   Well sir, we're a settin' down the second week in January. Soon as ever'one's spent their Christmas packet, you know? Soon's ever'one begins to think 'bout the spring layoffs—as you can't help doin' in the new year. You understand the beauty o' that.

JOE   Sure.

JAMES   National's allotin' considerable monies. You see, what you don't know is that this ain't no ordinary strike, nossir. What you don't know is that Number Six makes all the trim for the Bennett Autobody plants in three states. Do you take my meanin'? (*He looks at* JOE *and laughter spurts out of him. He pounds* JOE'S *knee.*)

SANDY   Loll, is that one a yore dirty jokes!

JAMES   (*to* JOE, *conspiratorially*) Number Six makes all the trim. Ever' bumper. Ever' hubcap. Ever' runnin' board. Ever' light. When we set down come January, ever' Bennett plant in Michigan, Ohio, and Indiana's gonna feel it.

SANDY   Come he'p, Loll, if 'n that's all you got to do.

JAMES   (*to* JOE) 'Course you can't tell *no* one. Mum's the word, right brother?

INT.   BENNETT AUTOBODY PLANT. ASSEMBLY LINE. DAY

JOE *works well, fully attuned, experienced, a confidence in his movements.*

The noon whistle blows, the belts slow down and stop. The pitch of the collective generating machinery drops and quiet comes to the plant, except for the shouts and laughs of MEN *glad to have their lunch break.*

JOE *grabs the paper bag that holds his lunch and heads down the line after the other* MEN *in his section.*

EXT.   LUNCH AREA. BENNETT PLANT. DAY

The MEN *have gathered in a kind of open space near a wall of lockers. They use unupholstered can seats for chairs. They're talking quietly, intently, some not eating.*

When JOE *arrives, he sees something is not right. He sits down next to* TWO OTHER MEN.

JOE   What's happening?

FIRST MAN   They're layin' off.

JOE   What? Who says?

SECOND MAN   Santa Claus.

VOICE   Hey!

A THIRD MAN *appears.*

THIRD MAN   They're pulling out machinery!

He runs off and MEN, *including* JOE, *get up and follow, some with sandwiches and thermos bottles in their hands.*

INT.   BENNETT FACTORY OVERVIEW. DAY

From all directions MEN *are streaming toward an unnaturally lighted part of the huge car-assembly plant. They climb over car bodies, tread the motionless belts as if walking railroad tracks.*

INT.   FACTORY AREA. DAY

A section flooded with bright daylight pouring through huge open corrugated sliding doors on wheels.

Outside a flatbed railroad car slowly moving alongside. We hear the chuffing of an engine.

Huge tool and die machines are being unbolted from the cement floor. One has already been hoisted up on a pulley by an overhead trolley.

MEN, *including* JOE *and others from his section, converging.* SECURITY GUARDS *come running.*

ONE GUARD   Here, you men, you don't belong here. Go on back!

JOE *and the others don't move, but gaze on the scene. A* FLOOR MANAGER *in white shirt and tie, holding a clipboard, assists the* GUARDS *in dispersing the* MEN.

MANAGER   Go on back where you belong, men. We've got too much inventory, that's all—we're cutting back. Go on, nothing to worry about.

SECOND MAN   (*to* JOE) Shit. Do you have to unbolt a machine when you're loaded up on inventory? You can just turn it off.

GUARDS   Break it up. Go on! Get back where you belong!

EXT.   MAIN GATE. NIGHT

Not the usual going-home rush. MEN *lingering in conversation. Everyone's talking layoffs.*

NEWSBOYS *doing a lively business with the evening papers.*

JOE *finds* LYLE RED JAMES *reading a paper, which he holds spread out in front of him, his arms wide.*

JOE   Hey, Red.

JAMES   Looky here. They're layin' off a hundred and twelve brothers. Merry Christmas!

JOE   I guess I'll be the next to go.

JAMES   Don't you worry none, boy. *(He folds up the paper.)* You want this? *(He drops it on the ground.)* They're just cuttin' the boys who worked the tool and dies they took off the floor. They're not gonna bother the likes a you.

They begin walking.

JOE   It's almost like they knew about the strike, ain't it.

JAMES   How so?

JOE   Everyone says they're shipping those tool and dies to other Bennett plants. Why would they do that all of a sudden? Like they found something out.

JAMES   Hell, they're no dopes. They knew they was vulnerable same as we. *(a side glance to* JOE*)* I figgered 'em to do this.

Trolley bell clangs.

JOE   There's our car. You comin'?

JAMES   You go on. I got some business to tend to.

EXT.   FRONT PORCH, RAILROAD STREET HOUSE. NIGHT

JOE *coming home, opens his front door. No lights on.*

JOE   Clara?

Loon Lake: A Screenplay

A note is tacked to the door. He reads it, closes the door, knocks on the James's door and goes in.

INT.   JAMES'S LIVING ROOM. NIGHT

Two of the UNION OFFICERS *(p. 399) are sitting on the sofa: the* PRESIDENT, *a dour, skinny man, and a younger, burlier* VICE-PRESIDENT. *They are dressed in their work clothes.*

  SANDY JAMES *stands rubbing her palms on her hips. She is nonplussed. Behind her is* CLARA, *in the kitchen doorway, holding the* BABY.

SANDY   (*to* OFFICERS) Um, this is Mr. Paterson from next door?

The MEN *rise, shake* JOE's *hand.*

PRESIDENT   Yeah, Paterson. I seen you around.

They sit back down.

VICE-PRESIDENT   We're waitin' fer Red James.

Pause.

PRESIDENT   (*to* JOE) You and him buddies?

JOE   Yes.

PRESIDENT   You ain't seen him, have you?

JOE   No.

PRESIDENT   Don't you ride home together?

JOE   Sometimes.

The phone rings. The PRESIDENT *jumps up and grabs the receiver.*

PRESIDENT   (*into phone*) Yeah. (*pause*) Yeah. That's it.

He hangs up, exchanges glances with his colleague, who rises.

  Well. I guess we'll be on our way. Sorry to bother you, Mrs. James.

SANDY   Red should be home right soon.

PRESIDENT   No, no, that's OK. Just tell him we were in the neighborhood. Nothin' important.

The two MEN *leave.* SANDY *locks the door after them.*

SANDY   Oh, it gives me the jitters—strangers comin' 'round and askin' questions.

JOE   Like what?

SANDY   Where we got our lovely furnishin's? How long we had the radio?

She takes the BABY *from* CLARA. JOE *goes to the phone: the space inside the dial where the number ought to be is blank.*

INT.   POLICE STATION. DAY (SILENT)

The POLICE CHIEF *of Jacksontown is sitting at his desk, facing us. He wears a short-sleeved white shirt with epaulets, a tie, a mechanical pencil clipped in his pocket, his garrison cap. He is enormous, with arms like trees, the same specie of life as* FANNY THE FAT LADY.
  He folds his hands on the desk, stares at us, waiting.

EXT.   MAIN GATE, BENNETT AUTOBODY. DAY

In the street, UNION REPS *are handing out flyers to the* MEN *arriving for work.*

REP   Emergency rally this Friday night! What you can do about the Christmas layoffs! Come to the rally! (etc.)

EXT.   RAILROAD STREET TAVERN. NIGHT

LYLE RED JAMES *is trying to persuade* JOE *to step in for a drink.*

JOE   No, Red, I gotta get home to Clara.

JAMES   Hell, jest one, brother. I'm gonna buy you a drink to celebrate the occasion.

JOE   What occasion?

JAMES   A new career move for yours truly.

INT. RAILROAD STREET TAVERN. NIGHT

The Railroad Street Tavern is filled with AUTO WORKERS. *Much noise, cigarette smoke. The camera finds* LYLE RED JAMES *and* JOE *in a plywood booth at the back. They're drinking shots with beer chasers.*

JAMES   See, Joe, it could've kept working. Hell, I had it so finely made I mighta run for somethin' someday in the National. But the client don't give a hoot for that. You give him the intelligence and he jumps in the air like a rabbit with buckshot up its ass.

JOE   What client? What are you talking about?

JAMES   I mean I'd laugh if I didn't feel like cryin'. *(He drinks.)* But hell, I'm thinkin' to drop industrial work anyways. You been to the city of Los Angeleez? (JOE *shakes his head.*) Well, they's a need for operatives there. They's so much messin' around what with them movie stars and all, you see, ever' good wife needs to make her case sooner or later, if you get my meanin'. As does ever' good husband. *(He laughs.)* Yessir, they's career opportunity in Los Angeleez.

He looks up, nervously checking the other faces in the room. The truth is beginning to dawn on JOE.

See *(leaning forward)*, if the union was smart they wouldn't never let on they knowed. Take their losses this hand, play for the next, use me against the Bennett and fake 'em right outta their shoes. An' shit—ever' one would've made out all around—the union 'cause they knowed about me, the Bennett still thinkin' "they" had their inside op and me still drawin' my pay in good faith and doin' my work. *(He slumps back in his seat.)* But you see, they let me know they know and the company knows they know, and I'm not good to anyone anymore, leastwise to myself.

JOE   Red, this is so fucking weird—you recruited me!

JAMES   I surely did. I brought in numbers a good men and true. An' what do I get fer my trouble—I gotta take that pore chile now and move her out of her home.

JOE   Does she know, Red? Does Sandy know?

JAMES   What—about me bein' a detective? Aw Joe *(he grins)*, the pore chile has so much of a man in me already, did I tell her the whole truth, she'd go out of her nateral mind with love! *(He holds up his fingers.)* Bartender! Two more, if 'n you please.

INT.   RAILROAD STREET TAVERN. NIGHT

The customers have thinned out somewhat.

The number of shot and beer glasses on JAMES's *and* JOE's *table has increased considerably. While not exactly drunk,* JOE *has lost his edge and sits bemused by the shock of revelation. He looks up as* LYLE RED JAMES *greets* TWO MEN *arriving at the table.*

JAMES   Set yourself down!

They are heavy, middle-aged MEN. ONE, *in a worn coat, a battered fedora slides in next to* JOE. *The* OTHER, *in a lumber jacket and blue wool cap over his white hair, sits next to* LYLE RED JAMES.

JAMES   *(to the* ARRIVALS) See, I ain't sayin' I didn't make a mistake. I don't want you to think that—whatever happens.

ONE   That's all right, Mr. James. *(points at* JOE *with his thumb)* And this is him?

JAMES   My good friend and neighbor who has taken sup at my table—Mr. Paterson.

ONE   I see. *(He pulls back to study* JOE, *laughs ruefully and shakes his head. He looks at* RED JAMES.)

OTHER   *(pulling off his cap, holding it in both hands)* Mr. James, there's a particular place in hell, in fact, its innermost heart, where reside the tormented souls of men of your sort. They freeze and burn at the same time. Their flesh is parboiled in sulphurous pools of their accumulated shit, the tentacles of foul, slimy creatures drag them under to drink of it. This region is presided over by Judas Iscariot. You know the name, I trust.

JAMES   Aw, come on now, that ain't no kind of talk.

OTHER   On behalf of every working man who has gone down under the club or been shot in the back, I consign you to that place. I may get there too,

Loon Lake: A Screenplay

but, God have mercy on my soul, it will be a joyful thing if I can hear your screams and moans of useless contrition till the end of time.

JAMES   Hey brother, come on now. You ain't even tried to see if 'n I'm tellin' the truth. That ain't exactly fair!

The TWO MEN *rise. The* MAN *with the blue wool cap leans over and spits in* JAMES's *face.*

The MEN *leave.* LYLE RED JAMES *splashes water from a glass on his handkerchief and he washes himself.*

JAMES   (*to* JOE) Catholic fellers.

EXT.   RAILROAD STREET. NIGHT

LYLE RED JAMES *and* JOE *are making their way home—*JOE *weaving a little from drink.*

JAMES *sings as they go down the dark street. The moon is out, snow is on the ground.*

JAMES   "The train I ride on is a hundred coaches long;
You can hear the whistle blow nine hundred miles . . . "
(*He looks at* JOE) What you doin' here, boy? Tryin' to keep up? You still tryin' to keep up with Lyle Red James? *(singing)*
"Ohh-oh me, Ohh-my,
You can hear the whistle blow nine hundred miles . . . "

A car pulls up silently alongside them. JOE *turns, too late, to find a mass of* DARK FIGURES *overwhelming them both, muscling them into an alley.*

We look into the darkness and hear sounds of brutal struggle—gasps, grunts, curses, retching.

EXT.   ALLEY. NIGHT

JOE *is under a mass of struggling bodies. He is bleeding at the mouth. Something cracks and his face twists in pain. He is flat on the ground, black figures above him. He cannot move.*

A sickening thud. Then we hear a long, high-pitched wail, the weight of bodies lifts, the assailants are gone. JOE *rolls on his back, sees the stars.*

EXT. JACKSONTOWN STREET. NIGHT

A green and white police car moving fast, its siren going.

INT. HOSPITAL EMERGENCY ROOM. NIGHT

Two COPS *in blue tunics over sweaters, their hips hung with gunbelts, holsters, cuffs, sticks, stand beside a table on which rests the body of* LYLE RED JAMES. *They are writing up their reports on pads wound with rubber bands.*

The camera finds JOE *on an adjoining table,* CLARA *standing beside him.*

JOE *is a mess, face swollen and discolored, teeth bloodied, one arm taped to his chest. He has trouble speaking.*

JOE   Where's Sandy?

CLARA   I told them to keep her outside.

JOE   He was a company op. A damn spy.

CLARA   *(glancing at the next table)* The poor dumb galoot.

JOE   None of this had anything to do with us. I danced us right into it.

CLARA *touches her finger to her lips. The* COPS *leave and an* ATTENDANT *pulls a sheet over the corpse of* LYLE RED JAMES. *The* ATTENDANT *leaves.*

CLARA   Some men came to their house this afternoon. Just when it was getting dark. Sandy was with me. She thought it was the radio, that she left it on.

JOE   Did you get a look at them?

CLARA   I didn't want us to. I heard what they were doing. They tore the place apart.

JOE   Jesus.

CLARA   It's lousy that she got hit with all this.

JOE   Now I see why they didn't believe him.

CLARA   What? I don't think you should talk.

JOE   No, it's all right, I'm doped up. I'm saying he was trying to pin it on me. I guess he couldn't think of anything better.

CLARA   What?

JOE   But they weren't buying it because they must have found proof—his reports, his files.

CLARA   You should rest. They're going to set your arm and keep you here for observation.

JOE   He tried to make me the fink! *(He is suddenly crying.)* The son of a bitch! The goddamn hillbilly son of a bitch!

CLARA *looks away.*

EXT.   RAILROAD STREET HOUSE. DAY

JOE, *walking slowly, arm slung in a cast, mounts the porch steps. Behind him the street is filled with the morning procession of* MEN *going to work.*
   JOE *opens the door, goes in.*

INT.   RAILROAD STREET HOUSE. BEDROOM. DAY

JOE *stands in the doorway of his bedroom.* CLARA *and* SANDY *are asleep on the bed, the* BABY *between them.*

EXT.   RAILROAD STREET HOUSE. DAY

JOE *comes out on the porch, closes the door. The James's front door is ajar. He pushes it open wider, stands in the doorframe looking in.*

INT.   JAMES'S LIVING ROOM. DAY

The place is a shambles—furniture overturned, braided rug bunched in a corner, papers everywhere, desk jimmied open, etc.
   A MAN (BUSTER) *in topcoat, hat pushed back on his head, is picking up loose papers and stuffing them in a briefcase. He has a heavy five-o'clock shadow, thick black eyebrows. He glances at* JOE, *keeps assembling papers. Looks under sofa cushions, riffles through pulp magazines. He is very thorough. As he works, he talks.*

BUSTER   What's the matter—the lady's husband come home early? You tell me: was it worth it? I'll tell you: no. It is seldom worth what you have to go through to get it.

JOE   Put that stuff back. It doesn't belong to you.

BUSTER   (smiling) That's where you're wrong. Where's the widow?

JOE   What?

BUSTER   His bereaved.

JOE   I don't know.

BUSTER approaches JOE.

BUSTER   Hey kid, look at you. Look how they worked you over. How much can you take? What's the matter with you? (pause) Listen. (He taps an envelope on JOE's cast.) I'm here with money.

INT.   RAILROAD STREET HOUSE. KITCHEN. DAY

The visitor, BUSTER, is holding legal-sized papers in one hand, an uncapped fountain pen in the other, addressing SANDY JAMES, who is large-eyed, mouth tremulous. She is holding her fretful BABY. Next to her is JOE, and off to the side, head bowed, face averted, is CLARA.

BUSTER   (to SANDY) Your husband was a brave man, Mrs. James. The company knows it has a responsibility to his family. It ain't somethin' we have to do, y'unnerstand, but in these cases we like to. If you will sign this waiver, both copies, I have a death benefit sum of two hundred fifty dollars for you. Cash on the barrelhead.

SANDY looks at JOE.

JOE   (to BUSTER) A waiver of what?

BUSTER   (to JOE) A waiver of all future claims against Bennett Autobody and its agent, CIS.

JOE   What is CIS?

BUSTER   Listen, are you Mrs. James?

JOE   What is CIS?

BUSTER   Crapo Industrial Services. (*to* SANDY) We were your husband's employer, Mrs. James.

SANDY   Not the Autobody?

BUSTER   Only secondarily.

JOE *is looking at* CLARA, *whose back is to them all as she stares out the window.*

JOE   (*to* BUSTER) What if she don't sign?

BUSTER   (*sweetly*) How old are you, Mrs. James?

SANDY   Fifteen.

BUSTER   This is a lot of money. If you don't sign, you don't get it.

SANDY *looks at* JOE.

JOE   But she don't waive her right to sue, neither.

BUSTER   You have a really sharp mind, kid. So this fifteen-year-old cracker is gonna sue the largest autobody company in the world. Terrific. You gonna be her lawyer for the eight or ten years it takes even to get to court?

JOE *stares at him, turns to* SANDY, *removes the* BABY *from her arms.*

JOE   Go ahead. Two fifty seems to be the going rate for these things.

SANDY *sits at the kitchen table, signs laboriously while* BUSTER *looks on. Then* BUSTER *lifts one copy, reclaims his fountain pen, counts out the money from his wallet into* SANDY's *hand. He sets his hat firmly on his head, buttons his coat. He glances with interest at* CLARA.

BUSTER   Well, my condolences again. (*He steps toward* JOE, *who is holding the* BABY, *sticks his finger in the* BABY's *cheek.*) Hey, Beauty! (*He laughs in* JOE's *face.*) Beauty and the Beast.

He exits. A moment later the front door closes.

SANDY   Two one hundred dollar beels. An' a fifty dollar beel.

CLARA *takes the* BABY *from* JOE. *She hugs it.*

JOE Red worked for Crapo Industrial Services. Did you know that, Sandy?

SANDY No, sir.

JOE Neither did I. Why should it surprise me? *(pause)* Clara? Does it surprise you? *(no response)* No? Then why should it surprise me? After all, Mr. F. W. Bennett needs his industrial services. Spying is an industrial service, isn't it? I suppose strike-breaking is an industrial service. Paying off cops, bringing in scabs. Let's see, have I left anything out?

CLARA You're frightening the kid.

SANDY *takes the* BABY.

SANDY Mah milk's dried up. She'll have to get on that Carnation.

JOE Sit down, Clara.

They face each other across the kitchen table. CLARA *sighs, folds her hands in her lap.*

You knew that joker. Who is he?

CLARA Just some guy. I used to see him around.

JOE A friend of yours?

CLARA Oh Christ, no. I don't think I ever spoke five words to him.

JOE What's his name? *(silence)* What's his name, Clara!

CLARA I don't remember. Buster. Yeah, I think they called him that.

JOE Buster. Well, what do you think? Did Buster recognize you?

CLARA You don't look so good. Why don't you take it easy?

JOE I'm trying to. I'm just a poor hobo boy. What else can I do? After all, your friend Tommy Crapo is big time. He probably doesn't even know the name of Red James. It's just bad luck that the fucking hillbilly next door was an operative of Crapo Industrial Services. It's not a plot against me. It's not the whole world ganging up on one poor hobo boy.

CLARA Look—

JOE For Christ's sake—answer me. Did that goon recognize you, or didn't he?

Pause.

CLARA   *(softly)* He may have.

JOE   Okay. Fine. *(He stands.)* That's what I wanted to know. We need to know the situation to know how to deal with it. Right? Now is Tommy Crapo in Jacksontown? You tell me.

CLARA   How should I know? I don't think so.

JOE   Well, where would he be?

CLARA   He could be anywhere. Chicago. He lives in Chicago.

JOE   Good. Fine. Now when Buster calls Mr. Tommy Crapo in Chicago to tell him where the missing Clara Lukacs can be found, what is Mr. Tommy Crapo likely to do?

CLARA   I don't like this. I don't want to talk about this.

JOE   Hey Clara. You want to talk about us? You want to talk about our staying alive? Answer the question. What will Crapo do?

CLARA   I don't know.

JOE   Will he hang up the phone and laugh and call in his manicurist? Or is he going to come get you? *(pause)* I mean, what happened at Loon Lake? Why did he leave you there? Did you make him mad? Or was it just a business thing?

CLARA *looks at* JOE.

CLARA   You fucking bastard.

JOE   Oh, swell. Let's hear it. Step a little closer, folks. Hear the Lady Clara speak!

SANDY, *looking shocked and on the verge of tears, runs out,* BABY *in arms. The sound of the front door closing.*

CLARA   You're terrific, you know? That kid has just lost her husband!

JOE   Don't I know it. And what a terrific guy he was. They're coming at me right and left, all these terrific guys. They run in packs, all your terrific friends and acquaintances.

INT.   POLICE STATION. CHIEF'S OFFICE. DAY (SILENT)

The enormous POLICE CHIEF *of Jacksontown at his desk (p. 406). A* PATROL-
MAN *puts an open cardboard box before him. The* CHIEF *examines the contents:
a wallet, a paper bag with a wad of bills, a .32-caliber pistol. Holding the pistol,
he looks up into the camera.*

INT.   JAMES'S LIVING ROOM. DAY

SANDY *is pushing the* BABY *to and fro in her carriage in the middle of the mess.*
JOE *comes in the front door.*

JOE   Sandy, I'm very sorry for all this, and when we have time we'll talk
    about it, if you want. I'll tell you everything I can. Did Red ever give you
    instructions to call or what to do in case something happened to him?

SANDY   Nossir.

JOE   Does he have family in Tennessee? Anyone who could come help you?

SANDY *shakes her head.*

  How about your family?

SANDY   They cain't do nothin'.

JOE   *(looking around)* Well, did Red carry life insurance?

SANDY, *her lower lip protruding, shakes her head.* CLARA *comes in the front
door.*

JOE   *(to* SANDY) Do you know what that is? Insurance?

SANDY   Nossir.

JOE   Well, where does he keep the family papers? I mean like the kid's birth
    certificate. He must keep that somewhere.

At this point, SANDY *begins to cry. She tries not to, rubbing her eyes with the
heels of her hands as if trying to press the tears back in.* CLARA *comes to comfort
her.*

JOE   Jesus!

He looks around the room and begins to go through the carnage—opening drawers, tossing things around. The two women shrink back out of the way and stare at him.

He owes me, you know? He owes me a broken arm and a busted face. He owes me my pride.

In the middle of this frenzy, JOE *stops and stares at something.*

INSERT: CLOSE-UP OF THE PHILCO RADIO

JOE *muscles the radio away from the wall. He yanks the plug out. He stares at* SANDY *and* CLARA *as he pulls a cardboard accordion file from the back of the radio.*

    He reaches inside and his eyes widen—he withdraws a .32-caliber pistol.

    He tucks the pistol in his belt. He takes the cardboard file and clears a place on the floor in the center of the room.

JOE   *(holding out file)* Open it, Sandy.

They kneel on the floor, while CLARA *stands watching.* SANDY *unties the strings, turns the file over—out fall some papers, snapshots, and something that clinks.*

Medals. Was Red in the war?

SANDY   Nossir.

JOE   Stupid of me to ask.

SANDY *looks at her marriage certificate, a wedding photo of herself and* RED. *Tears begin to fall.* JOE *picks up a printed insurance policy and examines it.*

Tennessee Mutual. Face value one thousand dollars. *(pause)* Aren't there people who cash these things right away? Wills, IOUs, stuff like that?

CLARA   Factors.

JOE   Yeah, factors. I bet I can get sixty, seventy cents on the dollar. This is as good as cash.

CLARA   It's not yours.

JOE   I didn't say it was. *(pause)* Would you come out on the porch a minute?

EXT. PORCH, RAILROAD STREET HOUSE. DAY

JOE *closes the door behind them. He looks up and down the street before facing* CLARA.

JOE   I don't know. Maybe you want to see your old sweetheart again. Have a few laughs.

CLARA   Is that what you think?

JOE   I don't know what I think. But I'll tell you, if we don't move our ass out of here, we're finished.

CLARA   Maybe so, but that's our problem, not hers.

JOE   If we are all tending to our own problems, we can walk out this minute. Let the fifteen-year-old widow shift for herself. Is that what you want?

CLARA   *(moving to door)* I'm getting cold.

JOE   *(grabs her arm)* Why do I have to explain these things!

CLARA   Let go of me. It was your idea, big boy. I didn't tell you to move to this shit-hole.

INT. JAMES'S LIVING ROOM. DAY

CLARA *and* JOE *coming back inside.*

JOE   Sandy, I'm prepared to take you back to Tennessee. I mean, we're all finished in Jacksontown. I assume you understand that. You will spend Christmas with your family in your ancestral home.

SANDY   My what?

JOE   I'm proposing we join forces—you, Clara, and me—pool what we have and help each other. I give you my word I'll make good on every penny of the whole thousand.

He waits for her answer.

SANDY   *(vehemently)* Well, I have to lay him in his grave 'fore I leave.

Her way of saying yes.

JOE   *(enthusiastically)* Of course, we got to do that! Of course! *(looking at* CLARA*)* In fact—hey, Sandy, I bet you didn't know we had a mortician among us.

CLARA *looks at* JOE, *then at* SANDY. *A slow, almost shy smile, an appreciative shake of her head.*

SANDY   *(tears welling)* Ah want the best!

CLARA   Why not? *(She kneels next to* SANDY, *puts her arm around her.)* You'll have the best. *(looking at* JOE*)* In Jacksontown it won't cost that much.

EXT.   CEMETERY. DAY

A modest graveyard, bordered by an iron fence, on a low rise that commands a view of adjoining streets. This is a marginal commercial neighborhood of warehouses, freight yards, etc.
    A train whistle is heard.

EXT.   GRAVESITE. DAY

JOE *and* CLARA *stand on either side of* SANDY *before an open grave—*JOE *in his khaki greatcoat, one sleeve pinned.* CLARA *wears her fur jacket.*
    On the other side of the grave, a MINISTER *in black coat and no hat stands with hands folded over a Bible.*
    It's cold. We see everyone's breath.

JOE   *(to* MINISTER*)* Could we get going, please?

MINISTER   One more moment, brother. People are hoping to pay their respects.

JOE *looks behind him. Several bystanders are coming through the gate, uphill toward them.*

EXT.   STREET ALONGSIDE CEMETERY. DAY

Two green and white police cars and a motorcycle with sidecar are parked aslant at the curb. POLICEMEN *in leather jackets, garrison caps, and boots are lounging about, leaning against fenders, talking, smoking cigarettes, etc.*

Also further down the street is a flatbed jalopy truck loaded with furniture and bedding.

EXT.   GRAVESITE. DAY

JOE *turns now to look directly behind him: several* UNION MEN *in lumber jackets and knit caps are standing in a group. One nods at him solemnly.*

JOE *now looks at* SANDY, *in profile, staring into the grave. The* BABY *fusses in her arms, obscuring* CLARA *on the other side of* SANDY.

When the STRAGGLERS *arrive at the site, the* MINISTER *smiles and opens his Bible.*

MINISTER   Our Father, who art in Heaven, Hallowed be thy name . . .

EXT.   STREET ALONGSIDE CEMETERY. DAY

A gleaming cream-colored La Salle turns into the street, and cruises silently past the police cars. It pulls up to the curb, in front of the flatbed truck, and the engine is cut. The wrench of a hand brake. No one gets out.

EXT.   GRAVESITE. DAY

JOE *has seen the car. He is not at ease. The* MINISTER's *voice drones on unintelligibly.* JOE *slides his good hand into his coat pocket.*

EXT.   CEMETERY (ANOTHER ANGLE). DAY

The service is over. Two GRAVEDIGGERS *shoveling dirt over the coffin. The* MINISTER *is consoling* SANDY. *The* UNION MEN *surrounding* JOE *and* CLARA.

EXT.   GRAVESITE. DAY

JOE *finds himself isolated among the* UNION MEN. *One of them steps forward— a* HEAVYSET MAN *wearing a blue wool cap.* JOE *recognizes him as the man who spat in* LYLE RED JAMES's *face the night of the murder.*

HEAVYSET MAN   *(removing his cap)* We don't want to disturb Mrs. James at this time. We have made up a pot *(he puts a wad of bills into* JOE's *hand).* From the boys from the local.

JOE *is stunned. The* MAN *moves closer to him, speaking right in his ear.*

Do you think, Paterson, that we would be so stupid as to permit ourselves to be overheard threatening a man in public not ten minutes before we meant to jump him in a dark alley?

JOE   Who did, then?

HEAVYSET MAN   Use yer brains, lad. I'm sorry for the beatin' you took but if it was us, we'd have had to put you in the grave beside him.

EXT.   CEMETERY. DAY

JOE *finds* SANDY *and* CLARA, *takes* SANDY's *arm and begins moving them both down toward the gate.*

ONLOOKERS *appear, offer condolences.* JOE *keeps his eye beyond them on the* COPS *in the street. One* COP *has stationed himself beside the flatbed truck.*

CLARA *has spotted the cream-colored La Salle.* JOE *does not miss this.*

EXT.   CEMETERY GATE. DAY

Somehow JOE *and* CLARA *and* SANDY *are finding it difficult to make progress: a knot of* PEOPLE, *including* THREE POLICEMEN, *has built up in front of them.*

FIRST POLICEMAN   *(tipping his hat to* SANDY) Pardon me, Ma'am. *(to* JOE) Mr. Paterson, I wonder if you'd mind coming to the station with us— answer a few questions.

JOE   What? What questions? I already told you guys in the hospital. I told you everything I know.

The procession has now halted.

FIRST POLICEMAN   We just want to talk to you a few minutes, clear up some things.

JOE *looks out to the street behind the police. A* NEWS PHOTOGRAPHER *holds his Speed Graphic over his head, snaps* JOE'S *picture.* JOE *turns around; the* UNION MEN *have come up behind them, hemming them in.*

JOE   (*to* POLICEMAN) What the hell is this?

FIRST POLICEMAN   Just a few questions.

JOE   I'm responsible for these ladies and this baby. I can't leave them alone here.

SECOND POLICEMAN   We'll take 'em to the stationhouse. They can wait where it's warm.

FIRST POLICEMAN   Just a few minutes.

JOE   I'm sorry. There's no time.

Someone in the crowd laughs. More flash pictures. The SECOND POLICEMAN *comes up to* JOE, *twists his good hand behind his back.*

SECOND POLICEMAN   Don't make it hard.

In the scuffle that follows, JOE *loses sight of* CLARA *and* SANDY.

JOE   Wait a minute—Clara!

EXT.   STREET ALONGSIDE CEMETERY. DAY

JOE *being led to a police car. He resists. His arm is twisted tighter. A roil of people, some shouting "Take it easy, let him go," etc.*

JOE   Clara!

The door of a police car is opened.

   FIRST POLICEMAN *whacks* JOE *below the belt.* JOE *doubles over and is shoved inside the car. The door is slammed.*

INT.   POLICE CAR. DAY

JOE, *holding himself, retching, falling to the side as the police car takes off, makes a* ∪-*turn—faces and figures going by the window. A siren is heard.*

The POLICEMAN *sitting next to* JOE *pushes him upright with the tips of his fingers.*

POLICEMAN   Relax, sonny. Enjoy the ride.

INT.   POLICE CHIEF'S OFFICE. DAY (PLAYOUT OF FLASH FORWARDS IN SCENES ON PP. 406 AND 416).

The POLICE CHIEF *of Jacksontown behind his desk. Cold as it is, he's in a short-sleeved shirt that exposes his enormous arms. Pencils clipped in his breast pocket. A blue garrison cap with lots of gold trim.*

Camera pulls back: the office walls are dark green to the waist, light green to the ceiling. Globe light on a chain, creaking oak chairs, big clock on the wall, a large window with bars.

JOE *is seated before the* CHIEF's desk and he is staring out this window.

EXT.   POLICE STATION COURTYARD (JOE'S POINT OF VIEW). DAY

Through the bars we see the cream-colored La Salle coming to a stop just outside. A CHAUFFEUR *gets out, opens the rear door: a* MAN *gets out wearing a dark overcoat with a fur collar, a pearl grey fedora* (TOMMY CRAPO).

A couple of COPS *standing in the courtyard greet him (silent). They seem eager to shake his hand. He says something to them and one* COP *moves off with alacrity.*

INT.   CHIEF'S OFFICE. DAY

CHIEF   Are you deaf, son?

JOE   What?

CHIEF   I said, where you from.

JOE *brings his attention back to the* CHIEF.

JOE   Paterson. New Jersey.

CHIEF   Like your name.

JOE   Yeah.

CHIEF   What was your last job before this?

JOE   What? I rousted for a carnival.

CHIEF   Whereabouts.

JOE   Uh, upstate New York. New England.

CHIEF   What carnival?

JOE *is looking out the window again.*

   Pay attention! What carnival? What was the name of it?

JOE   I don't remember.

CHIEF   You don't remember. Well, how long did you work for them?

JOE   I don't know. Listen, is this going to take much longer?

CHIEF   It's up to you. You worked at this carnival.

JOE   Yeah. Coupla months. It was a summer job. Some lousy carnival.

Again JOE *glances out the window.*

CHIEF   *(voice over)* And before that?

EXT.   STATION COURTYARD (JOE'S POINT OF VIEW). DAY

The MAN *in the fur-collared overcoat (*TOMMY CRAPO*) is standing beside the La Salle. He removes one grey kidskin glove, takes off his hat; he has shiny black hair, he is short, dark, polished—a smoothie.*

INT.   BENNETT LODGE, LOON LAKE. LIVING ROOM. NIGHT (SILENT)

Quick reprise of CLARA *and* TOMMY CRAPO *dancing in evening clothes (p. 320).*

EXT. STATION COURTYARD (JOE'S POINT OF VIEW). DAY

TOMMY CRAPO, *hat and gloves in hand, is shaking his head and smiling. A relieved expression on his face. He raises his arm in greeting, lets it fall.*
  CLARA *walks into the picture.*

INT. CHIEF'S OFFICE. DAY

JOE *is at the window, grabbing the bars.*

CHIEF *(voice over)* Sit down, son!

JOE CLARA!

EXT. STATION COURTYARD (JOE'S POINT OF VIEW). DAY

CLARA *and* TOMMY CRAPO *looking at each other. He hugs her. He holds her at arm's length and he laughs. He strokes her fur jacket. He shakes his head reproachfully as he smiles.* CLARA *grins.*

JOE *(voice over)* Cla-ra!

CHIEF Son of a bitch. What does he see out there?

INT. CHIEF'S OFFICE. DAY

JOE *is pounding on the window. The* CHIEF *is pressing a buzzer on his desk.*

JOE CLA-RA!

Two PATROLMEN *rush in.* ONE *grabs* JOE, *pulls him back, slams him in his chair. The* OTHER *yanks the shade down over the window.*

CHIEF Boy, don't you know you're being interrogated? Don't you understand that?

JOE I gotta talk to Clara Lukacs. She's out there.

CHIEF All in good time.

JOE Look, I'll answer anything—any goddamn questions you can think of. Just give me a minute with her.

Loon Lake: A Screenplay | 425

He attempts to rise from his chair. The COP *behind him presses him back down.*

Another COP *has come in with an open cardboard box and puts it on the desk. The* CHIEF *examines the contents—a paper bag with a wad of bills, a wallet, a .32-caliber pistol. He hefts the pistol.*

CHIEF   (*to* COP) A very serious piece of equipment. This is what the department should be carrying. Not the shit we got.

COP   Never been fired.

JOE *is sitting, leaning over, head in hands.*

CHIEF   Where'd you get this?

JOE   It's his. Red James.

CHIEF   Didn't do him much good, did it. You take it off him?

JOE   No. It was in his house. Inside the radio.

CHIEF   Yesterday you went down to Mallory the pawnbrokers.

JOE *lifts his head.*

You collected six hundred dollars on the deceased's insurance policy.

JOE   That's right. The money belongs to Mrs. James. I'm holding it for her. She's fifteen years old and we're taking her home to her folks.

Pause.

CHIEF   You expect them to give you trouble?

JOE   Who?

CHIEF   Her folks that you're taking her home to. That you were packing this thing.

JOE   It wasn't for that.

CHIEF   What was it for, then?

JOE   Protection. I was glad to have it.

CHIEF   Protection.

JOE   Until we got out of town. In case someone came after me.

CHIEF   Who?

JOE   I don't know who. Whoever killed Red.

CHIEF   Why would they do that?

JOE   I don't know. If they thought I saw them? If they thought I could pin it on them?

CHIEF   Could you?

JOE   I already told you. I didn't see anything. I got hit from behind and went down and it all fell on top of me. Could I see my girl, please?

CHIEF   Why would anyone want to kill him, anyway?

Pause.

JOE   I don't know.

The CHIEF *is going through* JOE's *wallet. He takes out a card.*

CHIEF   You carry a union card.

JOE   So?

CHIEF   Maybe you killed him.

JOE   *(rising)* What? Jesus H. Christ!

CHIEF   Sit down, son.

JOE   Oh, this is swell. This is really swell. No, I didn't kill him. We were friends, we lived next door.

CHIEF   Did you fool with his wife?

JOE *sinks into his chair.*

Did you?

JOE *cannot speak.*

OK. We could hold you for possession. But I think we have enough to hold you as material witness. You know what that is?

JOE *shakes his head.*

Loon Lake: A Screenplay   427

You're all we have to go on. You were there when it happened. It means we hold you while we work up the case. *(pause)* I make it you diddled the wife and decided you liked it too much. The insurance didn't hurt, neither.

Long pause.

JOE   Hey, mister, look at me. I don't look like much, do I. My arm's been broke, one side of my face is stitched up, I've been pissing blood . . . Jesus, since I came to this town I been short-paid, tricked, speeded-up, double-crossed—and your Jacksontown finest felt they had to work me over to get me here. I probably don't smell so good either. But I tell you something: you wouldn't hear from my mouth the filth that has just come from yours. I mean that is so rotten and filthy I'd get down on my knees and beg that little girl's forgiveness if I was you.

CHIEF   You oughtn't to tell me to do anything, son.

JOE   Or else you're being funny. Is that it, are you bein funny? I mean, what's the idea—that I killed him before he broke my arm? Or that I killed him after he broke my arm? After? Oh yes, it makes great sense, it really does. With my one arm I was able to get him to hold still so as I could bash his head in. And then just to make sure everyone would know it I lifted him on my back and took him out to the street to flag a police car to get him to the hospital. Smart!

CHIEF   *(to* COPS*)* He's pretty stupid if he thinks we have to be smart.

They all laugh. JOE *slumps in his chair.*

CHIEF   *(to* JOE*)* You don't like my story, maybe you have a better one.

JOE *realizes a deal is impending. Not good. The* CHIEF *is staring at him.*

JOE   *(new tone of voice—conciliatory)* Look, you're making it wrong. It wasn't like that. We were family friends, Red and me. My fiancée Clara and his wife, Sandy. We watched their baby for them when they went to the movies.

CHIEF   Your fiancée?

JOE   Yes sir—that's what I'm trying to tell you. Clara and me—we're engaged to be married. You don't know my Clara or you wouldn't think I had an eye for another woman.

CHIEF   She's something, eh?

JOE   *(sitting back, smiling)* Well—only the best, most beautiful girl in the world.

The CHIEF nods. One of the COPS leans over, whispers in his ear.

CHIEF   Maybe we ought to see the little lady.

The COP leaves the room, closes the door.
    Silence.
    The CHIEF sits with his arms folded. Joe glances at the blank shade over the window. The ticking of the wall clock seems to grow louder.
    JOE holds his aching arm.
    The waiting is unendurable.
    Finally footsteps are heard in the hall outside. JOE stands. The door opens—the COP is holding it. SANDY JAMES walks in holding her BABY.

JOE   Sandy—where's Clara!

SANDY looks at him with some sort of fierce joy overlaying her bereavement.
    JOE dashes to the window and, before he can be stopped, pulls up the shade.

EXT.   STATION COURTYARD (JOE'S POINT OF VIEW). DAY

The courtyard is empty.

EXT.   F. W. BENNETT LODGE, LOON LAKE. NIGHT

All the lights are lit. The music of a dance band can be heard on the breeze.
    The figure advancing over the meadow toward the house is JOE—just as in opening Loon Lake exterior scene (p. 320). Now he wears a cheap three-piece suit, shirt and tie, and he carries a valise tied with rope. (No cast is on his arm.)
    As he moves closer to the house we hear the music more clearly—it is the song "Exactly Like You."

INT.   POLICE CHIEF'S OFFICE. DAY

A goose-necked table lamp has been placed to shine in JOE's face.
    The room now has several COPS in it. The CHIEF has put on his tunic. There is

a middle-aged woman STENOGRAPHER. *Also a* TOWN COUNCILMAN *in a pin-stripe suit, prim and proper, stiff shirt collar, glasses, and with thinning grey hair.*

JOE *peers through the light at this audience convened for his official testimony. The* CHIEF *bends to his ear.*

CHIEF   *(sotto voce)* All right, son. You can get y'self outta big trouble you come up with the right answer. You take my meaning?

The CHIEF *steps back into the shadow.* JOE *is subdued. His expression is impassive. No sign of the loss he's sustained.*

JOE   All right. This is the straight story *(pause—he clears his throat.)* The F. W. Bennett Company employs an industrial espionage agency to keep track of what's going on inside the plants. The name of that agency is Crapo Industrial Services. Maybe you don't know this, but I think you do. They put their operatives on the line and into the union.

CHIEF   Let's not waste time, Mr. Paterson.

JOE   Red James—the deceased—was one of these detectives. He'd actually gotten to be an officer of the local. Secretary. He took minutes, kept records, and passed everything on to Crapo Industrial Services.

CHIEF   Get to the point, please. You say you can identify the men who murdered him?

JOE   The union board secretly planned a strike just after the new year. The idea was if one plant that made automobile trim was shut down, every other Bennett plant would have to shut down too because Number Six makes all the trim. So it was a big strategy of theirs—and Red got the word out. Right away there are layoffs, half the tool and die machines are shipped out to other plants. And the strike is up the creek.

CHIEF   And that's why the union goons killed him. (JOE *is silent.*) Speak up. That's why the union killed him.

JOE   Anybody got a Lucky?

A COP *steps forward, proffering a cigarette. He lights a match,* JOE *leans forward to it, glancing around at the faces he sees in the light. He takes a deep drag on the cigarette, leans back.*

Loon Lake: A Screenplay

Thanks. You know, it's hard to speak to faces you can't see. As long as I'm talking, why not put a little light on the subject?

The ceiling light goes on. The PEOPLE *in the room rearrange themselves.* JOE *fixes his attention on the* TOWN COUNCILMAN *as he speaks.*

JOE   I'll try to make this clear as I can. I know by sight most of the men in the plant—I mean, you learn these things, you get the feel of who's a worker and who isn't. There are people who wear the same clothes and talk the same talk who don't work the line and never will. And they are the men who jumped us.

The CHIEF *stands. He motions to the* STENOGRAPHER, *who closes her book.*

CHIEF   (*to* JOE) You better know what you're doing, son.

JOE   I made them for an out-of-town traveling band. One of Crapo's industrial services. I mean, if you really want Red James's killers, it's very simple. Speak to Mr. Thomas Crapo, president.

TOWN COUNCILMAN   (*stepping forward*) What is it you're trying to say, young man?

JOE   I'll spell it out for you, sir. The agency murdered its own operative.

TOWN COUNCILMAN   That's a most serious charge.

JOE   Yes, sir, it certainly is. But we're in a war, we're talking about war here! The company moving those machines meant Red's days were numbered. Once the union knew he was a spy he was no more use to Crapo. And that made him a dangerous man.

TOWN COUNCILMAN   I don't understand.

JOE   He knew probably about as much about Crapo as he knew about the local. He wasn't just your average fink, who's been hooked up for a few dollars and doesn't know what he's doing. Red was a pro, an industrial detective—and he was angry 'cause they'd left him to the dogs.

The CHIEF *shakes his head. He motions to the* STENOGRAPHER *and she leaves the room. When the door closes, he turns to* JOE.

CHIEF   All right, son.

JOE   *(continuing)* Look at it from the Chief's point of view, here. First he thinks: a Crapo man is killed; it's the union who killed him. Why not, who would think different! And if he can make that case, if Crapo can trick him into making it, look what's accomplished: he's set the union back twenty years. No working stiff wants hoods and killers for comrades. That's worth one op's life, I can tell you.

CHIEF   All right, this interrogation is over. Put him in the slammer.

JOE   *(raising his pitch)* I know my rights. You're all witnesses. I'm telling you the truth—it's out now and will be on every wire service in the country, you got any idea of changing my testimony.

CHIEF   *(to* COUNCILMAN*)* The boy lies. He lied before and he's lying now. He's a punk from New Jersey who we found with a gun and the widow's insurance money in his kick.

JOE   *(talking fast)* That's right. I made up Tommy Crapo and Crapo Industrial Services. Or did I get it from the newspapers. That's it—they must advertise in the newspaper. I can give you the Illinois plate number of a white La Salle, but that's made up too. It's all made up. Buster is made up too.

CHIEF   Who is Buster?

JOE   Buster who got Mrs. James to waive her rights for two hundred and fifty Industrial Service dollars. *(to* COUNCILMAN*)* Why doesn't anyone ask the right questions around here? A roomful of ace detectives and not one of them thinks to ask how I know so much, how I knew Red James, how I got to be his friend, what I'm doing here in this lousy town. You think I go around getting busted up for laughs?

CHIEF   What are you talking about?

JOE   *(spewing it out)* But if I was wearing a regular suit and tie like this gentleman, and my face was washed and my hair combed, you would listen. And if I told you Red James was a double-op—that he was on the take from the union—why, this strike at Number Six is a phony! They never intended to strike Jacksontown. That's a wild goose chase—look at the dumb Bennett shipping its machines all over the damn country! What a joke. Oh, yes, gentlemen, when the real strike comes—and it is coming—the birds will be singing in Jacksontown. It will be a peaceful day at Number Six and you won't know a thing till you hear it on the radio.

COUNCILMAN   What's this—what strike, where!

JOE   Or maybe that isn't a good enough reason for Crapo to rub out Mr. Red James—that he was a dirty double-crossing Benedict Arnold.

COUNCILMAN   (*to* CHIEF) How does he know these things! Who is this fellow! Damn it all, I want an explanation!

The CHIEF *sits down behind his desk.*

CHIEF   (*to* JOE) You don't like Crapo very much, do you?

Pause.

JOE   We fancy the same girl.

CHIEF   And that's why you're fingering him—or trying to.

JOE   No more than he's done to me, Chief. But I got a better reason. I don't condone killing, and neither does Mr. Bennett.

CHIEF   Mr. Who Bennett?

JOE   Mr. F. W. Bennett of Bennett Autobody. Is there any other?

Silence. JOE *looks around the room.*

I'm a special confidential operative. I was sent here by Mr. F. W. Bennett personally to check on the Crapo organization. Mr. Bennett takes nothing for granted—especially not the loyalty of gangsters. My target was Crapo's chief op at Number Six, Lyle Red James. Mr. Bennett himself suggested the disguise of a working-class couple—and so I brought with me a lady *(he clears his throat)* I happened to be serious about. Miss Clara Lukacs. This is the private personal part, Chief, and I expect every man in this room to keep quiet about his. I met this lady when she was with Mr. Crapo. We took to each other. We couldn't help it. And, well, he is not a man who forgives easily, as you can see by my condition and the circumstance of me being here before you.

Long silence.

CHIEF   It's too crazy. There are so many holes in this story it's like a punch-board. Why should Mr. Bennett need to do these things? And if he did, why would he find some kid like this, not old enough to wipe the snot from his nose! No, Jacksontown doesn't need this. I'm sorry, Mr. Paterson, you throw names around okay, but you were a punk when we pulled you in, and as far as I'm concerned, you're still a punk.

JOE   My name isn't Paterson. (*knowing smile to* COUNCILMAN) It's easy enough to check. In my billfold, which you are holding, is a piece of paper with the secret phone number of Mr. Bennett's residence at Loon Lake in the Adirondack mountains of New York. You may not know about this place—it's his retreat. Call him for me. I get a phone call of my choosing, isn't that the law? That's who I choose to call. (*pause*) Tell him I'm sorry about the Mercedes. He'll understand.

CHIEF   Yes sir. And who should we say is calling?

One of the COPS *laughs.* JOE *is livid with rage. Tears fill his eyes.*

JOE   (*to* CHIEF) You stupid son of a bitch. Tell Mr. F. W. Bennett it's his son calling. Tell him it's his son, Joe.

EXT.   TWO-LANE DESERT ROAD. DAY

A flatbed truck loaded with furniture, bedding, etc., going down the road. The landscape is hardscrabble flatland, tumbleweed, an occasional rotted-out car frame in a field, mountains in the distance.

Suddenly the truck slows, brakes screechingly to a stop. Door flies open (passenger side) and SANDY JAMES *jumps out and runs back along the shoulder of the road as if looking for something. She finds it, drops to her knees.*

INT.   TRUCK CAB. DAY

SANDY *climbs back in, joy and triumph on her face. She holds a sprig of tiny desert flowers.*

JOE *hands the* BABY *over to her, puts the truck in gear and starts off again,* SANDY *cooing to her* BABY *and showing her the modest desert blossoms.*

SANDY   It's spring, darlin'!

EXT. TWO-LANE DESERT ROAD. DAY

The late-afternoon sun casting a red glow over everything. JOE *and* SANDY *in their truck overtake and pass another vehicle just like it, similarly loaded with household possessions.*

INT. CAFE. EVENING

A Western roadside cafe: red-checked tablecloths, one candle stuck in a bottle for atmosphere, jukebox in the corner.

JOE *and* SANDY *are dining on fried steaks and potatoes.* SANDY's baby *sits in a highchair. The* WAITRESS *brings two bottles of beer. After she goes,* SANDY *leans across the table.*

SANDY   You sure we kin afford this?

JOE   I don't know if we can afford it. But I sure do need it.

SANDY *laughs.*

SANDY   Clara told me about you.

JOE   What?

SANDY   Oh, long before I dreamed anything like this. (*to* BABY) Hey honey, c'n you chew this french fry? Can you?

JOE   What did she say?

SANDY   Just that she was sweet on you. You know. The way girls talk.

JOE   (*clearing his throat*) Yeah, well I was sweet on her, too.

SANDY   And I thought you was married! I thought Clara was yore wife!

Pause.

JOE   Yeah, well, she'd be anything you wanted. If you wanted it badly enough.

He drinks his beer, looks out the window at the red glow in the western sky as SANDY *chatters happily to her* BABY.

EXT. ROADSIDE CABINS. NIGHT

The flatbed truck parked in front of a cabin.

INT. CABIN. NIGHT

JOE *is making love to* SANDY. *The* BABY *is crying.*

SANDY (*over* JOE's *shoulder, to* BABY) Hold on, honey. Momma'll be there in a minute.

JOE *curses, flings himself on his bed.* SANDY *immediately jumps up to attend to the* BABY.

JOE (*as he recovers*) Hey. Don't you have any manners?

SANDY Sir?

JOE I thought you told me you like it.

SANDY I do. I like it fine.

JOE I can see that. You really get involved.

SANDY I like it better than I did with Loll.

JOE You do?

.SANDY A' course! You leave all that other part out.

JOE What other part?

SANDY You know. The spankin' and the ticklin'. I hated that.

EXT. TWO-LANE DESERT ROAD. DAY

An old touring car, piled with trunks, boxes, etc. A MAN, *his* WIFE (NORA), *their young* BOY.

  JOE *slides out from under the car, stands.*

JOE Nothing moves. Your gears are locked.

MAN That's what I thought. (*to* WIFE) Nora, you go on the next town with these good people. Billy and me'll stay with the car. (*to* JOE) Everything we got is right here.

Loon Lake: A Screenplay

INT. TRUCK CAB. DAY (MOVING)

SANDY *has moved closer to* JOE *to make room for* NORA, *a middle-aged woman in a dusty black coat, a felt hat that has seen better times.*

NORA   (*to* SANDY) My Billy was just that baby's size seems like yesterday. But everything changes. And quicker than you think.

SANDY   Yes'm, sure does.

NORA   I never thought we'd lose our home. I never thought we'd have to pick up and take to the road like vagabonds.

SANDY   No'm.

NORA   My husband's a professional man. A pharmacist. We're on our way to San Diego. We hope to make a new start.

A light comes to SANDY's *eyes.*

SANDY   (*looking at* JOE) Why, that's what *we're* doin'! Makin' a *new start!*

EXT.   A WESTERN MAIN STREET. DAY

The truck pulls to the curb in front of a one-pump garage. The woman, NORA, *climbs out, shuts the door.*

INT.   TRUCK CAB. DAY

JOE *puts the truck into gear, moves out.* SANDY *enjoys the sights.*

SANDY   Nice li'l ol' town. Church, picture show! I hope they got 'em like this in California!

JOE   What do you mean we're makin' a new start?

SANDY   What?

JOE   All they want is to open another drugstore. They want to do what they've always done. That's what a new start means.

SANDY   Well, I was just chattin' with that lady.

JOE   You think I want a job in an automobile factory? Or is it just *your* new start you're talking about? I mean, this furniture of yours we're dragging two thousand miles—is that your new start? So you can find rooms and put the furniture in just the way you had it in Jacksontown? That kind of new start?

SANDY   I don't know why you're so put out with me.

JOE   Because if that's what you mean, say so. Let's settle it here and now. I'm not your husband. And even if I was, I wouldn't make my living as a stool pigeon.

SANDY *is bewildered. Tears come to her eyes. She hugs her* BABY *and stares out the window.* JOE *glances at her: so forlorn. He feels bad now.*

EXT.   TWO-LANE ROAD. DAY

The truck moving at a good clip.

INT.   TRUCK CAB. DAY

JOE   Shit. I'm sorry. *(no answer)* C'mon, Sandy, I said I'm sorry. Stop that sniveling and fight like a grown-up. Why don't you say who the hell do I think I am. Why don't you tell me it's your money we're living on. Why don't you say that. Why don't you tell me that's all I'm good for anyway— living off other men's money, other men's women.

SANDY   *(wiping her eyes)* I didn't think of it.

Pause.

JOE   *(staring at the road)* I did.

EXT.   TWO-LANE ROAD. DAY

The desert road—the truck going toward the distant western mountains.

INT.   TRUCK CAB. DAY

JOE   Let's get married.

SANDY *gasps, stares at him.*

We don't want a new start, Sandy. We want a new *life*. A whole new life in California. We'll get married in California, OK?

Suddenly she is all over him, grabbing him around the neck, kissing him.

JOE   Hey! Watch it! Hey!

EXT.   TWO-LANE ROAD. DAY

The truck veering from one side of the road to the other.

JOE   *(voice over)* Hey, watch it! *(laughing)* You're gonna kill us!

EXT.   JUNK STORE. DAY

At the edge of a small western farm town—tractors parked in the street, a railroad crossing down the block.

JOE and SANDY (with BABY) standing in the dusty street, watching her furniture being unloaded from the truck. The PROPRIETOR scrawls a chalk number on each piece as his HELPERS carry it inside the store.

SANDY   *(to BABY)* There goes the radio, darlin'.

JOE   Don't worry. I'll buy you ten radios. That's what a new life means. Giving up the past. Like me, I'm through living on the road. I'm going to make something of myself. A man can do a lot, starting from a small investment. More than one fortune has been made from nothing, I can tell you.

SANDY   Yessir.

The PROPRIETOR comes over, cash in hand.

PROPRIETOR   I'll give you sixty-five dollars.

JOE *holds out his hand. The PROPRIETOR counts the money into his palm.*

JOE   Where's there a used car lot?

PROPRIETOR   You lookin' to unload the truck too?

JOE   I am.

The PROPRIETOR *walks around the truck, kicks the tires.*

SANDY   *(dismayed)* How we gonna get to the state a' California?

JOE   In style, kid. You don't wanna ride in lookin' like an Okie, do you?

INT.   RAILROAD DEPOT. DAY

On the wooden bench in the small waiting room with wood-strip wainscotting and a potbellied stove, JOE *sits dandling* SANDY's BABY. *(Perhaps the* BABY *ought to have red hair.)*
      SANDY *comes out of the restroom. She carries a small bag and has an excited, hopeful expression on her face. She's wearing a tight dress, hose, shoes, a coat open to show her off.*

SANDY   You like?

JOE   Oh, my. That's something.

SANDY *totters on the high heels, grabs the bench.*

SANDY   I'm gonna fall! These are Clara's shoes 'n' everything. She gave 'em
      to me. You think it'll do fer the new life?

She is all smiles, full of delight, wobbly.

JOE   Sure. It'll do just fine.

EXT.   RAILROAD STATION (STREET SIDE). DAY

JOE, SANDY, *and the* BABY.

JOE   Well, the bags are checked and we've got a couple of hours till the train
      comes. Now what can I do for the new life, so I can look like I belong to the
      beauty I got standing here beside me?

He spots something across the street.

EXT.   MOVIE HOUSE. DAY

A small-town theater showing a double feature.

JOE   *(voice over)* Look, Sandy—Gary Cooper and Marlene Dietrich.

SANDY   *(voice over)* Oh, she's my favorite!

EXT.   RAILROAD STATION (STREET SIDE). DAY

JOE *taking* SANDY's *arm to lead her across the street.*

JOE   You and the kid can watch the picture while I do a few things.

MONTAGE: INT.   JOE ABOUT TOWN. DAY (MUSIC)

JOE *in the town drugstore, the* DRUGGIST *cutting off his cast, two or three* CUSTOMERS *looking on with great interest.*
    JOE *in the town barbershop getting a haircut.*
    JOE *in a haberdashery, standing in front of a mirror examining himself in a new three-piece suit, the* HABERDASHER *crouching, taking the measure of the cuffs.*
    JOE *likes what he sees. (End music.)*

EXT.   MOVIE HOUSE. DAY

JOE, *pale but groomed and well turned out in suit and tie, new shoes, looking like a new man, pays his ten cents to the* CASHIER *and goes into the theater.*

INT.   THEATER (DARK LIGHT, FLICKERING SCREEN LIGHT)

JOE *coming down the aisle, looking for* SANDY. *The seats are all empty.*

JOE   *(loud whisper)* Sandy?

SANDY   *(voice over)* Here we are!

He finds her sitting down in the front row, close to the screen. The sound is a voice-over newsreel narrator ("President Roosevelt dedicates Grand Coulee Dam ... In Germany, Adolf Hitler etc., etc. ... ")

JOE   You about ready to go?

SANDY   Yessir. I seen the whole show but for the newsreel.

JOE *sits beside her.*

NEWSREEL SEQUENCE (BLACK AND WHITE)

A shot of LUCINDA BENNETT *in flying regalia, holding a bouquet of flowers on a platform beside a runway. Smiling, receiving a silver cup to the applause of the people around her.*

ANNOUNCER   *(voice over)* The nations mourns its favorite aviatrix, Lucinda Bailey Bennett, holder of more flying records than any other woman, here shown in happier times, receiving one of her many prizes.

A shot of LUCINDA *shown standing under the wing of a two-engine seaplane, waving at the camera.*

ANNOUNCER   *(voice over)* Mrs. Bennett, on a record-breaking around-the-world flight in her latest plane, *The Loon*—a gift from her husband, auto magnate F. W. Bennett—disappeared on the Pacific leg of the journey, somewhere in the seas between Hawaii and Japan. No trace of the downed plane has been found.

WARREN PENFIELD *wanders into the shot, realizes he's being photographed, is horrified, climbs into the plane, tripping over himself in his haste to be out of sight.*

ANNOUNCER   *(voice over)* Lucinda Bennett's one companion on her journey, a family friend, Wilfred Greenfield, served as her navigator for the ill-fated flight.

The plane is shown taxiing over the water, lifting gracefully into the sky.

INSERT: CLOSE-UP OF JOE REACTING

A shot of F. W. BENNETT *reading a statement before a standing microphone.*

ANNOUNCER   *(voice over)* His voice cracking with emotion, the aviatrix's husband tells reporters the sad news.

BENNETT   —have accepted the inevitable and called off the search. I tell all who grieve for this gallant woman—my wife—that if she had to die, surely this is the way she would prefer—at the controls of her machine, flying toward some great personal ideal.

A plane seen going off into the sunset. Imposed over this is a close-up of the smiling LUCINDA, *hair blowing in the wind.*

ANNOUNCER   *(voice over)* All America bids "so long!" to its sweetheart of the skies.

INT.   TRAIN COACH (MOVING). DAY

JOE *and* SANDY *sitting stiffly in a coach seat at the rear of a crowded car.*
  The other PASSENGERS *in the car seem to know one another, be familiar with each other—*KIDS *run down the aisles, their* MOTHERS *wear slippers instead of shoes, seats are swung around for familiar chat like neighbors'.*
  A kindly, plump GREY-HAIRED LADY *wanders past, makes a fuss over* SANDY's BABY. *She calls a* FRIEND, *a group develops around* SANDY *and* JOE *and the* BABY—*everyone introducing themselves. All the* PEOPLE *in the car are members of the same Pentecostal church.* SANDY *introduces herself and* JOE *as Mr. and Mrs.*

SANDY   We're bound for California. To make a new life.

CHURCH ELDER   *(to* JOE *and* SANDY) Bless you, Brother and Sister. Through the divine love of our Lord Jesus Christ, we too are takin' up residence in the south of California.

OTHERS   Amen!

CHURCH ELDER   Yes, thank you Jesus! He is bringing us to the Pacific to be baptized in the waters of His ocean.

The church elder bursts into song, startling JOE. *Almost immediately, the whole car is singing, clapping hands. The plump* GREY-HAIRED LADY *lifts the* BABY *from* SANDY's *lap, swinging her in her arms in time to the music.*
  JOE *looks at* SANDY: *she is beaming, delighted to be part of this.*

INT. TRAIN COACH. (MOVING) NIGHT

Everyone in the car is asleep except JOE. *They lie under blankets, curled up on seats, children sprawled on parents, etc.*

SANDY *sleeps with her head on* JOE's *lap. The* BABY *sleeps in the arms of the* GREY-HAIRED LADY *across the aisle.*

The train is coming into a station. It slows, lurches to a stop.

JOE *slips out of the seat, pillowing* SANDY's *head on a folded blanket. He leaves the car.*

EXT. TRAIN STATION PLATFORM. NIGHT

JOE *steps down from the train, lights a cigarette. A pitch-black night. The platform is badly lit. Down at the end, at the front of the train, a* HANDLER *is tossing up a sack of mail. He leaves. The train remains motionless in the hiss of steam that floats back from the engine.*

JOE *hoists himself to a sitting position on a baggage cart. He takes out his thick wallet, removes a couple of bills, folds them into the handkerchief pocket of his jacket. He stares at the train. A* CONDUCTOR *up ahead is waving a lantern.* JOE *jumps down, grinds out his cigarette, goes back aboard.*

INT. TRAIN COACH. NIGHT

JOE *kneels down beside* SANDY, *gently, so as not to awaken her, tucks the wallet under her hands.*

He stands, grabs his roped valise from the rack, looks all around, gets out of there.

EXT. TRAIN STATION PLATFORM. NIGHT

JOE *stands on the platform as the train slowly pulls out. After it clears the station, he steps his way across the tracks toward the platform on the other side, glancing after the departing train, its red light fading from sight.*

EXT.   F. W. BENNETT LODGE, LOON LAKE. NIGHT
(PLAYOUT OF SCENE, P. 429)

All the lights are lit. Dance music fading in and out on the breeze.

   JOE *is advancing over the meadow toward the house. He carries his valise. He wears his suit, tie open.*

   The music becomes clearer: "Exactly Like You"—a strange song in a scene of menacing isolation.

INT.   BENNETT LODGE. LIVING ROOM. NIGHT

The song is playing loudly, but the room seems to be empty.

   JOE *stands in the entrance to the front hall.*

   The song comes to an end and we hear the scratching and clicking of the needle on the record. JOE *comes down the steps, into the great room, walks over the Victrola and removes the playing arm from the record.*

   When he turns, he finds BENNETT *sitting, small and shrunken, in a wing chair facing him.*

REPRISE: EXT.   SEQUENCE OF LOON SHOTS (P. 331). DAY

Two loons diving out of a bright morning sky. They skid into the water, sending up a spray. We hear their manic cry over the water.

EXT.   TERRACE OVERLOOKING LOON LAKE. DAY

The cry of the loons echoing up from the lake.

   BENNETT *and* JOE *are taking breakfast in the sun.*

   BENNETT *is unkempt. He wears sloppy clothes, has a stubble on his face. He looks older than we remember him. His hair is uncombed.*

   He glances up at the sky.

BENNETT   I half expect to see her plane coming over the hill. I find myself
   looking for it . . . I respect character in a man, but I revere it in a woman.
   That little doxy—what was her name—

JOE   Clara.

BENNETT   Yes. She had it in a cheap sort of way. But in Lucinda it tested like the best ore, through and through, in the bones and in the beam of the eye.

Pause.

Long ago she lost the pleasure of—what?—our connection. And I was able to appreciate her character in the depth of her withdrawal from me. And then, how I wished she had less of it!

A MAN *in a dark green shirt and pants comes out with a pot of coffee, which he puts down roughly on the table. He leaves.*

We see the breakfast: milk carton, fruit served from a can, a loaf of bread in its wax paper wrapping.

Poor Bob. Hasn't got the hang of waiting table. I don't care. I have no appetite.

JOE   Where's the rest of the staff?

BENNETT   Fired 'em. Couldn't bear the sight of 'em.

Once more BENNETT *looks into the sky over the lake. Dissolve to:*

EXT.   RAMP AND HANGAR, SHORE OF LOON LAKE. DAY

BENNETT *and* JOE *astride horses, overlooking the ramp and hangar. The sky this day is dark with an impending storm.*

BENNETT   She liked to go up in the rain. I never flew with her because I sensed it was her private realm. I told her she liked the sky because it was clean . . . She was a very orderly soul, Lucinda. Years ago she may have fallen in love with a fellow, some mail-service pilot, one of those adventurous types. And I was going to have it looked into. But when I thought about it, I knew she would never permit herself an affair. It was not something she'd give in to. And gradually she ceased to mention him. If it were possible for Lucinda to exist without a body, she would have chosen to. Her body was of no interest to her. She did not like it—what?—handled.

Distant thunder. The horses stir, JOE*'s is skittish.*

Just keep a tight rein on him. Let him know you're the boss.

JOE *does this—the horse settles down.*

Loon Lake: A Screenplay

That's it. Not bad for a tenderfoot. You learn quickly.

JOE I try to.

Dissolve to:

INT. DINING ROOM. NIGHT

BENNETT *and* JOE *are dining on food, uncooked, from cans. Packaged white bread. The table is a mess.*

BENNETT'*s dereliction is advanced: his white hair is longer, yellowish, he has a beard now, he wears a filthy flannel shirt.*

BENNETT *(looking over the terrain of the table)* There should be some of that evaporated milk.

JOE *gets up, goes off to kitchen.*

INT. KITCHEN. NIGHT

The once sparkling, gleaming kitchen is a ruin: stacks of unwashed dishes, bags of garbage, empty cans.

JOE *picks his way through, finds a tin of milk in one of the refrigerators. He looks around at the carnage, sees something on the floor, steps on it.*

INT. DINING ROOM. NIGHT

JOE *returns with the milk, places it before* BENNETT, *resumes his seat.*

BENNETT Thank you. Where was I?

JOE You never had a child.

BENNETT Actually, that's not entirely true. Lucinda became pregnant once—and immediately took measures to have it rescinded. She didn't want a child. On the other hand, I think she had a strong maternal instinct. For pets. For the help's children. In a way, Penfield was her child. She protected him. It was she who saved him from a jail sentence. I would have had him put away. He came to kill me. You knew that, of course.

JOE   I'd heard.

BENNETT   Well, the fellow was pathetic, but she kept him on to rehabilitate him—her cause. She decided the poor man was a poet. I got to like him myself. He read aloud very well—probably should have been an actor. Anyway, he settled in. I indulged Lucinda in this. But then of course I did something I shouldn't have. I took Penfield's poems that he'd written to the president of the New York Public Library, a friend of mine, and asked his opinion. He in turn got hold of some professor who was an expert in the field of literature. Oh, my. *(He laughs.)* And I showed Lucinda this fellow's letter. Without reading it, she threw it in the fire.

Dissolve to:

EXT. SPEEDBOAT, LOON LAKE. DAY

JOE *at the wheel,* BENNETT *beside him. They are racing along, the mahogany Chris-Craft planing the water.* BENNETT *taps* JOE's *shoulder, points at something. Joe throttles down.*

They watch a pair of loons flapping up from the water, beating their way into the sky.

BENNETT   I like those damn birds. You know why? They're convertible. They fly like hell and can swim faster than a fish. I like that. I like the way they move out of one element into another. *(looking at* JOE*)* Pretty as you please.

Dissolve to:

INT. LIVING ROOM. NIGHT

BENNETT *and* JOE *are drinking.* JOE *is fairly neat, presentably groomed, looking to the manor born in clothes from the Loon Lake haberdashery.*

BENNETT, *by contrast, looks like some bum who's wandered in off the tracks.*

BENNETT   She was a wonderful woman. Didn't give a damn for fashion, you know. Always wore her hair the same way: short, brushed back from the temples. Most seemly. She had a thin, fit body. Thin waist. Ribs showed. Good hands, small, squarish. Never painted her nails or wore makeup. I liked her mouth. A generous mouth. Lovely smile. A light in the eyes when she smiled. She had almost no bosom. Just a slight rise there with good, thick nipples. She told me once if I liked her body I must really like boys. *(pause)* Why am I telling you these things?

JOE   I don't know. Because I'm here.

BENNETT   Precisely. You're here. You've come here to kill me. Like Penfield.

JOE   What?

BENNETT   I suppose you think I've got something to live for.

Pause.

JOE   If you thought I would want to kill you, why did you tell them to let me go?

BENNETT   What?

JOE   When the cops called you from Jacksontown. You told them to let me go.

Pause.

BENNETT   Did they? Did I?

A pause. BENNETT *begins to laugh.* JOE *joins in. Soon they are laughing uproariously. The laughing sound echoes and gradually modifies into the manic laughter of the loons. This continues into next scene.*

EXT.   HILLSIDE, LOON LAKE. DAY

JOE *is running down to the lake from the main house. As he runs, he sheds his clothes.*
    By the time he reaches the boathouse deck, he is nude.

EXT.   LOON LAKE. DAY

The lake on this brilliant day glistens like a bowl of light.
    JOE *dives into the lake. He comes up in a great spray of water, dives down again, comes up out of the water again, water falling from him; he hoots, he calls, he spouts. He laughs, he dives again.*

EXT.   TERRACE OVERLOOKING LOON LAKE. DAY

Looking down at JOE *from this height is* F. W. BENNETT, *now decently dressed, combed, beardless, recovered from mourning.*
   He beams, enjoying the antics of the boy in the water. He waves.

EXT.   LOON LAKE. DAY

JOE, *rising half out of the water, waves back. Sound: the echoing cry of the loons.*

EXT.   TERRACE. DAY

BENNETT *(from the rear) laughing and waving.*

EXT.   LOON LAKE. DAY

JOE, *water falling from him, arms aloft, like wings about to lift him into the air. He falls back, surface dives, and disappears under the water.*

EXT.   TERRACE. DAY

BENNETT *(from the rear) waving.*

EXT.   LOON LAKE. DAY

The lake is still.

EXT.   TERRACE. DAY

A shift in the light. No sound. BENNETT *from the rear, his hands on the parapet. He turns around to us. It is not* BENNETT. *It's a man the same age, with the same white hair. It's* JOE. *He glances at us, anguished.*
   Stop frame.

END

Loon Lake: A Screenplay

Interview with E. L. Doctorow

My Life in the Movies

PAUL LEVINE   Let's talk about your life in the movies. A significant part of the education of your young heroes—I'm thinking of Joe in *Loon Lake* and Edgar in *World's Fair*—is the movies. For them, film is not simply escapist entertainment but also a way of learning about the social world. What part did movies play in your growing up?

E. L. DOCTOROW   My childhood in New York City in the 1930s was very much attuned to movies. As often as I went to the library and came home with an armful of books I went to the local movie theaters, of which there were three or four within walking distance. These were the days of the Hollywood studio system. There were A movies and B movies, or second features. You usually went on a Saturday afternoon, and you got to see two full-length films, one or two serial episodes, a batch of cartoons, a newsreel, and what was called a short, which was some silly farce with the Three Stooges or Lew Lehr's monkeys or something of that sort. So you went in about one in the afternoon and came out reeling at about five. If it was spring or summer and the sun was still out, you would immediately get a headache.

Basically, when a film opened, you had four or five different chances to see it over a period of six or eight weeks. You could go downtown to Manhattan to the Radio City Music Hall or the Roxy or the Paramount to see it for a dollar and a quarter. That was rare. Later it would open in the first-run houses in the Bronx, where the admission was seventy-five cents. Then it would come down through the system to the local smaller movie theaters, where a kid could see it for a dime. I would get twenty-five cents from my mother and father and I would go with my friends to the local delicatessen for lunch and have two hot dogs with sauerkraut and mustard and a Pepsi-Cola. That would use up fifteen cents. And then with the dime in change I would go to the movies.

Was I influenced by movies? Of course, I was. I loved all the films that everybody loved in those days. As I grew older, I came to appreciate the B movies because of the strange, sleepwalking kind of actor they usually featured, the clumsy sets, and the laughable plots. We became quite sophisticated moviegoers at a fairly early age. Then, by the time I was in my teens, there was an art house a subway stop away, the Ascot Theater, on the Grand Concourse. It was there that I first saw Noel Coward in *In Which We Serve,* Alec Guinness in *Kind Hearts and Coronets,* and Olivier's *Henry the Fifth.* The first art films that came to us and were sold that way were English. When I was in my teens, I discovered the beautiful collection of films shown at the Museum of Modern Art in their underground screening room. I saw some great French movies there: *Grand Illusion, Rules of the Game,* and *Harvest.* That's the way it went: a gradual sophistication of taste.

PL So your taste moved to the art cinema.

ELD Yes. I liked movies that were nonformulaic, that had some wit to them. I despised musicals and love stories with violin sound tracks. Was I influenced by film? Of course. But it was possible for me to love movies without compromising a deeper engagement with the written word. I'm not so sure that's possible for the younger generations now. A lot of films in those days were to a large extent dependent on theater for their conceptualization, as was radio. The people who worked on films were essentially theatrical in their imagination. That is not necessarily true now, when we see films being made by people who grew up on television.

Movies have been around long enough now to create their own traditions and recyclings. Although films sometimes rely on books for their stories, film is now a self-perpetuating culture and the dominant one.

PL Your first professional contact with film was when you were working as a reader. Could you tell us about that experience?

Interview with E. L. Doctorow

ELD I'd come out of the army, married and with a child, and got a job working for an airline company as a reservations clerk on the night shift, and that didn't seem to me to be quite the way to spend one's life. I was twenty-four or twenty-five. I was trying to write my first novel. Through a friend of mine I found out that a person could be paid by film companies in New York for reading books and writing synopses of them. Well, I had always been good at that at school. I wrote very good book reports. (*laughs*)

So I found work as a freelance reader. I would read a book and write a report and get paid ten or twelve dollars for it. Pretty soon I quit my job with the airline, having become a more experienced reader with a few more clients. I was reading a book a day seven days a week! I would write my two-page, single-spaced report and deliver my profound comments as to whether the book in question was or was not movie material, and turn it in and get another book. So my bias toward film has always been through texts, you see.

Eventually I was offered a staff job and didn't have to read quite as much because I wasn't paid per book but per week. I had a desk behind some filing cabinets at the end of a hallway. I was now given a lot of screenplays as well as books. You could knock off a screenplay in half an hour. At that time Westerns were very popular. I was writing reports on these rotten Westerns and that, of course, is how I was motivated to write my first novel, which I conceived as a parody of the genre. I would never have done that if I hadn't been working for a film company.

So I've always had something going with films, but, as an adult, in the literary end of it: the prefilm, the first stirrings of film possibility in the book the studio buys. That, to the extent that I have been participating in filmmaking, is where I've stayed, either by reading books to see if they are potential films or writing books that have been made into films. But the more I've participated in films the more alienated I've become from them.

How have movies affected my work? Someone else will have to figure that out. I will say, however, that everyone who writes now, everyone who has written since James Joyce, has been affected by films. It's inevitable. The twentieth-century novel learned from film not to do exposition, it learned to jump cut, it learned the possibilities of discontinuity and of shifting scenes without transitions. I think many of the techniques of what we call postmodern fiction may come of film watching.

As to whether my books are in any way more specifically cinematic, readers may think so. But directors who've tried to make movies out of them tell me how difficult they are to adapt. There's internal moral life and thought that is not at all cinematic.

PL   Let me return to *Welcome to Hard Times* for a minute. There's a kind of paradox. You wrote the novel partly in response to reading Western screenplays. You transformed that into a novel and then it was bought for the movies. How did that sale come about and what was your role in the making of that film?

ELD   I had no role in the making of it. I didn't want to participate and wasn't asked to. An agent sold it for a nominal sum to the MGM company. I suppose it appealed to them because it was in counterpoint to the usual Western. I think maybe they were influenced by Henry Fonda, who was very fond of the book and wanted to act in the film version, so they bought it for him. He told me that he hoped to make a picture as good as *The Ox-Bow Incident.* He was very enthusiastic. But, as it turned out, he had no more control over the film than I had. All his expectations were dashed. The picture was directed by an amiable journeyman named Burt Kennedy, who also did the screenplay. It was really bad, I thought, and of course missed the historical perception of the book, which didn't surprise me. Even then—this was the late sixties—I certainly knew what happened to novels when they were turned into films.

I remember being invited to a screening. I went with my friend the poet James Wright. There were two of us in the theater and maybe a couple of people who worked for the distributors. The movie began and there was mood music and it was windy or rainy, I forget which, and the Bad Man entered from right to left. At that moment I knew I was going to hate the movie because in my mind he'd always come in from left to right. (*laughs*) And pretty soon ridiculous things were happening in this film and Wright and I started to laugh. We were laughing at this movie. After a while I stopped laughing and got very gloomy, though he continued to laugh.

There are two or three good scenes in that movie. And they all happen to use the dialogue right out of the book. In one scene a circuit judge played by an old character actor, Edgar Buchanan, rides into town and sets up a portable desk in the middle of the street. He's come to give credentials to the town of Hard Times and establish it as a legal entity. And he makes this speech wondering why people come out west and how then towns rise up from the ground and then blow away. It's a beautiful set piece. There are one or two other moments like that, but for the most part it is an awful film. But the money I received—and it was very modest—allowed me to put a down payment on a house on Broadview Avenue in New Rochelle, New York. It was a fair trade: a lousy movie for a house. There ought to have been two stone MGM lions out by the front steps.

Daniel

P L   But the next time someone expressed interest in a novel, *The Book of Daniel*, you decided to write the script yourself. What made you change your mind?

E L D   After the book was published, Haskell Wexler, a very reputable cinematographer, approached me. He had made a film of his own called *Medium Cool*, which I'd seen and liked. He spoke very insightfully about the book. He was the first of a long line of Hollywood people I've dealt with who have spoken intelligently about my books. They may be the best readers in the country now. I mean, the days of the stupid studio head who couldn't read are past, though some of them are still around. But in my experience, people who produce and direct movies are smart readers.

Wexler came out to see me in Sag Harbor, where I was staying for the summer. I was very impressed because he had a small attaché case that held a radio phone. That was back in 1973, you understand. We talked about my novel and then he got a call on his attaché case. So I agreed to write a screenplay. (*laughs*) It was a modest option deal. The key thing was to make a serious movie that was faithful to the book. And I was willing to participate to make sure that it was done right. And I didn't need to do a treatment because I knew what it should be.

His response to the screenplay was critical. He said he would revise it himself by doing some research into the actual circumstances of the Rosenberg case. Then he submitted to me *his* screenplay. And I was really appalled because he had turned it into a documentary history of the actual Rosenberg case. He had completely misunderstood my purposes. He wanted to make a documentarily true film that would exonerate the Rosenbergs because he believed, along with many people, that they had been framed. This novel lives in its ambiguity. Daniel, the son of the executed couple, never discovers the truth of their innocence or guilt. And when Wexler said that he had tracked down the executioner, who lived in Yonkers, and was going to interview him, I realized that he and I had nothing in common on this. His option ran out. I refused to grant an extension.

Movie people can be terribly literal. My book is not a documentary. It does not portray the Rosenbergs. It's about what happened to them. It's about national states of mind and the historically sacrificial role of radicals in America. And it's told from the point of view of people intimately affected by events they find inexplicable—namely, children. I would get calls from other people with the same point of view as Wexler's. So I just put the thing away.

Several years later Sidney Lumet expressed an interest. We were sitting outdoors in someone's yard in Sagaponack having lunch. He knew the book and asked to see my screenplay. By that time I was wary. I was determined that if a picture were ever to be made, I wouldn't sell it in the usual way and cede all control. At this point, *Ragtime* was behind me. I didn't really need a picture to be made of *Daniel*. I didn't need money. In any event, there wasn't going to be very much money attached to this film.

But Lumet said he loved the script. That was the first thing that persuaded me that he might be the man for the job. (*laughs*) And, of course, he's a superb filmmaker. I wanted final cut—unheard of for a writer. What we worked out is that we would be partners. We would cast the film together. We would edit it together. And we would share Sidney's privilege of final cut. He had just made a very commercially successful movie and felt he was in a position to make a two-picture deal: he would make picture two, which is what the studio wanted, if they would let him make this one first. Well, that didn't turn out. Every studio turned us down, Sidney or no Sidney. So with Sam Cohn's help— my friend and agent at ICM—we found ourselves a third partner, John Heyman, who is essentially a film financier. John sold the cable rights around the world and that's how we put together the money. We ended up with eight million dollars. At that point, Paramount, who had turned it down, bought into it and took it over. So we were in business.

Sidney wanted a couple of changes in the script. He thought the opening scene, which shows a riot on Union Square, was too expensive and so we had to make it smaller. (That's the scene in the film on Greene Street.) I spent the summer of 1982 out at Sag Harbor. I rented a room down near the water and I revised the screenplay that we eventually shot. And I think that the first day of shooting was in September, on Yom Kippur, of 1982. That was chosen so the streets would be empty for our big production scene: a political rally for the Isaacsons. He's a very practical, knowledgeable filmmaker, Mr. Lumet. It was shot on 20th Street between Broadway and Fifth Avenue, I think, with lots of extras and 1950 vintage police cars. He had cameras everywhere—on the fire escapes, on rooftops, in the street. And when everything was ready to shoot somebody shouted "Stop!" and came running through the crowd and climbed up on the speaker's platform and held a little light meter up to the actor-speaker's face. Thousands of people rehearsed and waiting, and the cinematographer needs his light-meter reading. Migod, how we forget that it's photography, that all of it—Hollywood stars, movies, the gossip, the mythology—depends on a light-meter reading.

In June 1983 there was a big march in New York—an antinuclear march. I remember asking Lumet, "Isn't there some way we can use this? That's 750,000 extras we don't have to pay for." We thought about the ending, which took place at Columbia when Daniel goes out and there's a crowd there, and I said, "Maybe we could use this instead." And Sidney said, and this is about the day before the march, "Out of the question. I need three or four crews and I don't have time to get them." The next day he called me up and said, "It's all set." (*laughs*) And so he shot the great rally with 750,000 people. Well, actually, it turned out to make for a very soft ending. Or maybe we used it improperly. We might have done better.

PL   Was it difficult for you to transform your novel into a screenplay?

ELD   It was not difficult to do but it was unpleasant. I perceived it not as writing but as a kind of engineering job. All the powers you summon from words in writing a novel become somewhat irrelevant. You use words in a very functional, practical way to create images and perhaps small inspirations in the mind of the director. The words are like the rocket boosters in space launches: they get the film up and then they fall away. The only words left are the words that the characters speak.

This was the first screenplay I wrote by many, many years. But I guess generally that what I knew about movies and what I only learned to articulate later, with *Ragtime,* was that the words the characters speak are about the last of several means by which information is conveyed to the audience. Where will you put the camera? What is the set-up for the shot? Is it going to be down below and looking up at the actors? Is it going to be up looking down? Is it going to be close? Is it going to be distant? How is the scene lit? How are the people dressed? How is their hair dressed?

Of course, this is a generalization. There are directors whose pictures are talkative: Eric Rohmer, Ingmar Bergman. But, generally speaking, as the American movie has evolved, the dialogue is the icing on the cake. If you're a writer of books and you agree to write a script, especially based on your own work, you're in another world—a time-driven world of passing images. More relentlessly time-driven than theater, I think.

PL More relentless?

ELD Yes, I think so. Theater can be iconographic. And opera is a kind of theater in which the actual number of events is few but the reactions to them—the arias—are quite time consuming. But in film, especially in American film, ninety-nine percent of the time there's a presumption of ordinary reality: ordinary, literal reality, which is supposed to be no different from what we see when we step out in the street.

But writing *Daniel* took me back through the events and experiences of writing the book and that depressed me. That was an exhausting, emotionally depleting book. I threw everything I knew into that book. I expended myself. When it was finished I was not quite the same person I had been. Now I had to go back and look at this material objectively, as a craftsman, as someone who had an engineering problem in front of him, as someone who had to do a mechanical drawing for a piece of machinery. Or say I had to go back through it like an archeologist checking off and cataloging my previous life. Well, when you do that, you see, you're doing something risky, it's a kind of self-negation as a writer that you would do well not to do too often.

PL That I understand. But in a practical sense: The novel opens with Daniel speaking; the film script you wrote does not open with Daniel speaking. The whole voice of Daniel is in fact sublimated in the screenplay and subdued in the film version. And the voice is so important. I just wondered how you could enter the film if you couldn't enter through his voice.

ELD But you see that's always the problem—making the interior life *play*. That's what happens with movies. They externalize voice—you're looking at Daniel. We did do a few close-ups for periodic insertions in the picture—in which Daniel addresses the audience. But by and large we see him in the world—not as in the book, the world through him.

Ragtime

P L   How then did it come about that you wrote the *Ragtime* script?

E L D   Well, after deciding that it was not healthy to go back through the same experience—of course I would do it again! My agent was then the late Phyllis Jackson. At the time she had the manuscript in hand, Phyllis's agency happened to be merging with another agency. And she decided to liaise with a brilliant theatrical and film agent at this other agency, the aforementioned Sam Cohn. He became the film agent for *Ragtime*. Sam had a very close relationship with the producer Dino De Laurentiis, to whom he gave the manuscript. And De Laurentiis bought it immediately. Then Sam approached Robert Altman, who was about to release *Nashville*. Everybody thought that picture suggested our consanguinity. Altman said he would direct.

When I decided to write the screenplay for Altman, it was for the same reason I had written the *Daniel* script: to protect my work. I knew very well of his reputation as a mauler of written scripts. I was wary of him at the same time I liked him personally, very much. I wrote a script without any restraint whatsoever. That is to say, instead of writing an efficiently reductive script for a 120-minute movie, I wrote a 400-page script for an unreasonably expensive six-hour movie, putting in every conceivable scene from the book that seemed manageable, and with no regard for storyboard efficiencies. I explained my technique to him. I said, "This is the screenplay from which we will derive the finished screenplay. I want to make sure that no matter what you do and how you take off, you are still in my book." And he appreciated that. He understood that quite well. But instead of saying it was much too long, impractical, costly, talky, and all the things that it was, he said, "I want to shoot every page." Now this was before the concept of the TV miniseries had evolved, well before *Roots* came along—any of that. He proposed to make two three-hour theatrical films and to shoot an additional four hours, which could eventually be seen—all ten hours—over several nights on television. It was a grand vision he had. And I think that was the straw that broke Dino's back.

They had already had problems with a movie they were doing together, *Buffalo Bill and the Indians*. I think De Laurentiis felt that he was being treated with contempt, which he may very well have been. And then when Altman said he wanted to shoot all 400 pages of my *Ragtime* script, I think that about ended their relationship. Altman was taken off the film. I didn't want to lose him. In fact, I flew out to Hollywood to try to persuade De Laurentiis to reinstate him. But it was over. And afterwards, on reflection, it seemed to me possible that Altman had created the crisis with his producer as an act of either self-sabotage or self-preservation, it was hard to know which.

PL   From the point at which Milos Forman entered the project, what was your relationship to the film?

ELD   I had grave misgivings about Forman from our first meeting. It wasn't only that he was replacing Altman, that Altman was my man. Forman read my script and said he didn't like it—that it was impractical, which I knew, but that it was also too wide in scope. "A movie must be about one person," he said. I was appalled. He was only interested in the Coalhouse Walker story. This was a conceptual disaster the finished film could not survive. He wanted us to collaborate on a screenplay according to his notion—this deadly, depressing, pseudoesthetic notion that all movies had to fit the same formula, that there was this ironclad rule that must never be broken.

At that point maybe two years had gone by since the publication of *Ragtime*. I had done the screenplay for Altman. I had to make a decision now: to collaborate with Forman and fight to protect my work from his simplistic reduction or to abandon it and him and good riddance. So I told Milos I would not write the screenplay. I already had the idea for *Loon Lake* in my mind. And I was thinking about this play for which I had a rough draft, *Drinks before Dinner*. So I chose to move on.

But I was to have one more experience with the film of *Ragtime*. I was asked to arbitrate a dispute between De Laurentiis and Forman having to do with an eight-minute segment of film dealing with the character of Emma Goldman and her activities. Their basic dispute had to do with the length of the movie, and this suggestion for a cut was Dino's. Eight minutes is a lot of movie. I had seen the film with that sequence included. I then watched it without that sequence and felt that the film was better off without it. No question. It was poorly acted, clumsily directed, and it portrayed Emma Goldman as starting a riot when in fact all the riots at her public speeches were started by the police.

Forman had been appealing for artistic solidarity, that we two artists would stand firm against the commercially minded producer. That in itself was funny. Perhaps he also thought that, since I'd wanted more of the book filmed,

I would naturally see it his way. I was all for solidarity, but in this case the material was embarrassing.

Apparently, as the years have gone by, Forman has turned bitter about that episode. He has intimated that I had an ulterior motive in siding with the producer, a kind of a pathetic thing for him to say—pathetic and contemptible. I understand also that he feels now that he should have made the film even more purely about one man. But when the film was done, and about to be released, Forman sent me a handwritten letter in which he apologized for his work. He said he thought he'd made a pretty good movie, but not a great one. He said, after all, I'd been right, that too much of the book—the contextual life—had been cut away.

Loon Lake

PL   After that experience, how did you come to write the screenplay for *Loon Lake*?

ELD   *Loon Lake* was bought by Twentieth-Century Fox in partnership with De Laurentiis. I have the feeling that Fox put up the money. I'm not sure about that. In any event, they were both involved. I simply suggested that I get first crack at the screenplay. I had this feeling that things hadn't been going so well for me in the movies. After the experience of *Ragtime* I wanted as much control of this film as a writer could possibly have. You understand, though *Daniel* was the first adaptation I wrote, it was not filmed until well after *Ragtime* had been released. I had not yet come up with the idea of a creative partnership and shared final cut with a director. But I was under no illusions. I knew I could do the screenplay and they could put it on the shelf and find someone else to do it—find twelve people to do it. Do it for years and years and years. But somewhere along the line something about it might establish itself in the mind of a screenwriter they would hire.

So I did it and something significant happened. There's only one instance in which something came to me in the writing of a screenplay that I wished I'd known when I was writing the book, and that's in *Loon Lake*. At the very end, the Master of Loon Lake, the industrialist, Bennett, watching a pair of loons rising from the water, says that he admires loons because they're convertible. They fly, they swim, they move from one element into another. The image is made applicable to Joe, the young man who will become Bennett's heir and the Master of Loon Lake. That's the only instance in which a screenplay has advanced the creative understanding of the piece for me beyond the book.

P L   One more question about *Loon Lake*. Movies seem to play a great part in the novel. How self-conscious was this allusiveness to the movies on your part?

E L D   Even though Joe would have been older than I was in those days by about ten years, I think I was remembering my own experience going to the movies on Saturday and how important they were. Joe mentions Fred Astaire and Charlie Chaplin; they were key figures in a kid's awareness because they exemplified physical grace. It didn't matter whether Astaire was dancing and twirling a woman about or Chaplin was running from a cop or ducking when the guy swung at him. It had to do with physical competence, it was very joyful for a kid who could appreciate that kind of thing.

P L   There are other film references as well. There's the scene where Joe's being grilled while his girl is being taken away. And there's the scene when they're on the train and everybody breaks into song, which sounds like the bus scene in *It Happened One Night.* And, finally, there's the scene where Warren Penfield confronts the little girl in Seattle.

E L D   Oh, that one was quite deliberate. A remembrance of the actress Frances Farmer. The thing about Warren Penfield is that he goes the wrong way. Everyone of his generation is going to Paris. *He* goes to Japan. He never quite gets it right. En route he finds himself in Seattle at the time of the General Strike, which I wanted to write about, and he doesn't understand what's going on. I had known about Frances Farmer's terrible story. When I was young—ten or twelve—I saw a picture called *Come and Get It,* with Frances Farmer, in which she first plays a young woman and then the young woman's daughter a generation later. I thought she was the most beautiful woman I had ever seen. She may still be. I remembered that she grew up in Seattle and her mother ran a rooming house. Her monstrous mother, who had her committed and lobotomized. I realized writing the book that Frances would have been a little girl when Penfield was in Seattle. So I sent him to Mrs. Farmer's rooming house and put Frances in the book as the little girl. A small, private remembrance is what that is. A lighted candle.

PL   You have had one more novel adapted for the movies. What was your experience with the filming of *Billy Bathgate?*

ELD   That is a tale for another day. Let's just say here that as a result of my experience with the directors of *Ragtime* and *Billy Bathgate* I've come up with a theory: Directors are prone as a class—perhaps it's a genetic flaw, I'm not sure—but they will inevitably come up with and hold to the one idea about how a book should be treated that will sink their movie. It's my theory of *The Director's One Disastrous Idea.*

PL   Four of your novels have been turned into movies, yet all of them have proved difficult to translate into film. Why do you think that film directors and producers have been so attracted to your fiction?

ELD   I think one reason is that some of the books may participate in narrative conventions that filmmakers find very reliable. For instance, *Welcome to Hard Times* takes place in the West. Well, that's their native territory. They feel very comfortable dealing with that. However they might betray the piece—and they did—they would recognize it to begin with and that would give them a certain sense of security. By contrast, *Ragtime* was bought simply because it had a strong impact on the reading public. And it was probably bought for its scale—the scale of the thing—and a certain value that attached to the title itself. But again *Billy Bathgate* does participate, apparently, in the convention of the gangster story. And to the extent that I've always used our myths—and myths very often do descend (or ascend) into genre—to that extent, an unwary filmmaker might think he had something going here that could be done readily. I'm not sure *Loon Lake* is an example of this except that it's a kind of road story with archetypal figures in it that people in film might conceive of as having wonderful roles for actors.

PL   And it's very much a quest story.

ELD   Yes. Possibly that it's a search, just as *Daniel* is a kind of a search.
    People ask, "How does it feel to see your stories up on the screen?" Actually it often feels terrible. It's always wrong somehow. Even if it were a great movie, a superlative movie—and I've never had that good fortune—it would still be wrong. Something about your extremely personal, coded esthetic life is thrown up glaringly on the screen necessarily in a state of distortion.

PL   Why, then, are so many writers drawn to movies?

ELD   If you are talking about young writers, it's a very powerful thing in this culture to make a movie that's well received. Film dominates American culture. Have you ever seen a film company on location? They take over a street, a town, and everything stops. I think of moviemaking as a kind of military action. Materiel and troops are gathered, the supply lines are set up, someone says, "Go," and the shoot begins. It all has to be coordinated and can't be stopped. An enormous amount of the director's energies and talents simply goes into coordinating the skills and obligations of other people: employing them in the first place, choosing them and casting them, the myriad details. So it's a very executive sort of art, which reminds me of generalship more than anything else. And that may be attractive to writers who are drawn to directing. And the circulation that your work gets is, of course, much greater than in any other form. And, finally, the rewards can be astronomical. Even the ordinary wages of screenwriting are far in excess of what almost any other form of writing brings. So the money has to be a major factor.

And people just love the magnitude of the thing, the images up on the screen they're responsible for. They just love that, and the excitement of creating those images, composing their film from strips of film. When I was with Lumet editing *Daniel* it was a very recognizable process for me. I had never been in a film cutting room before. I caught on to it quickly enough. The same principles apply as when you compose a book. I would say that's where the real excitement is—in the composition of the film. That's the joy, I should think. Though I suppose yelling through a megaphone at four thousand extras streaming down a valley—that's fun, too.

PL   Last question. In *City of God*, you create a writer, Everett, who is both fascinated and appalled by movies. You've often expressed your own sense of frustration in working on films, but after each disappointment you return to the scene of the crime.

ELD   Simple recidivism is the explanation for that. (*laughs*)

PL   Do you think you will write any screenplays in the future?

ELD   I'm trying to go straight, but who knows if I'll be able to manage it?

Personal Implications

As you consider your study of the Gospel of Matthew as a whole, list the three or four primary ways that you may have been convicted to change.

Recall Jesus' gracious invitation to come to him to find rest, his specific commands to obey, and his commission to make disciples. Note at least one particular way in which you should respond to each of these three emphases in Jesus' teaching.

Note a few things you have learned that should lead you to thank God . . .

. . . for aspects of his character you have seen more clearly in this study:

. . . for particular things he has already done through Jesus:

... and for particular things he promises to be and do for us in the future:

As You Finish Studying Matthew . . .

We rejoice with you as you finish studying the book of Matthew! May this study become part of your Christian walk of faith, day by day and week by week throughout all your life. Now we would greatly encourage you to continue to study the Word of God on a week-by-week basis. To continue your study of the Bible, we would encourage you to consider other books in the Knowing the Bible series, and to visit www.knowingthebibleseries.org.

Lastly, take a moment again to look back through this book of Matthew, which you have studied during these recent weeks. Review again the notes that you have written, and the things that you have highlighted or underlined. Reflect again on the key themes that the Lord has been teaching you about himself and about his Word. May these things become a treasure for you throughout your life—which we pray will be true for you, in the name of the Father, and the Son, and the Holy Spirit. Amen.